Joan W Scott

The French Revolution of 1830

THE
FRENCH REVOLUTION
OF 1830

by David H. Pinkney

PRINCETON UNIVERSITY PRESS

NEW JERSEY

To

DAVID

1953-1969

PREFACE

In 1958 I presented a paper to the Second Newberry Library Conference on French History (later published in *French Historical Studies*, Fall 1958) in which I noted that American historians had almost completely failed to make contributions to French history comparable to the great works of the French themselves, such as Lefebvre's *Les Paysans du Nord* or Soboul's *Les Sans-culottes de l'an II*. I attributed this failure to the inability of Americans, owing to geographical separation, to do the sustained research in French archives that was the foundation of the great French books. I urged my American colleagues to cease trying to meet our French friends on their own ground with monographs but instead to write on broader subjects that are of interest to Americans concerned with European history and not merely to French historians, to draw on the detailed works of others, and to study in depth in archives only neglected or debated aspects of the subject—a possible task for an American on sabbatical leave and occasional summer research trips. I argued, too, that as outsiders we could bring to many subjects in French history valuable objective judgments that our more involved French colleagues could not.

I have taken my own advice. I have chosen to write on a major event in nineteenth century French history, and I have used monographs and articles in areas of the subject where they are available and researched in depth in archives and contemporary publications where little or no work had been done or where disagreement called for reexamination of sources. I wrote with Americans in mind as my principal readers yet with the conviction that I had something to say to Frenchmen, too. I hope that the result may prove instructive and interesting to readers on both sides of the Atlantic.

I am indebted to many persons and institutions for help in bringing this book to completion. A fellowship from the John Simon Guggenheim Memorial Foundation made possible a year of research in France, and a Faculty Fellowship from the Social Science Research Council helped finance a semester's leave for writing and a return trip to France. The University of Missouri and the University of Washington granted me sabbatical leaves, and the University of Missouri Research Council gave valued financial help. Many persons aided me, some in ways they scarcely knew through a question, a comment, or a suggestion; I think particularly of Louis Chevalier, Louis Girard, Raymond Grew, Daniel Resnick, Charles Tilly, and Charles Mullett. I am grateful to all of them and to others who go unnamed. To G. de Bertier de Sauvigny, Sherman Kent, and Helen R. Pinkney, who read and criticized the entire manuscript, I reserve a very special thanks.

David H. Pinkney

Seattle, Washington
July 1971

CONTENTS

Preface   vii

   I   Conflict without Compromise   3

  II   The Sources of Opposition   44

 III   Surprise, Confusion, Disorder,
         July 25, 26, 27   73

  IV   Days of Revolution, July 28 and 29   109

   V   Struggle for Power, July 30-August 9   143

  VI   The Revolution in the Provinces   196

 VII   The Little Things: Liquidation of a
         Revolution   227

VIII   The Crowd in the Revolution   252

  IX   Purge and Replacement   274

   X   Revolution Unresolved, August-
         November 1830   296

  XI   The Close of the Revolution,
         November-December 1830   330

Bibliography   369

Index   386

The French Revolution of 1830

ABBREVIATIONS

The following abbreviations of major source collections are used in the footnotes.

AHMG   Archives historiques du Ministère de la Guerre

AN   Archives nationales de France

AP   Archives de la Préfecture de Police de Paris

AS   Archives du Département de la Seine et de la Ville de Paris

BHVP   Bibliothèque historique de la Ville de Paris

BN   Bibliothèque nationale

I

Conflict Without Compromise

ON MONDAY morning, July 26, 1830, Parisians picking up the day's official newspaper, the *Moniteur universel*, noticed that the entire first page was devoted to a report to the King in which his ministers called for and justified extraordinary measures against the periodical press of the opposition, an opposition that in the preceding few weeks had won a resounding victory in the general elections. Turning the page they read the texts of royal ordinances—issued without parliamentary approval—instituting a rigorous censorship of the press, dissolving the newly elected Chamber of Deputies, changing the electoral law to favor conservative candidates, and ordering new elections. Here was the rumored royal coup d'état. Some had hoped for it. Many feared it. Probably most politically aware Frenchmen half-expected it yet thought that it would never occur.[1]

The ordinances of July 25 were the culmination of a conflict between the crown and the liberal majority in the Chamber of Deputies dating back to the liberals' victory in the general election of 1827 and in more exacerbated form to the appointment of the unpopular Polignac Ministry in August 1829. At the center of the conflict was the aging monarch, Charles X, seventy-three years old in 1830. He had fled the Revolution in 1789 and spent the next twenty-five years of his life in exile, escaping the fate of his brother, Louis XVI. He returned to France in 1814, and during the reign of his second brother, Louis XVIII, he earned a reputation for ostentatious piety and emerged as the leader of the dissident ultraroyalists who thought the regime too liberal. He hated the Revolution and all its works, and he tended to see in all liberal opposition a revolutionary threat

[1] See below, Ch. III.

to his throne. During the first three years of his reign a well-disposed royalist majority dominated the chamber, and the problem of harmony between the ministry and parliament had never arisen. By 1827, however, the majority was disintegrating, and elements of it were in rebellion against Comte Joseph de Villèle, who had been the first minister since 1822. Villèle, unwilling either to compromise or to give up the office and power he cherished, called a general election, hoping to win a renewed majority and perhaps, should the liberals gain additional seats, frighten dissident royalists into solidarity behind him. He set the election for November 17 and 24, but he made no announcement of it until November 5, intending to take his opposition by surprise and to allow them no time to organize a campaign. But the liberals were better prepared than he expected; a warning from the police told of an efficient organization that, they claimed, reached into every street of Paris and into every department.[2] Villèle probably discounted this report, but a committee of liberals, called "Aide-toi, le ciel t'aidera," did exist. It had been founded early in 1827 under the presidency of François Guizot, a popular professor and writer and a former official of the Ministry of the Interior, for the purpose of aiding liberal candidates and electors in combating official efforts to keep them off the ballot and electoral lists. Prefects and subprefects exhibited great ingenuity in exploiting all provisions of the electoral law that would permit disqualification of known opponents of the government and qualification of reliable supporters. When Villèle called his surprise election of 1827, the "Aide-toi" was ready to direct the liberals' resistance against these machinations and to support the campaigns of liberal candidates.[3] After all the

[2] AN, F⁷ 6772, Police générale, Affaires politiques, Préfet de Police to Ministre de l'Intérieur, Sept. 19, 1827.

[3] Guillaume de Bertier de Sauvigny, *The Bourbon Restoration* (Philadelphia, 1966), pp. 390-92; Achille de Vaulabelle, *Histoire des deux Restaurations jusqu'à l'avènement de Louis-Philippe (de janvier 1813 à octobre 1830)*, 5th ed. (Paris, 1860), VIII, 97-98; Charles H. Pouthas, *Guizot pendant la Restauration: préparation de l'homme d'état, 1814-1830* (Paris, 1923), pp. 370-80.

ballots had been counted, the Villèle royalists had won 150 to 180 seats in the new chamber. The liberals, who had elected fewer than twenty of their candidates in the preceding general election four years earlier, had as many seats as the Villèlists, and the right opposition had sixty to eighty seats.[4]

Repudiated by Right and Left and no longer able to command a majority in the chamber Villèle could not remain in office, and Charles X had his first opportunity to appoint a prime minister. Nonetheless, he parted with Villèle reluctantly, and he expected his new ministry to continue the policies of the old.[5]

The new council, named in January 1828, included several Villèlists, two opponents of the preceding ministry, and some officials without clear political affiliation, but it was Left-Center in political orientation. It had no president; Vicomte Jean-Baptiste Martignac, who took the Ministry of the Interior, became its spokesman in parliament. The King's hope to continue the Villèlist system was futile, for a majority in the chamber were anti-Villèlists, a combination of the Left and the Defection, a band of dissident royalists, followers of François Chateaubriand. The ministry found itself in an impossible position—if it satisfied the parliamentary majority, it would alienate the King, and if it followed the King's wishes, it would have no majority. Charles, adopting a neutral position, at first allowed the ministry to try to please the majority with concessions to the Left, but the results—a liberalized press law and measures against the Jesuits—did not please him, and he began to think of a new ministry based on all the elements of the shattered royalist majority of the early 1820s, a ministry that would take a hard line against what Charles saw as the revolutionary aspirations of the liberals.[6]

---

[4] Bertier de Sauvigny, *Restoration*, p. 392. Strict precision in determining the strength of each group is impossible because they were not organized and disciplined parties with each adherent unmistakably labeled.

[5] Bertier de Sauvigny, *Restoration*, p. 406.

[6] *Ibid.*, pp. 405-14; Bertier de Sauvigny, *Le Comte Ferdinand de*

The King wanted his good friend, Prince Jules de Polignac, a former émigré warmly devoted to the Bourbons and
sympathetic with Charles's conception of a strong monarchy,
to head the ministry. In January 1829 the imminent resignation of the Minister of Foreign Affairs, Comte Pierre de La
Ferronnays, due to ill-health, offered him an opportunity to
advance his plan. He proposed to name Polignac to the
vacant post and at the same time to replace Martignac in the
Ministry of the Interior with Auguste Ravez, an extreme
rightist. Martignac would move to the Ministry of the Navy.
The incumbent ministers protested this shake-up and threatened to resign, and Charles turned to the appointment of an
entirely new ministry. About January 20 Polignac was summoned back from London, where he had been serving as the
French ambassador, and immediately began a round of talks
with potential ministers. He made little progress, and the
date for the reconvening of parliament, January 27, was
approaching. Charles did not want to face the new session
with a ministry in formation or dissolution, and he ordered
Polignac back to London, putting an end to the Prince's
ministerial explorations.[7]

But the King did not abandon his hopes for a new ministry. In March he asked his close adviser, the ultraroyalist
Comte Ferdinand de Bertier, and Comte François de La
Bourdonnaye, another rightist, to draw up two ministerial
lists—one including some of the present ministers who
might be persuaded to stay on and the other composed of
new men. Thinking that circumstances would more likely
require the latter, Bertier wrote to the King on April 1
proposing a new ministry that included Polignac in Foreign
Affairs and La Bourdonnaye at the Interior. Within the
same week a ministerial crisis threatened to provoke Martignac's resignation, giving Charles the opportunity he

Bertier (1782-1864) et l'énigme de la Congrégation (Paris, 1948), p. 432;
Charles d'Haussez, *Mémoires du Baron d'Haussez, dernier Ministre de
la Marine sous la Restauration* (Paris, 1896, 1897), II, 86.

[7] Bertier de Sauvigny, *Restoration*, pp. 414-15; Bertier de Sauvigny,
Ferdinand de Bertier, pp. 432-34, 439.

sought, but the difficulty was resolved. Martignac agreed to stay on, and the King postponed his project until after the end of the parliamentary session in the summer. Bertier, nonetheless, continued his preparations and kept up a secret correspondence with Polignac, advising him on the names being considered in discussions centering around Bertier, La Bourdonnaye, and the King. They were thinking at this time not of a ministry that would defy the chamber in some kind of a coup d'état, as many of their enemies suspected, but of a combination that would win the support of a majority of the deputies. Bertier thought that they could count on a majority of forty votes in the lower house. The parliamentary session ended on July 31. Polignac, following Bertier's advice, had arrived in Paris a few days earlier and had at once entered into talks looking toward the formation of a new ministry.[8]

The results were announced in the *Moniteur* of August 9. Polignac and La Bourdonnaye stood out as the leading personalities of the new combination, the former taking the portfolio of Foreign Affairs, the latter that of the Interior. La Bourdonnaye opposed having a president of the council, perhaps because he objected to Polignac in that role, and the ministry had no president other than the King. The choice of the Minister of War had been left to the Dauphin, who controlled higher military appointments, and he chose Comte Louis de Bourmont, a high-ranking general in the royal army. The Ministry of Finance went to Comte Gilbert de Chabrol, a holdover from Martignac's ministry. Jean Courvoisier, a magistrate, former deputy, and a fanatical Catholic, took the Ministry of Finance. The King's choice for the Ministry of the Navy, Admiral Henri de Rigny, the hero of the Battle of Navarino in 1827, declined, and that post was filled by a career prefect, Baron Charles d'Haussez. Comte Guillaume de Montbel, a devoted partisan of Villèle and his successor as Mayor of Toulouse, completed the

8 Bertier de Sauvigny, *Restoration*, pp. 418-19; Bertier de Sauvigny, *Ferdinand de Bertier*, pp. 438-45; *Moniteur universel* (Paris), Aug. 1, 1829, p. 1366.

council, taking the Ministry of Ecclesiastical Affairs and Public Instruction. Bertier had hoped for a portfolio in return for his faithful services to the Bourbons, but La Bourdonnaye thought him too compromised by clerical connections and blocked his appointment.[9]

Guillaume de Bertier de Sauvigny, the historian of the Bourbon Restoration, has declared that Charles and his advisers could scarcely have put together a combination of men less competent for the tasks confronting the government or more likely to disturb and irritate public opinion. The appointments of Polignac, La Bourdonnaye, and Bourmont were capital blunders. Polignac had spent thirty of his fifty-eight years outside France; he was little attuned to the changes that revolution and war had wrought in his country since he fled it as a child in 1789. He had served in the army of Condé, returned to France in 1804 and was promptly arrested for his part in the Cadoudel Plot against Napoleon; he spent the next decade of his life in prison. After the Restoration Louis XVIII appointed him to the Chamber of Peers, but during Louis's reign he was one of the dissatisfied ultraroyalists who gathered around the King's brother, the future Charles X. From 1823 to 1829 he again lived abroad, serving as the ambassador to the Court of Saint-James's. He was a devout Catholic, a convert from eighteenth century skepticism, and his title of Prince, which he regularly used, had been bestowed by the Pope. He was an Anglophile and married to an Englishwoman, which endeared him to few Frenchmen. He had many admirable personal qualities, but, as Bertier observes, "there are few men in French history who have been so universally disliked." His unpopularity alone would probably have made him an ineffectual minister, but it was compounded by stubbornness, a supreme self-confidence, and an unwillingness—perhaps borne of his long imprisonment—to come to grips with reality.[10] La

[9] *Moniteur*, Aug. 9, 1829, p. 1395; Bertier de Sauvigny, *Restoration*, pp. 420-22; Bertier de Sauvigny, *Ferdinand de Bertier*, pp. 441-44.

[10] Bertier de Sauvigny, *Restoration*, pp. 420-21, Vincent W. Beach, "The Polignac Ministry: A Re-evaluation," *University of Colorado*

Bourdonnaye, a man of reactionary views and intemperate language, was associated in the public mind with the worst excesses of the White Terror after the defeat of Napoleon.[11] In a speech before a secret session of the Chamber of Deputies, which he himself later published, he called for "a salutary terror" against enemies of the monarchy. "To stop their criminal conspiracies we must have irons, executioners, torture. Death and death alone can put an end to their plots."[12] The appointment of Bourmont was an affront to all patriotic Frenchmen, for he had fought with the Chouans during the Revolution, later rose to high position in the Imperial armies, again rallied to Napoleon in 1815 only to desert him on the eve of Waterloo. In that same year he testified against Marshal Ney in the trial that ended in the condemnation and execution of the marshal, Napoleon's "bravest of the brave."[13]

The announcement of the new ministry was greeted with approval by royalists, by indignant outcries from the liberals. The Villèlist *Gazette de France* declared, "For all men not blinded by passion, the formation of the present ministry is the result of that cry heard from all friends of order: *no more concessions.*" The next day it categorically denied that the Charter was in any way threatened, this in response to the liberal press that was warning of an imminent coup d'état.[14] Most eloquent of the voices on the left was the *Journal des débats*. "So here again," it declared on August 10, "is broken that tie of love and confidence that unites the people to the monarch! Here again the court with its old rancors, the emigration with its prejudices, the clergy

---

Studies, Series in History No. 3 (Jan. 1964), pp. 95-96; Pierre Robin-Harmel, *Le Prince Jules de Polignac, ministre de Charles X, 1780-1847* (Paris, 1941), *passim.*

11 Bertier de Sauvigny, *Restoration,* p. 421; Beach, "Polignac Ministry," p. 93.

12 Prosper Duvergier de Hauranne, *Histoire du gouvernement parlementaire en France, 1814-1848* (Paris, 1857-71), III, 309, 310.

13 Bertier de Sauvigny, *Restoration,* p. 421; Beach, "Polignac Ministry," p. 93.

14 Charles de Rémusat, *Mémoires de ma vie* (Paris, 1958-67), II, 277.

9

with its hatred of liberty that come to interpose themselves between France and its King. . . . Unhappy France! Unhappy King!" A few days later it dramatically denounced the association of the three leading personalities of the ministry with three shameful episodes in France's history— the emigration, the defeat at Waterloo, and the White Terror. "Coblentz, Waterloo, 1815, there are the three principles, there are the three personalities of the ministry. Turn it to any side you wish, on all sides it irritates. It has no aspect that is not sinister, not one face that is not menacing."[15] The *Journal* joined other liberal papers in discovering an ominous English influence in the appointment of the Anglophile Polignac and of Bourmont, who had contributed to English victory at Waterloo.[16] However, interest in the responses of the articulate minority in Paris should not obscure the fact that the masses were indifferent. According to police reports the announcement of the new ministry caused no ruffle in the calm of the Parisian summer.[17]

The opposition attributed to the ministry a direction and sense of purpose that it sorely lacked. The ministers assumed office with only the vaguest conceptions of what they would do with the powers suddenly vested in them. In January 1829 the King, Polignac, La Bourdonnaye, and Bertier had agreed that a new ministry should strive to strengthen royal authority and to give the landed aristocracy a larger role in government while at the same time extending the suffrage, the four leaders being convinced apparently that the public was loyal to the monarchy and that, properly controlled, it would elect partisans of the King. In a memorandum dated September 10, 1829, Polignac declared his dissatisfaction with the power of the middle class in France, the abuses of the press, and usurpation of royal prerogatives by ministers,

[15] *Journal des débats* (Paris) Aug. 15, 1829.

[16] *Ibid.*, Aug. 16, 17, 25, 1825; Charles Ledré, *La Presse à l'assaut de la monarchie, 1815-1848* (Paris, 1960), pp. 90-91.

[17] AN, F⁷ 3883, Préfecture de Police de Paris, "Bulletin de Paris," Aug. 10-18, 1829.

and he expressed the wish that the doors of the Chamber of Deputies might somehow be closed to "mediocre men driven by turbulent and revolutionary passions." Their places, he obviously thought, should be taken by members of the aristocracy. But these were no more than aspirations, and in his memorandum Polignac put forward no specific program. The ministry certainly had no plan for a coup d'état or any other dramatic violation of the Charter, and as the weeks after August 8 passed into months with nothing attempted, nothing accomplished, it became apparent that the ministry had no plan of domestic action whatsoever.[18]

When the ministry was organized, the King and his advisers had counted on the support of a majority in the Chamber of Deputies, but Chateaubriand's refusal of his endorsement, dramatized by his resignation as Charles's ambassador in Rome, put his followers among the deputies into the opposition and ruined those hopes. The only practical course for the ministers, were they really determined to survive, would have been to use the King's power of issuing ordinances, granted by Article 14 of the Charter, to change the electoral law in a way that would assure the choice of sympathetic deputies in a new election. But this required resolute leadership and willingness to meet the charge of violating the Charter, for the power granted by Article 14 was ill-defined and doubtful, and Polignac was both irresolute and committed to respect the Charter.[19]

La Bourdonnaye, the most vigorous member of the council, might have been competent to lead it into a defiance of the parliamentary majority and their supporters, but he was a contentious and difficult colleague, soon at odds with his fellow ministers. Annoyed and frustrated, he used the min-

---

[18] Berthier de Sauvigny, *Ferdinand de Bertier*, p. 433; Vincent W. Beach, *Charles X of France: His Life and Times* (Boulder, Colo., 1971), pp. 296-97, 300; *Moniteur*, Dec. 17, 1830, p. 1728.

[19] Article 14 read, "The king is the supreme head of the state. He commands the land and sea forces, declares war, makes treaties of peace, alliance, and commerce, appoints all public officials, and makes all regulations and ordinances for the execution of the laws and the security of the state" (Bertier de Sauvigny, *Restoration*, p. 67).

istry's vote in November to reestablish the office of president of the council of ministers as the occasion to resign. Two of his colleagues, Chabrol and Haussez, anxious to be rid of him and knowing his strong opposition to the appointment of a president when the ministry was formed, may have initiated the proposal with the intent of forcing his resignation. Polignac became the titular head of the ministry. The Villèlists wanted to bring their chief, the former first minister, into the council as La Bourdonnaye's successor in the Ministry of the Interior, and Bertier had hopes of winning the portfolio denied him in August, but both projects foundered, the first owing to Villèle's unwillingness to cooperate and the second owing to opposition of the Villèlists and probably also to the reluctance of Polignac to have a colleague who possessed such close ties with the King. Montbel reluctantly moved up to the Ministry of the Interior. To his place in the Ministry of Ecclesiastical Affairs and Public Instruction the King named Comte Martial de Guernon-Ranville, the Procurer-General in Lyon, chosen for his reputed ability as a speaker, a talent in unfortunately short supply in a ministry that would soon need effective spokesmen before an unsympathetic parliament.[20]

The change in the ministry in November brought no alteration in its policy nor in the liberals' opposition to it. The council continued to meet in long sessions four times weekly—twice at the seat of a minister, all being visited in succession, and twice at the palace under the presidency of the King. The talk dragged on—Polignac drew doodles on a

[20] Bertier de Sauvigny, *Ferdinand de Bertier*, pp. 442, 453-54; *Moniteur*, Dec. 17, 1830, p. 1728; Haussez, *Mémoires*, II, 88; Montbel to Villèle, Aug. 1829, Joseph de Villèle, *Mémoires et correspondance* (Paris, 1888-90), v, 379; Montbel to Villèle, Nov. 16, 1829, *ibid.*, 391-92; Genoude to Villèle, Nov. 15, 1829, *ibid.*, 388; Villèle to Montbel, Nov. 1829, *ibid.*, 393; Montbel to Villèle [Nov. 1829], *ibid.*, 394-95; Rémusat, *Mémoires*, II, 279; Alexis de Tocqueville, *Oeuvres et correspondance inédites de Alexis de Tocqueville* (Paris, 1861), II, 6; Guillaume de Montbel, *1787-1831; souvenirs du Comte de Montbel, ministre de Charles X* (Paris, 1913), pp. 217-19.

tablet, ministers frequently went to sleep. They discussed the timing of the next session of the chambers, what bills to introduce that might have chance of approval by the almost certainly hostile deputies, and especially how to get the budget passed. Early in January they fixed the opening of the legislative session for March 2 and decided to offer it only the budget and one other bill, which they hoped could be noncontroversial.[21] Rumors of a coup d'état directed against the Chamber of Deputies continued to circulate, but the council did not at this time contemplate so drastic a step, preferring first to seek the cooperation of the existing chamber.[22]

The opposition was not idle. The liberal press kept up a barrage of attacks on the ministry and continually warned that the ministers would not hesitate to violate the Charter if the deputies refused their cooperation. It urged resistance by all legal means, including refusal to pass the budget and refusal to pay taxes, if the government should attempt to collect them without parliamentary approval. On January 3, 1830, a new journal appeared in Paris to add its persistent voice to the clamor against the ministry, and it did not spare the King himself. It was the *National*, founded by a group of journalists with the support of Talleyrand and the liberal banker, Jacques Laffitte, and edited by three bright young men, Adolphe Thiers, François Mignet, and Armand Carrel. In a cascade of brilliantly written and provocative articles they maintained that an acceptable monarchy must have as ministers only men enjoying the confidence of the Chamber of Deputies, argued that refusal of the budget was a constitutional right, and, drawing a parallel between France in 1830 and England in 1688, implied that if the

21 Haussez, *Mémoires*, pp. 128-31; Bertier de Sauvigny, *Restoration*, p. 426; Beach, "Polignac Ministry," p. 106; Montbel to Villèle, Oct. 28, 1829, Villèle, *Mémoires*, v, 386-87; Genoude to Villèle, Nov. 29, 1829, *ibid.*, 399.
22 Bertier de Sauvigny, *Ferdinand de Bertier*, p. 455; *National* (Paris), Jan. 5, 1830; AN, CC 547, Chambre et Cour des Pairs, "Note adressé à M. de Polignac par M. Guernon-Ranville," Dec. 15, 1829.

13

King violated the Charter he should be replaced by the head of the most closely related family, the Duc d'Orléans.[23] The opposition expressed itself in other ways, too. The society "Aide-toi, le ciel t'aidera" alerted its members and organized new committees in expectation of new elections. Associations of taxpayers committed to refuse to pay taxes not duly voted by parliament appeared in several departments. Throughout the autumn of 1829 and the succeeding winter and spring officers of the Gendarmerie in the provinces reported frequently on liberals' efforts to organize tax resistance. Many newspapers gave their support to the movement, and the courts blocked most of the government's efforts to silence them for violation of the press laws. On the other side of the political spectrum the rightist press heightened the fears of the opposition and added to the growing political tension by urging the King to use the powers authorized by Article 14 to deal with the revolutionary menace to monarchical government.[24]

While the ministry continued in its indecisive course in domestic affairs during the fall of 1829 and the succeeding winter, it did resolve on action abroad—the decision to send a combined naval and land expedition against Algiers. The French navy had been blockading the port of Algiers since 1827 in retaliation for an insult by the Dey of Algiers to the French consul and in an effort to coerce that ruler into acceptance of French proposals for settlement of disputes over France's long-standing fishing and trading rights in Algeria and over a debt that the Dey claimed the French government owed him. The blockade had been ineffective and costly, and the French were anxious to discontinue it, but the latest attempt to resume negotiations had ended on August 3, 1829, with the Algerians firing on the ship of the

[23] Bertier de Sauvigny, *Restoration*, pp. 426-27; Ledré, *Presse*, pp. 96-99; *National*, Jan. 3, 29, 1830.
[24] Bertier de Sauvigny, *Restoration*, pp. 426-27; Pouthas, *Guizot*, pp. 423-25; Daniel L. Rader, "The Breton Association and the Press: Propaganda for 'Legal Resistance' before the July Revolution," *French Historical Studies*, 2 (Spring 1961) 64-82; *National*, Jan. 6, 1830; AN, F⁷ 6777, 6778, Police gén., Rapports de Gendarmerie, 1829-30.

French representatives. The King in his opening address to parliament in 1828 and again in 1829 had called for action to terminate the intolerable situation across the Mediterranean, and the episode of August 3 gave new impetus to these proposals just as the Polignac Ministry took office. In October 1829 Haussez, the Minister of the Navy, urged the council of ministers to consider a naval expedition against the port. The Dauphin voiced his strong opposition, and the King decided to follow Polignac's counterproposal to attempt to induce the Sultan of Turkey to put pressure on his vassal, the Dey of Algiers, to negotiate a settlement. Polignac also toyed with the idea of using the forces of the Pasha of Egypt, supported by French money and ships, to attack the Dey, a fantastic scheme, which illustrates Polignac's frail grasp on reality. Neither plan materialized, and in mid-December the ministry agreed that force, applied by the French army and navy, offered the only solution. Formidable defenses of the port of Algiers ruled out either a naval bombardment or an effective naval siege. Bourmont, the Minister of War, recommended capture of the city from the land side by an army put ashore some distance away. This appealed to the ministers, and they instructed Bourmont and Haussez to examine the problems presented by such an expedition and to report back to the council. The proposal immediately ran into opposition from general officers of the navy, who claimed that the almost uninterrupted bad weather along the Algerian coast, the strong coastal defenses, the heat, the lack of water, the trackless sands and hostile tribes of the interior made the expedition impractical and dangerous. They warned that the government would be unable to find a general officer to command it. Haussez, nonetheless, was sure that a successful landing could be made, and he got support for his position from two captains who had served with the blockading squadron off Algiers and from a handful of other officers.[25]

25 Bertier de Sauvigny, *Restoration*, pp. 434-36; Haussez, *Mémoires*, II, 132-33, 160-61; Martial de Guernon-Ranville, *Journal d'un ministre* (Caen, 1873), pp. 10, 13-14, 27-29, 32.

The ministry discussed the arguments for and against the proposed expedition, and on February 6 voted unanimously to recommend to the King a landing on the peninsula of Sidi-Ferruch, twelve miles from Algiers, and an attack on the city from the land. The next day the King gave his approval. The expedition was to be ready to sail in six months—in August, when the weather along the Algerian coast was most propitious, and the city could be taken in no more than two months. The enthusiastic Haussez said the navy would be ready by May 15, even by May 1 if the weather were favorable.[26]

Polignac informed the principal foreign powers of his government's intention to send the expedition against Algiers. He assured them that it was punitive in purpose and that no change would be made in the regime of North Africa without consulting them. Russia, Austria, and Prussia readily gave their approval, but Britain, with more direct interests in the Mediterranean, was suspicious of French intentions. To the British, the extent of the preparations suggested more than a mere punitive expedition, and in both London and Paris they pressed for explanations and for a promise that France was not planning conquest and the establishment of a French colony. Despite their repeated *démarches* Polignac refused to give them any more precise assurances than he had offered to all the powers. The British government was annoyed, and its sympathies with the Bourbon regime, which it had helped to found only a decade and a half earlier, noticeably cooled.[27]

Neither the surviving records of the ministry's deliberations nor its official pronouncements permit a conclusive determination of the motives behind the decision to mount the expedition against Algiers. In his circular to the powers on March 12 Polignac declared that his government sought, in addition to redress of grievances arising from the dispute

---

[26] Guernon-Ranville, *Journal*, pp. 129-32; Haussez, *Mémoires*, II, 163.
[27] Bertier de Sauvigny, *Restoration*, pp. 436-37; Guernon-Ranville, *Journal*, pp. 38-39, 61, 78-79; Etienne d'Audiffret-Pasquier, *Histoire de mon temps: mémoires du Chancelier Pasquier* (Paris, 1895), VI, 210-13.

over French rights in Algiera and over the debt claimed by
the Dey, to put an end to piracy based on the Algerian
coast, to the enslavement of Christians, and to the exaction
of tribute from nations trading in the Mediterranean. An
official justification of the expedition published in the *Moniteur* of April 20, 1830, put little emphasis on the latter
humanitarian motives, and they may be regarded as window
dressing intended to win the sympathy of the great powers.
Economic motives seem to have played no significant part.
Villèle's Minister of War had in 1827 called attention to
economic advantages that possession of Algeria might bring
France, but little trade moved between the two countries,
and French businessmen, even in Marseille, showed almost
no interest in the opposite coast of the Mediterranean and
little enthusiasm for the expedition. Although a few Frenchmen saw an opportunity to establish a permanent foothold
across the Mediterranean, the government at this time had
no clear intent of winning a new colony for France. Among
the political opposition many feared that the real motive of
the expedition was to distract and mislead public opinion
and to corrupt the army and undermine its loyalty to the
laws in preparation for an assault on the Charter.[28] "They
have," warned the *Journal des débats*, "the insane hope of
making a victory against Algiers a victory against our
liberties. . . ."[29]

One student of the subject has argued that the principal
motivation behind the decision was the desire to gain possession of the Dey's treasury, estimated in 1827 to amount to
150 million francs. In their hands it would give Charles and
his ministers a measure of independence of the chamber
should it refuse to vote the budget. They may also have
thought to use it, the same author suggests, to assure the

---

28 Bertier de Sauvigny, *Restoration*, pp. 436-37; Guernon-Ranville,
Journal, p. 32; Marcel Emerit, "Une Cause de l'Expédition d'Alger: le
trésor de la Casbah," *Actes* du 79ᵉ Congrès national des sociétés savantes, Alger (1954), pp. 171-73; *Moniteur*, Apr. 20, 1830, pp. 434-35;
Pierre Renouvin, *Histoire des relations internationales* (Paris, 1953-58),
v, 108-09.

29 *Journal des débats*, May 17, 1830.

loyalty of key army officers in the critical days of confrontation with the deputies that perhaps lay just ahead. But this implies a clarity of purpose and a determination on the domestic political scene that the Polignac ministry lacked. The probable motive behind the expedition, aside from the desire to end the costly blockade and to settle immediate grievances with Algiers, was to enhance the prestige of the ministry by a demonstration of patriotic enterprise, to reassure its supporters, and to appeal to all who thought the Bourbons overly passive in foreign affairs. The hoped-for advantage was a general strengthening of the government's political position, not a preparation for a coup d'état, something the ministry did not then contemplate.[30]

Having decided upon the Algerian expedition and launched preparations for it, the ministry turned its attention to the chambers, scheduled to assemble in about three weeks. The ministry reaffirmed its earlier decision to limit its legislative program to the budget and a few noncontroversial bills. It took no steps, however, to win support even for this modest program, entered into no negotiations with influential deputies, offered no judicious persuasion in jobs or money, which, Haussez thought, might have assured a friendly majority. Several ministerial sessions were devoted to the address from the throne to be delivered at the royal session on March 2. All members brought their ideas for it to the meeting of February 13, where they discussed them and then charged Courvoisier, the Minister of Justice, to draw up a complete draft. All agreed that the ministry must demonstrate its firmness, and Courvoisier's text, presented on February 20, included a sharp warning that the government would not yield to any illegal pretensions of the chamber.[31] "If criminal maneuvers raise up obstacles against my government, which I hope will not be the case, I will find the strength to overcome them in my resolution to

[30] Emerit, "Expédition d'Alger," pp. 174-75; Renouvin, *Histoire*, v, 108.

[31] Haussez, *Mémoires*, II, 153, 154, 171-76; Guernon-Ranville, *Journal*, pp. 32-34.

maintain public order, in the just confidence of the French people, and in the love that they have always demonstrated for their kings."[32] Guernon-Ranville feared that the statement might be interpreted as a threat to govern by decree, and he suggested a milder version appealing for the chambers' cooperation. After the mention of the King's determination to maintain public order he would have put these words: "in the loyal support that I have the right to expect from the two chambers. . . ." This proposal stirred a long and heated debate, but it ended in the adoption of Courvoisier's original version.[33]

Only a handful of deputies and a few peers turned up for the traditional mass held at Notre Dame on the eve of the opening of parliament, but for the royal session of March 2 in the Louvre scarcely a seat on the floor was vacant; the galleries were overflowing, and crowds gathered in the streets around the palace. The King arrived shortly after 1 P.M., and after a ceremonial reception by delegations of deputies and peers, he was escorted to the throne, took his seat and began to read in his high-pitched voice the carefully prepared address. At one point he rasied his head in a gesture of emphasis, and his diamond-studded hat fell off, dropping at the feet of the Duc d'Orléans, who stood at his left; the Duke picked it up and held it until the King finished speaking. Most of the address was given over to a routine report on the nation's foreign relations and finances. Toward the end Charles spoke of "the sacred rights" of the crown and of his obligation to pass them on intact to his successors and then gave the warning that the ministers had agreed upon. At the end there were polite applause and a few "vives le roi."[34]

To the opposition deputies the King was threatening the dissolution of the chamber and perhaps resort to Article 14

[32] Guernon-Ranville, *Journal*, p. 35.

[33] *Ibid.*, pp. 35-36.

[34] Haussez, *Mémoires*, II, 177; Charlotte de Boigne, *Récits d'une tante: mémoires de la comtesse de Boigne, née d'Osmond* (Paris, 1921-25), III, 226; *Moniteur*, Mar. 3, 1830, p. 245.

to assure the return of a more amenable body of deputies in the next elections. In the succeeding days they proclaimed their refusal to be intimidated by naming two prominent opposition deputies, Pierre Royer-Collard and Casimir Périer, as their first choices for the presidency of the Chamber of Deputies and by electing only opposition members to the committee charged with drafting the reply to the royal address.[35]

This committee deliberated for several days, and on March 15 presented its text of the proposed reply.[36] The critical passage—the response to Charles's warning—came near the end.

Sire, the Charter, which we owe to the wisdom of your august predecessor, and which Your Majesty is firmly committed to defend, consecrates, as a right, the participation of the country in the discussion of public affairs. That intervention ought to be, it is in fact, indirect, wisely regulated, fixed within limits exactly drawn, and we would never permit that anyone dare violate those limits, but it is positive in its result, because it is based on the permanent accord between the political views of your Government and the wishes of your people, the indispensable condition of the normal conduct of public affairs. Sire, our loyalty, our devotion compel us to tell you that this accord does not now exist.

An unwarranted mistrust of the feelings and thoughts of France is today the fundamental attitude of the Administration. Your people are distressed by this because it is an affront to them; they are worried by it because it is a threat to their liberties.[37]

For two days the chamber discussed the proposed reply in secret session. The presence of virtually all the deputies and all save one of the ministers (Courvoisier was ill) attested to

[35] *Moniteur*, Mar. 5, p. 255, Mar. 10, 1830, p. 275; Pasquier, *Mémoires*, VI, 217.
[36] *Moniteur*, Mar. 15, 1830, p. 296.
[37] *Ibid.*, Mar. 19, 1830, p. 309.

the importance that all factions attached to the debate. Montbel and Guernon-Ranville spoke for the government. The former denied that the country was alarmed or even concerned and charged that the purpose of the proposed reply was to force the King to change the ministers against his will, and this was in violation of the Charter and of the royal prerogative. If the choice of ministers were given to the chamber, he said, the country would fall into anarchy. Guernon-Ranville insisted that the King's power to change his ministers was absolute; no limits could be imposed upon it. Both men avowed, moreover, that the ministers would not resign except on orders of the King. The liberal lawyer André Dupin replied that the chamber was not demanding that the King change his ministers; it was only pointing out that the country's distrust of the present government frustrated the essential cooperation between the crown and the legislative chambers. The resolution of the difficulty fell within the King's prerogative; the chamber was not prescribing it. But despite this disclaimer the opposition speakers left no doubt that in their view the only solution to the conflict was a change of ministers. Some deputies of the Right-Center proposed an amendment that would have tempered the defiance expressed in the committee's text while still affirming the chamber's dissatisfaction, but it won only thirty supporters. In the final roll call 221 deputies voted to support the committee's draft of the reply; 181 voted against it.[38] The next day the royalist *Quotidienne* declared, "Two hundred twenty-two [*sic*] men who swore fidelity to the King have sanctioned the first manifesto of the Revolution of 1830,"[39] a prophetic statement wholly unfounded at the time. The 221 thought of themselves as *defenders* of the constitution, not revolutionaries; few, if any, of them contemplated the overthrow of the King.

[38] *Ibid.*, Mar. 15, p. 296, Mar. 16, p. 300, Mar. 17, 1830, p. 303; *Journal des débats*, Mar. 16, 17, 1830; *Gazette de France* (Paris), Mar. 16, 17, 1830. The *Journal des débats* and the *Gazette de France* published lengthy accounts of the secret sessions of the chamber based on reports of persons present.

[39] *Quotidienne* (Paris), Mar. 18, 1830.

The lines of conflict between the crown and the majority in the Chamber of Deputies were now drawn. The 221 had declared that the ministers must be responsible to the majority in the chamber. The King and his partisans insisted that the ministers were his appointees, responsible to him alone. At a meeting of the council of ministers on March 17 the King declared that he would never submit to what he regarded as the illegal pretensions of the chamber. The parliament had a constitutional procedure, he continued, for expressing its lack of confidence in a ministry; it could reject the ministry's legislative proposals when they were submitted to it. The majority in the lower chamber was now refusing its cooperation without even knowing what the ministry's proposals were, and this was a defiance of royal power. Moreover, the King was convinced that the chamber was divided into so many factions that *no* ministry could win and hold a majority in it. Seeing that Charles would accept no compromise solution, Montbel proposed that he prorogue the chamber and prepare for new elections; counting on victories in almost all the departmental colleges, Montbel was confident of winning a majority favorable to the King and his present ministers.[40] Guernon-Ranville feared that a new assembly might be more dangerous than the present one, and he urged the King and ministers to make an attempt to work with the present chamber in the expectation that some deputies might be enticed away from the 221. He would introduce no legislation but the budget; he hoped that the chamber would approve it, but if not, rejection would be a clear violation of the Charter, and the King would then be justified in taking extraordinary measures. But only Chabrol endorsed Guernon-Ranville's proposals. The majority agreed to prorogue the chambers

---

[40] Elections took place in two stages. First, all electors met in the so-called "collèges d'arrondissement" and chose 258 deputies. Then the one-fourth most highly taxed electors in every department met in departmental colleges and elected 172 deputies. Peter Campbell, *French Electoral Systems and Elections Since 1789*, 2d ed. (London, 1965), p. 60.

until September; dissolution would be ordered only after completion of preparations for new elections.[41]

One minister wanted to emphasize the King's rejection of the chamber's pretensions by a royal refusal even to receive the reply, but the others decided that the King should hear it in the traditional manner. The next morning, March 18, a deputation from the lower chamber waited upon the King at the Tuileries; he received them seated on his throne, surrounded by his ministers and the officers of the court. Royer-Collard, the president of the chamber, read the reply. The King listened attentively, and when Royer-Collard finished, he read a brief statement drawn up the preceding day.[42]

> Sir, I have heard the address that you present to me in the name of the chamber of deputies. I had the right to count on the cooperation of the two chambers in order to accomplish all the benefits that I contemplated; my heart is grieved to see the deputies of the departments declare that, for their part, that cooperation does not exist.
>
> Gentlemen, I announced my resolves in my address at the opening of the session. These resolves are unalterable; the interests of my people forbid my deviation from them.
>
> My ministers will inform you of my intentions.[43]

The next day, when the Chamber of Deputies assembled just after noon, the visitors' galleries were filled, spectators unable to find seats crowded the corridors, and the gathering deputies talked animatedly among themselves. The session opened at 1:30, and the president had read letters from two resigning deputies, when ushers announced the arrival of

[41] Guernon-Ranville, *Journal*, pp. 40-51; Haussez, *Mémoires*, II, 179-80, 182; Pasquier, *Mémoires*, VI, 220.
[42] Guernon-Ranville, *Journal*, p. 51; *Courrier français* (Paris), Mar. 19, 1830; Pasquier, *Mémoires*, VI, 221; *Moniteur*, Mar. 19, 1830, p. 309.
[43] *Moniteur*, Mar. 19, 1830, p. 309.

the Minister of the Interior and the Minister of the Navy. They took their places on the ministerial bench, and Montbel drew a paper from his portfolio and handed it to the president. Royer-Collard, glancing at it, announced that he had received a proclamation of the King. "The session of 1830 of the chamber of peers and of the chamber of deputies of the departments," he read, "is prorogued until the first of September next." He announced that in conformity with law the session was immediately terminated. The deputies of the Right promptly rose and shouted, "Vive le Roi!" Those on the Left, apparently taken by surprise, remained silent in their seats until someone shouted "Vive la Charte!" All the Left rose and took up the cry. The galleries joined in, and the session ended in a tumult of shouting.[44]

After the burst of activity forced upon it by the meeting of parliament the Polignac Ministry subsided into its usual lethargy. It should, Ferdinand de Bertier thought, have ordered immediate elections while the opposition was still off-balance from the government's show of determination on March 19 and still unprepared, but it let this opportunity slip by. Polignac then accepted the advice offered by Bertier and two other friends who would shortly join the ministry, Comte Charles de Peyronnet and Baron Guillaume Capelle, to postpone elections until at least September. The electoral lists would be revised in August and September, and the government could assure revision favorable to its chances in the elections. Officers of the Army of Africa, most of whom were royalist electors, would by then be back in France, and the government could count on the support of a victorious army. The King and ministers at first agreed on this course but later decided that so long a postponement would, owing to the long delay in passing the budget, confront the government with grave financial difficulties. In early April they decided to hold the elections soon after the landing of the Algerian expedition, hoping to benefit from the success—

[44] *Ibid.*, Mar. 20, 1830, p. 315; *Courrier français*, Mar. 20, 1830; *Journal des débats*, Mar. 20, 1830; *Gazette de France*, Mar. 20, 1830; AN, F⁷ 6777, "Prorogation des Chambres, Correspondance particulière."

which seemed probable—of that operation. On April 17 the Ministers of War and the Navy reported that the landings would begin about May 20 or 22, and the ministry proposed to the King that he call elections for the end of June and set the opening of the new parliamentary session at the beginning of August. The enabling ordinance appeared in the *Moniteur* on May 17. It dissolved the chamber as of May 16 and called the arrondissement electoral colleges for June 23 and the departmental colleges for July 3. The delay in the publication of this decision is probably explicable as a move to reduce the time available to the opposition to prepare for the elections. Haussez urged the ministry to prepare for them and for the troubles that they were likely to excite by purging the high military commands and the top administrative posts of all men of doubtful loyalty or determination, strengthening garrisons in Paris and other cities, assembling additional troops within easy call of Paris, and drafting new electoral and press laws. The ministry endorsed his recommendations, but Polignac took no action.[45] Pressed by his colleagues and even by the King he would reply, "We will think of it, Sire, we think of everything, everything will come in time."[46]

While the council deliberated on the issue of elections, politicians both within and outside the government mounted an effort to effect a change in the ministry. Courvoisier, Montbel, and Chabrol urged that Villèle be brought in as president of the council. Two deputies of the opposition called on Villèle, who arrived in Paris on March 23, and promised that a majority of the centrist deputies would support a ministry headed by him. They feared that Polignac, too stubborn to compromise, would attempt a coup d'état and by his political ineptness throw the country into revolution. Villèle replied that he would return only if requested by the King to form a new ministry at his own

---

[45] Guernon-Ranville, *Journal*, pp. 62-63, 67-71, 76-77; Haussez, *Mémoires*, II, 183-85; Bertier de Sauvigny, *Ferdinand de Bertier*, pp. 456-58; *Moniteur*, May 17, 1830, p. 541.
[46] Haussez, *Mémoires*, II, 192.

choosing. The two deputies then attempted to put their proposal before the King but were rebuffed. Polignac himself, however, called on Villèle, asked for his help, and invited him to join the ministry, even as president; Villèle declined, not wishing to be involved in a combination in which he had so little confidence. He returned to his home in the south in mid-April, and the ministry remained unchanged. Polignac apparently still enjoyed the full confidence of the King.[47]

When it decided on the timing of the elections, the ministry agreed that if the electoral colleges should return a favorable majority, the government would seek enactment of a more restrictive electoral law and a more rigorous press law. But not all foresaw that the elections would be favorable. The advice from the prefects, although it included routine expressions of confidence, was not entirely reassuring. The possibility of a hostile chamber emboldened by its new mandate had to be considered, and the ministry was divided on how to deal with such a body. Guernon-Ranville thought that Polignac was prepared to use Article 14 and legislate by royal ordinance and that he could count on the support of the heads of the two military ministries, Bourmont and Haussez. Courvoisier opposed the use of such powers; he urged that the ministry resign if it were defeated in the elections and announced that he would certainly resign. Chabrol took the same position. Guernon-Ranville and Montbel would use the emergency powers only with great reluctance and as a last resort. Montbel, anxious to avoid association with such measures, recommended that after the elections but before the opening of the next session the King dismiss the present ministry and form a new combination more likely to win a majority in the new chamber. Chabrol, Courvoisier, and Guernon-Ranville favored his recommendation, he claimed, but the King showed no interest in it.[48]

[47] Montbel, *Souvenirs*, pp. 222-24; Villèle, *Mémoires*, v, 416, 418-21, 422-24; Bertier de Sauvigny, *Ferdinand de Bertier*, pp. 457-58.
[48] Guernon-Ranville, *Journal*, pp. 68-69, 72-74, 91; Montbel, *Sou-*

This division within the ministry could only render it more ineffectual and would certainly weaken it before the chamber. Guernon-Ranville confided to his diary on May 2 that the ministers were on the verge of quarreling. "This state of affairs," he wrote, "cannot last."[49] Polignac had already decided that it must be changed. Courvoisier and Chabrol were determined to resign, and Polignac wanted to bring Comte de Peyronnet to the Ministry of the Interior to direct the government's preparations for the elections. The Dauphin was planning a visit to the armed forces assembling at Marseille and Toulon for the descent on Algiers, and he would make stops in the principal cities and towns along his route. Assuming that this publicizing of the government's grand plans would enhance its prestige, Polignac apparently decided to delay announcement of the ministerial changes until the Dauphin returned.[50]

Angoulême was back in Paris on May 15, and four days later the King signed the ordinance effecting the new appointments. Peyronnet, who had served as Minister of Justice under Villèle, was named to the Ministry of the Interior. Montbel, the incumbent Minister of the Interior, asked to be permitted to resign when he learned of Polignac's intention to appoint Peyronnet, but on the personal appeal of the King, who was anxious to assure the support of the Villèlists for the new ministry, he agreed to move to the Ministry of Finance, replacing Chabrol but only with the understanding that he would resign after the elections. Courvoisier's replacement in the Ministry of Justice was Comte

---

venirs, pp. 225-26; AN, CC 546, Chambre et Cour des Pairs, "Déclaration de M. Courvoisier, ancien Garde des Sceaux," Dec. 2, 1830; Moniteur, Dec. 16, p. 1721, Dec. 17, 1830, p. 1728; AN F⁷ 6767, Police gén., Préfet de Seine-et-Marne to Ministre de l'Intérieur, Mar. 20, 1830; F⁷ 6770, Préfet de la Haute-Marne to Ministre de l'Intérieur, Mar. 22, 1830, Préfet de la Moselle to Ministre de l'Intérieur, Mar. 10, 1830; F⁷ 6772, Préfet de la Côte-d'Or to Ministre de l'Intérieur, Mar. 24, 1830.

49 Guernon-Ranville, Journal, pp. 79-80.

50 Ibid., pp. 77-78, 80; Haussez, Mémoires, II, 192-93; AN, CC 549, Chambre et Cour des Pairs, Polignac to Chantelauze, April 30, 1830; Montbel, Souvenirs, p. 228.

Jean de Chantelauze, President of the Royal Court of Grenoble and a deputy of the Right-Center. Polignac wanted to bring into the ministry to help prepare for the elections Baron Capelle, Prefect of the Department of Seine-et-Oise, who under Villèle had been a specialist of electoral affairs in the Ministry of the Interior. To accommodate him the Administration of Public Works was separated from the Ministry of the Interior and established as a separate ministry under his direction. Neither the King nor Polignac obtained from the three new appointees any formal commitment to agree to the use of Article 14 should the new chamber prove hostile, but in response to discreet inquiries all agreed that they would not oppose it should "energetic measures" become necessary.[51]

The changes did nothing, of course, to appease the opposition and scarcely strengthened the ministry or contributed to its unity. Polignac made his choices in consultation with the King and the Dauphin and never took his colleagues into his confidence on this matter of grave concern to them. The appointment of Peyronnet displeased the Villèlists, who hoped for the return of Villèle himself to this post. Peyronnet was, moreover, thoroughly unpopular, and the opposition considered his appointment an affront to them.[52] The *Journal des débats* called him "a man violent among the most violent, blind among the most blind."[53] Chantelauze, who had declined a portfolio in August 1829, joined the ministry without enthusiasm, and his colleagues had little enthusiasm for him. Montbel thought well of him but Haussez, a more acute judge, thought him lacking in dignity, without political standing, and naive in his judgments.

[51] Guernon-Ranville, *Journal*, pp. 89, 98, 100-101; Haussez, *Mémoires*, II, 201-3; Montbel, *Souvenirs*, pp. 229-33; *Moniteur*, May 16, p. 539, May 20, 1830, p. 553; Montbel to Villèle, May 24, 1830, Villèle, *Mémoires*, V, 434-37.

[52] Guernon-Ranville, *Journal*, pp. 95-96, 101; Montbel, *Souvenirs*, pp. 227-29; Haussez, *Mémoires*, II, 193, 199; *Gazette de France*, May 22, 23, 1830; *Journal des débats*, May 20-24, 1830; *National*, May 23, 1830; Villèle to Comtesse de Villèle, May 30, 1830, Villèle, *Mémoires*, V, 441; Pasquier, *Mémoires*, VI, 228.

[53] *Journal des débats*, May 20, 1830.

Haussez's opinion of Capelle was no more flattering. This new minister brought to the council a record of incompetence in the elections of 1827, a habit of talking too much, and a vexing affinity for contradiction. Moreover, despite the changes the ministry still lacked a really effective public speaker to represent it before the chambers. It was a combination ill-suited for the difficult and dangerous days that lay ahead.[54]

All the ministers, new and old, assembled for the first time, on May 20, at a special meeting under the presidency of the King at the Tuileries.[55] Charles opened the session with a short statement directed particularly to the new members.

> Gentlemen, I want to explain to you in a few words the system that I wish to follow and that I have already developed several times before the council; my firm determination is to defend the charter; I do not wish to deviate from it on any point, but I will not permit others to deviate from it. I hope that the chamber of deputies will be composed of sober men, sufficiently devoted to their country to second my intentions; if it should be otherwise, I will know how, while still respecting the constitution, to assure respect for my prerogative, which I regard as the best guarantee of public order and of the happiness of France.[56]

Charles was apparently prepared to use his ordinance power should the new chamber again be dominated by the opposition, a position now vigorously endorsed by the royalist press. At this time, however, the ministry did not even discuss resort to Article 14.[57]

[54] AN, CC 547, Chambre et Cour des Pairs, Chantelauze to his brother, May 18, 1830, Chantelauze to Polignac, May 9, 1830, Testimony of Chantelauze, Sept. 9, 1830; Montbel, *Souvenirs*, p. 228; Haussez, *Mémoires*, II, 203-7.

[55] Guernon-Ranville, *Journal*, p. 92.

[56] *Ibid.*

[57] *Gazette de France*, May 19, 1830; *Drapeau blanc* (Paris), May 18, 1830.

All energies not consumed by routine business were now concentrated on winning the elections, only a month away, and particularly on defeating the 221. At the preceding council meeting Montbel, still Minister of the Interior, had predicted a government majority of thirty to forty seats, but reports from the prefects and the Gendarmerie indicated that the liberals were actively preparing for the elections throughout the country and that the government could not count on a certain victory. The reporting officials expressed especial concern over the rumors that they attributed to liberal agents—reports that the Polignac government planned to restore the national lands confiscated from émigrés and the church during the Revolution, reestablish feudal dues and tithes, reinstitute primogeniture, and pay the clergy an indemnity for lost lands.[58] The government responded with efforts to marshal its supporters. Circulars were sent to government employees and to army officers informing them that the ministry expected their support. Bishops and other clergy, trusting not in prayer alone, publicly urged electors to cast their votes for government candidates.[59] Even before the shake-up in the ministry the King and Polignac had decided, without consulting the ministers, that Charles would make a direct appeal to the voters in a royal proclamation sometime before the election. The ministers were asked only to pass on the form and the timing of this dubious expedient. They agreed on a text early in June, and on June 13 the King issued it along with

[58] Montbel, *Souvenirs*, p. 234; Pasquier, *Mémoires*, VI, 231; AN, F⁷ 6740, Police gén., Papers on election of 1830, Préfet de la Haute-Vienne to Ministre de l'Intérieur, June 15, 1830; F⁷ 6768, Police gén., Préfet de Tarn-et-Garonne to Ministre de l'Intérieur, Mar. 4, 1830; F⁷ 6741, Police gén., Letter to electors of Boulogne (Pas-de-Calais), June 17, 1830; F⁷ 6777, Police gén., Reports of Gendarmerie royale, May, June 1830; F⁷ 6778, Reports of Gend. roy., Apr., May, June 1830.

[59] AN, CC 547, Circulars from officials of Ministry of Finance to employees, May 1830, Ministre de la Guerre to Lts.-gén. Cmdts. des Div. milit., May 1830, F⁷ 6741, Préfet du Var to Ministre de l'Intérieur, July 10, 1830; *Moniteur*, Dec. 19, 1830, pp. 1755, 1758; Paul Droulers, *Action pastorale et problèmes sociaux sous la Monarchie de Juillet chez Mgr d'Astros, Archévêque de Toulouse, censeur de La Mennais* (Paris, 1954), pp. 45-46.

the ordinance fixing the meeting places and naming the presidents of the electoral colleges.[60]

> Frenchmen, your prosperity is the source of my glory; your happiness is mine. At the moment when the electoral colleges are about to meet throughout my kingdom, you will harken to the advice of your king.
>
> . . . .
>
> Do not permit yourselves to be misled by the insidious words of enemies of public tranquility. Reject the groundless suspicions and false fears that would shake public confidence and excite grave disorders.
>
> . . . .
>
> Electors, hasten to your colleges. Let no reprehensible negligence deprive them of your presence! May a single sentiment move you, may a single flag rally you!
>
> It is your King who asks this; it is a father who calls you.
>
> Fulfill your duties. I will know how to fulfill mine.[61]

In issuing this public appeal for partisan support the King stepped down from his rôle of constitutional monarch above parties into the rôle of a party leader. A defeat for his party in the elections would be not merely a defeat for the ministry but a defeat for the crown. Charles would have either to accept humiliation or to resort to measures of dubious legality.

Prefectoral reports coming to the Ministry of the Interior about this time indicated that defeat was not unlikely, and on June 18 the ministry took the unusual step of postponing elections in twenty departments to July 12 and 19, nominally to gain time for the settlement of cases of disputed eligibility that were holding up completion of the electoral lists, but the opposition was strong in these departments, and the government probably feared the effect on the second round of the elections of a striking liberal victory on June 23, the first day of balloting. Perhaps also the ministers thought

[60] Guernon-Ranville, *Journal*, pp. 93, 108.
[61] *Moniteur*, June 14, 1830, p. 645.

that a strong governmental showing in the other departments on June 23 and July 3 might influence electors in the twenty affected departments to cast their votes for government candidates three weeks later.[62]

The opposition's electoral campaign was being directed by the "Aide-toi, le ciel t'aidera." Contrary to the insinuations of its enemies it was neither secret nor conspiratorial. It had a central organization in Paris that included the well-known liberals of the day, the Marquis de Lafayette, Jacques Laffitte, Guizot, Benjamin Constant, Jacques Dupont de l'Eure, General Etienne Gérard among others, and in the provinces it was represented by a network of committees and agents, most of them well-known to the local prefects, subprefects, and Gendarmerie. In the spring of 1830 the organization concentrated on the reelection of the 221 deputies who in March had voted for the reply to the address from the throne. It organized banquets and receptions for them when they returned to their home departments, made certain that no rival opposition candidates were presented in their colleges. Workers personally solicited votes and provided transportation to the electoral colleges and even lodging for electors who needed them. The organization's local committees advised electors on procedures to assure their inclusion on electoral lists and to eliminate unqualified government supporters. It republished an earlier manual for electors, which summarized in convenient form the required qualifications of voters and procedures on the formation and revision of electoral lists, pointing out that any elector had the right to demand the addition of qualified voters and the exclusion of the unqualified. A final section dealt with voting and offered advice on how to assure an honest count of votes. Both the *National* and the *Journal des débats* published the manual in its entirety, and the *National* announced that free copies were available at its office.[63]

---

[62] Guernon-Ranville, *Journal*, p. 109; *Moniteur*, June 20, 1830, p. 669; *Journal des débats*, June 21, 22, 1830; Bertier de Sauvigny, *Ferdinand de Bertier*, p. 460.
[63] Vaulabelle, *Histoire*, VIII, 97, 99-101, 128; AN, CC 549, Chambre

During the spring of 1830 public opinion, already disturbed by the quarrel between King and parliament and by the electoral campaign, was further agitated by the curious episode of an epidemic of fires in Normandy. They had started at the end of February, and within forty days thirty-four fires had occurred in two districts of the neighboring departments of the Manche and the Calvados. In May the number in those departments and in the adjoining Orne rose to seventy-two, and in June there were sixty-four. As the fires spread and the efforts to apprehend the suspected arsonists failed, local populations grew increasingly exasperated and even terrified. Peasants armed themselves and mounted watches. The Minister of the Interior sent investigators to the scene. Magistrates and peasants alike kept a close watch over peddlers and other strangers, all of whom were suspect, and police in Paris began special surveillance of salesmen who traveled in Normandy. But the fires, it seemed, could be neither explained nor stopped. Investigating magistrates thought that political opponents of the government were setting them to excite hatred and distrust of the government that might engender support for a refusal to pay taxes. Liberals accused royalists of trying to frighten citizens with the specter of revolution. Rumors spread that the fires were set by nobles and priests, and peasants blamed the government as at least an accomplice, since it did not put a stop to them. The Ministers of the Interior and Justice became involved in the matter in March, and in early May it came before the full council of ministers. They considered the dispatch of troops to the scene, but Polignac was opposed, holding that it was inappropriate to send the

---

et Cour des Pairs, "Comité directeur," n.d.; Pouthas, *Guizot*, pp. 432-34; *Gazette de France*, May 20, 1830; AN, F^7 6778, Reports of Gend. roy., Apr., May, June, 1830; F^7 6777, Reports of Gend. roy., May, June, July 1830; 149 AP 1, Papers of Jean-Claude Mangin, Préfet de Police, "Liste des membres composant la société *Aide-toi, le ciel t'aidera*," June 16, 1830; CC 549, Chambre et Cour des Pairs, Polignac, "Projet de note au Roi," Apr. 14, 1830; *National*, May 13, 1830; *Journal des débats*, May 14, 1830.

armed forces to apprehend a few miserable offenders. On May 16, however, after the Minister of Justice reported growing exasperation of the peasants over the government's inaction, they ordered two squadrons of cavalry and one battalion of grenadiers to the Department of the Manche and a second battalion to the Calvados. A week later two regiments of the Royal Guard were ordered to the two departments. The number of fires did not decline substantially until July, but the presence of the troops had a calming influence on the agitated population. No satisfactory explanation of the epidemic has ever been found. A committee of the Chamber of Peers in the autumn of 1830 conducted a searching examination of the available evidence but concluded only that no member of the Polignac Ministry could be charged with involvement in a plot "to deliver a province of France to flames."[64]

Concern over the fires in Normandy, the uncertainties of the Algerian expedition, and the darkening electoral prospect made June an anxious month for the Polignac Ministry. Just before the elections, however, a shaft of light cut through the darkness. News came that the Army of Africa had landed on the African coast. On May 16 Bourmont had reported from Toulon that the expedition was almost completely embarked and would be ready to sail in three days. Only three months had elapsed since the decision to prepare the expedition, and in that time the Ministers of War and the Navy had assembled 100 war vessels, 500 transports, more than 200 small craft, and 37,000 men. Bourmont, who had been selected over Marshal Auguste Marmont, who

[64] Cour des Pairs, "Rapport fait à la Cour par M. le Comte de Bastard," *Moniteur*, Dec. 4, 1830, Supplément A, pp. 1, 5-6; AN, CC 550, Chambre et Cour des Pairs, Cour royale de Caen, "Etat de tous les Incendies qui ont éclaté dans le Ressort de la Cour royale de Caen depuis 8 Août 1829 jusqu'au 5 Novembre 1830"; CC 550, Ministre de l'Intérieur to Préfets de la Manche et du Calvados, May 15, 1830; CC 548, "Resumé de la correspondance des Magistrats [July 1830]"; F7 6777-6778, Reports of Gend. roy. on fires, May, June, July 1830; F7 3883, "Bulletin de Paris," July 3, 1830; Guernon-Ranville, *Journal*, pp. 80-87, 90-91, 109-10, 123; AN, F7 6741, Préfet de la Manche to Ministre de l'Intérieur, June 9, 1830; *Journal des débats*, May 20, 27, 1830.

sorely wanted the post, was formally named commander in chief of the expedition on May 18. The leading division sailed on the first favorable wind, May 25, and by the twenty-seventh the entire fleet had departed. It approached the coast of Africa two days later, but adverse weather caused the cautious naval commander, Admiral Guy-Victor Duperré, who from the beginning had many misgivings about the expedition, to order withdrawal to the shelter of the Bay of Palma, off the island of Majorca. Here the fleet remained for more than a week awaiting a break in the weather. The delay aroused concern in France and encouraged those, particularly among the liberals, who opposed the expedition and had been predicting its failure. On June 13 the fleet again approached Algiers and this time dropped anchor as planned off the peninsula of Sidi-Ferruch. Disembarkation began at dawn the next day, and all troops were ashore by the sixteenth. They won their first engagement three days later while supplies and equipment were still coming ashore. Paris learned of the landing on June 18, and on the twenty-third Haussez formally reported to the ministry both the successful disembarkation and the first victory ashore. The ministry's plan to enter the elections with an initial success in Africa had been realized. A few days later, however, both Haussez and Duperré were defeated at the polls, suggesting that success in Algeria would not have the salutary effect that the ministry expected.[65]

On June 26 Peyronnet reported to the ministers that the returns from the arrondissement colleges showed the voting going against the government and that most of the 221 who were candidates at this level had been reelected. Additional

[65] Haussez, *Mémoires*, II, 189, 213, 215-17; Vaulabelle, *Histoire*, VIII, 119, 135-37, 139-41; BN, MSS Fr. 7986, Bourmont to Polignac, May 16, 1830; *Moniteur*, July 8, 1830, pp. 742-43; *National*, July 9, 1830; AN, F⁷ 6777, Gend. roy., 10ᵉ Légion, Cie. de la Gironde, "Rapport . . . ," Mar. 1, Apr. 1, 1830; Cie. des Bas-Pyrenées, "Rapport spécial . . . Juin 1830"; 19ᵉ Légion, Cie. de la Haute-Loire, "Rapport . . . ," July 3, 1830; Chef, 22ᵉ Légion, to Ministre de l'Intérieur, May 8, 1830; Cmdt., 24ᵉ Légion to Ministre de l'Intérieur, Mar. 10, 1830; F⁷ 3884, "Bulletin de Paris," June 19, 1830; Haussez, *Mémoires*, II, 224-25.

returns available at the two succeeding meetings were no more heartening. Almost certainly the government's hope for an electoral victory to resolve its conflict with the liberals was going to be frustrated, and it had either to accept defeat or to find another way to overcome the opposition in the chamber. At their session on June 29, when the ministers were exploring the paths open to them, Chantelauze, who had remained silent through most of the discussion, declared that he had a sure way. Acting under Article 14 the government should provisionally suspend the constitution and govern by decree, dissolve the chamber once the elections were completed, change the electoral law to assure a loyal majority, and order new elections. To forestall any resistance that these resolute measures might inspire and to counter it should it arise he would reenforce the garrisons of the four largest cities, giving each at least 20,000 to 30,000 men, and simultaneously with the publication of the ordinances declare a state of siege in these four cities. The other ministers were not at this time prepared to take such drastic measures, but after long discussion all agreed that under Article 14 the King might both suspend laws and legislate in order to save the state from imminent danger.[66]

For a week at the end of June and the first days of July the ministry reached no further decision. The Prefect of Police heard that men close to Polignac, including the Austrian ambassador, were pushing him toward a coup d'état. Bertier urged him to convoke the parliament in a provincial city far from the corrupting influences of Paris and coerce it with two reliable divisions recalled from the Army of Africa. But the ministers were awaiting the results of the departmental elections on July 3, in which they still had a forlorn hope of reversing the verdict of the balloting in the arrondissements. But as the returns came in, this last hope vanished. The government did win a majority among the departmental seats, but it was too small to overcome the

[66] Guernon-Ranville, *Journal*, pp. 120, 123-27; Montbel, *Souvenirs*, pp. 234-35.

earlier losses. The departments in which the elections had been postponed offered the government no hopes, for they were strongholds of the opposition; of the one hundred seats contested there the government won but nineteen. The final count for the entire country—known only in the third week of July—was 270 deputies for the opposition, including 201 of the 221, and 145 for the government.[67]

By July 4, when the first results of the departmental colleges became known, the King had concluded that his appeal to the country had failed, that his government would again face a hostile chamber. He emphasized to the ministry that day that he would not compromise; having staked the prestige of the crown, he would act vigorously against the seditious electors and deputies, who in his eyes were trying to usurp royal powers and disrupt constitutional government. He listened to Polignac's report on the council's deliberations at its preceding meeting and then ordered his ministers to discuss further the options open to the government and to bring a definite plan of action to their next meeting with him three days hence.[68]

The ministry's next session, on July 6, opened with more discouraging reports from the Minister of the Interior on election returns. Polignac declared that recourse to Article 14 was the only solution, and Peyronnet then presented— Guernon-Ranville thought the idea was Polignac's—a proposal that the King summon a Grand Council of France, a kind of new Assembly of Notables, composed of peers, deputies, magistrates, and members of departmental general councils under the presidency of the Dauphin. The King would report to it the problems he faced in dealing with the Chamber of Deputies and ask for its advice. Only Polignac and Haussez supported the proposal. The other ministers, including Peyronnet himself after he had heard the argu-

---

[67] AN, 149, AP 1, "Rapport du 22 Juillet 1830"; Bertier de Sauvigny, *Ferdinand de Bertier*, p. 462; Guernon-Ranville, *Journal*, pp. 121-29; *Journal des débats*, July 7, 25, 1830; *Temps* (Paris), July 12, 23, 1830.
[68] Guernon-Ranville, *Journal*, pp. 128-29.

ments of its opponents, agreed that the council would be powerless and that the summoning of it would only proclaim that the government lacked any plan to deal with the emergency. The Grand Council progressed no further, and Peyronnet brought forward a more substantial and practical suggestion. Under the authority of Article 14 the King would, as soon as the elections were completed, issue ordinances dissolving the chamber, changing the electoral law and ordering new elections, and suspending the freedom of the press. This was the program that the King and ministry eventually adopted, but not all ministers were convinced of its wisdom. Guernon-Ranville, arguing that the present situation did not justify resort to such a drastic and dangerous course, urged that the ministry first try to work with the new chamber. The opposition was not, he believed, a solid bloc, and confronted with the firmness of the King, on the one hand, and the threat of revolution posed by the Left, on the other, it might dissolve and make possible a government majority. If, despite the government's efforts, the chamber rejected the budget, a revolutionary act, the ministry would be justified in using Article 14. Moreover, the postponement of a confrontation would give the government time to repatriate the victorious Army of Africa to support its policy. Guernon-Ranville's colleagues were unconvinced by his arguments; all agreed to recommend Peyronnet's proposals to the King.[69]

An encounter later in the month between Bertier and Horace Sébastiani, a leading liberal deputy, suggested that perhaps Guernon-Ranville was right, that some of the opposition would welcome an accommodation. Sébastiani told Bertier that he and his friends were concerned by threats to public order; they were willing to accept changes in the electoral law and the press laws and the retention of Polignac at the head of the government in return for three ministries for opposition leaders including Casimir Périer and Sébastiani himself. Bertier carried the proposal to Po-

[69] *Ibid.*, pp. 129-41; Montbel, *Souvenirs*, pp. 235-36; *Moniteur*, Supplément A, Dec. 4, 1830, p. 2.

lignac, but the first minister rejected it on grounds that the time for accommodation had passed.[70]

The ministry met with the King at Saint-Cloud on July 7, and Charles heard its recommendations and Guernon-Ranville's reservations. He expressed his satisfaction that all agreed on his using Article 14 and differed only on timing. He would, he said, accept their recommendations, because their enemies threatened not merely the ministry but the monarchy itself.[71]

> The spirit of the revolution survives in its entirety in the men of the left [Guernon-Ranville recalled Charles's saying]; in assailing the ministry, it is the monarchy that they want to attack; it is the monarchical system that they want to overthrow.
>
> Unfortunately I have more experience on this point than you, gentlemen, who are too young to have seen the Revolution; I recall what happened then; the first retreat that my unfortunate brother made was the signal for his downfall. . . . They protested to him, too, their love and fidelity, they asked of him only the dismissal of his ministers, he gave in and all was lost.
>
> They claim to be angry only with you; they say to me: "Dismiss your ministers and we shall reach an understanding." I will not dismiss you; first because I have an affection for all of you, gentlemen, and because you have my full confidence; but also because, if I give in this time to their demand, they will end by treating us all as they treated my brother. . . .[72]

The ministry charged Peyronnet with the drafting of the ordinances on elections and Chantelauze that on the press and a statement justifying the King's use of the ordinance power. In their own view the ministry was not preparing to

[70] Bertier de Sauvigny, *Ferdinand de Bertier*, pp. 462-63.
[71] Guernon-Ranville, *Journal*, pp. 141-42; Montbel, *Souvenirs*, p. 238.
[72] Guernon-Ranville, *Journal*, pp. 142-43. Montbel's version of this declaration is substantially the same as Guernon-Ranville's. Montbel, *Souvenirs*, p. 238.

violate the Charter but only to restore the government, threatened by a factious majority illegally claiming the right to name and control the King's ministers, to the form envisaged by the Charter.[73]

Before the council met again news arrived of the capture of Algiers and the surrender of the Dey. A telegraphic dispatch from Toulon reached the capital on July 9. An artillery salute by cannon at the Invalides first broke the news to Parisians, announcements were made in the theaters that evening, and many buildings were illuminated. The next day the story appeared in the newspapers; the opposition dailies admitted on that and succeeding days their pleasure over the victory but refused to give credit for it to the Polignac Ministry and expressed concern over the use the government might make at home of its victory abroad. The King requested that a *Te Deum* be sung in all the churches of France, and on the next Sunday, July 11, the Archbishop of Paris presided over a great ceremony of thanksgiving at Notre Dame attended by the King. A procession of twelve carriages and their escorts moved through streets lined with the Royal Guard and troops of the Line from the Tuileries to the cathedral. The Archbishop waited at the portal to greet the King.[74] He had already in a pastoral letter acclaimed the victory in Africa and opined, "May the enemies of our God and King everywhere and always be so treated; may all those who dare to rise against him be thus confounded."[75] He now declared before the monarch, "May he soon come again to thank God for other marvels no less sweet and no less brilliant."[76] Enemies of the regime later

[73] Montbel, *Souvenirs*, p. 238; Haussez, *Mémoires*, pp. 231, 232, 237, 239.

[74] Haussez, *Mémoires*, II, 218; AN, 149 AP 1, Préfet maritime de Toulon to Ministre de l'Intérieur, July 9, 1830; F⁷ 3884, "Bulletin de Paris," July 10, 1830; *Moniteur*, July 10, p. 750, July 12, 1830, p. 758; *Drapeau blanc* (Paris), July 10, 1830; *National*, July 13, 1830; *Journal des débats*, July 10, 1830; *Globe* (Paris), July 12, 15, 1830; *Temps*, July 10, 1830; Guernon-Ranville, *Journal*, p. 145.

[75] *Moniteur*, July 11, 1830, p. 754.

[76] *Ibid.*, July 12, 1830, p. 758.

denounced these statements as counsel of a coup d'état, but the Archbishop was no adviser of the King, and he was probably only referring naively to his hopes for a victory in the elections. Official sources reported great enthusiasm among the crowds lining the streets of the royal progress, but Haussez and Etienne Pasquier, who were in the procession, reported that spectators were ominously silent and that the King was dismayed by the popular reaction to what was to him so glorious a victory.[77]

After the fall of Algiers the English renewed their representations for assurances on the French government's intentions in North Africa. The ministry had at the end of June considered its policy in event of conquest, and all had concurred that, the assurances given to the powers notwithstanding, the King's hands were free. A few days after word of the surrender reached Paris the King decided that France would keep Algiers as a colonial possession, and he informed the British ambassador, "In taking Algiers I considered only France's dignity, in keeping it or returning it, I shall consider only her interests." It was not a reply likely to win sympathy for the Bourbons for the trial of strength that the King knew lay just ahead. On July 25 Lord Aberdeen, the British Foreign Minister, told the French ambassador that never before, not even under the Republic or the Empire, had France given Britain such grave cause for complaint as she had in the past year.[78]

The news from across the Mediterranean briefly diverted the ministers from their domestic cares at their next meeting on July 10 and perhaps fortified their resolve, but certainly the success there did not determine them to use Article 14,

---

[77] Roger Limouzin-Lamothe, *Monseigneur de Quélen, Archévêque de Paris: son rôle dans l'Eglise de France de 1815 à 1839 d'après des archives privées* (Paris, 1955-57), I, 314; Pasquier, *Mémoires*, VI, 238-39; AN, F⁷ 3884, "Bulletin de Paris," July 12, 1830; *Moniteur*, July 12, 1830, p. 759; Haussez, *Mémoires*, II, 218.

[78] Guernon-Ranville, *Journal*, pp. 111-12; Bertier, *Restoration*, p. 439; Alfred Nettement, *Histoire de la Restauration* (Paris, 1860-72), VIII, 537-38.

that decision having been made three days earlier. Opposition leaders feared that the victory might encourage the
government onto dangerous paths. On July 10 a group of
forty to fifty deputies, peers, lawyers, and journalists who in
May had agreed to meet if a coup d'état seemed imminent
gathered at the home of Duc Victor de Broglie to discuss
what action they might take. They now decided that if the
coup were attempted they would refuse to pay taxes, campaign to persuade others to follow their example, and urge
the deputies to refuse to vote the budget.[79]

At the ministry's session of July 10 Peyronnet and Chantelauze presented drafts of the proposed ordinances, and that
meeting and all those for the next ten days the ministers
devoted to discussion of them. On Tuesday, July 20, they
agreed to the substance of four separate ordinances. One
dissolved the newly elected assembly. A second set September 6 and 13 as dates for new elections. An ordinance on the
press suspended the freedom of the periodical press and
required preliminary authorization to editor and printer
separately for every periodical publication, an authorization
granted for only three-month periods and subject to withdrawal at any time. Any journal published in violation of
these regulations would be seized and its presses put out of
operation. The fourth ordinance established a new system
of elections intended to return a more sympathetic chamber. The arrondissement colleges would henceforth only
nominate candidates; actual election of deputies would be
by departmental colleges composed of the one-fourth most
highly taxed citizens in each department, and they would
be required to take only half of their choices from among
the nominees of the arrondissement colleges. In determining
the eligibility of voters, which was based on taxes paid, the
prefects would henceforth exclude the *Impôt des patentes*
(a tax on businesses) and the doors and windows tax, the
purpose of this change being to disenfranchise urban voters,

[79] Guernon-Ranville, *Journal*, p. 145; Victor de Broglie, *Souvenirs,
1785-1870* (Paris, 1886), III, 260; Duvergier de Hauranne, *Histoire*, x,
507, 524.

especially lawyers and businessmen and to give more weight to the votes of rural landholders.[80]

The final drafts of the ordinances were read, reread, and approved at the council meeting on Saturday, July 24. They would be presented to the King the next day for signature. Chantelauze, still at work on the justification, promised to have it ready for presentation with the ordinances on the twenty-fifth. Apparently apprehensive that they were committing an illegal act despite Article 14, the ministers decided to submit their ordinances to the next session of parliament for approval.[81]

The ministry had given little thought to the possibility of violent resistance to its coup against the chamber. Peyronnet proposed that he discuss with the Prefect of Police measures to assure order in the capital, but his colleagues thought this unnecessary or not worth the divulging of the secret of the ordinances, which had been carefully guarded. Capelle suggested that the government send a special commissioner to each of the country's military districts to assist in the maintenance of order; the council approved but could not find qualified and reliable men on short notice, and nothing was done. Haussez expressed concern to Polignac, who was acting as Minister of War in Bourmont's absence, over lack of military precautions in Paris; the president offered only an evasive reply and, when pressed, an exaggerated report of the number of troops available in the capital.[82]

---

[80] Guernon-Ranville, *Journal*, pp. 143-44, 148-49; Montbel, *Souvenirs*, pp. 238-39; *Moniteur*, July 26, 1830, p. 814.

[81] Guernon-Ranville, *Journal*, p. 152.

[82] *Moniteur*, Dec. 16, 1830, p. 1719; Guernon-Ranville, *Journal*, pp. 151-53; Haussez, *Mémoires*, II, 241.

II

The Sources of Opposition

In the months after the formation of the Polignac Ministry the men of the opposition were vigorously active. They spoke out in the press, in parliament, and on public rostrums, contended with prefects and subprefects to get their candidates on ballots, their voters on electoral lists; they campaigned for liberal candidates, fought government prosecutors who tried in the courts to silence their journals, and considered resistance, even violent resistance, in which the populace might join if the government should violate the Charter. What moved these men to devote time and energy to political campaigning, to assume the onus of official and royal displeasure, to risk fortunes and careers, and even to contemplate popular insurrection with all its unpredictable perils?

By the spring of 1830 a constitutional issue set the opposition against the King and his government, and the division reflected a fundamental difference of opinion on how France should be governed. Charles X was determined that choice of ministers be his alone. The opposition was determined, not that it choose the King's ministers, but that they be acceptable to the majority of a freely elected parliament. This had been one of the objectives of the Revolution of 1789; it was sanctioned, they held, by the Charter. Now the King denied it, not only challenging the chamber but violating the constitution itself. Here the issue was joined. King and parliament confronted each other on a question of constitutional principle.

Abstract constitutional questions, however, rarely move large numbers of men to dangerous action. Certainly in France the constitutional question that historians have

44

made to appear so critical in the spring and summer of 1830 had lain dormant and unresolved for a decade and a half, since 1814, when Louis XVIII's constitutional commission wrote into the Charter the ambiguous Article 13, "The ministers are responsible," but failed to prescribe to whom they were responsible. Not until 1830 did any considerable body of men find it imperative to define that responsibility. After Charles had been driven from his throne in 1830 the revolutionary leaders promised a law establishing ministerial responsibility but never produced it; the constitutional question was apparently not of vital importance to them. Nonetheless, it is significant as an issue on which a variety of grievances, fears, and aspirations in France of 1829 and 1830 could focus. In these discontents and ambitions one must seek the forces that nurtured opposition and ultimately revolution.

Charles X feared for the very survival of the Bourbon monarchy, and at times he and his sympathizers suspected and even believed in the existence of a conspiracy to overthrow it. In 1827 the private office of the Minister of the Interior drew up a report on "the maneuvers of the revolutionary faction" and listed among its members Talleyrand, Lafayette, Laffitte, Guizot, Périer, Constant, Thiers, and a number of Napoleonic generals.[1] Six months later the Prefect of Police reported Constant as saying, "All is ripe for an accident," and the prefect had heard that five or six thousand former army officers, organized and armed with the help of Laffitte, were ready to act when an accident should occur.[2] Polignac's Minister of the Navy, Haussez, was sure when he wrote his memoirs two years after the Revolution that a minutely organized conspiracy against the Bourbon monarchy had by 1830 spread its operations over all France and even had connections abroad. It had collected

[1] AN, F⁷ 6772, Police générale, "Manoeuvres de la faction révolutionnaire . . . ," Mar. 4, 1827.

[2] AN, F⁷ 6772, Préfet de Police to Ministre de l'Intérieur, Sept. 19, 1827.

funds, enrolled workers to fight in the streets, and distributed weapons. The Duc d'Orléans, he charged, was their substitute for the legitimate King.[3] Rodolphe Apponyi, an attaché of the Austrian embassy and cousin of the ambassador, was sure that the French branch of that international conspiracy—the Carbonari—had since the formation of the Polignac Ministry organized in Paris a force of at least sixty thousand men to overthrow the Bourbons. The "so-called political faction" in the chamber, his name for the 221, was only an auxiliary of the Carbonari.[4] The police and the Gendarmerie, forever sniffing about for plots and conspiracies, far from sustaining Apponyi's fantasies, found only the "Comité Directeur" and its affiliates in the provinces. One Gendarmerie commander in Alsace called it the "Comité Révolutionnaire," but it was simply the central committee of the "Aide-toi, l'ciel t'aidera," which was, of course, a legal organization operating openly to support the electoral campaigns, not of revolutionaries, but of liberal monarchists, candidates for the chamber.[5]

Most feared of the alternatives to the Bourbon monarchy suggested by France's recent history was the republic, and some saw it as a real and present threat. The Gendarmerie officer who referred to the "Aide-toi" as a revolutionary organization believed it to be spreading republican propaganda in his district.[6] Charles X seemingly believed the republicans so strong that should he display the slightest weakness in his dealing with the liberal opposition France

[3] Charles d'Haussez, *Mémoires du Baron d'Haussez, dernier Ministre de la Marine sous la Restauration* (Paris, 1896, 1897), II, 231-33.

[4] Rodolphe Apponyi, *Vingt-cinq ans à Paris, 1826-1850: journal du Comte Rodolphe Apponyi . . .* , 2d ed. (Paris, 1913-26), I, 348-50; AN, 149, AP 1, Papiers de Jean-Claude Mangin, Préfet de Police, 1829-30, "Rapport du 22 juillet 1830."

[5] AN, F⁷ 6777, 6778, Police gén., Gendarmerie royale, "Rapports," Jan.-July 1830; F⁷ 6772, Report of Préfet de la Vendée, Aug. 25, 1829; AN, BB¹⁸ 1186, Ministère de la Justice, Correspondance gén. de la Division criminelle, Procureur-gén., Amiens, to Ministre de la Justice, July 9, 1830; AN, 149 AP 1, Ministre de l'Intérieur to Préfet de Police, April 17, 1830.

[6] AN, F⁷ 6778, Gend. roy., 22ᵉ Légion, "Rapport," Jan. 8, 1830.

would soon be a republic. His definition of a republican, ✓ however, apparently included almost everyone to the left of himself and Polignac.

France sheltered a few republicans in 1830, but the active minority of them had submerged themselves in the liberal opposition to the Polignac Ministry. In the early years of the Restoration "Republican" had been a nasty word, like "Communist" in America a century later, used in political debate to frighten or besmirch one's opponents. Napoleon had tried to efface the memory of the Republic, not a fanciful aim because most Frenchmen *wanted* to forget the Terror, which was then inseparably associated with the Republic. The historian Edgar Quinet recalled that as a boy during the Empire he was surprised to come upon the words "Jacobins," "Girondins," and "Montagnards" in a book, and he did not know what they meant. In the first years of the Restoration, too, most children and people grown to adulthood since the Revolution knew little of the Republic, and what they did learn was hostile to it. In the 1820s, however, ⌐ memoirs of participants in the Revolution and the Imperial wars appeared on the bookstalls along with popular histories that presented the Revolution and the Empire as a great epoch in French history. Adolphe Thiers's *Histoire de la Révolution française*, published between 1823 and 1827, and Mignet's history of the Revolution, which appeared in 1824, although partial to the constitutional monarchy, brought a new objectivity to the study of the Republic, and Thiers expressed his admiration of the Convention and excused the Terror.[7]

In the early twenties a few militant republicans had joined with Bonapartists and liberals in the Carbonari, a

[7] Georges Weill, *Histoire du parti républicain en France, 1814-1870* (Paris, 1928), pp. 1, 7, 16-17; Jean Lucas-Dubreton, *Le Culte de Napoléon, 1815-1848* (Paris, 1960), pp. 244-47; Stanley Mellon, *The Political Uses of History: A Study of Historians in the French Restoration* (Stanford, 1958), pp. 21, 28-30, 33-34; Jacques Godechot, *Les Révolutions, 1770-1799* (Paris, 1963), pp. 238-40; Alphonse Aulard, "Thiers historien de la Révolution française," *La Révolution française*, 66 (1914), 492, 494-95, 504, 506; 67 (1914), 18-21.

secret organization plotting the overthrow of the Bourbons, but the miscarriage of their plans discredited all illegal opposition. Georges Weill, the historian of the republican movement, thinks that republican secret societies probably continued to exist throughout the Restoration, apparently drawing most of their members from students in Paris. In 1827 a group of them attempted to set up a shadow municipal government of Paris prepared to take over the administration of the city in event of insurrection, but in the crisis of 1830 it proved to be only a shadow. Fear that Polignac might attempt a coup d'état inspired another group of republican students in January 1830 to organize a force to resist such an effort. They named Lafayette their commander in chief and recruited followers in the Latin Quarter, but the record of student participation in the fighting of July 1830 suggests that they were not a serious threat.[8] A number of republicans joined the "Aide-toi" in 1827, and they remained in it in 1828 when many of the moderates withdrew, thinking that the society's purpose had been accomplished with the liberal victory in the election of 1827. Direction of the organization, however, remained in the hands of Guizot, Odilon Barrot, and other constitutional monarchists who certainly had no commitment to a republic. A newspaper, the *Tribune des départements*, sympathetic to republican ideas, established in 1829, foundered after four months' existence for want of adequate financial backing. Revived by a group of republican students with financial help from Lafayette, it resumed publication in April 1830 and threw its support to the liberal coalition opposing Polignac. With a circulation of about 500—the liberal *Journal des débats* had a circulation of nearly 12,000—it was scarcely a formidable enemy.[9]

No evidence suggests that the republicans enjoyed any

---

[8] Cf. Chs. III and VIII.

[9] Weill, *Parti républicain*, pp. 7-11, 17-19, 21-23; Achille de Vaulabelle, *Histoire des deux Restaurations jusqu'à l'avènement de Louis-Philippe (de janvier 1813 à octobre 1830)*, 5th ed. (Paris, 1860), VIII, 98-100; Charles Ledré, *La Presse à l'assaut de la monarchie* (Paris, 1960), pp. 100, 243, 258.

consequential popular support. The Ministry of Justice kept a careful record of seditious incidents reported by its agents throughout the country, usually seditious cries or the distribution of seditious literature. In the five and a half years from the beginning of 1825 to the outbreak of revolution in 1830 the ministry took notice of 282 incidents. Two were pro-republican—one in 1826 and one in 1827; eighty-one were pro-Napoleonic. The monthly reports of the Gendarmerie throughout France during the first seven months of 1830, when political feelings ran high, noted not a single "Vive la République!"[10]

Both the dimensions and the organization of the republican movement in 1830 remain something of a mystery. With certainty one can say only that the handful of militant republicans were by themselves no threat to the Bourbon monarchy, but if the monarchy were overthrown by other more powerful forces, the republicans might, in the absence of any other substitute government, be able to impose a republic on France or on Paris. But lacking broad popular support they could not long maintain it. In 1830, moreover, there were other alternatives, and the strength of the forces favoring a reformed monarchy or a revived Napoleonic Empire far exceeded the strength of the republicans.

The renewal of interest in the Revolution and the Empire in the 1820s had contributed more to the revival of Bonapartism than to the revival of republicanism. The flood of memoirs by Napoleon and his associates and many histories began the development of the Napoleonic Legend, the legend of Napoleon as the defender of the benefits of the Revolution, the protector of the church, the advocate of a peaceful, united Europe, and as the general who had led France to the apex of her power and glory. Even illiterates received the same message from popular songs of Béranger— "Waterloo," "Les Deux Grenadiers," "Le Vieux Drapeau,"

10 AN, Inventaire de la Série BB[18], Tome 1, Nos. 1-1226 (1825-31); AN, F7 6777, 6778, Police gén., Gend. roy., Reports, July 1830. The other two hundred seditious incidents were various affronts or threats to the King, the royal family, or the government.

and others. A collection of them published in 1821 sold 11,000 copies in a single week, and an illustrated edition published in 1826 achieved even larger sales. One of the first acts of Polignac's new Prefect of Police in August 1829 was an order to stop street singers from glorifying Napoleon in song, and his order specifically mentioned one of Béranger's, "Les Souvenirs du peuple."[11]

Napoleon became a folk hero, at once the conquering Emperor and the Little Corporal who had brought his country glory and wise rule and whose defeat was the defeat of France. A measure of his popularity was the flourishing sale of Bonapartist symbols and likenesses of him and of his son, the Duc de Reichstadt. The police were constantly on the lookout for seditious objects, and among those reported in the Department of the Seine in 1828 and 1829 all but one were Napoleonic, and that one—a tricolored drum—could have been republican or Napoleonic. The others included engravings, medals, and busts of Napoleon and his son, reproductions of Napoleonic battle scenes, neckties decorated with Napoleonic eagles and hats, and liquor flasks shaped to resemble the Duke.[12] From Bordeaux came a report in June 1830 that "effigies of the usurper" were being sold everywhere in the department.[13] After the Revolution of 1830 a veritable parade of Napoleons moved across the stages of Parisian theaters, catering to an apparently boundless popular interest. The first play about him opened at the Cirque-Olympique on August 31; two more began on October 9, and before the year's end eleven additional dramas of Napoleon's life reached the capital's stages.[14]

Although the legend flourished, Bonapartism in 1830 was

[11] Lucas-Dubreton, *Culte de Napoléon*, pp. 238-39, 244-47; Suzanne d'Huart, "Le Dernier Préfet de Police de Charles X: Claude Mangin," *Actes* du 80e Congrès national des sociétés savantes, Dijon (1959); Section d'histoire moderne et contemporaine, p. 606.

[12] AN, F7 6706, Police gén., Objets séditieux, 1818-30, Seine-Yonne.

[13] AN, F7 6777, Gend. roy., 10e Légion, Cie. de la Gironde, "Rapport," June 1, 1830.

[14] Annie Marguerite Lafon, "Le Légende napoléonienne à Paris de 1830 à 1840 à travers le théâtre," typescript thesis. Diplome d'Etudes supérieures d'Histoire, Faculté des Lettres de Paris (1959), pp. 14-16.

not an organized political movement and in itself posed no
threat to the Bourbons. Occasionally one heard the Duc de
Reichstadt mentioned as a successor to the aging Charles X
preferable to either the heir-apparent, the Duc d'Angoulême, or his heir, the King's young grandson, the Duc de
Bordeaux, posthumous son of the late Duc de Berry, who
would not achieve his majority until 1836. Talleyrand once
raised the possibility of this succession with one of Charles's
advisers, the Baron Eugène de Vitrolles, and in 1825 Lafayette informed Joseph Bonaparte, then living in exile in
the United States, that in anticipation of the collapse of the
Bourbon regime he was prepared to work for the succession
of Napoleon II.[15] Occasionally his candidacy appeared at
humbler levels. On June 28, 1830, a sign posted on a village
church door in the Department of the Gers declared, "Vive
Napoléon! Roi de France. Il regnera malgré la fureur des
français," and at the opposite end of the country, in Brittany, the Gendarmerie reported a citizen's announcing the
imminent arrival of Napoleon II.[16] But the Duke himself, a
frail young man, was far away in Austria under the watchful
eyes of his Hapsburg relatives. In July 1830 the Prefect of
Police heard of a plot to kidnap him and bring him to
France, but this seems to have been only another of the
many baseless rumors that flowed across the prefect's desk.[17]
The Ministry of the Interior collected information from civil
and diplomatic officials at home and abroad on the activities
of members of the Bonaparte family, all banned from
France, or their friends and even on their servants and former servants suspected of maintaining any contact with the
family, but the result of their labors was only a mass of
trivia that revealed no serious political activity.[18]

Within France lived many Napoleonic marshals and

[15] Lucas-Dubreton, *Culte de Napoléon*, p. 262; Arnold Whitridge,
"Joseph Napoleon in America," *History Today*, 9 (1959), 308-18.
[16] AN, F⁷ 6777, Gend. roy., 13ᵉ Légion, Cie. du Gers, "Résumé . . .
juin 1830," July 4, 1830; 5ᵉ Légion, Cie. des Côtes-du-Nord, "Résumé
. . . mai 1830," June 4, 1830.
[17] AN, 149 AP 1, "Rapport du 22 juillet 1830."
[18] AN, F⁷ 6669, Police gén., Famille Bonaparte, 1818-30.

generals and high civil officials, some of them disgruntled and alienated by the Bourbons, but none emerged to lead a Bonapartist political movement. Indeed Bonapartism in 1830 was politically important primarily as a focus of discontent against the existing regime and as a reminder that a substitute for the Bourbons, short of the Republic, was possible. The liberal opponents of Charles appreciated the broad popular appeal of Napoleon and tried to join him to their own cause. The *National* declared in February 1830, "We profit from his wars, we are ruled in large part by his institutions. France is immensely indebted to the man who was everything in his time." Shortly before the elections in June Thiers wrote in the same journal, "Napoleon is the greatest man of his century...."[19] The "Aide-toi" welcomed Bonapartists into its ranks, and the Bonapartists, like the republicans, subordinated their unpromising cause to the practical objective of ousting the Polignac Ministry.[20]

The outcome of the Revolution of July—the substitution of King Louis-Philippe for King Charles X—suggests the existence of an Orléanist conspiracy against the Bourbons. Partisans of Charles X suspected, even believed in it. They accused the Duc d'Orléans of seeking popular favor by opening the garden of his residence, the Palais-Royal, to the public, of wooing Bonapartists by filling his military household with Napoleonic officers, by courting the middle classes by his affectation of bourgeois manners, of appealing to liberals by contributing generously to their campaign committees.[21] In 1827 after the elections of that year had returned a liberal majority to the chamber, a pamphlet that appeared in Paris aroused new alarms. "Let's go, Prince," it declared to Orléans, "have a little courage. In our monarchy there remains a good position for the asking . . . , that of first

[19] Lucas-Dubreton, *Culte de Napoléon*, pp. 269-70.

[20] Vaulabelle, *Histoire*, VIII, 99; Lucas-Dubreton, *Culte de Napoléon*, p. 266.

[21] Charles de Rémusat, *Mémoires de ma vie* (Paris, 1958-67), II, 289-90; Haussez, *Mémoires*, II, 234; Apponyi, *Vingt-cinq ans*, I, 244, 262; Lucas-Dubreton, *Culte de Napoléon*, pp. 253-54; AN, F⁷ 6772, Report of Préfet de Police, Sept. 7, 1827.

citizen of France." "Your highness has only to stoop to take the jewel that is there on the ground. . . ." The author later explained that that jewel was the leadership of the opposition, but the public prosecutor charged him with advocating the Duke's usurpation of the crown, and the court sentenced the author to fifteen months in prison.[22]

More serious support for Orléans in the early months of 1830 came from opposition newspapers, especially from the *National*. Its young editors developed a theory of the continuation of the French Revolution in the pattern of the English revolution of the seventeenth century.[23] The English revolution had achieved its ultimate goal—a representative monarchy—only with a second revolution, the Revolution of 1688, when, Thiers explained in the *National* in February 1830, "a dynasty did not know how to reign over a newly constituted society, and another family that knew better was chosen." England chose "the family closest to the deposed prince." France must have her peaceful Revolution of 1688, and her William and Mary could be only the head of the family closest to the Bourbons, the Duc d'Orléans.[24]

In the succeeding weeks the *National* continued to raise the question of the dynasty, and so, too, did the *Globe*, the *Journal du commerce*, and *France nouvelle*,[25] but the Duke himself had no part in this advocacy of his cause. He never conspired against his Bourbon relatives, but he did take care to disassociate himself from the unpopular policies of Louis XVIII and Charles X, and he was determined not to be a victim of their blunders. When Napoleon returned to France in 1815 Orléans had not accompanied Louis to Ghent but took refuge in London without the King's permission, and in May 1830 he exclaimed of his cousins, "God knows where they will be six months from now!" and

22 Ledré, *Presse*, pp. 84-85.

23 Prosper Duvergier de Hauranne, *Histoire du gouvernement parlementaire en France, 1814-1848* (Paris, 1857-71), x, 387; Rémusat, *Mémoires*, ii, 287.

24 Duvergier de Hauranne, *Histoire*, x, 402; *National* (Paris), Feb. 12, 1830.

25 Duvergier de Hauranne, *Histoire*, x, 403-5; Rémusat, *Mémoires*, ii, 287-89.

avowed that whatever might happen, "I will not budge from here."[26] He maintained outwardly friendly relations with the Bourbons but at the same time gathered around him in the Palais-Royal a circle of friends that included two Imperial marshals, Edouard Mortier and Jacques MacDonald, and several lesser Napoleonic officers, Talleyrand—anxious for new honors—and a number of opposition peers and deputies, among them Constant, Laffitte, and Périer. Many of these men later held high office in the Orléanist monarchy, but the Duke at least had no forethought of this in the 1820s, and the rumors of coup d'état and revolution that circulated in the late spring and summer of 1830 aroused only his anxiety. Guizot was convinced that he hoped for the consolidation of the Bourbon monarchy.[27] His friend Charles de Semonville, Grand Référendaire of the Senate, warned him on July 21, 1830, that within five days he might have to choose among Saint-Cloud, Paris, or London, among loyalty to the King, leadership of a revolution, or exile. Shocked and alarmed by the suggestion he thought only of flight—to Eu, his chateau in Normandy, or to his sister's seat in Auvergne. Semonville tried to persuade him to a more heroic course but with no success.[28] The royalist Vitrolles, openly prejudiced against Orléans, had had a conversation with him on July 25, and, looking back later, he was convinced that the Duke had not foreseen the events and the intrigue that brought him to the throne of France.[29]

The country swarmed with Orléanists in 1830, if one can

[26] François Guizot, *Mémoires pour servir à l'histoire de mon temps, 1807-1848*, new ed. (Paris, 1872), II, 13.

[27] André Marie Dupin, *Mémoires de M. Dupin* (Paris, 1855-61), II, 170; Guillaume de Bertier de Sauvigny, *The Bourbon Restoration* (Philadelphia, 1966), p. 105; Albert de Broglie, "Mémoires du Duc de Broglie," *Revue des deux mondes*, 94th year, 24 (Dec. 15, 1924), 781-82; J.E.B. Howarth, *Citizen King: The Life of Louis-Philippe, King of the French* (London, 1961), p. 136; Rémusat, *Mémoires*, II, 287, 289; Guizot, *Mémoires*, II, 14; Jacques Laffitte, *Souvenirs de Jacques Laffitte racontée par lui-même* (Paris, 1844-45), II, 46; Odilon Barrot, *Mémoires posthumes*, 3d ed. (Paris, 1875-76), I, 119-20.

[28] Charles de Semonville, "Mémoire sur la Révolution de 1830," *Revue de Paris*, 1st year, 5 (Sept. 1, 1894), 72-74.

[29] Eugène de Vitrolles, *Mémoires* (Paris, 1951), II, 372-73.

believe the claims of the thousands of men who after the
revolution inundated the new government with claims for
jobs.[30] Certainly the active Orléanists and the militant republicans and Bonapartists had among them men moved in
part by hope for official place or favor, and many thousands
of citizens, even without strong political convictions, might
hope to benefit from a change in regime that would involve
a purge in officeholders. "A taste for holding office and a
desire to live on the public money," wrote Alexis de Tocqueville in his *Recollections*, "is the great and chronic ailment
of the whole nation. . . ."[31] The Bourbons by their purges in
1814 and 1815 and occasional lesser ones later in the Restoration had set examples that raised expectations of another
change of regime and had also created a large body of
displaced and disgruntled officeholders anxious to recover
lost places. But these people, willing to support a revolutionary regime once it was in power and perhaps even to
lend a hand in the safe, later stages of revolution, were not
an active political force before the revolution. Knowledge
of their existence does little to explain the determined
resistance of the many liberal deputies and electors to
Charles X and Polignac, for these active opponents of the
ministry were men of substantial wealth, holding honored
places in their communities, fearful of disorder, and not
likely to defy the King for the sake of a better job.

Fears more than hopes surely inspired these men to resist
the established government. In the election campaign of
1830 as in 1827 they professed their fears of imminent
restoration of the *Ancien régime*. Charles intended, they
charged, to reestablish feudal rights, reinstitute the tithe and
the *corvée*, restore primogeniture, and return national lands
to their former owners.[32] These were obviously exaggera-

[30] See Ch. IX.
[31] Alexis de Tocqueville, *The Recollections* (New York, 1949), pp.
31-32.
[32] AN, F⁷ 6777, Gend. roy., 4ᵉ Légion, Cie. de la Mayenne, "Rapport,"
July 1, 1830, 9ᵉ Légion, Cie. de la Charente-Inférieure, "Rapport," July
5, 1830, 10ᵉ Légion, Cie. de la Charente, "Rapport," July 4, 1830; 8ᵉ
Légion, Cie. du Cher, "Rapport," July 6, 1830; 12ᵉ Légion, Cie. du Lot-

tions intended to frighten voters, but the Bourbon government had since 1814 encroached enough on rights and benefits won during the Revolution and preserved by the Empire to arouse the concern of many Frenchmen. Nominally the Charter guaranteed these rights, but the government had on occasion ignored the guarantees. Article 11 forbade all investigation and punishment of opinions held and votes cast in the past, but in 1816 the government had banned from French soil in perpetuity all members of the Convention who in January 1793 had voted for the execution of the late king and had rallied to Napoleon in 1815. Article 66 abolished confiscation of property as a legal punishment and expressly forbade its reestablishment. Yet only with difficulty did Louis XVIII prevent its application to the regicides, and courts did apply it in some criminal cases. The notorious *cours prévôtales* for two years after 1815 made a mockery of the Charter's guarantee against extraordinary courts outside the regular court system.[33]

Equality, probably the most cherished heritage of the Revolution, had not been safe from encroachment. The Charter restored the nobility of the *Ancien régime* to its titles and in creating a Chamber of Peers gave to them, along with the new Napoleonic nobility, a share in the legislative and judicial power denied to other Frenchmen. The government favored the old nobility over the new and over commoners in making appointments to public office, giving them a privileged position in administration as well as in lawmaking, and they were the advisers and companions of the

---

et-Garonne," Rapport," July 5, 1830; F[7] 6778, Gend. roy., 13e Légion, "Rapport," July 6, 1830; 14e Légion, Cie. du Tarn, "Rapport," June 4, 1830; 15e Légion, "Rapport," June 1-5, 1830, 20e Légion, Cie. de la Haute-Marne, "Rapport," July 5, 1830,; 22e Légion, Cie. de la Meurthe, "Rapport," [May 1830]; 24e Légion, Cie. de l'Aisne, "Rapport," Apr. 8, 1830; F[7] 6742, Police gén., Préfet de l'Haute-Vienne to Ministre de l'Intérieur, June 15, 1830.

[33] Pierre-Paul Viard, "Les Aspects juridiques de la Révolution de 1830," *Revue d'histoire moderne*, 6 (1931), 92-93; Paul Bastid, *Les Institutions politiques de la monarchie parlementaire française, 1814-1848* (Paris, 1954), pp. 99, 100; Bertier de Sauvigny, *Restoration*, pp. 131-32, 133.

King. Charles X and Villèle compounded these offenses in the eyes of many Frenchmen by indemnifying the old nobility for lands confiscated during the Revolution. Villèle had tried to reestablish primogeniture for large estates, and only an unexpected adverse vote in the Chamber of Peers had blocked this violence to the principle of equality of inheritance established by the Napoleonic Code. In August 1829 *The Times* of London, which was thought to have at least semiofficial sources of information, reported that the Polignac Ministry would attempt to change the law on the transmission of real property.[34]

Voters and deputies were substantial property holders and sensitive to threats against property. They could not be indifferent to the courts' occasional ignoring of the Charter's ban on confiscation of property, and those among them who held lands confiscated during the Revolution from the church or nobles could not feel wholly secure in their holdings. Article 9 of the Charter guaranteed the inviolability of these so-called national lands, yet the very wording of the article admitted a distinction between them and other lands. Many dispossessed owners were not reconciled to their losses, and the ultraroyalists had encouraged their hopes for restoration of their lands. Villèle's indemnity of 1825 did not wholly satisfy them. The church by the Concordat of 1801 had formally renounced its claims to its former property lost during the Revolution, but the negotiation of a new concordat, begun in 1817 and never completed, cast at least a shadow of doubt on the validity of that renunciation. The unconcealed aspiration of some of the clergy to recover the lost lands of the church and the close association of the throne and the altar throughout the Restoration kept that shadow from fading. The appointment of the ministry of August 8, 1829, including as a leading member the ardently Catholic Polignac and a number of others suspected of excessive devotion to the interests of the church, gave the

---

[34] Viard, "Aspects juridiques," pp. 90-91; Bastid, *Institutions*, p. 106; Bertier de Sauvigny, *Restoration*, pp. 76-77, 247-48; Alfred Nettement, *Histoire de la Restauration* (Paris, 1860-72), I, 372.

shadow a substance that it had lacked in earlier years. Not wholly unfounded, too, was fear of reestablishment of the compulsory tithe. Bishops demanded it from their flocks, and nothing in the Charter blocked its reenactment into law.[35]

The clerical bias of the new ministry of August 8 increased apprehension of encroachments on personal liberties. "Here again," exclaimed the *Journal des débats* on August 10, "is . . . the clergy with its hatred of liberty." Frenchmen recalled the Villèle government's harassment of the church's intellectual enemies and the Law of Sacrilege of 1825, which would have put the force of the secular arm behind the enforcement of religious conformity. *The Times* reported that Polignac's program included a more restrictive press law, and the Minister of Public Instruction, yielding to pressure from royalist newspapers, appointed a special commission to investigate the political and religious ideas expounded in the popular courses taught at the Sorbonne by Guizot, Victor Cousin, and François Villemain. During the royalist reaction of the early twenties Villèle's government had closed the courses, but the moderate Martignac had permitted their resumption in 1828. Now in 1829 the authorities again threatened freedom of speech, and the ultra journal, the *Drapeau blanc*, screamed at these professors, "On your knees, miserable rhetoricians! On your knees! Ask pardon of your king."[36] The government's overt actions proved mild enough. It proposed no new press law, and Guizot, Cousin, and Villemain continued to teach their courses peacefully at the Sorbonne. Nonetheless, the apprehension of something worse to come remained inseparable from the Polignac Ministry.[37]

[35] Viard, "Aspects juridiques," pp. 92-94; Bertier de Sauvigny, *Restoration*, pp. 302-5.

[36] Duvergier de Hauranne, *Histoire*, x, 329, 349; Bertier de Sauvigny, *Restoration*, pp. 342, 407.

[37] Charles H. Pouthas, *Guizot pendant la Restauration: préparation de l'homme d'état, 1814-1830* (Paris, 1933), pp. 326-29; Guizot, *Mémoires*, I, 335-38, 346; Jules Simon, *Victor Cousin* (Chicago, 1888), pp. 30-33.

Fear of encroachments upon personal liberties, upon property rights, upon equality did not provoke a revolution, but it certainly had a part in the motivation of the effort to establish responsibility of ministers to the chamber as a safeguard against arbitrary acts of the government. It may have made revolution seem acceptable, perhaps desirable, if revolution alone could remove the threat to cherished rights.

Voters may have listened more attentively to the opposition's warnings of imminent reestablishment of feudal dues, restoration of the tithe, and increased taxes to pay the costs of the Algerian expedition because economic depression in the late twenties had cut many a Frenchman's income.[38] After 1817 France had enjoyed almost a decade of prosperity marked by rising industrial prices and rising profits and wages. In 1826 prices began to decline, wages were cut, and in some places there was considerable local unemployment. The number of bankruptcies in the country rose by almost two-thirds over the preceding year and the total liabilities involved more than doubled, exceeding 100 million francs, a record for the decade. In the capital department alone 663 businesses failed that year, nearly double the preceding high figure of the twenties. The year 1827 brought some recovery, but the high level of bankruptcies both in Paris and in the country at large and the drop in the yield of the *octroi*—the tax on foods, fuels, and building materials entering Paris—reflected continuing difficulties. Stagnating business and a declining stock market disturbed investors and businessmen; they grumbled and read the opposition newspapers. In the general election in 1827 the same body of electors who in the prosperity of 1824 had returned a large majority of ultraroyalists, now elected a liberal majority hostile to Villèle, and the ministry resigned. The easy, prosperous years of the Restoration associated with the long

[38] AN, F⁷ 6777, Gend. roy., 10ᵉ Légion, Cie. de la Gironde, "Rapport," Mar. 10, 1830; F⁷ 6778, Gend. roy., 16ᵉ Légion, "Rapport," Mar. 10, 1830; 18ᵉ Légion, Cie. des Hautes-Alpes, "Rapport," June 1, 1830; 24ᵉ Légion, Cie. de l'Aisne, "Rapport," May 5, 1830.

ministry of Villèle, the years of full employment and cheap bread, had passed.[39]

In 1828 and 1829 an agrarian crisis stemming from a succession of poor harvests turned recession into grave depression. A failure of the potato crop in 1826 forced up prices of both potatoes and grain. In the succeeding year the grain harvest was poor, and in 1828 the average price of wheat throughout the country was 40 percent above the level of 1825 and in May 1829, 60 percent above. The price of the standard four-pound loaf of bread rose in Paris from the normal 60 or 65 centimes of the prosperous years of the Restoration to 95 centimes in 1828, and in the second fortnight of May 1829 reached 1 franc 05. As the product of the next harvest moved onto the market, the price of bread declined slowly, but the crop was far from abundant, and the bread prices never fell below 75 centimes in 1829 or in the first seven months of 1830. The French workingman of the 1820s spent a third to a half of his income on bread, the staple of his diet. A rise in the price of bread cut sharply into his budget and forced him to reduce other expenditures. One of the few additional expenditures his meager earnings could ordinarily afford was on clothing; reduction of that expenditure hurt the textile industry. In the late twenties cotton, wool, and silk industries fell into doldrums that lasted until 1831. Expansion of the heavy metal industries, in progress for a decade, reversed in 1828, and the demand for coal dwindled. Activity in the construction industry, particularly important to the prosperity of Paris,

---

[39] Ernest Labrousse, *Le Mouvement ouvrier et les idées sociales en France de 1815 à la fin du XIXe siècle*. Les Cours de Sorbonne (Paris, 1948), pp. 90, 95; Louis Girard, *Etude comparée des mouvements révolutionnaires en France en 1830, 1848 et 1870-71 (1830-1848)*. Les Cours de Sorbonne (Paris, 1960), pp. 51-52, 86; Labrousse, "Comment naissent les révolutions," *Actes* du Congrès historique du Centenaire de la Révolution de 1848 (Paris, 1948), pp. 5-6; AN, F^20 722, Ministère de l'Intérieur, Statistique, "Tableaux par départements et par années, des faillétés declarées . . . de 1820 à 1835"; Tableaux par années des faillétés declarées . . . de 1820 à 1835."

declined as demand for space fell off and as investors and speculators withheld commitments to new enterprises.[40]

The depression hurt the commercial middle class of bankers, merchants, and manufacturers in numerous ways. Profits declined, and the threat of failure weighed heavily on many businesses. Even though the first year of crisis had presumably weeded out the weakest enterprises, the number of bankruptcies in the country moved to a new high in 1828, and in the Department of the Seine remained at a high level throughout 1828 and 1829.[41] In January 1829 the Prefect of Police reported that almost all factory owners in Paris had offered their buildings to the city for use as charity workshops, so little use did they have for them.[42] Security values on the stock exchange of Paris declined, to the dismay and embarrassment of many investors. The police reported the suicide of a leading stockbroker in May 1830.[43] On the exchange government bonds alone rose during the prolonged bear market, and they were in unusual demand only as a refuge for funds withdrawn from industrial and commercial investment to await more promising prospects. Jacques Laffitte, the Parisian banker, was pushed to the edge of bankruptcy by the drop in the values of both his securities and his real estate holdings.[44]

The police noted a tendency among businessmen to blame the government for their economic difficulties.[45] In August 1829 with the depression at a low point they were in no mood to welcome the appointment of the new Polignac

[40] AN, F⁷ 3882, Préfecture de Police, "Bulletin de Paris," Jan.-Dec. 1828; F⁷ 3883, Jan.-Dec. 1829; F⁷ 3884, Jan.-July 1830; F⁷ 6777, Gend. roy., Cmdt., 1ᵉ Légion to Ministre de l'Intérieur, Nov. 4, 1829; Labrousse, *Mouvement*, p. 91; Labrousse, "Comment naissent les révolutions," pp. 5-6; Girard, *Etude des mouvements révolutionnaires*, pp. 50-55.

[41] AN, F²⁰ 722, Ministère de l'Intérieur, Statistique, "Tableaux des faillétés . . . 1820 à 1835."

[42] AN, F⁷ 3883, "Bulletin de Paris," Jan. 6, 1829.

[43] AN, F⁷ 3884, "Bulletin de Paris," May 5, 1830.

[44] Girard, *Etude des mouvements révolutionnaires*, p. 55.

[45] AN, F⁷ 3883, "Bulletin de Paris," Jan. 6, 7, Dec. 8, 1829.

Ministry, which seemed to foreshadow political adventures that could only aggravate the country's economic troubles. One of Polignac's first appointees, Jean-Claude Mangin as Prefect of Police, soon added to the grievances of Parisian businessmen by rigorously enforcing Sunday and holiday closing laws and regulations against the display of merchandise or the dispensing of coffee on the street outside shops. In March 1830 he imposed new and vexatious regulations on the butchers of Paris. He alienated another special interest—one with important if concealed ramifications and influence—when he forbade prostitutes to solicit in the streets. Jesuits, the women charged, "controlled . . . our venerable and sweet seigneur, the prefect of police," and pamphleteers, knowing a good cause when they saw it, turned out a dozen or more protests.[46]

Polignac believed in the spring of 1830 that the opposition to the King and his ministry was confined to a small minority. Its efforts to excite opposition among the masses had failed, and would continue to fail, because, he claimed, "the masses are concerned solely with their material interests," and these were completely guaranteed by the crown. Rarely, he added, had a country been more prosperous.[47] His belief in the political indifference of the masses had some foundation in the reports of the Gendarmerie, and as late as July 27, 1830, the opposition deputies doubted that the populace of Paris would support them in their confrontation with the crown.[48] Nonetheless, his assurance that the country was prosperous and the material interests of the masses guaranteed shows that he did not see—or that he ignored—

[46] Huart, "Dernier Préfet de Police," pp. 606-7; Girard, *Etude des mouvements révolutionnaires*, pp. 95-96; Bibliothèque impériale, *Catalogue de l'histoire de France* (Paris, 1861), VII, 668-69. One of the pamphlets had the title *Prière romantique . . . à tous les amateurs des prêtesses de Venus et aux augustes défenseurs de Thémis au sujet des ordonnances qui defend aux charmantes déeses de Paphos de sortir de leurs temples; publié par un amoureux en délire.*

[47] AN, CC 549, Chambre et Cour des Pairs, Jules Polignac, "Projet de note au Roi," April 14, 1830.

[48] Rémusat, *Mémoires*, II, 316; Louis Blanc, *Histoire de dix ans, 1830-1840*, 12th ed. (Paris, 1877), I, 181.

the contrary evidence that flowed into the ministries in Paris.

Urban workers suffered much more from the depression than did their employers. While their cost of living mounted ominously with the rise in the price of bread and of potatoes, declining wage rates and unemployment cut their purchasing power. Between 1825 and 1830 wage rates in the building trades of Paris fell off by 30 percent, in the metal industry by more than a third, and in the provincial textile industry by 40 percent. Accurate measurement of levels of unemployment is impossible, but individual reports of reduction in work forces and repeated references by the police and Gendarmerie to scarcity of jobs attest the seriousness of unemployment in 1828 and 1829. In October 1828 the Minister of the Interior instructed prefects to refuse passports to workers planning to come to Paris in search of jobs.[49] In the spring and summer of 1829 construction workers seeking employment at the open-air "hiring halls" on the Place de Grève in front of the city hall and on the Place du Châtelet usually numbered four or five hundred, occasionally seven hundred or more. The prefect's count of those hired ran 40, 60, 50, 80; once in July it rose to 125 and once in August to 150, a high point for the year.[50]

The winter of 1828-29 brought grave distress to tens of thousands of Parisians already afflicted by unemployment, reduced wages, and the high price of bread. The temperature dropped to exceptionally low levels in January 1829, and the cold was accompanied by heavy accumulations of snow and ice. Construction work, little active in the last months of 1828, was almost totally suspended. On one cold day, January 22, more than four hundred persons voluntarily entered the municipal hospital, the Hôtel-Dieu, which they ordinarily shunned even in sickness, seeking shelter

---

[49] Labrousse, *Mouvement*, p. 92; Labrousse, "Comment naissent les révolutions," p. 6; Paul Gonnet, "Esquisse de la crise économique en France de 1827 à 1832," *Revue d'histoire économique et sociale*, 33 (1955), 286; AN, F7 3882, "Bulletin de Paris," Jan.-Dec. 1828; F7 3883, Bulletin de Paris," Jan.-Dec. 1829.

[50] AN, F7 3883, "Bulletin de Paris," Jan.-Aug. 1829.

against the cold and relief from hunger. Others in the same desperate state pleaded to be sent to the *dépôts de mendicité*, workhouses for the poor. The price of bread was 19½ sous for a four-pound loaf in December 1828, 18½ in the latter half of January 1829. The city distributed bread cards to registered indigents enabling them to purchase the four-pound loaf for 16 sous, but the Prefect of Police warned that his commissioners lacked the means to aid all the poor who overflowed their offices. Fearful for public order he urged distribution of bread cards to all workers with families without the usual formalities of registration as indigents, and he recommended additional relief for the many who lacked even the 16 sous without which the bread cards were useless. The municipal government and some rich individuals opened soup kitchens for the hungry and warming rooms offering shelter against the excessive cold. The approach of spring relieved the distress from cold, but the price of bread rose, jobs remained scarce, and the number of applicants for bread cards increased. In May, when bread sold at its highest level, 188,000 Parisians received bread cards, and a month later the number reached 227,000, more than a fourth of the city's population. These measures relieved distress but fell far short of eliminating it. Scarcely a single number of the Prefect of Police's daily "Bulletin de Paris" in 1829 lacked a report of a suicide attributed to destitution, an unidentified body picked from the Seine or a canal, or a newly born child found dead in street or river.[51]

The police noted, too, an increase in petty thievery, which they attributed to misery and the exhaustion of savings. Bitterness, born of prolonged distress, acerbated by each

---

[51] AN, F⁷ 3882, "Bulletin de Paris," Dec. 1828; F⁷ 3883, "Bulletin de Paris," Jan.-Dec. 1829; A.S., Vᵇⁱˢ 255, Bienfaisance, "Préfet de Police to Maire,, 10ᵉ Arrond., Dec. 27, 1831, "Chauffoirs pour les Indigens," Conseil d'Administration, Caisse syndicale des Boulangers de Paris, "Règlement pour le service à organiser en cas de cherté du pain," Nov. 22, 1828; AS, VD⁴ 4826-4827, Mairies, Préfet du Département de la Seine to Maire, 6ᵉ Arrond., Jan. 15, Feb. 2, 1829; Dépt. de la Seine, *Recherches statistiques sur la ville de Paris et le Département de la Seine* (Paris, 1826-60), v, Tableaux 2, 3.

successive rise in the price of bread, occasionally turned against the government. In October 1828 police found a roughly lettered sign posted in the Faubourg Saint-Antoine. "Vive Napoléon," it read, "War to the death on Charles X and the priests who want to starve us to death." Copies of the sign turned up in several nearby streets and in two adjoining quarters.[52] The rise in the price of bread above one franc in May 1829 inspired seditious signs posted in the Faubourg Saint-Antoine and near the Bank of France in the center of the city, and, on May 1 motivated the gathering of small crowds of protesters in the populous quarters of the city. The police, recalling the rôle of food riots in the Revolution, took the precaution of dispersing them.[53] In the summer and fall, as the price of bread declined, the police noted no more incidents, and the prefect clearly took pride in reporting the good spirits and the orderliness of the population.[54]

The grain harvest of 1829 in the area that supplied Paris, more abundant than in 1828, and declining prices of bread and of dried beans and peas, important elements in the diet of the poor, raised hopes that the winter of 1829-30 would be less rigorous for Parisians.[55] In December and January, however, the temperature dropped, plummeting on the seventeenth of January to a record low for eleven years, and during a month or more the bitter winter of 1828-29 seemed to be repeating itself. Petty thievery again increased. The prefect's daily bulletin reported elderly persons found dead in their rooms, victims of the extreme cold, and the police on several occasions collected in the streets cold and starving children abandoned by their parents, who lacked the means to support them. The city and private charity again opened soup kitchens and warming rooms. The price of bread—at 80 centimes in the latter half of December and in January and 77½ in February—was below

---

[52] Louis Chevalier, *Classes laborieuses et classes dangereuses à pendant la première moitié du XIXᵉ siècle* (Paris, 1958), p. 319.
[53] AN, F⁷ 3883, "Bulletin de Paris," May 1, 2, 1830.
[54] *Ibid.*, June-Dec. 1829.   [55] *Ibid.*, Nov. 19, Dec. 8, 17, 1829.

the critical level that required the distribution of bread cards. Spring fortunately came early that year. March 1830 was much warmer than March 1829, and construction work vigorously revived in that month. On March 17 all of the five hundred construction workers who gathered on the Place de Grève and the Place du Châtelet found jobs. Three days later three hundred were there, and all were hired, and the demand remained at a high level through the succeeding months and on into the summer. Other industries revived, too. Food prices continued at relatively modest levels, and the police reported no repetitions of the "murmures" or seditious protests of the preceding winter. The reports on these matters came now from Polignac's new Prefect of Police, Mangin, and possibly he, sharing or wishing to flatter the uncritical optimism of his superiors, was unwilling to admit or failed to discern continuing unrest. It was he who wrote in the "Bulletin de Paris" of July 26, 1830, on the eve of revolution, "The most perfect tranquility continues to reign in all parts of the capital." Nonetheless, in the spring of 1830 he could reasonably believe that the prospects for the economy and for Parisians were growing somewhat brighter.[56]

The prospects appeared brighter, however, only relative to the somber months of 1828-29, not relative to the good years before 1826. Moreover, Louis Chevalier has maintained, Paris in 1830 suffered from an illness that no commercial revival could cure or police repression contain. The illness was social disorganization expressed pathologically by high rates of mortality, homocide, suicide, illegitimacy, mendicity, and crime. The cause was an increase in population larger than the city could assimilate into its normal life.[57] Between the censuses of 1800 and 1817 the city's population, after centuries of slow growth, rose by nearly a third

[56] AN, F⁷ 3884, "Bulletin de Paris," Jan.-July 1830; F⁷ 6777, Gend. roy., Col., 1ᵉ Légion to Ministre de l'Intérieur, Dec. 5, 1829, Mar. 5, Apr. 5, 1830; Seine, Recherches statistiques, II, Tableaux 1, 2; III, Tableaux, 1, 2, 3; IV, Tableaux 1, 2, 3; V, Tableaux, 1, 2, 3, 4.

[57] Chevalier, Classes laborieuses, passim.

and between 1817 and the next census—1831—by more than a tenth. In 1830 three quarters of a million people lived where half a million had lived three decades earlier.[58] In those thirty years neither the city's economy nor its urban equipment expanded to accommodate so explosive an increase. The number of jobs fell far short of needs. Thousands were forced to subsist on the most menial, unstable employment and on public relief and charity. Few new houses had been built in the working-class quarters, and newcomers found what accommodation they could in garrets and cellars, in teeming apartments and crowded furnished rooms. About two-fifths of the city's population crowded into the central and eastern quarters that comprised but an eighth of the city's area. No major street construction alleviated growing congestion in the alleylike streets or brought light and air into the overbuilt quarters. Few streets had underground sewers. Not one house in five had running water even on the ground floor.[59] "For 10 francs a month," declared a Parisian guidebook of 1828, "an entire household composed of husband, wife, and brood of children huddle into a room 8 feet square, furnished with a tattered bed and canvas sheets."[60] The death rate for all of France in the 1820s was about twenty-five per thousand; in Paris the rate stood at thirty-three in 1829 and rose to thirty-five in the next year. In the four poorest arrondissements the death rate probably ran 50 percent or more above the rate of the four wealthiest arrondissements. On the poverty-stricken Rue Mouffetard more than twice as many children perished in their first year than on the opulent Rue du Roule.[61]

[58] Seine, *Recherches statistiques*, VI, 6-7.

[59] Chevalier, *Classes laborieuses*, pp. 234-42, 312-13, 444-47, 465-66; Seine, *Recherches statistiques*, V, Tableau 65; Bertier de Sauvigny, *Restoration*, pp. 255, 258, 259; André Morizet, *Du vieux Paris au Paris moderne; Haussmann et ses prédécesseurs* (Paris, 1932), p. 94; *Moniteur universel* (Paris), Dec. 7, 1854, p. 1350.

[60] Chevalier, *Classes laborieuses*, p. 273.

[61] Edmonde Vedrenne-Villeneuve, "L'Inégalité sociale devant la mort dans la première moitié du XIXe siècle," *Population*, 16 (1961), 679, 698; Chevalier, *Classes laborieuses*, p. 415.

Middle-class Parisians might occasionally give alms to aid this wretched population in their midst, but they were frightened by them and confounded them with criminals—"the dangerous classes"—and treated them as outcasts. Victor Hugo referred to the people of the Faubourg Saint-Antoine as "savages." Balzac spoke of the women he saw on the Place Maubert in the impoverished Twelfth Arrondissement as a "horrible assemblage, which at first inspired disgust that quickly turned to terror. . . ." Daumier's "Parisian Types" were darkly hideous and repulsive.[62]

Insecure, wretchedly housed, undernourished, in precarious health, resentful against the city's more fortunate residents, who regarded them as savages and barbarians, these people, Chevalier maintains, lived on the margins of the city's life not only physically but morally as well. The moral standards of respectable society and especially its respect for property had little meaning to these men and women or to their children. For thousands crime was normal, a means of existence and a kind of individual settling of accounts between the outcasts and the society that had no honorable place for them. From crime to revolution—a kind of mass settling of accounts—was but a step.

Although Chevalier's picture, based largely on literary evidence, is perhaps overdrawn, the existence in Paris of a large body of men in chronic rebellion against society and potentially dangerous in time of crisis cannot be denied. No more can one deny that a much larger body of men and women in the depression years of 1828-30 lived in desperate poverty. In any critical trial of strength with its political opponents the established government could certainly not count on their support, and one might assume, as many have, that these people would take advantage of the crisis to avenge themselves against established authorities and institutions.

Outside the capital, distress and misery were ordinarily less concentrated, but the depression of the late twenties

---

[62] Chevalier, *Classes laborieuses*, pp. 451-55, 495-96, 511, 517, 525-27

had not spared the countryside or provincial towns and cities. Here, too, food prices rose while wages and employment declined, profits diminished, and business failures increased. Seventy-seven bankruptcies in Lyon in 1828 were double the numbers of 1824 and 1825; eighty-seven in Bordeaux in 1829 set a record for the decade there. Food riots and violent protests against taxes, occasionally reported in previous years, became in the first five months of 1829 the principal subject of the procurers-general's reports to the Minister of Justice. The ministry learned of ninety such incidents in 1829, almost all of them in the winter and spring before the new harvest, and twenty-five in the month of May alone.[63]

Most commonly food riots took the form of interference with shipment of grains or demonstrations to force down prices in local markets. Crowds, usually with women in the forefront, fearful that sale of grains out of their districts would raise the local price, stopped grain wagons, demanded local sale of the contents, threatened dealers and draymen. At Clermont in the Department of the Meuse a crowd stopped all the wagons bound for Paris. At Nevers demonstrators forced the prefect and the mayor to have grain removed from boats in the port and hauled to the local market. At Fougères in Brittany under cover of darkness some protesting citizens pushed a wagon loaded with grain into a ravine, and in the Loire valley villagers sacked the lodgings of grain merchants and haulers. Less frequent but nonetheless common in market towns were popular efforts, which occasionally developed into riots, to enforce the sale of grain at "fair" prices.[64]

Such demonstrations occurred largely in the cereal producing areas of the west and in the departments north of the Loire River. Bread riots and other less violent protests against the high price of bread in the late twenties occurred throughout the country, and they involved not only urban

---

[63] Gonnet, "Esquisse de la crise économique," pp. 249-91.
[64] *Ibid.*, pp. 250-53.

workers and agricultural laborers but also small tenants and sharecroppers whose tiny holdings produced no surplus for sale, and consequently they drew no benefit from the rise in grain prices. Increase in the number of beggars and of roaming bands of mendicants (much magnified as in 1789 by popular rumors), strikes, petitions for higher wages, a few cases of Luddism, and defiance of tax collectors were other manifestations of the economic malaise that touched the whole country in 1828 and 1829.[65]

After May 1829 interference with grain movements and market riots fell off sharply as the new harvest came on the market, but in the cold months of the next winter reports of misery among the poor were as common from the provinces as from Paris, and some incidents were again reported.[66] On March 8, 1830, some thirty women from the village of La-clayette, Saône-et-Loire, near Mâcon, stopped two wagons loaded with wheat, chased away the drivers, unloaded the wagons, and were preparing to sell the grain well below the market price, when gendarmes appeared on the scene, dispersed the crowd, reloaded the wagons, and sent them on their way. At the next market day in the area the subprefect, the procurer-general, and a squad of twelve gendarmes arrived on the market place, and no disorders recurred.[67] The liberal opposition's movement to encourage the refusal of taxes, if the King and Polignac persisted in their defiance of the parliamentary majority, revived tax protests of the preceding year.[68] In June 1830 carpentry workers in Lyon went on strike for higher wages, and early in July the Prefect of the Meuse, alarmed by rumors of imminent closing of several manufacturing plants in Bar-le-Duc asked that troops be stationed in that city to prevent disorders.[69] Freezing

[65] *Ibid.*, pp. 249-91; AN, Inventaire de la Série BB[18], Tome I, Nos. 1-1226.

[66] Gonnet, "Esquisse de la crise économique," p. 253.

[67] AN, F[7] 6778, Gend. roy., 19ᵉ Légion, Cie. du Saône-et-Loire, "Rapport," Apr. 1, 1830.

[68] AN, F[7] 6777, Gend. roy., "Rapports," Feb.-May, 1830; F[7] 6778, Gend. roy., "Rapports," Jan.-June 1830.

[69] AN, F[7] 9787, Police gén., Gend. roy., Cie. du Rhône, "Rapport,"

weather, excessive rains, and a pest ruined the wine crop in Burgundy.[70] Increase in the price of grain set off riots in Ussel in the Corrèze on May 19 and 22. On May 28 disturbances broke out at Mauriac in a neighboring department, revived three days later, and on June 4 flared up a third time.[71] But these isolated instances stand out as exceptions in a country much less agitated by economic troubles than it was a year earlier. Officers of the Gendarmerie, who watched for symptoms of dangerous discontent that spring, found little ground for anxiety.[72]

The depression in the provinces, by adding economic grievances to the political complaints of local electors and deputies, probably contributed to the growth of the opposition to Charles X and Polignac. However, economic distress among the mass of provincials had little influence on the revolution in Paris, for the revolution completed its most critical days almost wholly isolated from the provinces. The depression perhaps contributed to an atmosphere that facilitated the country's peaceful acceptance of replacement of the Bourbons. The popular disorders of the two prerevolutionary years may have accustomed more citizens to violent resistance to authority and conditioned them to accept it even at the highest levels of government. Moreover, resentment over economic troubles had occasionally been directed against the Bourbons. At a grain riot in Montmorillon in the Department of the Vienne, near Poitiers on April 25, 1829, the crowd grumbled that "the King and the Jesuits force up the price of grain."[73] Norman peasants sang in 1830

June 18, 1830; Préfet de la Meuse to Ministre de l'Intérieur, July 10, 1830; BB[24], Ministère de la Justice, Graces demandées, 1830-31, 1e Avocat gén., Cour royale de Lyon, to Ministre de la Justice, Sept. 30, 1830.

[70] AN, F[7] 6778, Gend. roy., 20e Légion, "Rapport," July 10, 1830.

[71] AN, F[7] 6777, Gend. roy., 11e Légion, Cie. de la Corrèze, "Résumé," June 4, July 1, 1830.

[72] AN, F[7] 6777, 6778, Gend. roy., "Rapports," Jan.-July 1830.

[73] Gonnet, "Esquisse de la crise économique," pp. 251-52.

Les pommes de terre sont en requisition
Car Charles X en mange comme un cochon.[74]

But "the rich," "monopolists," merchants, large proprietors, even bakers shared the popular blame for the high prices of food.[75] Such diffusely focused discontent was in itself no serious threat to Charles or his ministers.

[74] Georges Weill, "La Révolution de Juillet dans les départements (aôut-septembre 1830)," *Revue d'histoire moderne*, 6 (1931), 293.
[75] Gonnet, "Esquisse de la crise économique," pp. 255-56, 263; Labrousse, *Mouvement*, p. 94.

III

Surprise, Confusion, Disorder, July 25, 26, 27

SUNDAY, July 25, 1830, was a hot day in Paris. The temperature rose to near 90 degrees, a record for the year, and Parisians crowded the parks, the outdoor cafés, and the villages of the environs. Most of the rich and the well-born had left the city. The royal family was in residence at Saint-Cloud, the Duchesse d'Angoulême traveling in the south, the Orléans family visiting the Duc de Bourbon at Saint-Leu, where the Austrian and Swiss ambassadors joined them for dinner. Many electors had gone to their provincial properties to vote in the recent elections and had stayed on in the country. Outwardly the sweltering capital betrayed no anxiety over the country's political future. The rumor of a pending royal coup d'état, current since the formation of the Polignac Ministry nearly a year earlier, had revived after the elections, and during the past week the report of an imminent coup had spread on the stock exchange. The financier, Ouvrard, who reportedly had close connections with Polignac, speculated on the expectation of a drop in the market, and others with official connections were said to have unloaded all their *rentes*, but most investors and speculators, perhaps reassured by the dispatch that week of official summonses to deputies and peers to the session of parliament opening on August 3, had rejected the rumor. The *rentes* held firm throughout the week, and prices had closed on Saturday little changed from their positions a week earlier.[1] Even the opposition journal, the *Temps*, was re-

[1] A. J. de Marnay, *Mémoires secrèts et témoinages authentiques: chute de Charles X, Royauté de Juillet, 24 février 1848* (Paris, 1875), p. 10; Dépt. de la Seine, *Recherches statistiques sur la ville de Paris*

73

assuring that hot Sunday morning. Its editors, who had often warned of dire things to come from the Polignac Ministry, taunted the prophets of disaster. "The end of the Charter was first fixed for July 22 . . . ," they declared. "Now it is for the 26th, for next Monday. . . . The coups d'état are for tomorrow. . . . They will be postponed even longer until they are admitted to be useless and impossible forever."[2]

The ministry's secret had been well kept. During the drafting and revision of the ordinances Polignac had permitted the existence of only a single copy. As soon as the ministers completed a new version, the old was destroyed, and the one copy Polignac entrusted to no locked drawer or portfolio but kept always on his own person. No minister had let a word slip, and even the King's intimates seem to have gotten no more than hints of the ministry's decisions. Rumors of a coup d'état had spread among the royal household at Saint-Cloud during the preceding week, but they had no firmer substantiation than those current in Paris.[3]

The ministers met at Saint-Cloud that Sunday. About an hour before the appointed time they gathered in the royal study with the courtiers who were privileged to wait upon the King after morning mass. Two at least among the courtiers noticed that the ministers seemed anxious and preoccupied and that, contrary to their usual custom on these occasions, they were reluctant to talk with their friends. Their behavior at once revived fears of imminent action against the newly elected chamber and its supporters. The Baron Eugène de Vitrolles, himself an adviser of

---

et le département de la Seine (Paris, 1826-60), v, Tableau 4; Moniteur universel (Paris), July 18, 1830, p. 784, July 25, p. 812; National (Paris), July 10, 13, 18, 21-24, 1830; AN, CC 549, Chambre et Cour des Pairs, Commissaire de Police de la Bourse to Polignac, July 26, 1830; Deposition of Baudesson de Richebourg, Commissaire de la Bourse de Paris, Nov. 17, 1830; 149 AP 1, Papers of Jean-Claude Mangin, Préfet de Police, Reports of July 18, 22, and 25, 1830.

2 Temps (Paris), July 25, 1830.

3 Charles de Semonville, "Mémoire sur la Révolution de 1830," Revue de Paris, 1st year, 5 (Sept. 1, 1894), 75; Eugène de Vitrolles, Mémoires, 4th ed. (Paris, 1951), II, 366, 408; Ange de Damas, Mémoires, 1785-1862 (Paris, 1922), II, 176-77.

Charles X and a former minister, sought out Polignac and two or three other ministers and urged upon them extreme caution in undertaking any measures that might provoke the ministry's and the monarchy's enemies. They gave him only evasive replies.[4] His warning of a popular outbreak in Paris did, however, alarm Guernon-Ranville, the Minister of Public Instruction, and he went immediately to Mangin, the Prefect of Paris Police, who was among those awaiting the King, and quizzed him on the state of opinion in the capital. Mangin reassured him repeatedly and, finally with some annoyance, declared, "Whatever you do Paris will not move; act boldly. I answer for Paris with my head . . . , I answer for it."[5]

At this moment the King entered the room, and the courtiers took their accustomed places. Charles appeared as preoccupied as his ministers, and as he moved about the room he spoke more briefly than usual to those waiting upon him. The courtiers soon withdrew. The doors were closed, and the meeting began. Chantelauze read the justification of the ministry's imminent action against the press, which his colleagues had instructed him to prepare, and together with the King they now approved it. Polignac, who sat on the King's left, handed Charles the ordinances on the press and on elections. The King had them read aloud.[6] Guernon-Ranville described the scene in his diary.

Before signing, the King seemed absorbed in deep reflection; for several minutes he sat motionless, his head resting on his hand and his pen two inches above the paper; then he said, "The more I think about it the more I am convinced that it is impossible to do otherwise,"

[4] Vitrolles, *Mémoires*, II, 368-70; Martial de Guernon-Ranville, *Journal d'un ministre* (Caen, 1873), pp. 153-54; Guillaume de Montbel, *1787-1831; souvenirs du Comte de Montbel, ministre de Charles X* (Paris, 1913), p. 239; Semonville, "Mémoire," pp. 74-75.

[5] Guernon-Ranville, *Journal*, p. 154.

[6] *Ibid.*, pp. 154-55, 254; Montbel, *Souvenirs*, pp. 239-41; Charles d'Haussez, *Mémoires du Baron d'Haussez, dernier Ministre de la Marine sous la Restauration* (Paris, 1896, 1897), I, 243.

and he signed. We then all countersigned in the most profound silence.[7]

While the ministers affixed their signatures, Peyronnet gave the King the ordinances dissolving the recently elected chamber, ordering new elections, and summoning the new chamber to meet in September. These, too, the King and ministers signed in turn.[8]

Discussion turned to the possibility of popular resistance to the ordinances. Polignac reassured his colleagues. The country would accept the ordinances, he was confident, but adequate armed forces were on hand in Paris and nearby ready to repress any disorders that might develop. Polignac counted on the indifference of the mass of Frenchmen to the quarrel between crown and parliament and on the surprise announcement of the ordinances, which would, he hoped, catch the opposition unprepared. He had ordered no special military preparations beyond deciding that should an emergency develop Marshal Auguste de Marmont, Duc de Raguse, would take the command of the Subdivision of the Department of the Seine, First Military District, a post temporarily vacant owing to the absence of Comte Louis Coutard on vacation. Marmont knew nothing of the appointment, and the number of troops in Paris in late July was fewer than usual. A third of the army was in Algeria or in reserve in the south for this expedition. An unusually large number of troops were in camps near the eastern and northeastern frontiers because of apprehension of Prussian intervention in Belgium, and two regiments of the Royal Guard were still in Normandy in pursuit of arsonists.[9] So unsuspecting was Marmont that when his chief of staff asked on July 25 for permission to spend a day with his

---

[7] *Guernon-Ranville*, Journal, p. 155. [8] *Ibid.*

[9] *Ibid.*; Vitrolles, *Mémoires*, II, 408; Jean Vidalenc, "La Journée du 28 juillet 1830," *Annuaire-Bulletin* de la Société de l'Histoire de France, Années 1948-49, pp. 34, 41-42; Auguste de Marmont, *Mémoires du marechal Marmont, duc de Raguse, de 1792 à 1841*, 3d ed. (Paris, 1857), VIII, 238, 432; AN, CC 546, Chambre et Cour des Pairs, Testimony of Champagny, Nov. 5, 1830; CC 547, Chambre et Cour des Pairs, Testimony of Polignac, Aug. 28, 1830.

family some seventeen miles from Saint-Cloud, Marmont urged him to stay two days. Investigations by the Orléanist government in the autumn of 1830 uncovered a confidential order of the General Staff of the Royal Guard that prescribed positions in Paris to be occupied by the Guard in case of an alert. Dated July 20, 1830, and signed by Marmont it misleadingly suggested a degree of preparation of which the Polignac Ministry was scarcely capable. It was only a routine instruction in existence since 1816, revised in July 1830 to conform to recent changes in barracking of the Guard; when it was ready, the staff sent it to commanding officers wholly innocent of the ministry's plans.[10]

With the signing of the ordinances the ministry completed the day's business, and the King adjourned the meeting. As he left the council chamber, he turned to his ministers, Haussez recalled, and declared, "These are great measures! Much courage and firmness will be required to make them succeed. I count on you; you can count on me. We are united in a common cause. For us the issue is life or death."[11]

To avoid any leakage of the ordinances before their publication on July 26 the ministry withheld them from the official newspaper, the *Moniteur*, until the very latest moment at which they could be included in the next morning's edition. Sauvo, the editor of the *Moniteur*, was dining with his family that Sunday when a messenger delivered an urgent summons from the Keeper of the Seals to wait upon him at the Chancellery on the Place Vendôme at eleven o'clock that evening. Sauvo arrived promptly. An attendant ushered him into a room where he found Chantelauze and Montbel seated at a dimly lighted table. On his approach they arose, greeted him, then resumed their seats, and Sauvo stood between them. Chantelauze handed him a roll of documents.

[10] AN, CC 549, Choiseul to Achille de Guise, Oct. 19, 1830; CC 551, Cour des Pairs, Note concerning the Duc de Raguse and plans for an alert [1830]; AHMG, D³ 131, Garde royale, Etat-major gén. to Lt.-gén., 2ᵉ Div., Infanterie de la Garde, July 20, 1830.

[11] Haussez, *Mémoires*, II, 243-44.

"Sir," he explained, "Here are some important papers to publish in tomorrow's *Moniteur*."

Chantelauze showed him the order in which they were to be printed, and had Sauvo sign a receipt for them. Montbel, who had been watching the editor, said to him, "You are much disturbed."

Sauvo had seen enough of the papers given him to understand what they were, and he replied that it would be surprising if he were not disturbed. Montbel agreed that they were, indeed, a grave matter. For several moments none of the three spoke. Montbel broke the silence with a nervous, "Well?"

"Monseigneur," replied Sauvo, "after having recognized the purpose of the acts handed to me, I can only reply, 'God save the King. God save France.' "

Both ministers blurted out that they hoped for the best, but Sauvo thought their faces showed more fear than hope.[12]

In the early hours of July 26 the chief printer of the *Moniteur* received Sauvo's order to print the ordinances. About the same time two printers at the Imprimerie royale began setting them in type for the *Bulletin des lois*.[13]

The next morning the ordinances did, indeed, take Paris and the country by surprise. Men highly placed among the government's partisans and in the opposition routinely scanning the *Moniteur* or the *Bulletin des lois* were taken aback by what they saw. At Neuilly the Duc d'Orléans picked up his copy of the *Moniteur* and read with surprise and dismay the ordinances that he had long feared. He hurried, paper in hand, to his wife's apartment and told her of them. An intimate of the household reported that the Duchess exclaimed: "My happiness is ended!" an exclamation more theatrical than credible.[14] Marmont heard of the

---

[12] AN, CC 547, Chambre et Cour des Pairs, Sauvo to Berenger, Sept. 20, 1830; Montbel, *Souvenirs*, p. 242.

[13] AN, CC 547, Commission de la Chambre des Députés, Enquête, Testimony of Laurissent, Chef de l'Imprimerie du *Moniteur*, Sept. 3, 1830.

[14] Prosper Duvergier de Hauranne, *Histoire du gouvernement parlementaire en France, 1814-1848* (Paris, 1857-71), x, 593; Auguste Tro-

ordinances that morning at Saint-Cloud but could not find a copy of them. He came into Paris, borrowed the *Moniteur* from a neighbor, and read the ordinances for the first time.[15] The Vicomte Jacques de Foucauld, commander of the Gendarmerie in Paris, back in the capital after a week's leave, was working in his office about 10 A.M., when an adjutant arrived, picked up an unopened copy of the *Moniteur* on his superior's desk, saw what it contained, and showed it to the unsuspecting Foucauld.[16] About the same time the Prefect of the Department of the Seine first saw the new ordinances in the *Bulletin des lois*.[17] Charles de Rémusat was working in the office of the *Globe* between nine and ten o'clock when a journalist, Placide de Justin, entered and seeing Rémusat looking so unconcerned, exclaimed, "Don't you know? The coup d'état is in the *Moniteur*!"[18]

Leaders of "the faction," which haunted nervous royalists, were unconspiratorially in the country. Lafayette, at Lagrange, where he planned to remain until the opening of the next session of the chamber on August 3, wrote to a friend on that day, "It appears that it [a coup d'état] has been renounced for the moment; provisional moderation has been restored to the order of the day." Not until the next day, upon the arrival of the *Moniteur* and a note from Rémusat, did he discover how poor a prophet he was.[19] Laffitte, vacationing at Breteuil, his property in the Department of the Eure, nearly a hundred miles from Paris, first learned of the ordinances from a copy of the *Moniteur* that his nephew dispatched to him by special courier.[20] Guizot,

gnon, *La Vie de Marie-Amélie, Reine des Français* (Paris, 1872), pp. 179-80.

[15] Marmont, *Mémoires*, VIII, 237; AN, CC 547, Cour des Pairs, Col. Perrigaux to Berenger, Sept. 27, 1830.

[16] AN, CC 546, Juge d'Instruction, Tribunal civil de Chinon, Testimony of Foucauld, Nov. 28, 1830.

[17] AN, CC 549, Deposition of Chabrol de Volvic, Nov. 15, 1830.

[18] Charles de Rémusat, *Mémoires de ma vie* (Paris, 1958-67), II, 309-10.

[19] Marie de Lafayette, *Mémoires, correspondance et manuscrits* (Paris, 1837-38), VI, 380.

[20] AN, CC 549, Deposition of Laffitte, Nov. 11, 1830; Jacques Laf-

traveling up from Nîmes, where he had been for the elections, by chance picked up the news on the twenty-sixth from a southbound mail coach in a village near Nevers.[21]

Readers of the *Moniteur* of July 26 could see at first glance that it was no ordinary issue. The heading "Parti officielle," usually limited to a single column, this day spread across the top of the entire first page, and a decorative crown and orb, rare to this journal, stood between the two words. A "Rapport au Roi," Chantelauze's justification of the government's drastic measures against the press and the chamber, took up all of the page below that unusual heading except for five lines on the King's reception of the British ambassador. The report continued through most of the first column of the second page.[22]

Those who read this long report learned that in the judgment of the King's ministers the country was slipping into anarchy, that pernicious ideas undermined the foundations of order and sowed seeds of civil war. "It must be recognized," declared the report, "these agitations . . . are almost exclusively produced and excited by the freedom of the press." "At all times . . . ," it continued, "the periodical press has been, and it is in its nature to be, only an instrument of disorder and sedition." Then followed two columns of specific charges against the press: it had discredited public authorities, confused men's loyalties, distorted facts, infringed upon the sovereignty of parliament, encouraged defiance of the King, revealed military secrets, excited soldiers of the Algerian expedition to disobedience and desertion, and attacked the church and the religious bases of society. "Its destiny is, in a word, to begin anew the revolution, whose principles it boldly proclaims." Against this threat the existing laws and courts were impotent. The King

fitte, "Les Trois Glorieuses," *Revue des deux mondes*, 100th year, 58, (July 15, 1930), 301-2; Auguste Bérard, *Souvenirs historiques sur la Révolution de 1830* (Paris, 1834), p. 61.

[21] François Guizot, *Mémoires pour servir à l'histoire de mon temps, 1807-1848*, New ed. (Paris, 1872), II, 2-3.

[22] *Moniteur*, July 26, 1830, pp. 813-14.

must consequently, his ministers urged, return to the press law of October 21, 1814, which authorized preliminary censorship of periodical publications of fewer than twenty pages. Article 8 of the Charter, the report contended, guaranteed to the individual freedom to publish his opinions, but that had not been intended to guarantee to the newspaper industry the right to publish opinions of others, free from official surveillance. The need to defend the sovereign power of the state would justify revival of the law of 1814, even by extraordinary means. Fortunately, the report continued,

> Article 14 [of the Charter] invested Your Majesty with a power sufficient, not certainly to change our institutions but to consolidate them and render them more permanent.
>
> Commanding necessity no longer permits postponement of the exercise of this supreme power. The moment has come for recourse to measures that adhere to the spirit of the Charter but are outside the legal order, all of whose resources have been fruitlessly exhausted.

In the usual manner of makers of coups d'état the ministers justified violation of the constitution by an appeal to the constitution.

After this report the *Moniteur* printed the ordinances approved by the ministers at their session of July 24 and signed by the King the next day.[23]

Not until about 10 A.M. or later did news of the ordinances become current among Parisians. The *Moniteur*, even though a newspaper as well as the official journal, was not a popular paper. Many public reading rooms and cafés that furnished journals for their customers did not subscribe to

---

[23] Two additional ordinances approved by the King on July 25 appeared in the *Moniteur* of July 26, both of them making appointments to the Council of State. They had no direct connection with the critical matters of the first four ordinances. The phrase "The Five Ordinances" found in many accounts of the revolution is misleading. Six appeared on that day, but the first four alone embodied the royal coup d'état.

it. Two other morning papers published second editions carrying the ordinances, and they were quickly sold out. In the garden of the Palais-Royal young men read them aloud to silent and attentive groups of listeners. The evening papers appeared earlier than usual, and all reprinted the ordinances.[24]

The first popular reactions were surprise and stupefaction. Monday was a holiday for some Parisian workers, and on this hot summer day many of them gathered at cafés in the suburbs beyond the city's tax wall. There the printers, at once concerned because the first ordinance posed an immediate threat to their livelihoods, talked about the possibilities of protest. The majority among them agreed to stay away from work the next day, and they tried to induce construction workers whom they met at cafés later in the day to join them. These men, however, showed little concern for a matter that seemed in no way to touch their interests. Within the city the peaceful aspect of the streets confirmed the ministry's expectation of popular indifference to the political conflict of the day. Haussez walked about the populous streets and saw no unusual gatherings of people, not even around posted copies of the day's *Moniteur*.[25] Rémusat and Armand Marrast, editor of the *Tribune des départements*, found the city equally calm that afternoon. Marrast, regarding the tranquil Rue de Choiseul, just off the Boulevard des Italiens, exclaimed in anger and despair, "What can be done with a nation of shopkeepers?"[26]

The stock exchange at first exhibited more concern than did the streets. The 5 percent *rentes* opened at 103, down more than two points from the closing price on Saturday,

---

[24] BHVP, Victor Crochon, "Souvenirs," MS, II, 9-10; AS, Vᵇ¹ˢ 3, Commission des Récompenses nationales (hereafter cited as CRN), 4ᵉ Arrond., Dossier Raveneau; A. J. de Marnay, *Mémoires*, pp. 11-12.

[25] Charles de Semonville, "Mémoire," p. 74; Crochon, "Souvenirs," p. 25; Ladvocat, "Note pour Monsieur le Ministre de l'Intérieur sur les ouvriers imprimeurs," Sept. 4, 1830, in Paul Chauvet, *Les Ouvriers du livre en France de 1789 à la constitution de la Fédération du Livre* (Paris, 1956), pp. 645-46; Haussez, *Mémoires*, II, 247; Marnay, *Mémoires*, p. 12.

[26] Rémusat, *Mémoires*, II, 316.

and at the end of the day's trading they sold for 101.50. Rumors spread of imminent reestablishment of the dread *cours prévôtales* of 1815 and of the exile of the 221 opposition deputies. In the afternoon a considerable number of bankers and other businessmen gathered in small groups at the Bourse and talked earnestly among themselves, and the police commissioner stationed there thought at the close of the day that the most numerous opposition to the ordinances existed in the business community.[27]

A number of the leading businessmen of Paris met at the Hôtel de Ville on July 26 to complete the election begun the preceding Saturday of members of the Tribunal de Commerce. Haussez charged in his memoirs that "leaders of the conspiracy" here excited opposition to the ministry and induced the industrialists among the electors to close their plants in order to put their workers on the streets in support of violent resistance to the ordinances. Another group of businessmen, the proprietors of plants that printed the principal newspapers, met that evening, according to the Count Apollinaire d'Argout, a liberal peer and former prefect, at the Café de la Rotonde, summoned by a leader of the "Aide-toi," Félix Barthe. Certain to be hurt by enforcement of the first ordinance, they here agreed to close their shops the next day. This reported employers' conspiracy achieved wide currency in histories of the revolution, and it may have occurred, but no evidence beyond these two dubious sources confirms it. Printing establishments did close on July 27, but only after publishers, presumably fearful of prosecution, had cancelled their orders. The printing workers, moreover, had not awaited the action of their employers before going into the streets; only a few of the more cautious among them reported for work that Tuesday morning. Later in the day many shopkeepers closed their stores and put up their shutters, and more did so on Wednesday, but this was no conspiracy, simply a predictable response to

[27] Marnay, *Mémoires*, p. 12; Crochon, "Souvenirs," ii, 25, 27; AN, CC 549, Comm. de Police de la Bourse to Polignac, July 26, 1830; *Moniteur*, July 27, 1830, p. 820.

an obvious threat to property. They could recall the disorders in the rues Saint-Denis and Saint-Martin only three
years earlier, after the elections of 1827, and they feared
broken windows, damaged stock, and perhaps looting. A
"large number" of employers received decorations for throwing their employees into combat, Haussez declared, but the
surviving records of the Commission des Récompenses nationales and its local subcommittees in Paris, which determined the recipients of the decorations of the revolution,
contain only one claim for honors based on even a semblance of such activity. A candymaker on the Rue de la
Paix, acting simply as an individual, had led his workers to
join the crowd on the Place Vendôme on the evening of
July 26, and the next day he tried to induce a number of
other small employers to release their workers, too.[28]

To liberal journalists and publishers the first ordinance
presented a direct threat. Intended to silence them, it would,
if enforced, deprive them of their means of livelihood and
ruin their political hopes. It required them to apply for
authorization to publish, which would, they could assume,
probably be refused, and if they published without authorization, the government would seize both their publications
and their presses. The ordinances did not take them wholly
by surprise; a few months earlier a number of them had met
to discuss their response to such a move, but on July 26 they
had no plans ready. The proprietors of the *Constitutionnel*
immediately asked their counsel, the liberal lawyer and
deputy, André Dupin, for advice on the legal situation that
the ordinances created for the opposition press, and they
invited a number of their colleagues from other papers to
attend the conference in Dupin's office on the Rue Coq-
Héron near the Place des Victoires. A dozen or so turned up
about eleven o'clock: Dupin and two other lawyers whom

---

[28] Haussez, *Mémoires*, p. 252, n. 1; Paul Mantoux, "Patrons et ouv-
riers en juillet 1830," *Revue d'histoire moderne et contemporaine*, 3
(1901-1902), 293; Chauvet, *Ouvriers du livre*, pp. 92, 646; Achille de
Vaulabelle, *Histoire des deux Restaurations jusqu'à l'avènement de
Louis-Philippe de janvier 1813 à octobre 1830*, 5th ed. (Paris, 1860),
VII, 326; AS, V^{bis} 322, CRN, 1er Arrond., Dossier Marie.

he had summoned—Odilon Barrot and Joseph Merilhou; Rémusat and Pierre Leroux from the *Globe*; Victor Bohain, publisher of the *Figaro*; François d'Aubert of the *Constitutionnel*, and a number of lesser figures. No one came from the *Journal des débats* or the *National*. Dupin, although somewhat annoyed at the number of men, some of them unknown to him, who appeared at what he expected to be a consultation with a client, spoke to the assembled group. He reported the unanimous opinion of himself and his two colleagues that the royal ordinances were illegal and that the journalists had the right, even the duty, to disobey them. Rémusat remarked testily that they scarcely needed to be told so obvious a truth and that the question was what those hurt by the ordinances should do. Now was the time to agree on common action. Another, endorsing Rémusat's position, proposed that they draw up a joint protest. Dupin, a cautious man, warned them that he would not permit a political meeting in his office. Taking this as an invitation to leave, the journalists made their excuses and departed. As they walked away, Leroux sighed to Rémusat, "Oh, the lawyers, the lawyers."[29]

A few streets distant on the Rue Neuve-Saint-Marc between the Bourse and Boulevard Montmartre, the offices of the *National* had already begun to take on the appearance of the opposition's headquarters. When Rémusat arrived there shortly after leaving the abortive session at Dupin's, he found a crowd of journalists heatedly discussing the ordinances and what they might do to combat them. He noticed his friends Thiers, Mignet, and Carrel of the *National*, Cauchois-Lemaire and Evariste Dumoulin of the *Constitutionnel*, Léon Pillet of the *Journal de Paris*, and René Chatelain of the *Courrier français*. Achille Treilhard, a former imperial prefect and a judge of the Royal Court of Paris, was attempting to preside over the noisy gathering. The *National*'s editors had already brought out an extra

[29] Rémusat, *Mémoires*, ii, 310-13; André Dupin, *Mémoires de M. Dupin* (Paris, 1855-61), ii, 138-39; Odilon Barrot, *Mémoires posthumes*, 3d ed. (Paris, 1875), i, 101.

edition calling for resistance to the ordinances. "The ministry of August 8 . . . ," they declared, "has just defied all the laws that France has learned to live with, to respect, and to cherish for fifteen years. . . . France . . . falls back into revolution by the act of the government itself. . . . What can still be done in France is to refuse to pay taxes. The chamber . . . has done its duty; the electors have fulfilled theirs; the press also has done all that could be expected of it; it is now up to the taxpayers to save the cause of the law."[30]

This recommendation conformed to the ideas of peaceful resistance most favorably regarded by liberals in the discussions of the past year, but the journalists assembled at the *National*, seeing their jobs about to be destroyed, could not await the results of such gradual methods of redress. The majority agreed on the need for an immediate and united protest by all the opposition press. Many, however, objected that they were present only as individuals and could not speak for their papers. Pillet proposed that all sign a common protest as individuals; their papers, he hoped, would publish it, but in signing they would not be committing their publishers. Thiers enthusiastically endorsed this compromise, and, the practices of citizens' meetings in 1830 being no different from those of today, the gathering immediately charged him with the drawing up of the protest. Cauchois-Lemaire and Chatelain were named to assist him, and Thiers asked Rémusat to join the three of them in his office. Cauchois-Lemaire and Chatelain then gave *carte-blanche* to Thiers and withdrew, and Rémusat, although he remained, contributed no more than his absent colleagues. The room was very hot, and while Thiers poured onto the paper before him his passionate words of defiance, Rémusat poured—and drank—"an excellent orangeade" that someone had thoughtfully placed on Thiers's desk. When Thiers had completed his draft, he read it aloud to Rémusat, who suggested but a single minor change. Later Cauchois-

[30] Rémusat, *Mémoires*, II, 313; Duvergier de Hauranne, *Histoire*, x, 535-36; *National*, special edition, July 26, 27, 28, 30, 31, 1830.

86

Lemaire and Chatelain returned, listened to Thiers read the protest, and they, too, found little in it to alter.[31]

While the drafting committee was at work two deputies, Alexandre de Laborde, representative of Paris, and Auguste Bérard, newly elected deputy of the Department of the Seine-et-Oise, arrived at the *National*. They had come from a gathering of half a dozen prominent deputies at the town house of Casimir Périer on the Rue Neuve-du-Luxembourg. All of them except Laborde and Bérard, fearful of compromising themselves, contended that although they opposed the ordinances they lacked authority to protest them until the meeting date of the chamber to which they had been elected. The two dissenters, acting on the proposition of one of the conferees that the initiative should come from Paris, left to organize a meeting of the deputies and electors of Paris that evening. Anyone who contemplated resistance on this first, confused day apparently thought of the *National*, and Laborde and Bérard went first to the busy office on the Rue Neuve-Saint-Marc. The assembled journalists gave the two men a warm welcome, and as the session was about to resume to consider Thiers's draft, they invited both deputies to join them and asked Laborde to take the chair.[32]

Thiers read his protest to the assembled journalists and their two guests from the Chamber of Deputies.

People have often predicted, during the past six months, [he began] that the laws would be violated, that a coup d'Etat would be attempted. The public, with good sense, refused to believe it. The ministry rejected the prediction as a calumny. Nevertheless, the *Moniteur* has finally published these memorable ordinances, which are the most flagrant violation of the laws. The legal regime is now interrupted, that of force has begun.

In this situation obedience ceases to be a duty. The citizens first called upon to obey are the journalists; they

31 Rémusat, *Mémoires*, II, 313-14; Vaulabelle, *Histoire*, VIII, 188-89.
32 Duvergier de Hauranne, *Histoire*, X, 535; Bérard, *Souvenirs*, pp. 61-64.

ought to give the first example of resistance to the authority which has defied the law.[33]

The succeeding paragraphs argued that the Charter guaranteed the press and electoral laws against change except by joint action of crown and parliament. Then came a declaration that the signers' newspapers would defy the first ordinance and an exhortation to the deputies to join them in resistance to the ministry's violation of the laws. "The government has today lost the character of legality that requires obedience," the proclamation concluded. "We will resist in so far as we are concerned; France must judge how far it ought to carry its resistance."[34]

After a lively discussion over the form of signature that would be most effective in giving weight to the protest, Rémusat came forward first to affix his signature, signing, he said, both for himself and for his newspaper. Forty-three others followed him. They represented eleven Parisian papers: the *National*, the *Globe*, the *Constitutionnel*, the *Temps*, the *Courrier français*, the *Journal du commerce*, the *France nouvelle*, the *Tribune des départements*, the *Courrier des électeurs*, the *Figaro*, and the *Sylphe*.[35]

After signing, the journalists dispersed to prepare the next day's editions of their papers and some of them, at least, to wonder how soon they would be arrested. Later in the day Thiers remarked to Rémusat that within twenty-four hours they might well be locked up in the fortress of Vincennes.[36]

Laborde and Bérard left the offices of the *National* to invite deputies of Paris and any other deputies who happened to be in the city to meet at Laborde's home that evening. About eight o'clock fourteen men turned up at the house on the Rue d'Artois. Presumably they were the most concerned of the considerably larger number of deputies present in the capital, and their number included three men who only three days later became members of the revolu-

[33] Duvergier de Hauranne, *Histoire*, x, 536-37.
[34] *Ibid.*, pp. 537-38.
[35] Rémusat, *Mémoires*, II, 317-18; Vaulabelle, *Histoire*, VIII, 191-92.
[36] Rémusat, *Mémoires*, II, 319.

tionary Municipal Commission of Paris, but this evening they could agree on nothing except to meet again the next day. Bérard, warmly supported by De Schonen, a former leader of the Carbonari, one of the founders of the "Aide-toi," and a deputy of Paris, urged that they make a formal protest against the ordinances. Casimir Périer opposed any such precipitous action and argued that this tiny minority had no right to speak for the deputies. Périer's caution prevailed. The group set a second meeting for three o'clock the next afternoon, and each agreed to bring as many of his fellow deputies as he could. Périer reluctantly opened his house to the meeting. As the deputies were leaving Laborde's, three delegates from a meeting of electors arrived hoping to join with them in making common cause against the ordinances. Bérard and his friends invited them to come to Périer's house the next day.[37]

While "the faction," reportedly so well prepared to subvert the monarchy, floundered about in search of some effective but not too dangerous means of resisting the government, the ministers and the administration went serenely about daily business and making routine arrangements for application of the ordinances. The Minister of the Interior ordered all prefects and subprefects presently on leave to return to their posts. The Ministry of War sent a dispatch to the commanding-generals of the nation's twenty-one military districts advising them that the King had been obliged to take extraordinary measures to protect the rights of the crown and that he counted on them to maintain order in their districts and discipline among their men. No orders for unusual movement of troops appeared. The Minister of Justice gave instructions to the prosecuting attorney of the Royal Court of Paris, on whom would fall responsibility for pressing charges brought under the new ordinances. Prefect of Police Mangin warned proprietors of reading rooms and cafés that if they furnished customers with papers printed in violation of the royal ordinance of July 25 they would

[37] Bérard, *Souvenirs*, pp. 65-70, 73; BHVP, Série 23, Carton 1830, "Note remise à P . . . par Casimir Périer."

be prosecuted as accomplices of the journals and their establishments would be closed. About 1:30 in the afternoon Foucauld, commander of the Gendarmerie, found Mangin in his office relaxed and unconcerned. He saw no reason why Foucauld should not dine out that evening as he had planned nor hold the inspection scheduled for the next day.[38] Marmont, still ignorant of his appointment to the command of Paris, attended a session of the Academy of Sciences at the Institute that afternoon. Encountering his friend François Arago, the astronomer, he exclaimed, "Well! you see, the lunatics, as I foresaw, have pushed things to the extreme. [I] will perhaps be obliged to get myself killed for acts that I abhor and for acts of persons who have long . . . filled me with disgust!"[39]

At Saint-Cloud the routine of mass, hunting, and cards proceeded undisturbed. After morning mass the King and the Dauphin went to Rambouillet to hunt and did not return until late in the evening. The Duchesse de Berry drove into Paris after lunch. The royal children, the Duc de Bordeaux and his sister, spent the afternoon at the Trianon Palace. In the evening the court busied itself with the customary games of whist.[40]

While the courtiers shuffled their cards under the flickering candles at Saint-Cloud the first acts of violence broke out in Paris. After the dinner hour the usual summer evening's crowd had gathered in the garden of the Palais-Royal. Small groups formed here and there—at cafés, in front of reading rooms, and around young men who read newspapers aloud. Sometime after eight o'clock a police commissioner

[38] *Moniteur*, July 26, 1830, p. 816; AHMG, D³ 131, Ministre de la Guerre to Lts.-gén. Cmdts. des Divs. milit., June 26, 1830; AN, CC 546, Testimony of Champagny, Nov. 5, 1830; CC 549, Deposition of Georges Bayeux, Avocat gén. à la Cour royale de Paris, Nov. 13, 1830; CC 550, Préfecture de Police, "Ordonnances sur les Escrits imprimés," July 26, 1830; CC 546, Testimony of Foucauld, Nov. 23, 1830.

[39] AN, CC 549, Deposition d'Arago, Oct. 30, 1830.

[40] Ange de Damas, *Mémoires*, II, 177; Semonville, "Mémoire," p. 76; *Moniteur*, July 27, 1830, p. 818; AN, CC 550, Sous-chef de la police municipale to Préfet de Police, July 27, 1830.

arrived with an order to seize the printing press in a shop in the Galerie d'Orléans at the garden's southern end. A crowd, already attracted by some verses posted in the window of the shop, quickly grew. They watched the police break in and make an arrest, and as the commissioner withdrew they booed and shouted "Vive la Charte!" "A bas les Bourbons!" and "Vive le 221!" In the next hour or so the crowd in the garden grew larger and more unruly, although its activities were still undirected. Gendarmes took over peace-keeping duties from police, brought in forty additional men, and at 10:30 closed the gates and cleared the garden, arresting seven or eight persons who resisted. The crowd re-formed in the Place du Palais-Royal in front of the palace, and when police chased them from there, one group went up the Rue de Rivoli, breaking street lamps and shouting "A bas Polignac!" "A bas les ministres!" "Vive la Charte!" to the Ministry of Finance, on the site of the present Hotel Inter-Continental, where they threw stones at the guards and broke a few windows. Another group marched up the Rue Castiglione, past the Ministry of Justice, on the Place Vendôme, where Polignac and four of his ministers had just met to discuss measures to contain the crowds reported around the Palais-Royal, and on up the Rue de la Paix toward the boulevards. Polignac, concerned for the security of his own ministry on the Boulevard des Capucines, insisted on returning there. He and Haussez got into the former's carriage and set out. In the Rue Neuve des Capucines, about a hundred feet from the ministry, they encountered some of the demonstrators, who recognized them and greeted them with shouts of "A bas les ministres!" and "A bas Polignac!" and a hail of stones that broke the glass in the carriage and struck Haussez, who happened to be sitting on the side whence they came. The coachman whipped the horses, and they dashed to the ministry and into the courtyard, as the guards quickly closed the gates behind them. The crowd stood around the building shouting and throwing stones at windows and street lights for about half an hour, then moved off into the boulevards and dispersed.[41]

When they could safely leave, Polignac and Haussez walked to the headquarters of the commander of the "Place de Paris," Comte de Wall, on the Place Vendôme to learn what measures he had taken for the security of the capital. To two men who had just been stoned by a mob the headquarters seemed scandalously relaxed. The sentries sat at the door or stretched out on camp beds, and Wall had retired for the night. Routed out of bed he learned for the first time of the crowds that had attacked two ministries within a few hundred feet of his headquarters and streamed past his own door. He promised to order out patrols immediately; he would have 150 men on the streets within two hours. One hundred fifty men afforded little reassurance to Haussez, and even the imperturbable Polignac decided that he ought to take the precaution of alerting regiments of the Royal Guard in Paris, which were not under Wall's command.

"Hasn't that already been done?" exclaimed the incredulous Haussez.

"You're always worrying," replied Polignac.[42]

About the same time at Saint-Cloud the King and the Dauphin returned from their day of hunting at Rambouillet. As he alighted from his carriage, Charles turned to Marmont and asked if he had any news of Paris. "Great consternation, great dejection, Sire," replied the marshal, "an extraordinary drop in securities." The Dauphin wanted to know how much of a drop. Marmont told him it was 4 percent. "They will go back up," replied the Prince and

<hr/>

[41] AN, CC 546, Testimony of Foucauld, Nov. 28, 1830; CC 548, Wall, "Rapport analytique de l'Etat-major de la 1er Div. milit. du 26 au 27 juillet 1830," Cte. de Quinsonas to Raguse, July 27, 1830; CC 550, Rapport de Groufier, Officier de Paix, July 26, 1830; Carton, Officier de Paix, to Chef de la Police municipale, July 26, 1830; Boussiron, Officier de Paix, Rapport, July 26, minuit ½; Préfecture de Police, "Rondes du soir," 2e Arrond., July 26, 1830; AN, F7 4174, Gendarmerie royale de Paris, "Rapport général du 23 au 24 juillet 1830 . . ."; Haussez, *Mémoires*, II, 249-50; Montbel, *Souvenirs*, p. 243.

[42] Haussez, *Mémoires*, II, 250-51.

moved on. The King retired without any further consideration of the day's events.[43]

By midnight calm had returned to the capital, its streets
were deserted. The ever-confident Prefect of Police wrote
in the "Bulletin de Paris," his daily report to the Minister
of the Interior, for July 26, "The most perfect tranquillity
continues to reign in all parts of the capital. No event
worthy of attention is recorded in the reports that have come
to me."[44]

On Tuesday morning, July 27, Lady Aylmer, hurrying from
Italy to England to join her husband, the newly appointed
governor of Canada, drove into Paris accompanied only by
her maid. Noticing as they passed through the Faubourg
Saint-Antoine the more than ordinary number of people
standing about in the streets and soldiers posted at the
corners, she asked her maid to inquire of the postilion what
this meant. "Madame," he replied, "it is a revolution." But
Paris was not yet in revolution. Indeed, few men had even
thought of revolution. The journalists, the deputies, the
electors, even the most belligerent among them, had contemplated only peaceful protest to persuade the King to
withdraw the offending ordinances and perhaps to change
his ministers. The disorders around the Palais-Royal and at
the ministries were not unprecedented and promised nothing that a routine show of force could not contain. Not
unreasonably did Polignac remark to the Russian ambassador that Tuesday morning, "I *was* more fearful than I am
now!"[45]

Despite the resolution of the journalists in the offices of
the *National* on Monday, the opposition press on Tuesday
presented no united front to the government, the *National*,
the *Globe*, the *Temps*, and the *Journal du Commerce* appeared in defiance of the first ordinance, all of them carrying

[43] Marmont, *Mémoires*, VIII, 238.

[44] AN, F⁷ 3884, Préfecture de Police, "Bulletin de Paris," July 26,
1830.

[45] R. Anchel, "Un Témoinage anglais sur les journées de Juillet:
souvenirs de Lady Aylmer," *Revue d'histoire moderne*, 6 (1931), 350;
Rémusat, *Mémoires*, II, 319, 322; Semonville, "Mémoire," p. 75.

the protest signed the preceding day, although the latter two omitted the names of the signers. The printers of the *Tribune,* the *France Nouvelle,* and the *Courrier français* refused to print the papers. The proprietors of the *Constitutionnel* and the *Journal des débats,* having failed to obtain authorization to publish, canceled the day's issues.[46]

The authorities moved quickly to silence the four recalcitrant journals that had appeared and were being freely distributed in Paris. Before 8 A.M. the prefect had issued a list of authorized journals for the guidance of proprietors of reading rooms and had ordered the search of offices of stage coach lines for copies of the *National* and the *Temps* awaiting dispatch to provincial subscribers. The Minister of the Interior sent a circular to all prefects ordering them to make certain that stage coaches delivered no newspapers or periodicals from Paris. Mangin dispatched police commissioners, supported by gendarmes, to seize the presses of the four defiant papers. The editors of the *National* refused to open their door and obliged the police to break in to accomplish their mission. At the office of the *Temps* on the Rue de Richelieu the police, arriving about noon, found the door to the printing shop locked and the approach to it barred by the editor, Jean-Jacques Baude; Baude threatened the commissioner with prosecution for burglary if he broke in and removed the presses and reminded him that the law punished burglary with forced labor. A crowd had gathered in the courtyard, and it cheered Baude, threatened the police and gendarmes, and intimidated two locksmiths summoned in turn to force the door. Finally, near six o'clock, the locksmith who riveted irons on criminals arrived to do the job, and the commissioner's men seized the type and parts of the presses to render them inoperable.[47]

[46] Charles Ledré, *La Presse à l'assaut de la monarchie, 1815-1848* (Paris, 1960), p. 108.

[47] AN, CC 550, Sous-chef de la Police municipale to Préfet de Police, July 27, 1830; Testimony of Comm. de Police, Qtr. de la Banque de France, Nov. 3, 1830; Marnay, *Mémoires,* pp. 12-13; CC 546, Testimony of Foucauld; Suzanne d'Huart, "Le Dernier Préfet de Police de Charles X: Claude Mangin," *Actes* du 84ᵉ Congrès national des sociétés savantes,

The police confined their initial actions to the seizure of presses and illegally printed papers. Owners and editors they left alone. Later in the day, however, the ministers ordered the arrest of the journalists who had signed the protest of July 26. Warrants were drawn up, and between 8 and 9 in the evening the public prosecutor of the Tribunal de Première Instance delivered them to the Prefect of Police for execution the next day.[48]

The accomplishments of the meetings of deputies, electors, and journalists on the twenty-seventh were scarcely more effectual than Baude's haranguing of the hapless police commissioner at the doorway of the *Temps*. An almost continual meeting went on in the office of the *National*, and one observer that day found sixty to eighty people there, all talking at once. Although he overheard drastic proposals to recall Napoleon II or to reestablish the republic, the decision reached was much more modest—to urge the electors of Paris to reestablish in each electoral district the committees that had managed the recent elections. These committees, the meeting at the *National* thought, could organize and coordinate the opposition to the ordinances in every district of the city. To present this proposal to the deputies in Paris and to urge them to assume leadership of the opposition the gathering appointed a delegation of five of its members headed by Thiers. A meeting of electors, deputies, and journalists was set for that evening at the house of Charles Cadet-Gassicourt, a member of the executive committee of the "Aide-toi."[49]

Dijon (1959); Section d'histoire moderne et contemporaine, p. 608; AN, F⁷ 6969, Police gén., Préfet de Loir-et-Cher to Ministre de l'Intérieur, July 29, 1830; Alfred de Saint-Chamans, "Le Combat pour le roi, juillet 1830," *Revue de Paris*, 3d year, 1 (Feb. 1, 1895), 489-90; Duvergier de Hauranne, *Histoire*, x, 544-45.

48 Montbel, *Souvenirs*, p. 243; AN, CC 547, Comm. de la Chambre des Députés, Enquête, Testimony of Crosnier, Chef de Division, Préfecture de Police, Sept. 8, 1830; CC 549, Mangin to Prés., Cour des Pairs, Dec. 9, 1830.

49 Rémusat, *Mémoires*, II, 320-21, 323; Hippolyte Bonnelier, *Mémorial de l'Hôtel-de-Ville de Paris, 1830* (Paris, 1835), pp. 9-11; Henri Vienne,

At 3 P.M. thirty to forty deputies gathered at the residence of Casimir Périer, where they engaged in lively but inconclusive discussion. Bérard again pressed his colleagues to issue a formal protest. Most of them agreed in principle but shied away from the positive act, which, they feared, might compromise them, a fear heightened by the spreading rumor that the government planned to arrest and exile all recalcitrant deputies. To await further developments seemed the prudent course. The deputies designated three of their number, and not the most audacious—Guizot, Dupin, the lawyer who had ordered the militant journalists out of his office, and Villemain, who had joined Périer in opposing any overt action, to draft an address of protest expressing the sentiments of the gathering. After agreeing to meet at noon the next day at the house of Pierre Audry de Puyraveau on the Rue du Faubourg-Poissonnière, the assemblage adjourned, some of its members prudently leaving by a back door because they had heard that gendarmes were at the front entrance.[50]

The deputies had just departed when Thiers's delegation from the *National,* accompanied by Rémusat, arrived at Périer's door. Thiers explained their desire to arrange for cooperation of electors and deputies in resisting the ordinances. Chevalier, one of the delegates, added that the people of Paris were beginning to move and that they must not be left without leadership. The exchange grew heated, and Périer asked what they expected the deputies to do; they were only a few individuals against a government with all the official machinery of coercion at its disposal. "Do you think we have a thunderbolt?" he asked. Most earnestly he

---

"Dix jours à Paris du dimanche 25 juillet au mardi 3 août 1830," *Mémoires* de la Société bourguignonne de géographie et d'histoire (1892), VIII, 81-82.

[50] Bérard, *Souvenirs,* pp. 71-74, 76; Dupin, *Mémoires,* pp. 138-39; BHVP, "Note remise à P . . . par Casimir Périer"; AN, CC 549, Déposition of Casimir Périer, Nov. 6, 1830; Guizot, *Mémoires,* II, 5; BHVP, Série 23, Dossier Laffitte, "Notes prises chez M. De la Borde."

urged that they not incite the people to rebellion without first warning them of what they faced.[51] "I am informed," he continued, "that troops are being assembled, that a confrontation is wanted and that it has been decided to strike a great blow. We shall do by law, and by moral resistance, all that can be done. Knowing what I do I would not push anyone to attempt more."[52] The conversation quickly ended, and the delegates left without having accomplished more than an exchange of divergent views. As they walked away, Rémusat defended Périer's position to his colleagues, arguing that the sole strength of the deputies lay in their claim to be the *legal* representatives of the country opposing the *illegal* acts of the government; in abandoning legality they would make themselves powerless. Chevalier, an ex-Carbonaro, scorned such caution and declared that despite Périer he believed in the possibility of a victorious insurrection. Thiers and Marrast were less confident and opposed exciting violence, but even an unsuccessful uprising would, they cynically thought, serve a purpose in alienating people from the Bourbon monarchy.[53]

In the early evening forty or fifty deputies, electors, and journalists found their ways through the growing crowds and the patrols on the streets to the house of Cadet-Gassicourt on the Rue Saint-Honoré about a quarter of a mile to the east of the Place du Palais-Royal. The meeting began about eight o'clock in one or two stifling rooms on the second floor, and the host, an elector of the Fourth Arrondissement, presided. The historian Vaulabelle has presented this gathering as a critical episode in the revolution, holding that the men here assembled made the decision to organize violent resistance and to prepare arms.[54] Rémusat, who was there, has left a description of the meeting that reveals it as another indecisive session.

[51] Rémusat, *Mémoires*, II, 323-24.   [52] *Ibid.*, p. 324.

[53] *Ibid.*, pp. 324-25; Bonnelier, *Mémorial*, pp. 11-12.

[54] Rémusat, *Mémoires*, II, 327; Jacques Laffitte, *Souvenirs de Jacques Laffitte racontés par lui-même* (Paris, 1844-45), II, 68; Vaulabelle, *Histoire*, VIII, 219-20.

How many useless words are spoken in this kind of meeting cannot be imagined by a person who has not attended one. There are the earnest and the impetuous, who want to speak to satisfy their temperaments and to sooth themselves by declaiming at random. There are the boobs, who want to tell what they have seen or heard, believing it very important because it is all that they know. There are the vain, who, preoccupied with themselves, insist upon explaining their conduct. . . . I recall that a large part of the time was spent in listening to Durosoir. He was a former professor of history, who after having been a liberal, like all his fellows, left us to become an assistant in the Faculty of Letters. He made both an apology and a *mea culpa*, explained to us that events had enlightened him, and swore to us that he was now really one of us.[55]

This kind of talk might have gone on for hours had not late arrivals reported troops moving in the Rue Saint-Honoré; they would soon reach the house and might block the exit, making departure hazardous. Some flatteringly professed to believe that the force was on its way to arrest everyone at the meeting; earlier a report that police spies sat among them had made them feel importantly conspiratorial. Now all hurriedly left the house. The only decisions to emerge from the wordy gathering were an agreement to keep in contact with the deputies in Paris and an endorsement of the proposal to reestablish the electoral committees as centers of resistance and direction in each district.[56]

While the deputies, electors, and journalists talked and temporized, the workingmen of Paris acted. Early in the morning bands of printing workers were on the streets urging others to join them. Their number multiplying, they converged on the garden of the Palais-Royal, where illegal newspapers were circulating freely, and men were reading aloud the protest of the journalists. Before nine o'clock Polignac reported these crowds to the Comte de Wall and

<hr>

[55] Rémusat, *Mémoires*, II, 327.   [56] *Ibid.*, p. 328.

asked him to look to the protection of the vulnerable ministries, and about 9:30 an aide interrupted Foucauld's
inspection at the Saint-Martin Barracks to deliver a request
from Wall for 100 mounted gendarmes. Foucauld ordered
out this force, and, divided into three detachments, it took
up positions at the Ministry of Foreign Affairs, the Ministry
of Justice, and at the headquarters of the "Place de Paris" on
the Place Vendôme. Wall also alerted the 1st Battalion of
the 5th Regiment of the Line and 500 men of the 1st Regiment of the Royal Guard.[57]

The crowd in the garden of the Palais-Royal continued
to grow throughout the morning, but without any threatening incidents until news arrived shortly after noon of the
police seizure of newspaper presses. Then the police heard
cries of "A bas les ministres!" and saw people chalk un-
complimentary remarks about the King on walls and
columns. The forbidden journals continued to circulate and
to be read aloud. Alarmed shopkeepers along the galleries
began to close their shops, and itinerant merchants gathered
up their wares and departed. About one o'clock the police
closed the gates and cleared the garden. Some of the crowd
moved up the Rue de Richelieu, where Baude was defying
the police at the offices of the *Temps*; others went to the
Rue Neuve des Capucines, where they cheered deputies
arriving at Périer's residence; but the largest concentration
formed on the Place du Palais-Royal, then only about half
its present size, on the Rue Saint-Honoré on both sides of
the *place*, and in other streets that converged on it. Anxious
shopkeepers here, too, closed their shops, adding their employees to the crowds, and removed signs bearing the compromising adjective "royal" or the royal arms. Posts manned
by the Royal Guard in the court of the palace were doubled,
and the Comte de Wall sent sixty men of the 5th Regiment

[57] AN, CC 550, Sous chef de la Police municipale, "Rapport au Préfet de Police," July 27, 1830; Vaulabelle, *Histoire*, VIII, 205; Vienne, "Dix
jours," p. 79; AN, CC 546, Testimony of Foucauld, Nov. 28, 1830; CC
549, Wall to Polignac, July 27, 1830, 9 A.M.; AHMG, D⁸ 131, Wall
to "Mon cher général" [?], July 27, 1830.

of the Line to support them. About three o'clock a detachment of mounted gendarmes, ordered to clear the *place*, charged the crowd with drawn sabers, and the retreating demonstrators showered them with stones. Two detachments from the 3d Regiment of the Royal Guard then occupied the *place*. An hour or so later the Guard fired on the crowd. The inconclusive evidence suggests that the stones and the taunts of the crowd lurking in the edges of the *place* and in nearby streets exasperated three or four guards into firing without orders. Then the whole troop moved into the Rue Saint-Honoré and discharged several volleys into the Rue de Valois and the Rue du Croix des Petits Champs. Men picked up the bodies of victims, placed them in stretchers, and paraded them through the streets shouting "Mort aux Ministres!" and "Mort à Polignac!"[58]

Boniface, the harried police commissioner of the Quarter of the Palais-Royal, already at odds with the gendarmes over their handling of the crowds, hurried to the Prefecture of Police to report on the ominous developments in his quarter and to obtain orders. Mangin informed him that he had none to give, that responsibility for maintenance of order in Paris now rested with the army. That morning Marmont had just called his carriage to go to Saint-Germain for the day, when an attendant brought word that the King would see him after mass. Charles received the marshal about 11:30 and calmly told him, "It appears that there is some concern for the tranquillity of Paris. Go there, take

[58] AN, CC 547, Testimony of Odieuve, Chatet, Joly, DeMauroy, and Poisson, Sept. 16, 1830; CC 548, "Rapport du 27 Juillet 1830" [source not identified; apparently from Garde royale]; CC 549, Mangin to Polignac, July 27, 12 noon; Deposition of Victor Boniface, Comm. de Police, Qtr. de Palais-Royal [n.d.]; Sous-chef de la Police municipale, "Rapport au Préfet," July 27, 1830; CC 550, Mondor, Officier de Paix, "Rapport," July 27, 1 P.M., 4 P.M.; Monnet, Officier de Paix, "Rapport," July 27, 1 P.M.; S. Ansart, avocat, to Prés., Cour des Pairs, Dec. 18, 1830; AN, 149 AP 1, Mangin Papers, Police reports, July 27, 1830; AS, DM[13] 1, Venard to CRN, Feb. 7, 1831; V[bis] 3, CRN, 4e Arrond., Dossier Meline; VD[3] 3, "Renseignements fournis par M. Bertrand, Chef, 3e Bat., 12e Légion, Garde nationale" [n.d.]; Crochon, "Souvenirs," II, 103; Herbert P. Gambrell, "Three Letters on the Revolution of 1830," *Journal of Modern History*, 1 (1929), 597; Barrot, *Mémoires*, I, 102.

command, and see Prince Polignac on your way. If all is in order in the evening you may return to Saint-Cloud." He left immediately for Paris, accompanied only by an aide-de-camp, stopped at the Ministry of Foreign Affairs, where Polignac informed him of the order approved by the ministers two days earlier giving him command of the Subdivision of the Seine of the First Military District. By one o'clock he was installed in the headquarters of the subdivision in the Tuileries Palace overlooking the Place du Carrousel.[59]

The choice of Marmont, Duc de Raguse, to command in the capital at this critical time was ill-advised. His defection to the allies in early April 1814 had, in the popular view at least, undermined Napoleon's plans to recover Paris and forced his abdication. "Ragusard," an adaptation of his title, had been adopted into the language as a synonym for traitor. In the summer of 1830 he was out of sympathy with the government's policy toward the Chamber of Deputies, and he thought Polignac and the other ministers incompetent if not stupid. He was embittered against the Duc d'Angoulême and the ministers for their parts in withholding from him the command of the Algerian expedition. Marmont coveted the assignment and believed that it had been promised him. When it went to Bourmont, he thought of resigning his commission, but he was deeply in debt and could not forego the salary, almost all of it pledged to his creditors. He looked forward that summer to the end of his present assignment on September 1. He planned to leave Paris in October to go to Italy for several months, allowing the government to reap the fruits of its foolishness without compromising him. He was scarcely an auspicious choice to defend a government and a crown in a moment of supreme crisis, but as a loyal soldier or, his enemies said, as a man already too compromised to defect again, he accepted the command of Paris and carried out his assignment probably as well as any man could with the forces available.[60]

[59] Marmont, *Mémoires*, VIII, 238-39, 257; AN, CC 549, Déposition de Louis de Komierowski, a.d.c. de Raguse, Nov. 9, 1830.
[60] Marmont, *Mémoires*, VIII, 212-30, 324-37; AN, CC 547, Perrigaux to Berenger, July 27, 1830.

In the postmortem debate on the army's failure to hold Paris, Polignac and Marmont clashed over the number of troops he had at his disposal. Polignac held that the garrison of Paris numbered 13,000 men. Marmont, charging that Polignac was too ill-informed to distinguish between nominal strength and men actually present and armed, declared that he had only 9300 men under arms in Paris. Independent sources suggest that the truth lay between the two claims. The order of battle in Paris for Marmont's command in the afternoon of July 27 can be reconstructed in this form.

Royal Guard	
Infantry—8 battalions from 1st, 3d, and 7th (Swiss) Regiments	3800 men
Cavalry—8 squadrons, Lancers and Cuirassiers	800
Line	
Infantry—11 battalions from the 5th, 15th Light, 50th, and 53d Regiments	4400 to 5400
Gendarmerie	
Mounted	600
Foot	700 to 900
	10,300 to 11,500

About 1500 of these men ordinarily manned guard posts throughout the city and were not available for emergency duty, and the loyalty of the troops of the Line in an insurrection was not certain. Moreover, the 7th Regiment (Swiss) had only recently been transferred to Paris after several years of duty in the provinces, and its noncommissioned officers were not yet familiar with the city and its streets. Marmont admitted that he had 1700 additional men available in four nearby towns—Saint-Denis, Versailles, Rueil, and Courbevoie—and on July 28 elements of the 2d Guard Regiment from Versailles and the 6th Guard Regiment from Saint-Denis joined his command in Paris.[61]

[61] AHMG, D³ 131, 1ᵉ Div. milit., Etat-major gén., "Rapport journalier . . . du 27 Juillet 1830," signed by Wall; AS, D 4AZ 1181, "Précis

Until his interviews with the King and Polignac on Tuesday, the twenty-seventh, Marmont had received no warning of the heavy responsibility now placed upon him nor had he been informed of threats to the peace in Paris and the measures taken to contain them. He arrived at his headquarters on the Place du Carrousel without plans and handicapped by the absence of his principal staff officer, who was on leave. Here he learned of the crowds around the Palais-Royal, but in the early afternoon, as seen from the headquarters, they seemed to pose no threat, and he only continued and at some points reinforced the patrols that Wall had already put on the streets. As soon as he learned that troops had fired on the crowd, he reacted vigorously, ordering out virtually the entire garrison of Paris to occupy strategic positions in the city. By five o'clock two battalions of the 1st Infantry Regiment of the Guard, fifty Lancers, and two artillery pieces were on the Place de la Madeleine and the Boulevard des Capucines. Further to the east along the boulevards the 50th Regiment of the Line occupied the section between the Rue Montmartre and the Porte Saint-Denis, and the 53d Regiment of the Line supported by the Cuirassiers of the Guard were on the Place de la Bastille and nominally, at least, in communication with the artillery regiment garrisoned in the fortress of Vincennes about four miles to the east. The 5th Regiment of the Line took up its position of the Place Vendôme; the 15th Regiment at the Pont-Neuf, and the 3d Regiment of the Guard, 150 Lancers, and four cannon were on the Place du Carrousel. The Swiss and six artillery pieces remained in reserve on the Place Louis XVI, the present Place de la Concorde. All these units

des événemens aux quels à pris part la troisième regiment d'infanterie de la garde royale depuis le vingt-six juillet jusqu'au jour de son licenciement par un officier," p. 2; AN, CC 549, Place de Paris, Etat-major, "Casernement des differens Corps Stationnés dans la Capitale à l'époque du 21 Juillet 1830"; *Almanach royal pour l'an MDCCCXXX* (Paris, 1830), p. 619; Marmont, *Mémoires,* VIII, 242, 268-69, 316, 431; *La Garde royale pendant les événemens du 25 juillet au 5 août 1830; par un officier employé à l'Etat-major* (Paris, 1830), p. 5. Vidalenc, "Journée du 28 juillet," p. 42.

had moved to their positions without encountering any resistance, and patrols maintained communications among them.[62]

In the next hour or two Marmont drew from troops on the Place du Carrousel small detachments to demolish barricades and to disperse crowds in the neighborhood of the Palais-Royal. Captain de Blair led about thirty men to destroy a reported barricade in the Rue Saint-Nicaise, a narrow street, now gone, that ran between the Rue Saint-Honoré and the Rue de Rivoli. The first barricade they encountered scarcely slowed them down, but a large crowd behind two overturned omnibuses at the end of the street near the Rue Saint-Honoré assailed them with stones and paving blocks. The Guards advanced with fixed bayonets, and the crowd fled. The troops opened the barricade, and Blair sent mounted gendarmes through to clear the adjoining streets. About 6 P.M. a squad of thirty guardsmen on their way to reinforce the guard at the Palais-Royal encountered a barricade made of an omnibus and a water porter's cart on the Rue Saint-Honoré, and when they stopped to dismantle it, they were stoned, and several guardsmen were hit. The squad was, nonetheless, able to continue on to its assigned position. A few minutes later a detachment of Lancers charging the crowd on the Rue Saint-Honoré near the Rue de l'Echelle withdrew under a hail of stones and bricks.[63]

Beginning around seven o'clock the exasperated guardsmen started to use their firearms, under orders, although Marmont had issued instructions to fire only as a last resort. About 7 a captain and some thirty guards were the tar-

[62] Marmont, *Mémoires*, VIII, 239-40, 268; Albert Maag, *Geschichte der Schweizertruppen in französischen Diensten während der Restauration und Julirevolution, 1816-1830* (Biel, 1899), p. 374; AN, CC 550, Choiseul to Préfet de Police, July 27, 1830; Vidalenc, "Journée du 28 juillet," pp. 41-42. In disposing his troops Marmont did not follow the order issued over his name by the General Staff of the Royal Guard on July 20, 1830.

[63] AN, CC 546, Testimony of François de Blair, Nov. 13, 1830; Testimony of Charles de Saint-Germain, ex-lt., Garde royale, Nov. 12, 1830; CC 551, Pigon to Prés., Cour des Pairs [Dec. 1830].

get of bricks thrown from houses overlooking a barricade on the Rue de Rivoli near the Rue des Pyramides, and he ordered his men to fire on anyone who showed himself at a window. About the same time two other Guards officers in the Rue Saint-Honoré, thinking they had been fired upon from houses, ordered their men to fire on windows.[64]

As darkness came on, the crowds continued to grow, and increasing disorders and acts of violence threatened to overwhelm the government's ability to keep the peace. Reports of broken street lamps, pillaged arms shops, and ominous crowds streamed to the Prefect of Police. Between 8 and 8:30 a band of men moved through the Rue de l'Arbre Sec and the Rue Baileul, cutting the ropes suspending the street lamps, and moved on to continue their work in the adjoining section of the Rue Saint-Honoré. About the same time two or three hundred men, armed with sticks, sabers, and muskets invaded the Rue de Richelieu; they broke into shops in search of arms, and destroyed street lights until troops from the boulevard cleared the street, as the crowd shouted "Vive la Ligne!" "A bas les Gendarmes et la Garde!" and leaders tried to induce troops of the Line to join them. At nine o'clock the police commissioner of the Quarter Saint-Eustache reported a crowd destroying street lamps in the Rue Montmartre; at 10:30 the prefect heard it was on the Boulevard des Capucines and half an hour later on the Rue Saint-Honoré near the Palais-Royal. The first report of pillaging of arms had come at 6:30, when men broke into a shop on the Quai de la Megisserie near the Pont-Neuf; the police commissioner rushed additional agents to the spot to guard three other shops on the same quai. At a number of other points neither police nor troops were on the scene in time to prevent violent seizure of arms—on the Rue du Faubourg Saint-Martin, on the Rue Coq-Héron, and on the nearby Rue du Bouloi.[65]

---

[64] AN, CC 546, Testimony of Delaunay, Nov. 15, 1830; CC 551, Terrier to Prés., Cour des Pairs, Dec. 17, 1830; BHVP, Révolution de 1830, Carton 23, Dossier Vallée II, "Rapport de M. Antoine Martinet."

[65] AN, CC 548, Comm. de Police, Qtr. du Louvre to Préfet de Police,

At 9 P.M. a company from the 3d Regiment of the Guard sent to the rescue of the hard-pressed Gendarmerie post at the Bourse discovered all the street lights broken along its route up the Rue Saint-Anne and the Rue Neuve Saint-Augustin. They moved in darkness and in silence broken only by the sound of falling glass in nearby streets. A picket of mounted gendarmes hurrying to the Bourse found its way barred by ropes stretched across the Rue Vivienne. The crowd at the Bourse dispersed on the arrival of the troops, but after the Guards had withdrawn it returned and set fire to the guard post and prevented firemen from coming close enough to extinguish it.[66]

Beyond the central quarters crowds posed the threat of spreading disorders. Early in the evening a large number of miscellaneously armed men gathered in the Place de Grève and moved toward the Place de la Bastille. Here by 10 P.M. a large crowd had assembled, largely unarmed but increasingly hostile to the troops posted there. The Cuirassiers drove them out of the *place* and into the Rue du Faubourg Saint-Antoine and the Rue de Charonne, where they cut the cords of the street lamps and under cover of the darkness threw stones at the Guards who pursued them. The troops then blocked the two streets to prevent the demonstrators from marching to the center of the city. On the Left Bank no large crowd formed, but even small groups that gathered in the streets worried the police.[67]

July 27, 1830, 6:30 P.M.; CC 550, Police report, illegible signature, July 27, 1830, 8:30 P.M.; Comm. de Police, Qtr. Saint-Eustache to Préfet de Police, July 27, 1830, 9 P.M.; Comm. de Police, Qtr. de la Banque de France to Préfet de Police, July 27, 1830; F⁹ 1158, Dommages de Juillet, Dossier Sattler d'Argent, Dossier les Sieurs Fleron et Cie.; AS, D 4AZ 1181, "Précis des événemens . . . ," pp. 6-7.

[66] AS, D 4AZ 1181, "Précis des événemens . . . ," p. 6; VK³ 17, Récompenses nationales, Account of an "attaché à la rédaction du Figaro," n.d.; AN, CC 548, Gend. d'Elite, "Rapport du 28 Juillet 1830," 8 A.M.

[67] Gambrell, "Three Letters," p. 596; AN, CC 548, "Rapport [of police to Garde royale] du 27 Juillet 1830," unsigned.

Marmont admitted no serious alarm over the disorders of that evening, but officers actually in the streets grew less confident as the disorders increased. Among the papers found at the Prefecture of Police after the revolution is a police agent's hastily scrawled note, dated 8:30 P.M., July 27, and addressed to the prefect. "We are attacked," he wrote. "We need help without delay. The Gendarmerie itself (poste Chatelet) is not secure."[68] About the same time, when disorder approached a peak, the Viscomte de Vougy, Major of the Gendarmerie, informed the Prefect of Police that the detachments that he had requested for the Place de la Sorbonne, the Rue Vertbois near the Porte Saint-Denis, and other streets were on their way but that they had been drawn from reserves desperately needed on the Place du Palais-Royal. "We are at the end of our resources," he wrote, "and you can no longer count on the forces at the disposal of the Gendarmerie of Paris."[69]

Fortunately for the hard-pressed Gendarmerie the demonstrators grew tired and after about ten o'clock began to go home. Within an hour or two the darkened streets in the center of the city were deserted. Between 11 and 12 Marmont ordered his troops back to their barracks, leaving patrols on the streets near the Tuileries and fifty Cuirassiers on the Place de la Bastille to watch over the Faubourg Saint-Antoine. The marshal dictated a letter to the King, who had spent the day in routine business at Saint-Cloud, informing him that the crowds had been dispersed and peace and order restored in the capital.[70] A few hours earlier Charles had listened to an alarming report brought from Paris by the Duc de Duras, and when the Duke urged him to call troops

---

[68] AN, CC 550, Note to Préfet de Police, signature illegible, July 27, 1830, 8:30 P.M.

[69] AN, 149 AP 1, Vougy to Préfet de Police, July 27, 1830.

[70] Marmont, *Mémoires*, VIII, 241; AN, CC 546, Testimony of Foucauld, Nov. 28, 1830; CC 549, Deposition of Achille de Guise, Nov. 2, 1830; CC 548, Col., Rgt. de Service, Garde royale, to Raguse, July 28, 1830; BHVP, Crochon, "Souvenirs," II, 186, back of page; *Moniteur*, July 28, 1830, p. 822.

from the provinces and to alert his faithful followers in the Vendée, the imperturbable Charles replied, "You are mad, my dear duke. I repeat to you for the hundredth time that there is nothing to do or to fear; it is a straw fire that will make only smoke."[71]

[71] Semonville, "Mémoire," pp. 78-79; AN, AP 115, Archives des familles de Montholon et Semonville, "Récits des entrevues avec Charles X."

Crowd action builds in context of employers reaction, newspapers protest - questioning legitimacy of King & Ministers.

(cf. Tilly - crisis of gov't in rel. to outbreaks & protest by workers.)

IV

Days of Revolution,
July 28 and 29

ON THE morning of July 28 the gathering crowds in the central and eastern quarters, the circulation of inciting leaflets from the pens of opposition journalists, the "murmures" against the Royal Guard, the construction of barricades, all proclaimed that the efforts of police, Gendarmerie, and troops had not extinguished the fires of popular resistance. Marmont, in his headquarters at an early hour, received reports of these ominous developments and, seeing that his reassuring message of the preceding evening, which would only then be reaching the King, would be misleading, he dictated a new letter advising Charles of the present menacing state of the capital. The gendarme charged with delivering the letter mysteriously lost it, and its exact content remains unknown. At nine o'clock Marmont, informed of the miscarriage of his message, dictated another. By this time the reports coming to his headquarters had thoroughly alarmed him. He knew that ordinary methods of pacification would no longer suffice, and he wanted additional instructions.[1] His new letter to the King was brief and blunt:

> Wednesday at 9 o'clock in the morning I have already had the honor of reporting to Your Majesty the dispersal of the groups that disturbed the peace of Paris. This morning they are forming again, more numerous and more threatening than before. This is no longer a riot, this is a revolution. It is urgent that Your Majesty decide

[1] Auguste de Marmont, *Mémoires du maréchal Marmont, duc de Raguse, de 1792 à 1841*, 3d ed. (Paris, 1857), VIII, 242-43; AN, CC 549, Chambre et Cour des Pairs, Deposition of De Guise, Nov. 2, 1830.

on the means of pacification. The honor of his crown can still be saved; tomorrow perhaps it will be too late. For today I am taking the same measures as I did yesterday. The troops will be ready at noon, but I await with impatience the orders of Your Majesty.[2]

Even as he wrote, his troops were taking their positions in the city. The 1st Regiment of the Guard and 100 Lancers returned to the Boulevard des Capucines, and the 3d Regiment with 200 Lancers and the 2d Regiment of Horse Grenadiers were on the Place du Carrousel. The 6th Regiment of the Guard from Saint-Denis was assigned to a position at the Madeleine. The 15th Regiment of the Line returned to the Pont-Neuf, the 50th and the Cuirassiers to the Place de la Bastille, and the 5th and the 53d to the Place Vendôme. Marmont hurried couriers off to nearby cities—Orléans, Fontainebleau, Compiègne, Beauvais, Melun, and Provins—with orders to the garrisons to proceed to Paris, and he sent an officer to the 4th Regiment of the Guard en route from Caen and due in Paris on August 3 to hasten its march. From Vincennes he ordered four batteries of artillery into the city, but not until evening could he spare the cavalry necessary to escort them.[3]

Shortly after 9 a messenger from the Prefect of Police arrived at headquarters to ask if Paris were still under civil law. Marmont, seemingly fated to be the last to hear important news, sent an aide to inquire of Polignac. The first minister told him that the King had indeed that morning signed an ordinance placing the city under martial law. Informed of this the marshal hurried to the Ministry of Foreign Affairs, to take formal delivery of the ordinance. He now had command of all peace-keeping forces in Paris and authority to administer justice through courts martial. Both Polignac and Marmont ordered Mangin to print the ordinance and to post copies throughout the city, and the Under Secretary of State for the Ministry of War called

[2] AN, CC 549, Raguse to Roi, July 28, 1830.
[3] Marmont, *Mémoires*, VIII, 242-43, 432-33; AN, CC 548, Chambre et Cour des Pairs, Choiseul to Gouverneur de Vincennes, July 28, 1830.

together officers of his ministry's Bureau of Military Justice to draw up instructions for the establishment and operation of military courts. Mangin printed the ordinance as instructed, but hostile crowds gave bill posters in the pay of the police a difficult time in Paris that day. Most of the bills confided to them ended up in gutters.[4]

Through the morning hours while Marmont awaited instructions from Saint-Cloud the crowds had grown larger and more menacing. Only in the area west of the Louvre and the Tuileries and north to the boulevards did observers find the streets quiet and deserted. Near the present Place de l'Opéra a double rank of Guards barred the Boulevard des Capucines, but beyond that point on the Boulevard des Italiens, under the passive eye of soldiers, men and women were pulling up paving stones and felling trees to block the roadway. Further along near the Rue de Richelieu scores of hands had toppled into the streets two iron lampposts and their large supporting stone blocks. Overturned wagons and buses completed this barricade. Two-thirds of a mile on to the east a crowd at the Porte Saint-Denis threw stones at the gendarmes stationed on the boulevard and taunted them with shouts of "Mort aux gendarmes!" On the Place du Palais-Royal demonstrators piled up shop signs bearing royal symbols and set them afire under the noses of a battalion of the Royal Guard. Crowds milled about in the Rue Saint-Honoré, read inflammatory single-sheet editions of opposition papers, shouted revolutionary slogans, "Vive la Charte!" and "A bas la royauté!" and chalked them on walls.[5]

[4] AN, CC 546, Chambre et Cour des Pairs, Testimony of Champagny, Nov. 15, 1830; CC 549, Deposition of De Guise, Nov. 2, 1830; CC 547, Chambre et Cour des Pairs, Chef, Bureau de la Justice milit., Ministère de la Guerre, to [Ministre de la Guerre], Sept. 1, 1830; CC 550, Chambre et Cour des Pairs, Raguse to Mangin, July 28, 1830, 12:45 P.M.; Préfet de Police to Prés., Cour des Pairs, Nov. 7, 1830; AS, D 4AZ 259, Polignac to Préfet de Police, July 28, 1830; AN, 149 AP 1, Papers of Jean-Claude Mangin, Royal Ordinance of July 28, 1830.

[5] R. Anchel, "Un Témoinage anglais sur les journées de Juillet: souvenirs de Lady Aylmer," *Revue d'histoire moderne*, 6 (1931), 353; Charles de Rémusat, *Mémoires de ma vie* (Paris, 1958-67), II, 328-29;

Nearby on the Place des Innocents a band of angry men had dumped in front of the guard post the body of one of the victims of the preceding day's shooting. "This is your work!" they shouted. "He demands vengeance!" About ten o'clock they reappeared, reinforced in numbers and better armed, and sacked and burned both the guard post and the adjoining office of the district police commissioner. The gendarmes on the scene offered no resistance. Their fellows at the nearby Halle aux Blés had abandoned their post early in the morning without waiting to be attacked. On the Place du Chatelet a crowd disarmed the guard post and fired on mounted gendarmes trying to clear the place, killing two of them. A squad of fifteen guardsmen sent to the Place de Grève found 700 or 800 men, most of them armed with muskets, on the scene. The lieutenant in command of the Guards advanced alone to induce the crowd to disperse, and they fired, killing two guardsmen and wounding others including the lieutenant. The Guards returned the fire, but, in danger of being overwhelmed, they hastily withdrew westward up the quai to the protection of a battalion of the Guard just arrived on the Place du Chatelet. The wounded lieutenant was placed in a cab to be taken from the scene, but when several shots hit the cab, the driver forced him to get out, and he had to make his way back to the Carrousel on foot.[6]

About eleven o'clock the ministers, who had met with Polignac at the Ministry of Foreign Affairs, alarmed by

---

AS, DM[13] 1, Venard to Commission des Récompenses nationales (hereafter cited as CRN), Feb. 7, 1831; V[bis] 3, CRN, 4° Arrond., Dossier Méline; BHVP, Révolution de 1830, Série 23, "Les Trois glorieuses vues par De Creuze, peintre"; *Temps* (Paris), July 28, 1830; *Courrier français* (Paris), July 28, 1830.

6 BHVP, FGms 443, "Precis des Evénemens de Juillet 1830, Rédigé et Publié par le Sr. Duplessis, Pharmacien . . ."; AN, 149 AP, 1, Report to the Préfet de Police, July 28, 1830, 6 A.M.; CC 546, Testimony of Charles de Saint-Germain, ex-lt., Garde royale, Nov. 12, 1830; Testimony of De Launay, Nov. 15, 1830; CC 551, Chambre et Cour des Pairs, Maréchal *et al.* to Prés., Cour des Pairs, Dec. 17, 1830.

reports reaching them, moved to Marmont's headquarters in the Tuileries. As they walked through the Rue de la Paix and the Place Vendôme they saw troops of the 5th and 53d Regiments fraternizing with residents who offered them wine and brandy.[7]

Across the river a crowd had gathered on the Place de l'Odéon shouting for arms. Another at the Gobelins factory demanded removal of the white flag of the Bourbons, and yet others disarmed guard posts on the Rue des Saints-Pères and on the Place Maubert and broke into the mayor's office on the Rue de Grenelle in search of arms. Back on the Place de Grève about 11 A.M. the crowd had forced the guards of the Hôtel de Ville to withdraw. National Guardsmen in uniform took over from them but could not prevent the demonstrators from forcing the gates. The prefect abandoned the building to the invading crowd, which quickly overran it and raised the tricolor on the central cupola. The same revolutionary symbol soon appeared on one of the towers of Notre Dame.[8]

Shortly before noon Marmont, still without orders from Saint-Cloud but hearing that the Line had begun to defect, decided to take the offensive against the mounting insurrection while he could still depend on his troops. He abandoned his earlier practice of sending out small patrols to particular trouble spots and now ordered three powerful columns to move across the city to subdue the principal areas of revolt. General Emmanuel Quinsonnas with the 2d and 3d Battalions of the 3d Regiment of Guards, two cannon, and fifteen Elite Gendarmes was to clear the Rue Saint-Honoré east of the Palais-Royal and occupy the Place des Innocents. Comte de Wall received orders to support this

[7] Charles d'Haussez, *Mémoires du Baron d'Haussez, dernier Ministre de la Marine sous la Restauration* (Paris, 1896-1897), II, 255; Martial Guernon-Ranville, *Journal d'un ministre* (Caen, 1873), pp. 168-69.

[8] BHVP, "Les Trois glorieuses vues par De Creuze," "Rapport de M. Martinet"; AN, CC 548, Chef, Cie. des Fusiliers sédentaires, Garde royale, to Col. [unidentified], July 28, 1830, 12:15 P.M.; CC 549, Deposition of Chabrol de Volvic, Nov. 15, 1830.

113

operation by occupying the nearby Place des Victoires with infantry of the Line and Gendarmes from the Place Vendôme. After reaching the Place des Innocents a part of Quinsonnas's force was to proceed up the Rue Saint-Denis to the boulevards. The second column, under General Mathieu Talon, composed of the 1st Battalion of the 3d Guards Regiment, fifty Lancers, and two cannon, was ordered to move along the quais of the Right Bank and the Cité to the Place de Grève. General Alfred de Saint-Chamans commanded the third column, composed of two battalions of the 1st Regiment of the Guard and one from the 6th Regiment, 150 Lancers, and two pieces of artillery. Marmont ordered him to lead the force along the boulevards to the Place de la Bastille, where he was to take command of the Cuirassiers and the 50th Regiment of the Line already on the scene, watch over the Faubourg Saint-Antoine, and establish communications with General Talon on the Place de Grève. Marmont directed each column to destroy the barricades it encountered, but he forbade the troops to use firearms against crowds unless they were the targets of fusillades of at least fifty shots. They might, however, fire at windows from which attackers fired or threw stones.[9]

The columns quickly moved out, marching under the blazing sun of another hot summer day. Wall's troops proceeding to the Place des Victoires encountered no more resistance than a few scattered shots. Quinsonnas's force crossed the Place du Palais-Royal, passed an undefended barricade on the Rue Saint-Honoré, and entered the Place des Innocents by the southwest corner unopposed except for some shots fired at the rear guard of gendarmes. The troops found on the *place* only half a dozen National Guardsmen defending a tricolor flying atop Goujon's Fountain of the Innocents in the center of the *place*. A few Guards quickly disarmed them and sent them home, but the narrow streets running into the *place* from the west were

[9] Marmont, *Mémoires*, VIII, 245-47; AN, CC 546, Testimony of Saint-Chamans, Nov. 16, 1830; Alfred de Saint-Chamans, "Le Combat pour le roi, juillet 1830," *Revue de Paris*, 3d year, 1 (Feb. 1, 1896), 492.

filled with what a lieutenant of the Guard called "a disgusting populace."[10]

Four companies of infantry, the gendarmes, and two artillery pieces, useless in this confined area, took up positions around the fountain. The "populace" as quickly improvised barricades across exits to the *place* and opened fire on the troops. Soldiers found what shelter they could behind market stalls but, largely unprotected and unable to drive off their attackers firing from barricades and adjoining buildings, they suffered heavy casualties. The sound of musket fire from the Rue Saint-Denis and the quais and of artillery fire from the Place de Grève and the ringing of the tocsin on scores of church bells told these isolated units they were but single points in a spreading battle. The 2d Battalion of Guards and two companies of the 3d, following Marmont's instructions, had proceeded to the Rue Saint-Denis and turned left toward the boulevards; blocking their march was barricade after barricade, and at each, gunfire from surrounding houses took its toll of the exposed guardsmen. They eventually fought their way to the boulevard, barricades going up behind them as they advanced, but there they found all avenues of escape blocked. About 5:30 the commanding officer of the 3d Battalion got a small boy to smuggle a message through to Marmont requesting instructions.

By five o'clock the hard-pressed guardsmen on the Place

[10] The account of Quinsonnas's column is based on the following sources: AS, D 4AZ 1181, "Précis des événemens aux quels a pris part la troisième régiment d'infanterie de la garde royale depuis le vingt-six juillet jusqu'au jour de son licenciement par un officier du régiment," pp. 10-12, 14-15; V^{bis} 3, CRN, 4e Arrond., Dossier Saunière; V^{bis} 1, A. Duvergier to CRN, Dec. 28, 1830; BHVP, Série 23, FGms 443, "Précis des Evénemens de Juillet 1830, Rédigé et Publié par le Sr. Duplessis . . ."; AN, CC 548, Chef, 2e Bat., 3e Rgt., Garde royale to Chef d'Etat major, July 28, 1830; CC 549, Choiseul to Wall, July 27 [*sic*; correct date is July 28]; Marmont, *Mémoires*, VIII, 246-48; Albert Maag, *Geschichte der Schweizertruppen in franzosischen Diensten während der Restauration und Julirevolution, 1816-30* (Biel, 1899), plan opp. p. 396, pp. 395, 396, 400-401; Raymond Lecuyer, *La Révolution de Juillet . . . impressions et récits contemporains: Mémoires d'Alex. Mazas—Chronique de Rozet* (Paris, n.d.), pp. 84-86.

des Innocents were running low on cartridges. An aide of Quinsonnas, disguised in civilian clothes borrowed from a sympathetic resident, made his way through the insurgents' lines with an appeal to Marmont for relief. The marshal ordered two companies of the 15th Light Infantry from the Pont Neuf to the rescue. The 15th, advancing northward from the quai, got caught between two barricades on the Rue des Prouvaires and, under heavy fire from hidden assailants, could not advance except at prohibitive cost and would be decimated if it held to its exposed position on the street. Some of the soldiers apparently defected—the evidence is not clear—and the colonel withdrew his companies to the Rue Saint-Honoré. A battalion of Swiss ordered up from the Quai des Ecoles fought its way through the Rue de la Monnaie to the Rue Saint-Honoré, where it should have turned right to proceed directly to the Place des Innocents, but its officers were unfamiliar with the maze of streets of central Paris, and they moved their force on northward to the Church of Saint-Eustache. Missing another turn the battalion circled around a number of streets north of the church, attacked and harried all the way, and eventually entered the Place des Innocents from the northwest.

The combined force on the *place*, still surrounded, for the Swiss had not opened a line of communication, and with only a few cartridges remaining for each man, faced surrender or extinction if it remained there. Quinsonnas decided to break out by forcing passage down the Rue Saint-Denis to the quais. The wounded were loaded on artillery caissons, and the troops moved out of the east end of the *place,* turned right on the Rue Saint-Denis and, led by the Swiss Guard, fought their way through a succession of barricades, assailed by musket fire from corners, windows, and rooftops and by a rain of stones, furniture, and household utensils. But they did get through, and, reaching the quai, the column reformed near the Pont des Arts. Here it remained, occasionally exchanging shots with snipers on the opposite side of the Seine or in boats along the bank, until midnight, the whole time without food and drink except

DAYS OF REVOLUTION

what the men could obtain from nearby shops and friendly householders. The troops surrounded on the Boulevard Saint-Denis broke out to the north along the Rue du Faubourg Saint-Denis and returned to their base at the Ecole militaire by a circuitous route outside the city and through the Bois de Boulogne.

A detachment of Lancers led Talon's column out of the Place du Carrousel and along the quai toward the Cité and the Place de Grève. Pausing only to disarm three National Guardsmen on the Quai des Ecoles and to toss their bearskin hats into the Seine, the column marched unopposed to the south end of the Pont Notre Dame. Here it divided, part to cross this bridge and part to continue along the quai of the island to the suspension bridge that connected with the Place de Grève, where the two parts were to reunite. The Lancers leading the first force met a formidable fusillade from the narrow street at the opposite end of the bridge (now the much wider Rue Saint-Martin). The artillery moved to the head of the column and, firing from the bridge, cleared the street while the infantry returned the fire of the insurgents along the quai and in the Place de Grève, but heavy fire from all sides of the *place* obliged them to withdraw. Again the artillery took over and, firing grapeshot, forced the crowd into the shelter of buildings and adjoining streets. The infantry moved into the *place*, but they were assailed by firing from the Hôtel de Ville and other buildings overlooking the *place* (then an irregularly shaped area scarcely a fourth its present size), from the parapet of the quai across the river, and from the opposite end of the suspension bridge.[11]

11 The account of Talon's column is based on the following sources: AN CC 546, Testimony of De Launay, Nov. 15, 1830; Testimony of Fr. de Blair, Nov. 13, 1830; CC 548, Talon to Raguse [July 28, 1830]; CC 551, Tillette to Prés., Cour des Pairs, Dec. 17, 1830; AS, VD³, "Renseignements fournis par M. Bertrand"; Hauchecorne to Prés., CRN, 11ᵉ Arrond., Jan. 29, 1831; BHVP, Série 23, "Historique des faits qui sont passés dans le 7ᵉ arrondissement les 28-29-30 juillet et 3 août 1830"; "Rapport de M. Martinet"; Marmont, *Mémoires*, VIII, 256; AS, D 4AZ 1181, "Précis," pp. 14-15; Maag, *Schweizertruppen*, pp. 384-89; plan opp. p. 384.

117

In early afternoon Marmont ordered a battalion of the Swiss Guard in reserve on the Place Louis XVI to go to the support of Talon's hard-pressed men. Together the French and the Swiss Guards sealed off the streets leading into the *place* and kept crowds out of the square, but their attempts to penetrate into the streets and disperse their assailants all failed. Only the route along the Right Bank quai, by which the column had advanced, remained open, and bands of armed men at the south ends of the suspension bridge and the Pont Notre Dame threatened to cut it at any moment. The Swiss broke into the Hôtel de Ville, and Talon stationed some infantrymen of the Line newly sent to his support in its windows to repulse an expected attack. Toward evening the general ordered all his troops into the building. Firing had been intense throughout the afternoon and casualties heavy; the soldiers had been without food since early morning and without wine to quench their thirst, made more intense by exertion under a blazing sun. Supplies of cartridges were nearly exhausted, and two detachments sent for additional supplies failed to return. No one from Saint-Chamans's column, expected to establish contact with the forces on the Place de Grève, had yet appeared. Cut off from headquarters and virtually besieged in the Hôtel de Ville the troops confined themselves to firing from the windows on insurgents who dared to show themselves on the *place* or at the ends of impinging streets.

Talon had received instructions not to withdraw until joined by Saint-Chamans, but sometime after 10 P.M. an officer in disguise got through to Talon with an order from Marmont to return his troops immediately to the Place du Carrousel. The wounded were placed in commandeered cabs for evacuation, Talon's request to Marmont for carriages and stretchers having gone unanswered, and between eleven and twelve o'clock the troops left the Hôtel de Ville and marched westward along the quais. Quinsonnas's troops, bivouacked on the Quai du Louvre, sprang to the alert when its sentries spotted the column moving silently toward them.

They watched Talon's disheveled men file wearily past, then followed them to the Place du Carrousel.

Saint-Chamans's column had met no resistance until it reached the Porte Saint-Denis. Here his infantrymen, dismantling a barricade across the boulevard, were fired upon by assailants hidden in adjoining buildings or sheltering in the narrow streets leading off the boulevard. The column continued to be the target of sporadic fire as it moved on down the boulevards to the Place de la Bastille, and the troops returned the fire although rarely able to spot their attackers. Two battalions had exhausted their supplies of cartridges before they reached the Place de la Bastille, and the artillery, Saint-Chamans learned, had only the munitions they carried with their pieces. He dispatched a messenger to Raguse with a request for more supplies, but the man never reached his destination, and a second messenger arrived at headquarters only after the insurgents had cut off all routes to the east end. Meanwhile Saint-Chamans led his troops into the Rue du Faubourg Saint-Antoine. They passed a few barricades and encountered some firing from windows, but it soon stopped, and residents came into the streets and mingled with the troops. Finding no serious resistance in this area and having received no additional orders, Saint-Chamans withdrew to the Place de la Bastille intending to return to the Tuileries, but he learned that insurgents had felled trees and built barricades behind him as his column moved eastward along the boulevards, cutting off his line of retreat.[12]

He then undertook to push through the Rue Saint-Antoine to join Talon's forces on the Place de Grève. Expecting this move, people in the area had built a barricade

[12] The account of Saint-Chamans's column is based on the following sources: AN, CC 546, Testimony of Saint-Chamans, Nov. 16, 1830; CC 548, Choiseul to Saint-Chamans, July 28, 1830; Marmont, *Mémoires*, VIII, 256; Saint-Chamans, "Combat," pp. 494-95, 500, 502-3; BHVP, Série 23, "Historique des faits . . . 7ᵉ arrondissement"; AN, F¹ᵈ III, 81, Deposition of A. Trousseau, Jan. 24, 1831, Deposition of J. Gaudiot, Jan. 23, 1831; AS, DM¹³ 1, Venard to CRN, Feb. 7, 1831.

across the Rue Saint-Antoine about 350 yards to the east of the Hôtel de Ville. The Rue Saint-Antoine in 1830 was narrower than it is today, and in the section behind the Hôtel de Ville it followed a different route, the present Rue François Miron being the Rue Saint-Antoine of 1830. The insurgents chose for their barricade the point where the street narrowed just to the west of its junction with the Rue de Jouy. When Saint-Chamans's column left the Place de la Bastille, its drums rolling, armed men gathered in overlooking houses and in nearby streets; others collected stones and other projectiles at windows and on rooftops. They allowed the infantry leading the column to break through the barricade unopposed and to continue on toward the Hôtel de Ville, but as the cavalry, slowed by the debris in the street, moved through, the people opened fire and rained paving stones, roof tiles, and pieces of furniture on the exposed men in the streets. The column hastily withdrew. The cavalry made a second attempt to pass but was again forced back. With the street again clear people swarmed out of the houses, and, spurred by their first success, built seven new barricades in about 1000 feet of the Rue Saint-Antoine between the Rue du Jouy and the Church of Saint-Paul. In the early evening Saint-Chamans received new orders from Marmont. He was to send his Cuirassiers to Vincennes to obtain four batteries of artillery and every available cartridge and to bring them with all speed by the exterior boulevards to the Champs-Elysées. Saint-Chamans himself was to lead his infantry, cannon, and gendarmes to the Place de Grève to join Talon's force and then return to the Place du Carrousel.

At twilight the column again started down the Rue Saint-Antoine, led by infantrymen of the 1st Guard Regiment in skirmishing formation, keeping close to the buildings to avoid objects thrown from rooftops and windows. When the head of the column reached the original barrier at the Rue du Jouy, three officers in the lead fell, two struck by balls, one by a paving stone. The firing suddenly ceased, people swarmed into the street and called on the leaderless troops to withdraw and tried to seize their arms. Another officer rushed forward and took command of the faltering troops, and the artillery and other soldiers and gendarmes hurried to the scene. The people retreated to the houses, and the battle resumed, the troops now using their cannon. After about twenty minutes the entire column turned about and withdrew eastward, leaving its dead and wounded in the street. Frustrated in this attempt to break out of his position Saint-Chamans now led his battered command across the Pont d'Austerlitz and thence by the exterior boulevards of the Left Bank to the Place Louis XVI.

By early morning all the troops had returned to their barracks or bivouacked on the Champs Elysées or the Esplanade des Invalides, and the city quieted down. The official lists included the names of 496 citizens killed during the three days of fighting and 849 wounded who subsequently received aid from the Commission des Récompenses nationales; probably about half of these casualties occurred on the twenty-eighth, the day of heaviest fighting. The army lost about 150 dead and 580 wounded in the three days and another 137 missing. Neighborhood doctors and medical students cared for wounded on both sides in dressing stations established in public buildings, churches, and even private houses near the scenes of the fighting. Charles Cadet-Gassicourt, the host to the first meeting of electors and journalists on July 26, opened his pharmacy on the Rue Saint-Honoré to the wounded. Another pharmacist hung above his door on the Rue Saint-Denis a black flag inscribed "Secours aux blessés" and received more than eighty victims of the fighting. The Church of Saint-Germain l'Auxerrois, the *mairie* of the Ninth Arrondissement near the principal barricade on the Rue Saint-Antoine, and the Halle aux Draps opposite the Fountain of the Innocents became first aid stations, and the Church of Saint-Eustache and the fire station on the Place des Innocents were used as morgues.[13]

13 AN, F1d III, 33, CRN, 2e Etat des citoyens tués . . . ; F1d III, 34-37, Etats des sommes payées aux combattants blessés et non blessés . . . ; CC 548, Cmdt., Hôpital milit., le Gros Caillou to M. de Bouchet, July

The supply of food and wine to the troops engaged in fighting had completely broken down early in the day. The army had no field kitchens available, and men could not be spared to return to company kitchens in their barracks. Bakers in the military bakehouse of Paris prepared bread during the night of July 27-28, but no transportation was available to deliver it, and in the course of the day insurgents captured the bakehouse. Forage for horses was stored at Bercy, across the city from most of the troops, and insurgents in villages near Paris held up convoys of both forage and food ordered into Paris by the army. Throughout the day and evening the troops had to depend on what bread and wine they could buy, beg, or pillage from citizens. An officer of the 3d Regiment of the Guard who served with Quinsonnas's column reported that while the top floors of houses spewed shot and stones on the guardsmen, residents of the lower floors freely offered them refreshments and shelter, a reflection of the characteristic distribution of tenants in Parisian apartment houses, which put the well-to-do on the lower floors, the poor on the top. The Ministry of War authorized unit commanders to obtain wine from the nearest wine merchants for distribution of a daily ration to their men, an expedient that proved ineffective in the confusion of the day. In the evening the King on the advice of Marmont granted a bonus of one and a half month's pay to all troops on duty in Paris, and the Ministry of Finance authorized its immediate payment to enable the hungry men to buy provisions. By that time most of them had been without food or drink since early morning.[14]

28, 9:30 P.M.; F[1d] III, 33, "Rapport dressé par le Maire de Neuvième Arrondissement," Sept. 25; F[9] 1154, Combattants de Juillet; F[9] 1158, Dossier Couturier; AS, V[bis] 1, CRN, 4e Arrond., Dossiers Barthez, Brunet et Dubois, Gendrin, Giniez, Guillemot; V[bis] 3,4e Arrond., Dossiers Hébert, Moulin; BHVP, Carton 23, "Historique des faits . . . 7e arrondissement"; FGms 784, "Rapport de M. Censier sur les journées de Juillet 1830; FGms 443, "Précis des evénemens . . . par Duplessis."

[14] Marmont, *Mémoires*, VIII, 284-85; AN, CC 548, Ministre de la Guerre to Raguse, July 28, 1830; CC 551, Montbel, "Note sur les paiements faits aux troupes les 28 et 29 juillet 1830"; Guillaume de Mont-

While the activists fought, the deputies continued to talk, but under pressure of events in the streets and of the arguments of the bolder among them they moved nearer to positive action. At noon they met at the house of Audry de Puyraveau, their number including for the first time Lafayette and Laffitte. First in the afternoon's business came a decision to seek the cooperation of Marmont in putting an end to the bloodshed in Paris. Laffitte, who presided over the meeting, asked Périer, Benjamin Delessert, General Etienne Gérard, and General Georges de Lobau to join him in a deputation to call on the marshal in his headquarters. Guizot then presented the protest that the preceding meeting had instructed him to prepare. Carefully worded to express the opinion not of the Chamber of Deputies but only of the signers, it protested against the overthrow of the legal system of elections and the violation of the freedom of the press, which it blamed on the King's advisers.[15]

> The said measures . . . are in the eyes of the undersigned directly contrary to the constitutional Charter, to the constitutional rights of the Chamber of Peers, to the public law of the French people, to the jurisdiction and orders of the courts, and are capable of throwing the state into confusion that will compromise both the peace of the present and the security of the future.[16]

The protest moved on to a defiance of the crown, not a very bold defiance compared to the violence in the streets but a commitment to resistance nonetheless.

---

bel, *1787-1831; souvenirs du Comte de Montbel, ministre de Charles X* (Paris, 1913), p. 246; Guernon-Ranville, *Journal*, p. 173; AN, F^{1d} III, 81, P. Dellacelle to Roi, Sept. 2, 1832; Deposition of citizens of Versailles on activities of H. Maziere, Sept. 18, 1830; AS, D^{8} 1-2, Préfet de la Seine to maires de Paris, Aug. 28, 1830; D 4AZ 1181, "Précis," p. 13.

15 Auguste Bérard, *Souvenirs historiques sur la Révolution de 1830* (Paris, 1834), pp. 80-82; Marie de Lafayette, *Mémoires, correspondance et manuscrits* (Paris, 1837-38), VI, 384-85; AN, CC 549, Deposition of Laffitte, Nov. 11, 1830.

16 Bérard, *Souvenirs*, p. 82.

And, whereas, on the one hand, the Chamber of Deputies not having been constituted cannot be legally dissolved, and on the other hand, the attempt to form another chamber of deputies by a new and arbitrary procedure is in formal contradiction to the constitutional Charter and the acquired rights of the electors, the undersigned declare that they consider themselves legally elected . . . and as being replaceable only by virtue of elections held according to the principles and forms prescribed by law.[17]

The assembled deputies endorsed the protest and authorized its printing. The meeting then adjourned until four o'clock, and the delegation set out for the Tuileries.[18]

The anterooms of the marshal's headquarters that afternoon were filled with officers, many of them in civilian clothes, come to offer their services or to seek news of the fighting. Couriers arrived and departed. Aides-de-camp, less haughty than usual, Haussez thought, talked anxiously among themselves. In an adjoining room the ministers, informed of the fortunes of the government's forces only by the sound of cannon and musket fire and by fragmentary reports from Raguse and from a few devoted royalists, and powerless to influence the course of events, had little to do but to grow annoyed with each other.[19] The sharp-tongued Haussez described the scene in the ministers' quarters:

The president . . . was dreamy; he paced the apartment, sat down at the desk, wrote, went out, returned, and answered none of the questions that were addressed to him. M. de Chantelauze, so energetic two days earlier, was lying on a sofa, overwhelmed and pensive. M. de Peyronnet, faithful to his character, treated with disdain the resistance whose seriousness was attested every instant

[17] *Ibid.*, p. 83.

[18] *Ibid.*, pp. 81, 83-84; AN, CC 549, Deposition of Laffitte, Nov. 11, 1830.

[19] Haussez, *Mémoires*, II, 257-59; Guernon-Ranville, *Journal*, p. 169; Montbel, *Souvenirs*, pp. 244-46.

by the sound of gunfire heard from all sides. . . . M. de Ranville seemed to take upon himself the task of irritating our impatience by the flood of bad jokes with which he inundated us. Each event, each word inspired a fancy that we had not previously known in him.[20]

The five deputies arrived at the Tuileries about 2:30 P.M., and the Governor of the Palace took them directly to Marmont. The marshal received them politely and assured them that as a private citizen he sympathized with their efforts to end the fighting but that as a military commander he had no choice but to carry out his orders to suppress the insurrection. He urged them to use their influence to calm the people, and he insisted that submission was the first condition of a cease-fire. They replied that the people had revolted spontaneously against the ordinances and the ministers and that the deputies could do nothing with them until the King rescinded the ordinances and dismissed the ministers. Half an hour earlier Marmont's friend Arago had urged upon him the imperative necessity of just these steps, but Marmont had replied to him, as he did now to the deputies, that these were political matters beyond the limits of his authority. He promised the deputies, however, that he would inform the King of their representations and advise Laffitte of any reply he might receive. He then asked if they would be willing to see Polignac. They agreed, and he went into the ministers' room and had a long, whispered conversation. He returned to tell the deputies that Polignac thought a meeting would be useless, and they departed.[21]

At the moment the deputation arrived Marmont had been writing a letter to the King. All his forces, he reported, had reached their assigned objectives and, so far as he knew, stood in no danger of being forced to evacuate, but they were

20 Haussez, *Mémoires*, II, 258-59.
21 AN, CC 549, Depositions of Arago, Oct. 30; Lobau, Nov. 2; Périer, Nov. 6, Gérard, Nov. 11, Laffitte, Nov. 11, Baron de Glandevès, Nov. 6, 1830; BHVP, Série 23, Dossier Laffitte; Marmont, *Mémoires*, VIII, 249-51; Bérard, *Souvenirs*, pp. 86-87; Guernon-Ranville, *Journal*, pp. 171-72; Haussez, *Mémoires*, II, 259-60.

encountering almost universal opposition, and he would not conceal the increasing gravity of the military position in Paris. Plans and forces prepared to control a riot could not suppress a revolution. Marmont now added to the letter a paragraph on the deputies' démarche, and he concluded, "I think that it is urgent that Your Majesty profit without delay from the overtures that are made to him." He gave the message to his first aide-de-camp, Colonel Louis Komierowski, for delivery to the King, and Komierowski left immediately for Saint-Cloud with an escort of twenty-five Lancers.[22]

The colonel reached the palace about 4 P.M. The King received him in his study, read Marmont's dispatch, and heard the colonel's report on what he had seen in Paris. He then asked Komierowski to await a reply. Charles had just spent two hours with the Baron Eugène de Vitrolles, a trusted adviser who was in touch with General Gérard, a liberal deputy, through an intermediary and who pleaded with him to open negotiations with moderate members of the opposition who wanted to stop the popular insurrection. Charles had listened patiently but unmoved. He would not, he emphasized, negotiate with subjects in armed revolt. He assured Vitrolles, moreover, that Marmont had the city under control and that the leaders of the revolt had been arrested. Marmont's warning failed to shake the King's confidence. After talking with the Dauphin and the Duchesse de Berry, he recalled the colonel and instructed him to tell Marmont to concentrate his troops on the Place de Carrousel and the Place Louis XVI and to "hold firm." Marmont suspected that Polignac, on learning of the proposal of the deputies, had sent a message ahead of his, advising the King to continue the battle. Polignac's confidence remained unbroken. When told of troops' fraternizing with the insurrectionaries he was reported to have replied calmly, "Very well, you must fire on the troops!"[23]

[22] AN, CC 549, Raguse to Roi, July 28, 1830; Deposition of Komierowski, Nov. 9, 1830; Marmont, *Mémoires*, VIII, 248, 249, 251.

[23] AN, CC 549, Deposition of Komierowski, Nov. 9, 1830; Deposition

About the same time that Komierowski was talking with the King thirty to forty deputies reassembled in the house of Bérard on the Rue Neuve des Mathurins, north of the Madeleine, to hear Laffitte report on the inconclusive interview with Marmont. Having heard it they could only await the King's reply, which the marshal had promised to relay to them. Jacques Coste, editor of the *Temps*, soon arrived with the printer's proofs of the protest approved earlier in the day. He had shortened it slightly and removed all the respectful references to the King, and he insisted that he would not print it without signatures. Many of the deputies feared to sign it. Someone proposed that a list of deputies present at the meeting be placed at the bottom of the protest without anyone signing it, but for some even this was too dangerous. Finally all agreed to append the names of those who had attended the meeting of Périer's on the twenty-seventh, the meeting that had approved the principle of a protest, and of those now gathered at Bérard's and any other deputies in Paris and its environs whose support might be assumed. Laffitte observed cynically, "In this way, if we are defeated, no one will have signed; and if we win, we won't lack for signers." The protest appeared the next day in newspapers and on placards above the names of sixty-three deputies. During this meeting a stream of combatants came to Bérard's door asking for a leader and for direction of their efforts, but no one with a name well enough known to be an effective popular leader would assume so risky a task. The meeting adjourned until nine o'clock, having accomplished no more than the approval of the formal protest. As Gérard, Lobau, and Horace Sébastiani, all veterans of the Napoleonic wars, left the house a number of young men in the court berated them for their lack of courage and patriotism.[24]

---

of Arago, Oct. 30, 1830; Eugène de Vitrolles, *Mémoires de Vitrolles* (Paris, 1950, 1951), II, 377-82; Marmont, *Mémoires*, VIII, 251-54.

24 Bérard, *Souvenirs*, pp. 86-90; André Dupin, *Mémoires de M. Dupin* (Paris, 1855-61), II, 141-42, 497-98; François Guizot, *Mémoires pour servir à l'histoire de mon temps, 1807-1848*, New ed. (Paris, 1872), II,

In the evening only ten or eleven deputies made their way through the barricades to a gloomy session at Audry de Puyraveau's house. All the news was disheartening. The Royal Guard held the Hôtel de Ville; additional troops would arrive in the city tomorrow; the combatants were discouraged and resentful at being left without leadership; the government had issued warrants for the arrest of Laffitte, Lafayette, Gérard, Audry de Puyraveau, and two other opposition deputies; Thiers, fearful of arrest, had left the city, and Rémusat had gone into hiding. No message came from Saint-Cloud or the Tuileries in reply to the deputies' démarche of the afternoon. This rebuff, Laffitte insisted, was a declaration of war. They must find a new ruler. "William," he declared, using the historical parallel dear to the Orléanists, "must replace the Stuarts." Tomorrow, he announced, his house would be the headquarters for the war against the Bourbons. But others present favored accommodation with the Bourbons. Some would recall Napoleon II, and some, restore the Republic. While the deputies debated a crowd of workingmen, youth, and even children gathered in the street and in the courtyard of Audry de Puyraveau's house. Through the open windows they shouted their threats, their advice, and their determination to defend the deputies against police and soldiers. The deputies were in a dilemma. If the revolution should prevail over the Bourbons, the fragile coalition of divergent opposition elements, freed of its one cohesive force, would break into hostile factions, and popular violence might be directed to less moderate ends than defense of the Charter. If the revolution failed, and it seemed about to be overwhelmed by the repressive power of the government, those active in the opposition could expect no quarter from Polignac. Bérard, after picking his way home across the barricades, ordered the porter to admit no one, and before going to bed he planned an escape route

5; France, *Bulletin des lois*, 9th Series, Vol. 1, Part 1 (Aug. 9, 1830), pp. 1-3.

through a neighbor's house and put his pistols and a sword on his bedside table.[25]

Had Bérard known the disarray on the side of the government he might have slept soundly without his many precautions. Marmont had refused to execute the warrants for the arrest of prominent deputies, and the Prefecture of Police had returned the warrants against the journalists as unenforceable. The hungry, exhausted troops were in no mood to resume the distasteful duty of fighting their fellow citizens. Marmont had informed the ministers that he lacked sufficient forces to resume the offensive the next day. He would, therefore, concentrate his available strength on defending the Louvre and the Tuileries and his communications with Saint-Cloud. He could hold this defensive position for three days, he believed, awaiting the arrival of reinforcements from the provinces.[26]

At five o'clock the next morning, July 29, Rémusat left his hiding place with the Duc de Broglie near the western limits of Paris and walked along the river toward the center of the capital. He seemed to be alone in a deserted city. "The heat was already heavy," he wrote, "the sky was a pale gray, as it is in the summer before the sun has pierced the morning's mists; as far as the eye could see, to the east, along the river and its banks, the same emptiness, the same silence."[27] "It's all over," Broglie had said to him when he set out, and Rémusat could only agree. But the silence was misleading. During the night Parisians had barricaded almost every street in the city. A traveler coming to the central quarters from the north had encountered, he declared, a barricade about every thirty feet, and Rémusat found them blocking his way even in the hitherto peaceful Faubourg

[25] Bérard, *Souvenirs*, pp. 92-95; Lafayette, *Mémoires*, VI, 386-87; Guizot, *Mémoires*, II, 5-7; BHVP, Dossier Laffitte; Marmont, *Mémoires*, VIII, 254.

[26] Haussez, *Mémoires*, II, 264; Montbel, *Souvenirs*, pp. 246-47; Marmont, *Mémoires*, VIII, 254-55, 257; AN, CC 549, Testimony of Billot, Sept. 10, 1830.

[27] Rémusat, *Mémoires*, II, 338.

Saint-Honoré. A few were formidable accumulations of wagons, carts, barrels, furniture, market stalls, and building stones, others no more than two or three courses of paving stones laid across the street, but all could delay the passage of troops and make them more vulnerable to harrying attacks.[28]

The experience of the preceding day justified the construction of these defensive works, but on the twenty-ninth they were little more than symbols of popular resistance, for Marmont had abandoned offensive operations. Soon after daybreak he disposed his troops for defense of the fortress of the Louvre and the Tuileries. In the Louvre itself he placed two battalions of Swiss to command the quais on the south, the Place du Louvre on the east, and the Place de l'Oratoire on the north. Behind them to the west on the Place du Carrousel were the 3d and 6th Regiments of the Guard with six pieces of artillery and one battalion of Swiss. Small detachments from the Guard took positions in houses along the streets leading from the Place du Palais-Royal and the Rue de Rivoli to the Place du Carrousel and in buildings overlooking this *place* on the east. A battery of artillery in the Rue de Rohan commanded the Rue de Richelieu, an approach to the palace from the north. The 5th and 53d Regiments of the Line on the Place Vendôme protected the left flank. The 15th and 50th Regiments were in the Tuileries Garden; they guarded the terrace overlooking the quais and placed two cannon at the gate opposite the Rue Castiglione, which led to the Place Vendôme. The 1st and 2d Regiments of the Guard occupied the Place Louis XVI and the Boulevard de la Madeleine. About eight o'clock Saint-Chamans took part of this force to reopen and protect the line of communications with Saint-Cloud along the quais. Marmont had received some reinforcements during

[28] *Ibid.*, 338-40; Emmanuel Viollet le Duc, "Lettres d'Emmanuel Viollet le Duc à sa femme," *Revue de Paris*, 69ᵉ Année, No. 6 (June 1962), 98; BHVP, "Historique des faits . . . 7ᵉ Arrondissement"; AS, Dᵃ 1-2, Préfet de la Seine to Maires de Paris, Aug. 28, 1830; Lamotte to CRN, Oct. 7, 1830; Vᵇˡˢ 1, CRN, 4ᵉ Arrond., Dossier Boulanger.

the night, but they scarcely balanced the losses on the twenty-eighth. The insurgents had probably grown in numbers, the successes of Wednesday overcoming the fears of many who had hesitated to join the battle. A few National Guardsmen and some cadets from the Ecole polytechnique joined them and provided additional skilled leadership. Small groups of insurgents captured a number of outlying and largely undefended barracks. One band of about 300 men with 100 rifles harried troops on the Place Louis XVI, and Marmont sent a battalion of the 3d Regiment of the Guard across the river to disperse them. Another group of 350 to 400, fewer than half of them with firearms, tried to cross the Pont Royal to the Tuileries, but heavy fire from the windows of the Louvre and the terrace of the Tuileries Garden drove them back to the shelter of the opposite quai. Others gathered in the narrow streets around the Louvre, fired on the buildings occupied by the Guard but ventured no frontal attacks on their better-armed adversaries. Ill-equipped with muskets and cartridges and without artillery, they had little chance of dislodging the professionals of Marmont's command.[29]

The tenuous security of the moment could not hide the peril in which the monarchy lay. All of Paris except the corridor from the Louvre westward to the Etoile was in the hands of revolutionaries. Appeals to them without substantial concessions were meaningless. Military subjugation of the entire city would be prohibitively expensive in blood, in treasure, and in bitter resentment, and it was probably not even possible. Individual soldiers of the Line had defected on the twenty-eighth, and by the twenty-ninth the command could no longer count on the loyalty of entire regiments.

[29] Marmont, *Mémoires*, VIII, 257-58, 432; Maag, *Schweizertruppen*, pp. 418-19, 421; AN, CC 546, Testimony of Saint-Chamans, Nov. 16, 1830; Saint-Chamans, "Combat," p. 505; Haussez, *Mémoires*, p. 264; BHVP, Rapport de M. Martinet; AHMG, D³ 131, "Rapport du poste de Garde nationale établi à la Caserne de la Gendarmerie . . . rue des Francs-Bourgeois," July 31, 1830; BHVP, Dossier Vallier II, "Bulletin pour la Journée du 29 Jᵉᵗ 1830 du Corps parisien de la Partie ouest du Faubourg Saint-Germain"; AS, D 4AZ 1181, "Précis."

Even the Guard had been infected; guardsmen of the 1st Regiment protested to their colonel on the morning of the twenty-ninth that they would no longer fight against Parisians. The expectation of large reinforcements from the provinces faded as revolutionary sympathizers in villages and towns harried troops marching to the capital and denied them supplies.[30]

On Wednesday the delegation of deputies had urged upon the King and Marmont the withdrawal of the ordinances and the dismissal of the ministry, and at 7:30 on Thursday morning the Marquis Charles de Semonville, Grand Référendaire of the Chamber of Peers, and Comte d'Argout, arrived at the Tuileries to press the same course upon Polignac and his fellow ministers. After a heated exchange between Semonville and the first minister, the ministers withdrew. The excited Semonville, scarcely expecting to be taken seriously, proposed to Marmont that he place the ministers under arrest and stop the fighting on his own authority. Both Argout and Georges Glandevès, Governor of the Tuileries, warmly supported the proposal, and Semonville thought Marmont on the point of accepting it, when Polignac and his colleagues reentered the room and announced that they were going to Saint-Cloud to consult with the King. Semonville had already asked Glandevès for a carriage to take him and Argout to Saint-Cloud. The two men now dashed to the entrance. A carriage, called for the first minister, waited at the bottom of the stairs. They leaped into it, tossed out Polignac's portfolio, and galloped through the Tuileries Garden toward Saint-Cloud. Polignac followed close behind in the carriage called for the two peers, and both carriages clattered up the hill and into the courtyard of the Palace of Saint-Cloud almost side by side.[31]

---

[30] Marmont, *Mémoires*, VIII, 258, 432; Saint-Chamans, "Combat," pp. 505-6; Guernon-Ranville, *Journal*, p. 180; AN, F¹ᵈ III 81, J. Lemenager to G. de Lafayette, Sept. 3, 1830; CC 546, Testimony of Foucauld, Nov. 28; CC 549, Deposition of De Guise, Nov. 2, 1830; AS, D 4AZ 259, Proclamation, "Le Préfet de Police aux habitants de Paris," July 28, 1830; Maag, *Schweizertruppen*, p. 512.

[31] Charles de Semonville, "Mémoire sur la Révolution de 1830,"

Polignac went first to see the King, but in a few minutes
an attendant summoned Semonville to the King's study.
Here the two old men—Charles was seventy-two, Semonville,
seventy-six—angrily confronted each other. The marquis
urged upon the King the perilous position of Marmont, the
growing strength of the revolution, the threat to the monarchy itself if the fighting were not soon stopped. In his
Mémoire of the revolution Semonville recalled that their
exchange was "long and painful" and that both went beyond
the usual proprieties of royal interviews.[32]

At the end Charles slouched at his desk, his head in his
hands, and in a scarcely audible voice replied that he would
consider the matter with his ministers. But revolution could
not interfere with court routine, and the ministers waited
while King and courtiers trooped off to eleven o'clock mass.
On his return the council assembled in the King's study.
Charles reported his conversation with Semonville. The
Dauphin scoffed at the peer's warning and demanded an
attack on Paris. Haussez favored negotiations with the rebels
to gain time in which to move the government and to organize resistance in the Loire valley and the Vendée. Guernon-
Ranville protested that negotiation was capitulation to a
Parisian revolution, and he, too, would continue the struggle
in the provinces. The others favored withdrawal of the
ordinances and the appointment of a new ministry. Their
discussions were interrupted by a scratching on the door—
court etiquette forbade knocking on the closed door of a
room occupied by the King. Haussez opened the door and
found there a disheveled man in general's uniform. He was
panting, his face covered with dust and sweat, his uniform in
disarray. The King bade him enter, and he gasped out that
Marmont had been forced to abandon the Louvre. The
withdrawal of the Swiss from the palace had started a panic
among the other troops, and the entire command had fled

Revue de Paris, 1st year, 5 (Sept. 1, 1894), 80-85; Marmont, *Mémoires,*
VIII, 258-59; Montbel, *Souvenirs,* pp. 247-48; Guernon-Ranville, *Journal,*
pp. 176-78; AN, CC 549, Deposition de Semonville, Nov. 16, 1830.
    32 *Ibid.*; Semonville, "Mémoire," pp. 85-88.

in disorder to the Etoile. Only there did Marmont succeed in stopping the flight and reestablishing a semblance of order.[33]

Marmont's serious troubles had started when the 5th and 53d Regiments on the Place Vendôme were persuaded to join the opposition. Assured that they would not be used to fight against their fellow soldiers, the two regiments marched to Laffitte's house and placed themselves under the command of General Gérard, who ordered them to their barracks.[34] This exposed Marmont's extended left flank and at the same time raised new doubts of the loyalty of the 15th and 50th Regiments holding the Tuileries Garden. The marshal shifted these two regiments to a less critical position on the Champs Elysées, replacing them with a single battalion of Swiss drawn from the Louvre. Earlier in the morning he had issued a proclamation to the people of Paris appealing for an end to the fighting, and he asked the mayors to tell their people that the troops would stop firing. The Swiss holding the Louvre, on orders from the marshal, did cease fire, but the attackers did not reciprocate. The commander of the Swiss in the palace, on his own authority, decided about eleven o'clock to withdraw his men from the building. His battalion left the palace in good order, but when they were fired on by insurgents who swarmed into the building and into the court, he ordered them to quicken their pace, and they hurried down the Rue du Carrousel to get out of range of the firing. The troops on the Place du Carrousel, seeing the Swiss fleeing from the Louvre, panicked and began to run to the court of the Tuileries, across the court, and on into the Tuileries Garden. Here they were joined by the Guards stationed in the garden, and what had begun as an orderly withdrawal of one battalion from an exposed position turned into a rout of almost all Marmont's command. Despite his personal efforts to stem the flight the troops fled

[33] Haussez, *Mémoires*, II, 270-74; Guernon-Ranville, *Journal*, pp. 179-87.

[34] Marmont, *Mémoires*, VIII, 259; Odilon Barrot, *Mémoires posthumes*, 3d ed. (Paris, 1875), I, 107-8; Bérard, *Souvenirs*, pp. 100-110; AS, V^bis 322, CRN, 1e Arrond., Dossier Medoc.

precipitously through the garden to the Place Louis XVI and up the Champs Elysées, fired on by armed men in the adjoining streets. Some of the Guards in the houses along the Rue de Rivoli and the Rue Saint-Honoré saw the fleeing troops in time to join them; some did not and later had to fight their way out to the west, and others remained to be captured or killed by insurgents in fighting that continued in this area until mid-afternoon. Marmont sent ahead orders to stop at the Etoile. Here he intended to remain and by the threat of his presence give the government at least some power of negotiation.[35]

A guard hastily improvised from the victors protected the collections of the Louvre, but the crowd pillaged the Tuileries Palace, including the wine cellar, which ended the effectiveness of many of the "heroes of July" for the remainder of that day.[36]

Across the river a band of several hundred men led by students of the Ecole polytechnique attacked and captured the barracks of the Swiss Guard on the Rue de Babylone. Most of the Guards in the building escaped. Another group of insurgents broke into the barracks of the Royal Garde du Corps on the Quai d'Orsay and seized weapons but allowed twenty guards and thirty men of the 15th Regiment of the Line who had taken refuge there to depart unharmed. Anyone of this band who turned from the barracks to look at the river might have seen floating on the water furniture, pictures, books, and manuscripts; a crowd had sacked the Arch-

---

[35] Marmont, *Mémoires*, VIII, 262-66; Maag, *Schweizertruppen*, pp. 425-27, 433-37, 442-47, plan opp. p. 416; AN, CC 549, Deposition of De Guise, Nov. 2, 1830; AS, D 4AZ 1181, "Précis"; BHVP, Série 23, "Dossier Vallée II"; "Bulletin pour la Journée du 29 Juillet . . . ," "Note sur la garde du Chateau des Tuileries . . ."; Viollet-le-Duc, "Lettres," p. 99; *Dix jours de 1830, souvenirs de la dernière révolution, par A.S. . . .* , *officier d'infanterie d'ex-garde royale* (Paris, 1830), pp. 48-52.

[36] AS, VD³ 3, Bala to Prés., CRN, 12ᵉ Arrond., Jan. 25, 1831; BHVP, Dossier Vallée II, "Bulletin pour la Journées du 29 Juillet . . . ," "Note sur la garde du Chateau des Tuileries . . ."; "Rapport de M. Leconte, père, concierge-comptable du Chateau des Tuileries, sur le Evénemens du 29 Jᵉᵗ 1830"; "Les Trois glorieuses vues par De Creuze"; AN, AB XIX 15, "Papiers . . . de l'administration provisoire de l'Ancienne Dotation de la Couronne après la chute du Roi Charles X."

bishop's Palace and thrown furnishings and library into the river, and for two or three hours they floated downstream across Paris.[37]

Few people in the city that afternoon and evening believed that the battle was over. Reports spread that the Guard, reinforced by regiments from the provinces, was re-forming in the Bois de Boulogne and that artillery units would soon occupy Montmartre to cannonade the city. Against the impending assault Parisians built new barricades and strengthened the old and mounted guard at the city gates and on the approaches to Montmartre. Re-formed National Guard units patrolled the streets. At nightfall citizens placed lamps in their windows to reduce the peril of surprise attack under the cover of darkness. Everyone who could find a musket, legally or illegally, kept it in hand and seemingly fired it frequently. To one American student in Paris the streets that evening seemed more dangerous than during the heavy fighting of the twenty-eighth.[38]

At Saint-Cloud after confirmation of the disastrous news from Paris Charles declared to his ministers, "Let's proceed, gentlemen. We must decide." But the ministers and especially the Dauphin found formal admission of error and defeat a repulsive dish, and not until after four o'clock did Polignac emerge to inform the waiting Semonville, Argout, and Vitrolles that the King, with the agreement of the

[37] BHVP, "Rapport de M. Martinet"; Radiguel to Prés., CRN, Aug. 31; Dossier Vallée II, "Bulletin pour la Journée du 29 J^{et} du Corps Parisien . . ."; "Rapport de M. Bassire," Aug. 14, 1830; AHMG, D^3 131, Constant-George to Gen. Gérard, Aug. 3, 1830; Herbert P. Gambrell, "Three Letters on the Revolution of 1830," *Journal of Modern History*, I (1929), 602; AN, F^{1d} III 82, "Etat récapitulatif des citoyens tués ou blessés mortellement dans les journées de Juillet. . . ."

[38] Rémusat, *Mémoires*, II, 342-44; Hippolyte Bonnelier, *Mémorial de l'Hôtel de Ville de Paris 1830* (Paris, 1835), p. 60; Gambrell, "Three Letters," p. 604; Henri Vienne, "Dix jours à Paris du dimanche 25 juillet au mardi 3 août 1830," *Mémoires* de la Société bourguignonne de géographie et d'histoire, VIII (1892), 102; BHVP, NA 153, Folio 143, Chef, Garde nat., Montmartre, to Lafayette, July 30, 1830, 6 A.M.; AN, F^{1d} III 81, Brunet-Duplantis to Maire de Sèvres, May 25, 1831; Vitrolles, *Mémoires*, II, 402, 406; Dupin, *Mémoires*, I, 146; AS, VD^3 3, "Renseignements fournis par M. Bertrand. . . ."

council had asked the Duc de Mortemart to head a new ministry that would include Casimir Périer and Gérard. The Duke had reluctantly accepted, and his ministry would withdraw the offending ordinances and summon into session the newly elected Chamber of Deputies and the Chamber of Peers.[39]

The Duc de Mortemart was a noble of the old regime who also held a Napoleonic title of nobility as a reward for his services as an ordnance officer during the Russian campaign of 1812. In 1830 he held the rank of lieutenant-general in the army, and he had just returned from two years as ambassador in Saint-Petersburg. When summoned by Charles on July 29, he was ill with a fever and dubious of his ability to save the dynasty, scarcely a happy choice.[40]

The King and Polignac urged the three nobles to carry news of their concessions to Paris at once in the hope of stopping further bloodshed and protecting the crown. The three men set out, crowded into a one-horse chaise intended for two. They were ignorant of developments in the city since its abandonment by Marmont and did not even know to whom they should report the news they carried.[41]

Semonville's and Vitrolles' accounts of their adventures on this journey into the city differ so strikingly, despite their having been seated side by side in the same carriage, that the reader might think them to be writing of different events. They do agree that, although stopped and threatened at least once along the way, they did reach the Quai des Tuileries unharmed. Their destination was the Hôtel de Ville, where, they learned, a new government had established itself, but between the Tuileries and the Hôtel de Ville a throng of dangerous looking men, gathered in groups of thirty or forty, occupied the quais. Each group stopped

[39] Guernon-Ranville, *Journal*, pp. 182-88; Haussez, *Mémoires*, II, 274-75; Vitrolles, *Mémoires*, II, 394; Semonville, "Mémoire," pp. 91-92; Casimir de Mortemart, "Un Manuscrit sur les journées de juillet," *Le Correspondant*, 321 (Dec. 1930), 653-55.

[40] Vitrolles, *Mémoires*, II, 507n.; Haussez, *Mémoires*, II, 278, n. 2; Mortemart, "Manuscrit," pp. 653-55.

[41] Vitrolles, *Mémoires*, pp. 394-96; Semonville, "Mémoire," p. 92.

the emissaries, threatened them, insulted them, and demanded explanations of their presence. Semonville and Argout explained that they brought peace and the concessions that the people sought; then amid cries of "Vive la Charte!" "Vive l'Empereur!" and an occasional "Vive le Roi!" the crowd would permit the peers to move on, opening a passage for them through the next barricade or, taking the light carriage in hand, lifting it over the barrier. As they approached the Place de Grève, the crowd grew more densely packed, the progress slower, and the shouts of "Vive le Roi!" less frequent. Arrived before the Hôtel de Ville the trio alighted, pushed their way through the throngs that crowded the corridors and stairways to an ante room of the office of the Prefect of the Seine, where the provisional Municipal Commission was installed. They waited ten minutes, still not knowing whom they would find on the opposite side of the door. Admitted to the room they saw the commissioners, a group of men well known to them— Périer, Audry de Puyraveau, De Schonen, François Mauguin, and Lobau—seated round a table and Lafayette standing nearby. These men, although in the political opposition, belonged to the tiny establishment of wealthy taxpayers who ruled France, as far removed from the throngs on the streets as were the three peers come from Saint-Cloud. They received the emissaries as old friends and politely listened to their explanation of the mission that brought them here. Nothing decisive came of the meeting, for the peers had authority only to inform; they lacked both written credentials and the critical ordinances that would formally rescind the ordinances of July 25 and call the chambers into session. On the other side, the Municipal Commission disclaimed any power to negotiate.[42]

The aged and exhausted Semonville returned to his apartment in the Luxembourg Palace to await the arrival of Mortemart, who did not appear until ten o'clock the next morning. Argout toiled across the barricades to Laffitte's

[42] Vitrolles, *Mémoires*, pp. 396-403; Semonville, "Mémoire," pp. 94-98; Bonnelier, *Mémorial*, pp. 54-58.

house, now the headquarters of the opposition—"the Hôtel de Juillet." Here he informed the banker and his associates of the change of ministers and the withdrawal of the ordinances, and he asked that the deputies in Paris enter into negotiations with the new first minister. Argout had the impression that Laffitte, troubled by the spreading revolution, would accept these concessions as the basis for ending resistance to the King. Bérard urged him to bring Mortemart to Laffitte's house without delay, and the deputies present agreed that they would wait for him until one o'clock. The hour was striking ten as Argout left to rejoin Vitrolles and to return to Saint-Cloud. Delayed by drunken guardians of the Etoile gate and by Royal Guards beyond the Bois de Boulogne they did not reach the sleeping palace until the small hours of July 30.[43]

Since early morning on July 29 Laffitte's spacious house at the corner of the Rue de Provence and the Rue d'Artois (now the Rue Laffitte) had become the headquarters of the noncombatant opposition. Deputies, lawyers, businessmen, journalists, many of them wearing tricolor ribbons on their coats, moved in and out of his open door, crowded his salons, and overflowed into the courtyard and garden. At noon some thirty deputies who had gathered there resumed their deliberations of the preceding day as to what they should do in the spreading crisis. The past twelve or fifteen hours had done nothing to narrow the split between those who would contain the revolution and those who would continue and direct it. Lafayette arrived shortly and took the floor to inform the deputies that a number of citizens had offered him the command of the National Guard of Paris, disbanded since 1827, and that despite his seventy-three years he considered it his duty to accept.[44] While Lafayette spoke, an

43 Vitrolles, *Mémoires*, pp. 404-7; Semonville, "Mémoire," p. 98; Dupin, *Mémoires*, pp. 143-44; BHVP, Série 23, Dossier Laffitte, "Mémoire de J. Laffitte"; Raymond Lecuyer, *Révolution de Juillet*, p. 44.

44 Louis Girard in his book on the National Guard wonders who made this offer. A manuscript in the Bibliothèque historique de la Ville de Paris offers a possible answer. According to its anonymous author Etienne Garnier-Pagès and his brother invited notables of the

officer came with news of the Royal Guard's abandonment of the Louvre, a development that gave new urgency to the demand for revival of the National Guard under a responsible command. The deputies endorsed Lafayette's decision, and Guizot, supported by Louis Bertin de Vaux and Alexandre Méchin, urged the establishment of a provisional municipal authority to assure the defense, the provisioning, and the safety of the capital, deserted by its royal officials. The meeting unanimously approved this proposal, and after Lafayette declined the invitation to appoint the members of the Municipal Commission, the deputies elected to it Laffitte, Périer, Gérard, Lobau, and Antoine Odier, a deputy of the Department of the Seine. Laffitte, unwilling to exchange the political leadership of the revolution, which he thought he held, for mere municipal administration, used his sprained ankle—turned in climbing over a barricade the preceding evening—as an excuse to remain at "the Hôtel de Juillet." Odier declined to serve, and Gérard, who had accepted the command of troops in Paris, refused additional duties that might interfere with his military assignment. Audry de Puyraveau, De Schonen, and Mauguin, all prominent deputies, took their places.[45]

In the middle of the afternoon Lafayette and the five commissioners installed themselves in the Hôtel de Ville. An ex-captain of the Imperial Navy named Dubourg, who had assumed the title of general, purchased a uniform from

---

Seventh Arrondissement to their house in the morning of July 29, and there all agreed to proceed to the reorganization of the National Guard and the establishment of a provisional government. A delegation went to Laffitte's house, where they met Lafayette and offered to him and to Gérard "the government of the city." Lafayette then informed the assembled deputies of the offer, and they appointed him to the command of the National Guard. Louis Girard, *La Garde nationale* (Paris, 1964), p. 162; BHVP, Série 23, "Historique des faits . . . le 7° Arrondissement."

45 BHVP, "Mémoire de J. Laffitte"; BHVP, Série 23, Dossier Laffitte, "Notes prises chez M. De la Borde"; Lafayette, *Mèmoires*, VI, 388-90; Bérard, *Souvenirs*, pp. 103-4; Dupin, *Mémoires*, II, 144-46; Barrot, *Mémoires*, I, 108-9; Jacques Laffitte, "Les Trois Glorieuses," *Revue de deux mondes*, 100th year, 58 (July 15, 1930), 312-13.

an old clothes dealer, and moved into the Hôtel de Ville that morning as the leader of the popular movement, readily surrendered his position to Lafayette, and other improvised officials were persuaded to follow his example. The deputies had named Odilon Barrot, who had been acting as secretary of their meeting, to be secretary of the new commission, a duty that he shared with Jean-Jacques Baude of the *Temps* and Hippolyte Bonnelier, who had come to the city hall with Dubourg. Alexandre de Laborde, deputy of Paris, happened on the scene at the right moment and was pressed into service as Prefect of the Seine, and at the Prefecture of Police Nicolas Bavoux, a deputy and member of the Faculty of Law of Paris, took over the duties of Mangin, who at dawn that morning had burned his compromising papers and fled. The commission began its functions in a building overrun by combatants, petitioners, and curious of every description amid the sounds of the vast and elated throng that milled about the Place de Grève. Its first public act was to proclaim the museum of the Louvre and other public buildings under "the safeguard of the citizens." It called on the tellers in the recent elections in each arrondissement to reorganize the administration in their districts, arranged for free distribution of bread to combatants and their dependents, and appointed one of their visitors to reestablish the postal services. Lafayette announced the immediate reorganization of the National Guard of Paris, committed to it the responsibility for maintaining order in Paris, and directed the colonels or their deputies to come to the Hôtel de Ville for instructions.[46]

The election of the Municipal Commission, although the

[46] Bonnelier, *Mémorial*, pp. 19-42; Lafayette, *Mémoires*, VI, 388-92; Barrot, *Mémoires*, I, 109, 113-14; Laure d'Abrantes, *Mémoires sur la Restauration* (Paris, 1835-36), VII, 219; Rémusat, *Mémoires*, II, 343-44; *Moniteur*, July 31, 1830, p. 827; BHVP, Série 23, "Notes prises chez M. De la Borde"; FGms 321, Victor Crochon, "Souvenirs," II, 565; AS, D³ AZ 162, Laffitte to MM les membres de la Commission municipale, July 29, 1830; Huart, "Mangin," p. 608; CC 547, Dubourg au Rapporteur, Comm. d'Enquête, Sept. 25, 1830; Jean Tulard, *Préfecture de Police sous la Monarchie de Juillet* (Paris, 1964), p. 41.

most positive action the deputies had yet taken, was essentially a postponement of decision that reflected their continued division. Some wanted to carry on the revolution but differed on its ultimate objective. Others wanted to stop it before it grew even more dangerous. They could agree only on the rejection of a provisional government, which might imply a commitment for the future, and on the creation of a municipal authority charged with reestablishment and maintenance of order but that would involve no commitment whatsoever on the future government. The membership of the commission was itself a compromise—two conservatives who wanted to contain the revolution, Périer and Lobau, balanced two activists who would push it further, Audry de Puyraveau and Mauguin. De Schonen stood between them.[47]

[47] Barrot, *Mémoires*, I, 109-10; Bonnelier, *Mémorial*, p. 30. The *Moniteur* of July 30, a single-page edition, announced the formation of the commission under the heading "Gouvernement provisoire," but the next day the paper carried a notice that this announcement had not come from the Municipal Commission.

V

The Struggle for Power,
July 30–August 9

WHEN THE army fled Paris on July 29, leaving the capital to its insurgent citizens, the sovereign power of France lay abandoned. The Bourbons could still recover it, but should they falter or delay, the Bonapartists, the Orléanists, the republicans might grasp it, win popular endorsement, and make it theirs. Or rival aspirants for power might contest it by force, plunging France into civil war and inviting foreign intervention. Charles X in the evening of July 29 still refused to admit that the crown was slipping from his head, but many of his advisers understood, and they sought to restore it by concessions—concessions that Charles had avowed he would never make—to the parliamentary opposition, who, they hoped, might be able to calm the revolutionary populace. Should this maneuver fail, abdication might yet save the crown for the dynasty in the person of the young Duc de Bordeaux, the King's grandson.

The Bonapartists enjoyed widespread popular support. In the streets during the days of fighting "Vive Napoléon!" and "Vive l'Empereur!" had probably been the most frequently heard political cries fixed on any individual, and the tricolor, which flew from every staff on July 29, reminded beholders of the Empire as well as of the Republic. A few men whose names recalled imperial glories still passed as friends of the Empire—the Duc de Bassano, Marshal Remi Exelmans, General Gaspard Gourgaud, and the Comte de Lobau. One of them might contrive to seize control of the popular movement and use it to restore Napoleon II, but a formidable handicap weighed upon them all. Half a continent and the almost certain opposition of the anti-

143

Napoleonic coalition of 1814 and 1815 separated their candidate from the scene.

The republican bid, which looms large in some histories of the revolution, was largely the creation of the Orléanists, a menace from which they alone could save France, a bogey to frighten legitimists, Bonapartists, and the uncommitted into supporting the Duc d'Orléans. All the hopes of the republicans turned upon the leadership of Lafayette, and after he very early threw his support to Orléans, they could do no more than demand "republican institutions" around the throne.

The Orléanists had the advantage of a popular and well-placed leader in the person of Laffitte, a number of skillful publicists, notably Thiers and Mignet, and the ability to pose as both revolutionaries and conservatives, as defenders of both liberty and order. But all their hopes, too, could be reduced to ashes by one man, the Duc d'Orléans himself. Only a few miles separated him from the scene, but on July 28 and 29 his supporters had no assurance that he would play the role they were preparing for him.

The insurrection in Paris had shattered the orderly structure of government in France, and in the succeeding days half a dozen institutions shared its fragments. The Chamber of Deputies, led by the three score deputies who on July 28 had protested against the ordinances and refused to surrender their electoral mandates, assumed the right not only to govern the country but also to dispose of the crown and to revise the constitution. Lacking its support no contestant could expect to achieve power without renewed violence. At the Hôtel de Ville sat the provisional Municipal Commission, installed by the same deputies who dominated the chamber, but with its authority resting as much on the combatants of July, who controlled the Hôtel de Ville and permitted the commission to function, as on the deputies' formal appointment. The deputies had charged the commission with the maintenance of order and the provisioning of the city, but on July 30 it began to act like a national provisional government. Without consulting the deputies it

appointed commissioners to administer the national ministries, issued orders to officers of the royal army, and in conjunction with Lafayette ordered the creation of the Garde
nationale mobile for the defense of the frontiers, a veritable
new army outside the established military structure. The
royal army, nonetheless, remained important in the contest
for power. The troops of the Line in Paris had ceased to be
an effective force, and units of the Royal Guard that fought
in Paris had begun to waiver in their loyalty, but these did
not constitute the entire army. The 4th Regiment of the
Guard, on the march from Normandy, and the 8th from
Orléans had not yet been committed nor had the troops in
the camp at Saint-Omer in the east nor the garrisons in
provincial cities. Across the Mediterranean waited the victorious Army of Africa under the command of Bourmont,
himself a member of the Polignac Ministry and the holder
of a marshal's baton newly presented by Charles X. Within
the capital itself the only effective armed force was the
National Guard. Charles had disbanded it three years
earlier, but officers and men retained their arms and their
uniforms, and on Lafayette's order they quickly re-formed
their units and appeared on the streets and at the city's gates
as guardians of order within and as defenders against attack
from outside. Their adherence or opposition might determine the fate of any government established in the capital.
The armed people of Paris formed yet another force within
the city. Unorganized except in a few random units they
could, nonetheless, prevent the military reconquest of the
city and block the imposition of any government unacceptable to them. On the other hand, their political aims scarcely
went beyond the popular cry of "A bas les Bourbons!" Some
undoubtedly thought of themselves as republicans, more as
Bonapartists, and a few as Orléanists. Divided and inexper-
ienced they could impose no solution of their own, but any
successful aspirant for power would have to win at least
their consent.

The army's sudden evacuation of Paris on July 29 had
caught all parties by surprise. No one had thought of such

an abandonment of power as even a remote possibility. No one among the opposition had any considered idea of what advantage his party might obtain from it—no one, that is, except Thiers and perhaps Laffitte. As early as the morning of July 28 Thiers had attempted to inject the name of the Duc d'Orléans into the discussions of the deputies, and that evening at Audry de Puyraveau's house Laffitte, according to his own account, had urged the Duke upon his colleagues as France's William III. The next day Laffitte summoned Oudard, the Duke's private secretary, and asked him to determine if the Orléanists could count on Orléans; if they did not act, the Bonapartists or the republicans would, he warned, and the Duke could not expect to remain in France under the Empire or the republic. He must choose between a crown and a passport. Orléans would never willingly take the crown from the head of his cousin, Laffitte thought, but faced with exile and loss of his property he might accept it "to avoid becoming a school teacher a second time." The Duke, however, did not see his choice so narrowly limited, and he sent back a noncommittal reply, "I thank you." That evening Laffitte, Thiers, and Sébastiani, and other Orléanists gathered at Laffitte's house, decided that they could proceed no further in their project without assurance that Orléans would play his part. They chose Thiers to go at once to Neuilly to present their plans to Orléans.[1] Laffitte gave him a note recommending him to the Duke. "I beg M. le Duc d'Orléans," it read, "to hear in all confidence M. Thiers and what he is charged to say on my behalf."[2]

At Neuilly, Thiers found the gates of the park barred. After he had induced a guardian to let him pass, he learned at the chateau that the Duke had fled earlier in the day, probably more to forestall seizure by royal troops than to escape from revolutionaries, to his residence at Le Raincy,

[1] Charles de Rémusat, *Mémoires de ma vie* (Paris, 1958-67), II, 341; Jacques Laffitte, "Les Trois Glorieuses," *Revue des deux mondes*, 100th year, 58 (July 15, 1930), 311; BHVP, Série 23, Dossier Laffitte, mémoire headed "J. Laffitte"; BN, Dépt. des MSS, NA Fr. 20601, "Récit de la visite de M. Thiers à Neuilly. . . ."

[2] BN, Dépt. des MSS, NA Fr. 20601.

ten miles to the east of Paris. The Duchess and Madame Adélaïde, the Duke's sister, received him and promised to report his propositions to the Duke. Thiers then spoke to them earnestly of the crown of France. He explained that Laffitte and his party hoped to use the opportunity provided by the popular victory in Paris to establish a genuinely parliamentary monarchy, and they sought a dynasty willing to play the rôle of parliamentary monarchs. Not everyone favored this solution to the present crisis, he warned; legitimists, Bonapartists, and republicans were at work, too. At the moment Orléans could command the most support, but this could quickly change. "We must act quickly," he admonished, "thrones belong to their first occupants." Madame Adélaïde feared that a change of dynasty might bring foreign armies into France, but Thiers argued that Europe would be so relieved to see the revolution stop short of a republic that it would readily accept a new monarch. Now was the critical time for the Duke to come to Paris and put himself at the head of the revolution. Having heard his proposals Madame Adélaïde, a much more ambitious woman than the Duchess, replied, "If you believe that the support of our family could be useful to the revolution, we gladly give it." Thiers, equal to the drama of the occasion, declared, "Today you have acquired the crown for your house." He hastily sketched out the arguments to be conveyed to the Duke, bade goodbye to the ladies of Orléans, and hurried back to Paris. It was after midnight when he arrived at Laffitte's house, where a group of deputies vainly awaited the arrival of Mortemart, Charles X's new first minister. He reported his interview to Laffitte and Sébastiani, and they agreed to accept Madame Adélaïde's declaration as a commitment of the family. Laffitte, who a few hours earlier seemed to despair of foiling the efforts of Charles X to recover power, took heart. His party could now vigorously press their campaign for Orléans.[3]

About the same time in the early hours of July 30 the royal emissaries, Argout and Vitrolles, arrived at the Palace

[3] *Ibid.*

of Saint-Cloud to report the results of their mission and to escort Mortemart back to the deputies of Paris. They found Mortemart awake in his room; he had waited all evening for their return, but inexplicably he had done nothing to prepare the ordinances that were essential preliminaries to negotiation with the deputies. Argout and Vitrolles insisted that the minimum concessions that must be granted without haggling were a new ministry, withdrawal of the ordinances of July 25, the summoning of the chambers to meet on August 3, and the reestablishment of the National Guard of Paris. Shortly after dawn the two peers, Mortemart, his secretary, Alexandre de Mazas, and Langsdorff, a friend of Vitrolles who had accompanied him back from Paris, gathered around the table in the first minister's apartment to draft the ordinances. At 7 A.M. the King, still in his nightcap, received Mortemart and soon called Vitrolles to join them. Charles listened with ill-concealed distaste to the ordinances brought for his signature, and when he heard the proposal to re-form the National Guard, the usually regal Charles bounced up and down in his bed to emphasize his displeasure. Vitrolles argued that the King had no power to resist the changes pressed upon him, that refusal would lose the crown not only for himself but for his family. The old king signed.[4]

Mortemart, accompanied by Argout, Mazas, and Langsdorff set out for Paris in the Duke's open carriage but abandoned it as too conspicuous a conveyance when they encountered a band of armed men on the Versailles road at Sèvres. They proceeded on foot to Auteuil, crossed the river, and entered the city by the Grenelle Gate near the Ecole militaire. Their first destination was Laffitte's "Hôtel de Juillet," but as they neared it about 10 in the morning, they met Bérard, who informed them that the meeting of deputies there had broken up. He invited them to his house nearby for refreshments. Here he told them that accommo-

[4] Eugene de Vitrolles, *Mémoires* (Paris, 1950, 1951), II, 407-11; Raymond Lecuyer, *La Révolution de Juillet . . . impressions et récits contemporains: Mémoires de Alex. Mazas—Chronique de Rozet* (Paris, n.d.), pp. 44-45.

dation between the Bourbons and the deputies, difficult but still possible twelve hours earlier, was no longer possible. To Mortemart's protests of legitimate rights, the danger of embroilment with Europe, the promise of satisfaction of all demands, Bérard replied that the Duke's arguments had no relevance to the altered political scene. The choice no longer lay between Charles and Orléans but between Orléans and a republic, and the republicans grew stronger by the hour. "The only way for us to escape the republic," he warned, "is to accept the Duc d'Orléans as King. . . ." Bérard, the Orléanist, was proselytizing the King's first minister himself, attempting to frighten him with the republican menace. He knew that a majority of the deputies in Paris still opposed a change of dynasties, and even so ardent an Orléanist as Thiers thought the Bourbon cause not lost until August 3.[5]

The emissaries then separated, fearful of the attention they might attract if they walked together, and Mortemart proceeded alone through the barricaded streets to the Luxembourg Palace, seeing posted on walls bills acclaiming the virtues of the Duc d'Orléans and his qualifications for the throne. Arriving at the apartment of Semonville, who had been awaiting him since the preceding evening, he found the Duke under the care of his doctor, whom Lafayette, concerned for the effects of the preceding day's exertions on the old man's health, had sent to him. The doctor, seeing the pale and exhausted Mortemart, at once ordered a bath for him and insisted that he remain quietly at the Luxembourg lest he become dangerously ill. Some twenty peers whom Semonville had summoned to the palace agreed that the new ordinances should be presented to the deputies and to Lafayette and the Municipal Commission, and one of their number, Jean-Baptiste Collin de Sussy, undertook to deliver them. Mortemart ordered the *Moniteur* to publish the ordinances, but Sauvo, the editor, replied that armed men sent by the Municipal Commission occupied his

[5] Lecuyer, *Révolution de Juillet*, pp. 46-48; Auguste Bérard, *Souvenirs historiques sur la Révolution de 1830* (Paris, 1834), pp. 114-16; Alfred de Falloux, *L'Evéque d'Orléans* (Paris, 1879), pp. 100-101.

offices with express orders to prevent publication of any papers coming from royal officials. Other journals and printers asked to print the ordinances refused, citing the threat of broken presses if they did. The unhappy Mortemart, confined to the Luxembourg Palace, still tried to act like a first minister—he sought to establish communications with the diplomatic corps, he proclaimed the end of martial law, he ordered the opening of public works to provide employment—but these were meaningless gestures without influence on the course of events that were shaping the future of the country.[6]

At eight o'clock that morning, July 30, some forty deputies had met at Laffitte's house. Some of them brought copies of an unsigned placard extolling the Duc d'Orléans that they picked up in the street.

> Charles X can never again enter Paris; he caused the blood of the people to be shed.
>
> The republic would expose us to frightful divisions; it would embroil us with Europe.
>
> The Duc d'Orléans is a prince devoted to the cause of the revolution.
>
> The Duc d'Orléans never fought against us.
>
> The Duc d'Orléans was at Jemappes.
>
> The Duc d'Orléans carried the tricolor under fire; the Duc d'Orléans alone can carry it again; we want no others.
>
> The Duc d'Orléans has declared himself; he accepts the charter as we have always wanted it.
>
> It is from the French people that he will hold his crown.

This manifesto came from the pens of Thiers and Mignet, and during the night thousands of copies had been run off and were now broadcast across the city.[7]

[6] Lecuyer, *Révolution de Juillet*, pp. 51-54; Hippolyte Bonnelier, *Mémorial de l'Hôtel de Ville de Paris* (Paris, 1835), pp. 85, 87; Charles de Semonville, "Mémoire sur la Révolution de 1830," *Revue de Paris*, 1st Year, 5 (Sept. 1, 1894), 99.

[7] Bérard, *Souvenirs*, pp. 111-12; Prosper Duvergier de Hauranne, *Histoire du gouvernement parlementaire en France, 1814-1848* (Paris, 1857-71), X, 590.

Some deputies proposed to their assembled colleagues that they invite Orléans to assume the office of Lieutenant-General of the Kingdom, an office used on occasion in the past when circumstances prevented the King from governing. Charles X, then the Comte d'Artois, had held the title in 1814 when he returned to France in advance of his brother, Louis XVIII. Many of the deputies would have issued the invitation on the spot, but Bérard, who was presiding, refused to put the question to a vote until it had been debated by a meeting called specifically for that purpose. They agreed to assemble again that afternoon in the usual meeting place of the chamber, the Palais-Bourbon.[8]

Dupin, the Duc d'Orléans' lawyer and close adviser and a deputy, hurried out to Neuilly to inquire specifically if the Duke would accept the lieutenant-generalcy. Orléans had not returned from his retreat at Le Raincy, and Dupin could report back to his colleagues only the misgivings and the tears of the Duchess and the assurance of Madame Adélaïde that she thought they could depend on her brother.[9]

About noon between forty and fifty deputies gathered at the Palais-Bourbon. On the proposition of the legitimist Jean Hyde de Neuville they elected a committee of five members to confer with the delegates of the Chamber of Peers on a solution to the crisis. The choice of committee members—Augustin Périer, Sébastiani, Guizot, Benjamin Delessert, and Jean Hyde de Neuville—revealed the conservative temper of the chamber; four more liberal candidates won but nine votes. Shortly after the committee left for the Luxembourg, the Comte de Sussy arrived to inform the assembly of the new ordinances signed by the King and Mortemart. He was permitted to read them (he actually read only five, omitting the sixth on the reestablishment of the National Guard), but when he attempted to deliver them to Laffitte, the presiding officer, Laffitte refused to accept them. Sussy, unable to accomplish more, left for the Hôtel de Ville, hoping for a better reception from the

---

[8] Bérard, *Souvenirs*, pp. 113-14.
[9] André Dupin, *Mémoires de M. Dupin* (Paris, 1855-61), II, 147-49.

Municipal Commission and Lafayette, but he there met with a similar rebuff. In the subsequent debate at the Palais-Bourbon a consensus emerged that France must have a government at once, that postponement of decision even until the meeting of the chambers on August 3 would play into the hands of Charles and encourage renewed violence in Paris. The deputation to the Luxembourg returned to report that the twenty or twenty-five peers gathered there agreed that the appointment of Orléans as Lieutenant-General offered the best assurance for the maintenance of order. They did not mention that Mortemart had denounced it as illegal and "prejudicial to the majesty of the throne." Laffitte put the question of Orléans' appointment to a vote, and all the deputies present, save three, voted affirmatively. Constant and Sébastiani drew up a declaration of the assembly's wishes to be presented to the Duke.[10]

> The meeting of the deputies at present in Paris begs His Royal Highness Monseigneur the Duc d'Orléans to come to the capital to exercise the functions of lieutenant-general of the kingdom and expresses to him the wish to retain the national flag.
>
> The deputies have been concerned, moreover, with assuring to France in the next session of the Chambers, all the indispensable guarantees for the full and complete execution of the Charter.[11]

This unrevolutionary letter avoided any allusion to a change of dynasty. The ambiguous second paragraph was a concession to Lafayette, who had sent Odilon Barrot to the deputies' session to warn them that they would lose popular support should they designate a new chief without first obtaining guarantees of the liberties for which the people had fought. The next day, Laffitte, ashamed of his colleagues' timidity, Bérard thought, ordered that the decla-

10 Bérard, *Souvenirs*, pp. 117-24, 480-90; Marie de Lafayette, *Mémoires, correspondance et manuscrits* (Paris, 1837-38), VI, 395-402; Lecuyer, *Révolution de Juillet*, pp. 56-57; Bonnelier, *Mémorial*, p. 87.
11 *Archives parlementaires*, 2d Series, Vol. 61 (July 31, 1830), 644.

ration not be published, and it never appeared in the *Moniteur* nor in the *Bulletin des lois*. On the thirtieth, however, forty deputies affixed their signatures to it; seven, in addition to the three who voted against the invitation to the Duke, withdrew without signing. After choosing a delegation of twelve members to inform the Duke of their action, the deputies adjourned until the next day.[12]

The delegation went at once to the Palais-Royal and there confided to a member of the Duke's household a letter signed by all the delegates urging him to come to Paris. They awaited his reply at Laffitte's house, and it came promptly—the Duke would be in Paris the next morning. "It's not tomorrow," exploded Laffitte, "it's this very instant that he must come. There's not a moment to lose!" The messenger carried this advice back to Neuilly, and shortly before midnight the Duke, accompanied by two aides, arrived at the Palais-Royal.[13]

While the deputies sought to save France from the republic, Bonapartists prepared to reestablish the Empire. The principal activist of the movement was a journalist named Evariste Dumoulin, who had installed "General" Dubourg in the Hôtel de Ville. Despite a long and fruitless effort during the night of the twenty-ninth to win Casimir Périer to his plan, Dumoulin drew up and delivered to the printer the next day a proclamation summoning Napoleon II to the throne. Dated July 30 at the Hôtel de Ville and headed "Gouvernement provisoire" it declared to Parisians, "Napoleon II is the heir of your glory; he is our emperor." Dumoulin organized demonstrations to agitate for the Empire on the Place de Grève and solicited the support of several notables of the Empire. With them he had no success, but he thought that at least two members of the Municipal Commission, Audry de Puyraveau and Mauguin, and several lesser figures at the Hôtel de Ville would back him. Later in the day he received a summons from Lafayette.

12 Bérard, *Souvenirs*, pp. 124-25, 454-55, 493-94; Lafayette, *Mémoires*, VI, 398-99.
13 Bérard, *Souvenirs*, pp. 125-27; Dupin, *Mémoires*, II, 150.

The bearer of the message led him down long corridors of the Hôtel de Ville and finally left him in a small chamber with the word that Lafayette would join him in a few minutes. He waited a quarter of an hour in solitude and silence, dreaming perhaps of himself and Lafayette leading Napoleon II into Paris. But he grew impatient and opened the door; it was blocked by two National Guardsmen. He rushed to a window; it was heavily barred. The room's other window looked out onto a deep court. The emperor-maker realized that he had been tricked, and here he languished until seven o'clock in the evening, and his campaign came to an ignominious end. The prominent Bonapartists were joining the Orléanists, and no other leader came forward to rally latent support for Napoleon II.[14]

At Saint-Cloud the court had spent the thirtieth awaiting word from Mortemart of the deputies' acceptance of the new ministry. A seemingly formidable barrier of troops stood between the King and his rebellious capital, and Angoulême himself had taken over command of them after Marmont's disaster in Paris. The four regiments of the Guard that had fought in Paris, reenforced by the 4th, which arrived during the day, occupied the palace park along the Seine from Sèvres to Saint-Cloud and controlled the two bridges. Still-loyal elements of the 5th and 50th Regiments of the Line were in Sèvres. The Garde du Corps and cadets from the military school at Saint-Cyr, anxious to cross swords with their arch-rivals, the Polytechnicians, guarded the palace itself. Cavalry distributed along the roads from Saint-Cloud and Sèvres to Versailles protected a line of retreat. But during the day the dependability of these troops, subject to the blandishments and taunts of insurrectionaries who infiltrated their ranks, grew more and more doubtful. Twenty grenadiers of the 1st Guard Regiment posted on the Saint-Cloud bridge deserted. A battalion of Swiss surrendered

14 Bonnelier, *Mémorial*, pp. 74-77; Laure d'Abrantes, *Mémoires sur la Restauration* (Paris, 1835-36), VII, 221-24; Odilon Barrot, *Mémoires posthumes*, 3d ed. (Paris, 1875), I, 114.

their arms to rebellious citizens of Sèvres. In the evening the 50th of the Line laid down its arms. Marmont heard a report that the 3d Guard Regiment would desert during the night, and a number of colonels of the Guard warned Angoulême that they could no longer promise the loyalty of their men. A report of insurrection in Versailles raised the specter of encirclement by revolution. Marmont had already urged the King to leave Saint-Cloud at once while he still had loyal troops and to withdraw to the Loire valley, and at Blois or Tours, far from the corrupting influence of Paris, establish his government, summon the diplomatic corps around him, and convoke the chambers. The King still professed faith in Mortemart's negotiations and refused to leave Saint-Cloud, but the reports of growing desertions and the arrival of the ominous news that the revolutionaries of Paris were planning an attack on Saint-Cloud changed his mind.[15]

That night candles burned late at the palace, lighting the vast task of moving the court and all its retainers. Servants packed trunks, secretaries assembled papers, coachmen brought out carriages and wagons, grooms harnessed horses, and fearful men slipped pistols into their pockets. At 3 A.M. on July 31 a file of some twenty carriages and an innumerable baggage train moved out of the palace courtyard and headed westward along the road to Versailles. Two companies of the Royal Bodyguard led the way; two other companies brought up the rear. The infantry of the Guard, under command of the Dauphin, remained behind to hold

15 Charles d'Haussez, *Mémoires du Baron Haussez, dernier Ministre de la Marine sous la Restauration* (Paris, 1896, 1897), II, 283-87; Auguste de Marmont, *Mémoires du maréchal Marmont, duc de Raguse de 1792 à 1841*, 3d ed. (Paris, 1857), VIII, 289-91, 315; Martial de Guernon-Ranville, *Journal d'un ministre* (Caen, 1873), pp. 194-97; Alfred de Saint-Chamans, "Le Combat pour le roi, juillet 1830," *Revue de Paris*, 3d year, 1 (Feb. 1, 1896), 512-14; AS, D 4AZ 1181, "Précis des événemens aux quels a pris part le troisième régiment d'infanterie de la garde royale depuis le vingt-six juillet jusqu'au jour de son licenciement par un officier du régiment," pp. 21-23; BHVP, NA 153, Papiers Odilon Barrot, Folios 118, 120, 124, 129; AN, F1d III 81, Maire de Sèvres to Commission des Récompenses nationales (hereafter cited as CRN), Jan. 7, 1831.

the line of the river.[16] "The march resembled a funeral procession," wrote Haussez; "there was the same silence, an equal gravity, as great a sadness. . . . Independent of the attachment one had for the monarchy and for the monarch, each one had a special motive of regret in the loss of his position, the change of his habits, the ruin of his future."[17]

At the opposite end of the political spectrum the republicans hoped to pluck victory for themselves from the confusion of the monarchy's collapse. The evidence of their strength and activities is thin and dubious, coming largely from men who exaggerated either to win votes for its opponents, as did Bérard, or to advance the republican cause itself, as did Alexandre Dumas. Bérard avowed his belief in the existence of a network of republican societies, directed from a single headquarters on the Rue de Richelieu, already organized and at work on July 30. That evening, he heard, several thousand young men came to the Hôtel de Ville to petition Lafayette to accept the presidency of a provisional republican government. At noon the next day on the Place de Grève, Bérard's informants told him, the republic would be proclaimed. Numerous republican deputations did call on Lafayette and the Municipal Commission in the first days at the Hôtel de Ville, but for only one of them can the membership and demands be defined. On July 30 a delegation of six men, some of them former Carbonari, appeared at the Hôtel de Ville. Dumas, who was not present, wrote that they pressed Lafayette to make himself dictator of France, but Mauguin, who heard them when they came before the Municipal Commission, declared that they insisted on only two points—that firm guarantees of the "public liberties" be obtained preliminary to the creation of a new government and that the nation be "consulted" on the form of the new regime whatever it might be. Others may have made more far-reaching demands, but without Lafayette's support none had a chance of success. On the morning of the thirtieth Rémusat, anxious to know the old

[16] Haussez, *Mémoires*, II, 289-92; Marmont, *Mémoires*, VIII, 297.
[17] Haussez, *Mémoires*, II, 292.

republican's intentions, sought him out at the Hôtel de Ville and told him that if the government were changed the choice of a new chief could be only between him and Orléans. Lafayette had replied without hesitation, "Not I, . . . the Duc d'Orléans will be king, as sure as I shall not be."[18] The presidency of a French republic did perhaps tempt him—Bérard heard that it did—but on the morning of the thirty-first, after a long discussion with Barrot, he again declared his support for a constitutional monarchy. The party of the Hôtel de Ville could no longer be republican if, indeed, it ever had been. It did distrust the deputies and thought they moved too quickly to vest powers in the Duc d'Orléans without adequate guarantees against revival of the very abuses against which the revolution had protested, and it directed its energies toward inducing the chamber and Lafayette to obtain the guarantees it thought essential.[19]

At nine o'clock Saturday morning, July 31, the Duc d'Orléans received the delegation of deputies at the Palais-Royal. He told them that he had no hesitation about coming to Paris to share their dangers (although he had in fact hesitated for several days), but that ties of family and duty, not to be lightly broken, made it impossible for him to accept the office of lieutenant-general immediately. Orléans in these first hours was torn between his obligations to the Bourbons and the temptations of the crown. Shortly after his arrival at the Palais-Royal he had summoned Mortemart to his apartment and declared to him emotionally that he would never take the crown but would accept a regency for the Duc de Bordeaux if the King asked him. Now on Saturday morning he told the deputies that he saw no pressing need for immediate action on their invitation. The delegates protested that the republic might be proclaimed at any moment, that only prompt announcement of the appointment of the

18 Rémusat, *Mémoires*, II, 345.

19 Bérard, *Souvenirs*, pp. 117, 128-31; Alexandre Dumas, *Mes mémoires*, New ed. (Paris, 1884-92), VI, 255-59, 297-98; Barrot, *Mémoires*, I, 120-21, 126-29; Rémusat, *Mémoires*, II, 346-47.

lieutenant-general could save the country from civil war and reversion to absolutism. Asking the delegation to wait, Orléans withdrew accompanied by Sébastiani. Dupin soon joined them. The Duke probably sent Sébastiani to seek the advice of Talleyrand, a trusted counselor, who had earlier urged Orléans to come into Paris but to accept only the innocuous title of "Commandant de Paris." Now, however, Talleyrand advised him to accept the lieutenant-generalcy. The Duke, Sébastiani, and Dupin then drew up a proclamation to the people of Paris announcing Orléans's acceptance of the proffered office and returned to the waiting delegation. The deputies asked and obtained a few minor changes, then accepted the declaration.[20]

Residents of Paris,

The deputies of France, at this moment assembled in Paris, have expressed the desire that I come to this capital to exercise here the functions of lieutenant-general of the kingdom. I have not hesitated to come to share your dangers, to place myself in the midst of your heroic population, and to exert all my efforts to preserve you from civil war and anarchy. In returning to the city of Paris I wear with pride these glorious colors that you have again taken and that I myself have long carried. The chambers will meet; they will consider the means to assure the rule of law and the maintenance of the rights of the nation. A charter will henceforth be a reality.[21]

[20] Bérard, *Souvenirs*, pp. 132-37; Etienne Audiffret-Pasquier, *Histoire de mon temps; Mémoires du Chancelier Pasquier*, 3d ed. (Paris, 1895), VI, 291-301; Casimir de Mortemart, "Un Manuscrit sur les journées de juillet," *Le Correspondant*, 321 (Dec. 1930), 812, 814; Paul Mantoux, "Talleyrand en 1830 d'après des mémoires contemporaines," *Revue historique*, 78 (Jan.-Apr. 1902), 277-78, 283-84.

[21] *Archives parlementaires*, 2d Series, Vol. 61 (July 31, 1830), 644-45. The final line in the original of Orléans' statement read, "A charter will henceforth be a reality." It appeared that way in the *Moniteur*, on placards posted on walls, and in all newspapers except the *Journal des débats*, which printed "The Charter will henceforth be a reality." On August 3 the *Moniteur* published a correction, changing the initial article to "La" and stating that this was the original form. According to Bérard this correction was the work of Doctrinaires who wanted

STRUGGLE FOR POWER

When the deputies met early that afternoon, their number almost doubled since their preceding meeting, they heard and acclaimed this declaration of the Duke and ordered that it be printed in 10,000 copies. On the proposal of Laffitte, again in the president's chair, the assembly charged Guizot, Bérard, Constant, and Villemain to draft a proclamation to the French people explaining the measures the deputies had taken to resolve the crisis. Two deputies of the Left insisted that the proclamation must include specific guarantees of the "public liberties" demanded by the party of the Hôtel de Ville, and the presence of Bérard, Constant, and Villemain on the committee assured that they would not be forgotten. The committee's draft, approved by acclamation, began with praise for the heroic population of Paris, announced and justified the appointment of Orléans as lieutenant-general, and continued in these words:[22]

The Duc d'Orléans is devoted to the national and constitutional cause; he has always defended its interests and professed its principles. He will respect our rights, because he will derive his rights from us. We shall assure by laws all the guarantees necessary to make liberty strong and durable:

The reestablishment of the national guard with the participation of national guards in the choice of officers;

The participation of citizens in the formation of departmental and municipal administrations;

Trial by jury for press offenses;

Legal responsibility of ministers and of secondary agents of the administration;

to limit the consequences of the revolution. Guizot, one of the Doctrinaires, denied Bérard's charge. "La" was the original article, he declared, and some of the members of the delegation of deputies to the Palais-Royal changed it to "Une." When Bérard sought the original document in the archives of the Chamber of Deputies, he learned that it had been removed. Bérard, *Souvenirs*, pp. 179-80; *Moniteur universel* (Paris), Aug. 2, 1830, p. 833, Aug. 3, p. 837; François Guizot, *Mémoires pour servir à l'histoire de mon temps, 1807-48*; New ed., (Paris, 1872), II, 22.

[22] *Moniteur*, Aug. 1, 1830, p. 829; Aug. 2, pp. 833-34.

Pay and promotions of the military to be determined by law [and not by the pleasure of the King];

The reelection of deputies appointed to public office.

We shall provide, in concert with the chief of the State, for the continuing development of our institutions.[23]

Ninety-five deputies affixed their signatures to this declaration and resolved to proceed in a body to the Palais-Royal to present it to the Duke. Bérard, informed that Orléans was preparing to leave for the Hôtel de Ville, hurried across the river to ask him to await the arrival of the deputies. The procession set out from the Palais-Bourbon led by a tipsy drummer, four black-garbed *huissiers* of the palace, and Laffitte carried in his sedan chair, the barricades in the streets preventing the use of a carriage. All the deputies followed on foot surrounded by a swarm of gamins. Arrived at the Palais-Royal and admitted to the Duke's apartment, the deputies formed a semicircle around him, and Laffitte stood before the Duke to read the proclamation. Balanced on one foot and a crutch, trying to hold both his hat and the declaration, and made nervous by the gravity of the occasion Laffitte dropped the paper. The Duke stooped to pick it up and returned it to him.[24] Laffitte, seeing the Duke at his feet, said to him in a loud whisper for all to hear, "Don't look at my leg: two slippers, one sock, and no boots! God, if the *Quotidienne* [a royalist journal] saw it! It would say that we are going to make a sans-culotte king. But raise your eyes higher, to my arm. On it is the crown of France."[25]

Laffitte read the proclamation. The Duke replied with an invitation to accompany him to the Hôtel de Ville. Orléans in his few hours in Paris had learned enough of the confusion of powers in the capital to understand that appointment by a minority of deputies did not assure his authority. Without the support of Lafayette and the National Guard and at least the acquiescence of the armed population his

[23] *Ibid.*, p. 829.
[24] Jacques Laffitte, "Les Trois Glorieuses," pp. 319-20; Bérard, *Souvenirs*, pp. 141-46; Dupin, *Mémoires*, p. 153.
[25] Laffitte, "Trois Glorieuses," p. 320.

elevation might lead only to civil war. He knew that pro-Orléanist posters had been ripped from walls, that cries of "Plus de Bourbons!" and "Mort aux Bourbons!" included the younger as well as the older branch of the family, and Bérard had warned him that only quick action could fore-stall the proclamation of the republic. From Barrot he had learned that Lafayette had that morning expressed his favor for a constitutional monarchy, and he resolved to make a bold bid for the general's endorsement, hoping to win with it the support of the National Guard and the approval of the people of Paris.[26]

With no escort save a single aide-de-camp Orléans, mounted on his mare, appropriately named "Clio," led the procession of deputies, Laffitte in his sedan chair at their head, out of the palace, through the crowds of the Place du Palais-Royal, across the Place du Carrousel to the quai. The cheers and applause that heartened them at the outset of their journey dwindled as they moved eastward past the Pont-Neuf, and on the Place de Grève the hostile crowd greeted them with cries of "A bas les Bourbons!" "A bas le Duc d'Orléans!" A single ball fired from a musket easily concealed in an overlooking window or from a bystander's pistol could have ended the life of the Duke and the hopes of his supporters, but he rode forward with remarkable courage and coolness and dismounted before the entrance to the Hôtel de Ville.[27] Lafayette, together with the members of the Municipal Commission, stood there to receive him, and the two walked arm in arm up the steps and to the great hall, thronged with men of all ranks and conditions, some of them republicans who made little effort to conceal their hostility. Orléans, Lafayette, the municipal commissioners, and the deputies formed a semicircle facing the others, and Jean Viennet, deputy of the Hérault (apparently chosen

---

[26] Bérard, *Souvenirs*, pp. 142-45; Barrot, *Mémoires*, I, 123, 129; BHVP, Série 23, "Les Trois Glorieuses vues par De Creuze, peintre," MS, p. 3; Lafayette, *Mémoires*, VI, 410.

[27] In the Musée Carnavalet is a three dimensional diorama of the scene in front of the Hôtel de Ville as Lafayette welcomed Orléans.

because he had, in Laffitte's words, "a superb voice") read the proclamation of the deputies. The promise of the "public liberties" at the end won applause and bravos, and when the Duke reaffirmed his commitment to them, Lafayette advanced and shook his hand warmly. Within this room the Duke's cause seemed assured, but through the open windows came a chorus of "Vive la République" and "A bas le Duc d'Orléans!" Someone produced a large tricolor flag, and, taking it, Lafayette and Orléans advanced together (the sources do not permit saying who led whom) to a balcony overlooking the Place de Grève. On seeing the pair the crowd shouted, "Vive Lafayette!" but ignored his companion. The two men dramatically embraced, and from the crowd below came a thunderous response, "Vive le Duc d'Orléans!" "Vive Lafayette!"[28]

"The republican kiss of Lafayette," wrote Lamartine long after the event, "had made a king." But at the time the issues at stake had not been so clearly resolved. Metternich, hearing of the episode from the French ambassador, observed cynically, "A kiss is a small effort to smother a Republic; do you believe that you can attribute the same power to all kisses in the future?"[29] Orléans did not carry away from the Hôtel de Ville that day, as Barrot avowed, "the most beautiful crown in the world." He had by his visit achieved only a popular investiture in the office of lieutenant-general, affirming the investiture by the deputies. The lingering menace of the proclamation of a republic, the threat of the Municipal Commission's becoming a new commune had for the moment been eliminated. Orléans could confront the Bourbons and their ministers as the spokesman of a nominally united revolution, and with the double authority of popular and quasi-parliamentary sanction he could take into his hands the instruments of governmental authority.

Even Lafayette's endorsement did not swing all popular

[28] Laffitte, "Trois Glorieuses," pp. 323-28; Lafayette, Mémoires, VI, 409-10; Bérard, Souvenirs, pp. 146-48; Barrot, Mémoires, I, 124-25; Bonnelier, Mémorial, pp. 109-16; Guizot, Mémoires, II, 28-29.

[29] Clemens von Metternich-Winneburg, Mémoires, documents et écrits divers (Paris, 1880-84), V, 22-23.

support to Orléans. Proclamations announcing his designation as lieutenant-general were torn from walls, and men
charged with posting them were beaten up in the streets of
Paris. An officer who attempted to go from quarter to
quarter to read the proclamation in the streets was seized
by "a furious crowd," relieved of his horse and sword, and
held prisoner for a time at the Hôtel de Ville. Hostile
placards appeared on walls. Young republicans protested to
Lafayette against the direction that he had given to events,
and he, apparently having misgivings, decided that he must
make clear to the Lieutenant-General his political stand and
the guarantees that he expected as the price of his and his
followers' support. On August 1 the general, accompanied
by members of the Municipal Commission, adorned for the
first time with their tricolor sashes of office, called upon the
Lieutenant-General in the Palais-Royal. Here the Duke
charmed the naive General, and the General coined a
phrase that perhaps did as much as the famed kiss to
reconcile republicans to the newly emerging regime.[30]

"You know," declared Lafayette, "that I am a republican
and that I regard the constitution of the United States as
the most perfect that ever existed."

"I think as you do," replied the Duke; "it is impossible to
have spent two years in America and not to be of that
opinion; but do you believe that in France's situation, in the
present state of opinion, it would be proper for us to adopt
that constitution?"

"No, what the French people must have today is a popular
throne surrounded by republican institutions, completely
republican."

"That is precisely what I think," replied Orléans.[31]

[30] Lafayette, *Mémoires*, VI, 410-11; BHVP, Série 23, Armand Marrast, "Document pour l'histoire de France," MS: Armand Marrast,
*Programme de l'Hôtel de Ville ou récit de ce qui est passé depuis le
31 juillet jusqu'au 6 août 1830* (Paris, 1831), pp. 5-7; Barrot, *Mémoires*, I, 125-26.

[31] Lafayette, *Mémoires*, VI, 411. A letter in the Lafayette Papers, AN,
252 AP 2, confirms this version of Lafayette's statement concerning
the throne. Lafayette insisted that he did not say, "a popular throne
is the best of republics," a statement frequently atributed to him.

Lafayette returned to the Hôtel de Ville and assured his followers that the Duke shared their views on the future of France.[32] During the succeeding week they directed their belligerence against the Bourbons and their political energies toward reminding the deputies engaged in revising the Charter of the wishes of the party of the Hôtel de Ville.

On July 31 the Municipal Commission issued a proclamation addressed to "the people of Paris." "Charles X," it began, "has ceased to reign in France." On the same day an officer of Lafayette's staff who was attempting to win over troops covering Saint-Cloud asked the general for a statement on the present situation of the Bourbons, and Lafayette made an even more sweeping declaration, "The royal family has ceased to reign."[33] Both pronouncements expressed a wish rather than a fact, for Charles X, surrounded by the elite troops of his army and by his faithful ministers, remained at Versailles only eighteen miles from Paris, and his new chief minister was in the capital itself. Mortemart's midnight interview with Orléans had led him to believe that the Duke would support the accession of the Duc de Bordeaux.[34] Throughout the day, however, while the deputies and the Municipal Commission and Lafayette installed Orléans as lieutenant-general, with ominous implications for the Bourbons, Mortemart failed to establish effective contact with a single *de facto* authority in the capital. In his brief appearance in history Mortemart tried to carry out the mandate that the King had given him, but he was unable to master the swiftly moving events. In the morning of August 1 he conceded to a group of peers gathered in his apartment, "I have resisted the torrent as long as I could; it has overthrown me." The deputies, he said, had pronounced the dethronement of Charles X, which was not yet true. "I hope, nevertheless," he added, "that with the aid of the Chamber of Peers I can establish

[32] Lafayette, *Mémoires*, VI, 411, 581; Lecuyer, *Révolution de Juillet*, p. 124.

[33] *Moniteur*, Aug. 1, 1830, p. 829; Lafayette, *Mémoires*, VI, 405.

[34] Pasquier, *Mémoires*, VII, 299-301.

the rights of the Duc de Bordeaux." But the statement carried little conviction; he knew that Orléans had asked for the return of the letter he had written to Charles declaring his resolution never to accept the crown. The next royal moves in the struggle for power came from the King.[35]

The court had ended its nocturnal retreat from Saint-Cloud at the Trianon Palace about 7 in the morning of Saturday, July 31. The King called his old ministers around him and told them that he had given up almost all hope of an agreement with Paris. At the moment, however, he had no alternative to propose, and the meeting adjourned to await the arrival of Angoulême from Saint-Cloud and Sèvres. The ministers agreed among themselves that salvation lay in resisting the revolution, and they resolved to recapture initiative for the King. Their plan, informally discussed among themselves in the preceding two days, was to move the seat of the government immediately to Tours, to call to the scene the diplomatic corps, the law courts, and the principal administrative bodies, to summon the chambers to meet there on August 15, and to quarantine the revolutionary contagion in Paris by intercepting all communications between the capital and the provinces. The ministers drew up ordinances to put the plan into effect and drafted instructions to prefects, procureurs-general, tax collectors, and military and naval authorities. Peyronnet composed a proclamation to the French people announcing the determination of the King to combat the revolution with all his resources and calling on all citizens to rally to the support of the monarchy.[36]

[35] Lecuyer, *Révolution de Juillet*, p. 65; Pasquier, *Mémoires*, VI, 301.
[36] Guernon-Ranville, *Journal*, pp. 197-98, 201-3; Haussez, *Mémoires*, II, 293, 295, 298; Guillaume de Montbel, *1787-1813: souvenirs du Comte de Montbel, ministre de Charles X* (Paris, 1913), p. 250. The ministers' hope of winning support of the foreign diplomats in Paris to the royalist cause was stillborn. On July 30 the diplomatic corps in Paris had met to determine what actions its members should take in the revolutionary circumstances. Only the papal nuncio and the ambassadors of two secondary powers wanted the corps to join the King at Saint-Cloud. The English and Russian ambassadors, having been convinced by Talleyrand that the Orléanist solution of-

The ministers' bold initiative rested on two assumptions—that the Royal Guard and the Line outside Paris would fight for the King and that the provinces were loyal to the Bourbons. Reports of disaffection in Versailles and Rouen raised doubts of the latter, and defections among the Guards belied the former. On the Pont de Sèvres that morning Angoulême had ordered a battalion of the 3d Regiment of the Guard to fire on a crowd of armed men attempting to force the bridge. The guardsmen had refused. Six companies of Swiss, attacked in the Park of Saint-Cloud, threw down their arms, and artillerymen commanded to fire on them took their pieces across the bridge and joined the insurgents. The Dauphin soon ordered his troops to withdraw to Versailles, and in early afternoon they arrived at the Trianon hot, hungry, and discouraged. In Versailles they found the tricolor flying, the National Guard organizing, and a population eager to subvert royal troops.[37]

Angoulême's retreat had left Saint-Cloud undefended, and shortly after his departure a column of insurgents from Paris broke into the palace and pillaged parts of it before National Guard and Polytechnicians could restore order and mount guards over the building.[38]

The ministers had nearly completed their drafting of the ordinances and the proclamation when a messenger interrupted them to inform them that the court was leaving for Rambouillet. The arrival of Angoulême's discouraged troops had apparently determined the King to seek a more secure refuge and to remove the army from the corrupting

---

fered the best guarantee against the republic and against war, won the others to remaining in Paris, which was tantamount to repudiating Charles and endorsing his most potent rival. Mantoux, "Talleyrand en 1830," pp. 280-81.

[37] Marmont, *Mémoires*, VIII, 298-99, 315; Montbel, *Souvenirs*, p. 250; AS, D 4AZ 1181, "Précis," pp. 23-28; AHMG, D⁸ 131, Gentil to Gérard, July 31, 1830; BHVP, NA 153, Folio 381, Membre du Conseil municipal du 10ᵉ Arrond. to Commission du Gouvernement provisoire, Aug. 2, 1830.

[38] AN, F¹ᵈ III 81, Maire de Sèvres to CRN, Jan. 7, 1831; J. Bouer to CRN, May 28, 1831; BHVP, NA 153, Folio 325, Lt. 9ᵉ Légion, Garde nat., to Lafayette, July 31.

influence of Paris. Again grooms and coachmen prepared carriages and baggage wagons and harnessed horses, and about three o'clock in the afternoon the royal procession resumed its flight westward from revolution. By the time the main body of troops left in the early evening most of the men were drunk. Many of them slipped away in the darkness. Some, firing their weapons wildly into the air, almost started a battle with troops of the Line encamped along the road. Charles and the court escorted by the Garde du Corps reached Rambouillet in the evening and established themselves as best they could in the palace. In recent years the King had maintained it only as a hunting lodge, and the sudden decision to leave the Trianon allowed no time to prepare it to receive the entire court and its retainers. Angoulême with the troops bivouacked for the night at the village of Trappes about twelve miles from Rambouillet. The next day he moved the infantry and light cavalry on to Rambouillet and stationed the 2d Swiss Regiment in the village of Le Perray at the point where the highroad to Versailles and Paris emerges from the forest of Rambouillet. A few miles farther east at Cognières the heavy cavalry division guarded the Paris road. This division, already corrupted while in Versailles, remained at its outpost only a day. On Monday morning, the three regiments of the division, their own colonels in the lead, regimental standards flying, left for Paris to join the emerging government. Before the Guard regiments left Trappes the colonels, alarmed by the increasing desertions of their men, met and discussed means of arranging with Paris for the rallying of their troops. They took no action at the moment, but the colonels of the two Swiss regiments, especially concerned lest the disbanding of the French regiments leave the Swiss alone exposed to popular hatred, asked for and obtained from the Lieutenant-General in Paris safe conducts for their troops to withdraw into Burgundy.[39]

[39] Guernon-Ranville, *Journal,* pp. 203-6; Montbel, *Souvenirs,* pp. 251-52; Marmont, *Mémoires,* VIII, 299-302, 315-16; AS, D 4AZ 1181, "Précis," pp. 27-29.

At the palace on Sunday morning the two remaining ministers, Montbel and Capelle, met with the King—after mass, as usual—and persuaded him that Mortemart's mission had failed and that the King must reaffirm the royal power by some conspicuous act of authority. They proposed vigorous measures to provide for the provisioning and payment of troops, an appeal to all faithful Frenchmen and especially to the Army of Africa and the troops at Saint-Omer and Lunéville, and to the royalist Vendée and Midi. Charles authorized them to draw up the necessary proclamations at once. The two ministers, filled with determination, lacked even pens and paper, and their first task was to seek out the subprefect of the arrondissement to borrow these most elementary tools of government. When they returned to the King with the proclamations for his signature, they found him with the Dauphin, sad and dejected. He now knew of the spreading dissolution of the army, and he had just learned of a plan to direct the population of Paris on Rambouillet in a repetition of the march of the women on Versailles on October 5, 1789. "Gentlemen," he said, "it is no longer a matter of proclamations. I have to read to you a very different act by which I appoint Monsieur the Duc d'Orléans lieutenant-general of the kingdom." To the ministers' dismayed protests the old king replied that this alone offered an alternative to his falling into the hands of Lafayette and becoming, like his brother forty-one years earlier, a prisoner of the people. He might, he hoped, by this appointment shame Orléans into abandoning his present course and induce him to defend the monarchy. Unable to dissuade Charles, the ministers copied the letter to Orléans as he dictated it, and a few minutes later a courier bearing the letter hurried through the palace gate and took the road to Paris.[40]

No reply had arrived by the succeeding morning, but news had come of the defection of the heavy cavalry division and

[40] Montbel, *Souvenirs*, pp. 258-62; Bérard, *Souvenirs*, pp. 158-69; Ange Maxence de Damas, *Mémoires, 1785-1862* (Paris, 1922, 1923), II, 183.

of retreat of the Swiss from their advanced post at Le Perray to Rambouillet, leaving the town and the ill-deployed troops in it uncovered. Marmont, supported by the Baron Maxence de Damas, a former minister of Charles and governor of the Duc de Bordeaux, now pressed upon the King their earnest judgment that the dynasty itself was mortally threatened and that the only hope for its survival lay in Charles's immediate abdication in favor of his grandson. The King hesitated, asked for an hour to consider. In the delay he drafted an act of abdication, which Damas found unacceptable, and in the end he affixed his signature to a text drawn up by Damas. The Dauphin signed it in turn, giving up his rights to the throne in favor of the young duke, his nephew. The document was both a formal abdication and, in giving orders to Orléans, an attempt to recapture control of events.[41]

Rambouillet, August 2, 1830

My cousin, I am too profoundly grieved by the troubles that afflict and could threaten my people not to have sought a means to prevent them. I have now resolved to abdicate the crown in favor of my grandson, the Duc de Bordeaux.

The Dauphin, who shares my views, also renounces his rights in favor of his nephew.

You will now, by virtue of your office of lieutenant-general of the kingdom, proclaim accession of Henry V to the crown. You will take, moreover, all measures that concern you to determine the forms of government during the minority of the new king.

. . . .

You will communicate my intentions to the diplomatic corps and you will inform me as soon as possible of the proclamation by which my grandson will be recognized King under the name of Henry V.

. . . .

41 Marmont, *Mémoires*, VIII, 300, 303-5; Damas, *Mémoires*, II, 183-84.

I renew to you, my cousin, the assurance of the sentiments with which I am your affectionate cousin.

Charles
Louis-Antoine[42]

An hour short of midnight the King's courier arrived at the Palais-Royal to deliver the act of abdication. He found Orléans alone with Dupin, the two of them working on the Duke's address to the opening session of the chambers the next afternoon. In the hours and days since his double investiture on the thirty-first the Duke had moved resolutely to establish his hold on the instruments of authority. He had not long been back at the Palais-Royal that afternoon when the arms of the telegraphic semaphores began to move, dispatching to the commanding generals of three critical military districts announcement of the appointment of the lieutenant-general and orders to suspend all troop movements and to raise the tricolor. In the evening the same orders went out to five additional district commanders and to the general commanding the Department of the Finistère in royalist Brittany. The next day the new provisional minister of war, General Gérard, repeated the order to all nineteen military districts. He gave emergency command over five districts in the Vendée to General Maximilien Lamarque, who had suppressed the royalist rising there during the One Hundred Days. On August 2 Gérard advised Bourmont, commander of the army in Algeria, of events in Paris and ordered him to raise the tricolor and to suspend orders for the return of troops to France.[43] After the Duke left the Hôtel de Ville on July 31 the Municipal Commission in a final gesture as a *de facto* government appointed seven

[42] *Bulletin des lois du Royaume de France,* 9th Series, Vol. 1, Part 1, pp. 18-19.

[43] Dupin, *Mémoires,* p. 156; AHMG, D³ 131, Ministère de la Guerre to Cmdts. des 3ᵉ, 4ᵉ, 5ᵉ, 8ᵉ, 11ᵉ, 16ᵉ, 18ᵉ, 19ᵉ Divs. and to Gén. Cmdt., Dépt. du Finistère, July 31, 1830; Commissaire du Dépt. de la Guerre to MM les Lts.-gén. Cmdts. des Div. milit., Aug. 1, 1831; H 4, Algérie, Correspondance gén., Gérard to Bourmont, Aug. 2, 1830; AS, VK³ 17, Rejon to CRN, 12ᵉ Arrond., April 13, 1831; Charles Lesur, *Annuaire historique universel pour 1830* (Paris, 1832), pp. 261-62.

commissioners to manage temporarily the affairs of the national ministries.[44] The next day the Lieutenant-General named commissioners for four ministries and pointedly made no reference to the designations of the Municipal Commission, proclaiming by his omission that the executive power resided in his hands alone. To avoid any appearance of defiance he named Gérard, Louis, and Dupont de l'Eure to the posts given them by the Commission but as a reminder that the choices were his he moved Guizot from Public Instruction to the Interior. At the same time he appointed a new Prefect of Police in Paris, Amédée Girod de l'Ain, replacing Bavoux, the commission's appointee. Hereafter the commission confined its activities to municipal affairs. On August 1 Orléans exercised yet another royal power by summoning the Chamber of Peers and the Chamber of Deputies to meet on August 3. The next day he appointed a liberal lawyer and deputy, Louis Bernard, Procurer-General of the Royal Court of Paris and readied an ordinance, issued a day later, ordering the law courts henceforth to administer justice in the name of Louis-Philippe d'Orléans.[45]

By the time the King's abdication reached the Duke on August 2 the balance of power had shifted to his hands. He need treat the King's message only as an appeal, not as a command, and he and Dupin, discussing his response, never seriously considered obedience to the royal orders. Even had Orléans been disposed to become regent for the young Henry V, Lafayette, the National Guard, the activists among

[44] War: Gérard; Foreign Affairs: Edouard Bignon; Finance: Baron Joseph Louis; Justice: Dupin; Interior: Périer; Public Instruction: Guizot; Navy: Henri de Rigny. Dupin refused the appointment on the grounds that the commission had no authority to appoint a ministry; the commission replaced him with Jacques Dupont de l'Eure. Périer, apparently fearful that the Bourbons might yet prevail, managed to have his name removed from the list but not before the evening edition of the *Moniteur* for July 31 and the *Bulletin des lois* had published it. The *Moniteur* of August 1 reported the appointment of the Duc de Broglie to the Interior. *Moniteur*, August 1, 1830, p. 829; *Bulletin des lois*, 9th Series, Vol. 1, Part 1, p. 9; Dupin, *Mémoires*, p. 155; Bonnelier, *Mémorial*, pp. 118-28.

[45] *Moniteur*, Aug. 2, 1830, p. 833; Aug. 3, p. 836, Aug. 4, p. 841.

the people of Paris, and a powerful block of deputies, he knew, would never accept such a conclusion to the revolution. In his reply the Duke responded to both the recent messages from the King—the one appointing him Lieutenant-General of the Kingdom, the other the abdication. He declared that he was already Lieutenant-General by act of the deputies and could not accept the office from the King. He acknowledged receipt of the act of abdication but ignored the instruction to proclaim Henry V and the implication that the abdications were conditional on his acceptance of the Duc de Bordeaux as the new King. He gave his message to an aide to carry to Rambouillet, and he himself penned an ordinance formally transmitting the act of abdication to the archives of the Chamber of Peers. The next day he announced the double abdication to the assembled deputies and peers but spoke not a word of the Duc de Bordeaux.[46]

In the morning of August 3 a rumor spread across Paris that Charles had refused to leave Rambouillet and that royal troops had murdered emissaries sent to him by the Lieutenant-General. The cry "To Rambouillet! To Rambouillet!" echoed through the city's streets, and men took what arms they could find—muskets, swords, pikes, and kitchen skewers—and hurried to the Place Louis XVI and the Champs-Elysées, where they joined the National Guard ordered out by Lafayette. Commandeering buses, carriages, and wagons a crowd of 14,000 to 20,000 set off to drive the Bourbons out of France. Mystery still shrouds the origin of the movement. It was in part a spontaneous protest against the unpopular and recalcitrant ruler who seemed to be threatening the country with renewed troubles. Some royalists charged, however, that Orléanists staged the march to free Paris of its most turbulent population on the day of the opening of parliament. Odilon Barrot, returning early that morning from Rambouillet and an unsuccessful effort to induce the King to leave the country, did advise Orléans to

[46] Dupin, *Mémoires*, pp. 157-58; *Bulletin des lois*, 9th Series, Vol. 1, Part 1, p. 18; *Moniteur*, Aug. 4, 1830, p. 841.

172

coerce the King into leaving, presumably, although his explanation is obscure, because he feared that delay might aid the royalist cause or disturb the still precarious peace and order of Paris. The Duke sent instructions to Lafayette to call up 600 men from each of the twelve legions of the National Guard to march to Rambouillet, and he ordered Barrot together with De Schonen and Marshal Nicholas Maison to precede the column and to urge Charles to depart peacefully. Lafayette's orders to the legions went out that morning, and armed and unarmed guardsmen proceeded to the Champs-Elysées, their drums attracting hundreds of irregulars. The motley force that marched and rode away from the Champs-Elysées was described as "the most peculiar and the most interesting army ever seen." Along the way it acquired new recruits, including 2000 National Guardsmen from Rouen, who made it no less peculiar.[47]

Most of the men, one eye-witness recorded, carried chunks of meat and loaves of bread on their bayonets, but the provisioning of this irregular force posed formidable problems for the authorities along its route. The Prefect of the Seine-et-Oise, fearful of the depredations of the hungry horde moving across his department, appealed to his superior, the Commissioner of the Ministry of Interior, for a staggering quantity of bread. Paris could not furnish it, but Guizot did inform the prefect that the government would open a credit of 150,000 francs to pay the expenses incurred by the expedition, and in the departmental archives of the Seine-et-Oise are two fat bundles of claims filed against this credit, some of them unsettled three years later.[48]

[47] Henri Vienne, "Dix jours à Paris du dimanche 25 juillet au mardi 3 août 1830," *Mémoires* de la Société bourguignonne de géographie et d'histoire, VIII (1892), 115; A. J. de Marnay, *Memoires secrets et témoignages authentiques: chute de Charles, X, Royauté de Juillet; 24 février 1848* (Paris, 1875), pp. 22-23; Barrot, *Mémoires*, pp. 132-38; Lafayette, *Mémoires*, VI, 413, 415; Bérard, *Souvenirs*, pp. 170-72; *Moniteur*, Aug. 6, 1830, p. 850; Bonnelier, *Mémorial*, pp. 191-94; AS, VD⁴ 5870, Commission municipal de Paris to Maire, 2ᵉ Arrond., Aug. 3, 1830; BHVP, Série 23, "Historique des faits qui sont passés dans le 7ᵉ arrondissement les 28-29-30 juillet et 3 août 1830."

[48] Archives du Dépt. de Seine-et-Oise, IV.M.I³⁰, Comm. de l'Inté-

Barrot, De Schonen, and Maison left the column at Sèvres after urging General Claude Pajol, the nominal commander of "the most peculiar army," to halt its advance at Trappes lest closer approach to Rambouillet compromise their efforts to persuade Charles to withdraw peacefully. When the commissioners themselves arrived at Trappes, they sent to Marmont a request for a safe conduct, and within an hour mounted guards arrived to escort them to the palace. As they moved on, darkness had already fallen over the forest and park, but they could see the fires of the bivouacked troops and hear the cavalry horses stomping in their corrals, and they noticed some forty pieces of artillery emplaced around the chateau. Charles received them alone and asked brusquely, "Well, what do you want from me?" Barrot replied that a few miles behind them moved an armed force of Parisians and that they had come ahead to persuade him to avoid a new and useless conflict in which his most faithful supporters would perish.[49]

"I have abdicated, it is true," declared Charles with a vigor that seemed to preclude compromise, "but it is in favor of my grandson, and we are all determined here to defend his rights to the last drop of our blood."

Barrot argued that the catastrophe of civil war, which now confronted them, begun in the name of the young heir, would destroy forever his chances of occupying the throne. After some further exchange Charles asked to speak with Maison alone, and the others withdrew.

"How many are there?" he asked the old marshal.

Maison responded that he had no count but that he would estimate 60,000 to 80,000, probably two to three times the actual number. Charles then excused the marshal, saying he would announce his decision in fifteen minutes. A quarter of an hour later a note from Marmont informed the com-

rieur to Préfet de Seine-et-Oise, Aug. 3, 1830; Commune de Trappes, Etat récapitulatif des fournitures faites . . . pour les subsistences des troupes . . . , Aug. 8, 1830; the two bundles in the archives of the Seine-et-Oise are catalogued as IV.M.1[30-31].

[49] Barrot, *Mémoires*, pp. 139-40.

missioners that the royal family would leave immediately for Maintenon and that Charles would accept the escort and directions of the commissioners. In a few minutes the roll of drums and the call of cavalry bugles echoed across the park summoning the troops to the road, and at eleven o'clock the royal carriages escorted by the Garde du Corps moved out of the palace yard. After them followed a still lengthy baggage train and the remaining Guards and gendarmes. By 1 A.M. August 4 Rambouillet was deserted of its erstwhile inhabitants.[50]

The three commissioners preceded the ex-King to Maintenon, but before leaving Rambouillet Barrot sent an urgent, almost a desperate, message to Pajol. "The king has just decided to leave. Our mission has achieved this first happy result; but, for God's sake, give the firmest orders that your men not follow us." The advance elements of the column had reached Le Perray in the evening of August 3, and the next morning about 300 men came into Rambouillet. Officers of the National Guard posted sentries around the palace and saved it from devastation. A baggage wagon carrying the crown jewels, which was surrendered to Barrot the night before and confided to the mayor of Rambouillet, was turned over to the Parisian volunteers along with several carriages to escort back to Paris. The main body of the "peculiar army" never reached Rambouillet. Its mission accomplished and—perhaps more decisive—its enthusiasm eroded by heat, hunger, and blistered feet, it turned about and straggled back to the capital.[51]

Charles, some contemporaries and some historians have charged, blundered when he decided against using the troops with him to disperse the disorderly column of insurgents from Paris. But renewed bloodshed would surely only have

50 *Ibid.*, pp. 140-42; Marmont, *Mémoires*, VIII, 317; AS, D 4AZ 1181, "Précis," p. 36.
51 Barrot, *Mémoires*, p. 142; Marmont, *Mémoires*, VIII, 314, 317; *Moniteur*, Aug. 5, 1830, p. 845; AN, F1e III 81, Deposition of Pajol [1831]; Deposition of Lt.-gén. Boyer, May 25, 1931; Deposition of Lt.-col. Dégousée, May 15, 1931; Lafayette, *Mémoires*, VI, 415; Bonnelier, *Mémorial*, pp. 205-11, 253-58.

added to the hostility against the Bourbons. Marmont, who on August 2 had resumed command of the forces around the King, concluded, and with good reason, that resistance was militarily impossible. A thousand cavalrymen and half a dozen artillery pieces could have put the Parisian army to flight in open battle, but Marmont that evening had neither a thousand cavalry nor the choice of suitable terrain. Of the cavalry units at Rambouillet only the Garde du Corps, fewer than 700 men, was certainly loyal, and they could not be spared from guarding the person of the King. Cavalry, moreover, would be ineffectual against an enemy dispersed and hidden in a wood, and the first units of the insurgent force had by the evening of August 3 reached the Forest of Rambouillet. The town of Rambouillet itself, "a funnel in the middle of the woods," Marmont called it, offered no conditions favorable for a defensive stand, and the troops there, discouraged by the indecision of the royal government and decimated by mass desertions, formed but a shadow of an army. The infantry regiments of the Royal Guard combined could muster but 1350 men; one regiment, the 6th, had only 120. The only course that offered the Bourbon cause even a hope of recovery was, in Marmont's judgment, withdrawal to Maintenon and on to the Loire valley, where amid a friendly population faithful royalists might yet proclaim King Henry V.[52]

The next morning, August 4, at Maintenon when Marmont waited on the King to receive orders for continuation of the march to the Loire, Charles informed him that he had accepted the commissioners' urgent proposal that he leave the country. The royal party would proceed not to the Loire and the Vendèe and to a renewal of the struggle but to Cherbourg and to exile. Charles agreed to dismiss all his troops except the four companies of *Gardes du Corps*, the *Gendarmerie d'élite*, about 200 cavalrymen and an equal number of infantry of the Guard, and a battery of artillery—

[52] Damas, *Mémoires*, II, 189, 191-92; Paul Thureau-Dangin, *Histoire de la Monarchie de Juillet* (Paris, 1888-1900), I, 28; Marmont, *Mémoires*, VIII, 313-18.

about 1200 men in all, who would escort him to the frontier. When the family and the court resumed their journey at noon that day the remaining Guards, the remnants of the infantry of the Line, the Lancers, the Hussars, and the artillery drew up along the road to Dreux and rendered a final salute to the old King and the young heir. As the royal family disappeared over the hill, the troops turned in the opposite direction, to Chartres, where provisions awaited them and where the next day Gérard informed them that the new government would shortly dissolve the Royal Guard and incorporate into the Line its men who wished to remain in service.[53]

For the royal family the journey to Cherbourg was a calvary. Every village and town flew the tricolor from its highest tower or steeple; sullen crowds lined streets to watch the sad procession pass. At some stops loyal nobles called to pay their respects, but in public the only greetings that broke the silence were hostile or insulting. National Guardsmen assembled ominously in some larger towns; in Carentan National Guards and troops of the Line tried to take over the escort of the party from the Garde du Corps. Despite the trials of the journey Charles insisted on proceeding by very short stages, nominally to spare the horses but also in the forlorn hope that some miracle would yet save the crown for his family. In the first five days after leaving Maintenon the party never traveled more than twenty-two miles, and on Sunday, August 8, they settled down for a day of rest at Argentan, still not 120 miles from Paris. The party's slow progress disturbed the new authorities in the capital, and Guizot pressed the commissioners to speed the King on his way. The sojourn in Argentan stirred suspicion in the neighborhood that the royal family might flee into Brittany and inspired a company of National Guard from Alençon, twenty-seven miles to the south, to march on the

53 Marmont, *Mémoires*, VIII, 318-21; Barrot, *Mémoires*, I, 143-44; Damas, *Mémoires*, II, 192; AS, D 4AZ 1181, "Précis," pp. 36, 38-40; Jean Vidalenc, *Le Département de l'Eure sous la monarchie constitutionnelle, 1814-1848* (Paris, 1952), p. 278.

town. The King and his party, now escorted only by the *Garde du Corps* and a few gendarmes, left Argentan on August 10, apparently unaware of the approaching guard, and advanced nearly thirty miles that day. On the thirteenth the reduced party reached Valognes, only twenty miles from Cherbourg, and remained there while the commissioners completed the arrangements for embarkation. Jules Dumont d'Urville, among the first naval officers in Paris to rally to Orléans, had leased for the new government two American ships, the "Charles Carroll" and the "Great Britain," at Le Havre and brought them to Cherbourg. Here he prepared two naval escort vessels for a voyage to Naples, where, the government at first believed, the King wished to go. Subsequent instructions authorized him to land the party at any destination Charles might choose save the Channel Islands or the Low Countries. On Sunday, the fifteenth, the four companies of the Garde du Corps turned their standards over to the King. He thanked each company for its fidelity and, moved to tears, expressed his hope that the Duc de Bordeaux would in time return the standards to them.[54]

At nine o'clock in the morning of August 16 the party left Valognes accompanied by the Garde du Corps, who, Marmont insisted against the protests of the commissioners, must escort the King to his ship. At the city's gates they ignored the warning of the local National Guard that it could not answer for the party's safety if the Guard did not wear the tricolor cockade. Along the streets some hostile shouts greeted them, but the column reached the military port, where the ships awaited, without delaying incident. The two leading companies of the Garde du Corps lined the quai. The carriages of the entourage arrived, and the handful of faithful supporters gathered opposite the "Great

[54] Marmont, *Mémoires*, VIII, 321-30; Barrot, *Mémoires*, I, 147-75, 567-91; Damas, *Mémoires*, II, 192-93, 195-97; Guizot, *Mémoires*, II, 38-39; AN, F¹ᵈ III 81, Hervé Hamel to Ministre de l'Intérieur, Oct. 3, 1831; Achille de Vaulabelle, *Histoire des deux Restaurations jusqu'à l'avénement de Louis-Philippe (de janvier 1813 à octobre 1830)*, 5th ed. (Paris, 1860), VIII, 433-36.

Britain." At Argentan Charles had asked the commissioners to provide for a party of two or three hundred exclusive of servants; fewer than seventy arrived at Cherbourg, so little appealing was the cause of a fallen king. Amid a silence broken only by the sobs of the faithful, Charles and the Dauphin alighted from their carriage; next came the Duchesse d'Angoulême, the daughter of Louis XVI, dressed all in black, fleeing a revolution for the fourth time in her life. For the young Duc de Bordeaux walking hand in hand with his governor, the Baron de Damas, the Garde du Corps, forbidden to make any shout of loyalty, silently presented arms. Aboard the "Great Britain," which flew the white flag of the Bourbons, Charles bade farewell to the officers of the Guard and to others who would remain in France, thanked the government's commissioners for their attention and their consideration, and at 2:30 told Dumont d'Urville that he was ready to leave. Within a few minutes the two ships, moved by a brisk offshore breeze and an ebb tide, pulled away from the quai and made for the open sea. By six o'clock the two vessels and their escort had disappeared over the horizon. The next morning the ships were off the Isle of Wight, and late that evening the "Great Britain" and the "Charles Carroll" and the larger of the two escort vessels dropped anchor in the harbor of Cowes. Negotiations with the British authorities for Charles's asylum in Britain consumed the next several days. The ladies and children took quarters in Cowes, but Charles and the Dauphin remained aboard the "Great Britain" until the twenty-third. On that day the royal party boarded a British naval yacht and sailed for Weymouth, whence they traveled overland to Castle Lulworth in the county of Dorset, put at Charles's disposal by its owner, Sir Thomas Weld, a prominent English Catholic. Five hundred bottles of Bordeaux thoughtfully placed aboard the "Great Britain" and the "Charles Carroll" by Dumont d'Urville and now moved to Lulworth eased the family's adaptation to English life and fare.[55]

55 Barrot, *Mémoires*, I, 178-85; Marmont, *Mémoires*, VIII, 330-33;

Charles's ministers emerged from the ordeal less well than he. They became scapegoats of popular resentment against the Bourbons and the fallen ministry, and the new government offered them no safe conducts into exile. Leaving the King at the Trianon or at Rambouillet they fled from one uncertain refuge to the next until they reached the frontier or submitted to arrest.

In mid-August an ill-dressed servant whose mistress was stopping at a leading hotel in Granville on the Normandy coast attracted attention in a disreputable café of the town by his well-bred manner. Questioned, he eventually admitted to the Mayor of Granville that he was Prince Polignac and that he had hoped to embark for the island of Jersey. The mayor and the National Guard, concerned for his safety, hurried him off to Saint-Lo. Here Barrot and the other commissioners returning from Cherbourg saw him, and, fearful that the Garde du Corps, which had been ordered to Saint-Lo for disbanding, might make an effort to release him or that he might fall victim of the hostile population, they ordered the commander of the Gendarmerie at Caen to proceed at once with all available troops to Saint-Lo, and they advised the government in Paris to move the prisoner without delay to a safer confinement.[56]

Guernon-Ranville and Chantelauze left Rambouillet at dawn on August 1 and walked to Chartres without incident, but the next day a band of armed men detained them on the outskirts of Tours and the following morning turned them over to the National Guard of Chartres, who held them prisoners until authorities in Paris decided on their disposition. On August 26 several officers of the National Guard of Paris arrived to escort the two ministers together with Peyronnet, whose flight had ended in the same district even

---

"Journal de Dumont d'Urville" in Vaulabelle, *Histoire*, VIII, 456-60, 471, 476; Damas, *Mémoires*, II, 198-99, 201-6; AHMG, E⁵ 1, Gén. Cmdt., 14ᵉ Div. milit. to Ministre de la Guerre, Aug. 19, 1830.

[56] AHMG, E⁵ 1, Gén. Cmdt., 14ᵉ Div. milit. to Ministre de la Guerre, Aug. 18, Aug. 19, 1830; *National* (Paris), Aug. 20, 1830; Barrot, *Mémoires*, I, 187-91, 593-94, 595-96.

more quickly than theirs, to the fortress of Vincennes. They reached the fortress the next day, rejoining Polignac, who arrived at the same time from Normandy. Haussez left the King at the Trianon on July 31, found his way to the coast and across the Channel, and on August 19 boarded the "Great Britain" in Cowes harbor to pay his respects to Charles. Montbel and Capelle made their separate ways in disguise from Rambouillet to the eastern frontier and crossed, the one into Switzerland, the other into Luxembourg. Capelle and Marshal Bourmont—the government relieved him of his command but pressed no charges against him—followed Haussez to England and joined the exiled court.[57]

At mid-day on August 3, when Charles was still at Rambouillet and National Guards and armed citizens were streaming out of the western gates of Paris to administer another dose of revolution to the King, the deputies and peers converged on the Palais-Bourbon for the opening session of the chambers. The deputies, more than 200 of the 417 elected in June and July, wore street clothes, having decided against donning their uniforms embellished with *fleurs de lis*. A few peers—only seventy of the 331 appeared— wore the informal dress of their office with *fleurdelisés* collars and cuffs, but each had a tricolor ribbon in his coat or hat. Spectators had early filled the public galleries; the space reserved for the diplomatic corps remained empty save for a few junior secretaries. At the front of the chamber carpenters had erected a temporary platform, and on it now stood a throne and two stools. Three large tricolor flags hid the *fleurs de lis* on the hangings above the throne. At 12:30 the sound of saluting cannon announced the departure of the Lieutenant-General from the Palais-Royal, and about twenty minutes later the deputies could hear the approaching National Guard band that led the Duke's procession.

[57] Haussez, *Mémoires*, II, 323-55; "Journal de Dumont d'Urville," p. 467; Montbel, *Souvenirs*, pp. 249, 265-88; Damas, *Mémoires*, II, 215-25; AHMG, H⁴, Gérard to Bourmont, Aug. 2, 1830; Gérard to Comte de Clauzel, Aug. 11, 1830.

The Duchess and the younger children arrived first and occupied seats in the visitors' gallery. At ten o'clock the Duke, wearing the uniform of the National Guard and with a tricolor ribbon in his tunic, entered the chamber accompanied by a delegation of deputies and peers, his second son—the Duc de Nemours (his eldest son had not yet arrived in Paris), General Gérard, and the Prefect of the Seine. To the applause and cheers of the assembly he mounted the platform, saluted the deputies and peers several times, and took his place on the stool to the right of the throne. The Duc de Nemours sat on the stool opposite him.[58]

When the ovation had subsided, Orléans invited his auditors to be seated, and he delivered a short speech, a substitute for the customary address from the throne. The Duke himself had written the original text, but Guizot and Dupin rewrote it, and their revision, which the Duke read to the chambers, reflected their conservative view of the revolution. He accepted, he declared, all the consequences of his attachment to "the principles of a free government," but in his explanation of his present stand he made clear that he saw his rôle as defensive. "I hastened [to Paris], firmly resolved to devote myself to all that the circumstances would demand of me, . . . to reestablish the rule of law, to save threatened liberty, to render impossible the return of such great afflictions, by assuring forever the power of that Charter, whose name invoked during the battle was again invoked after the victory."[59] Beyond calling the attention of the chambers to the need to revise Article 14 of the Charter and reminding it of three of the six measures on which the deputies themselves had proposed action in their declaration of July 30, the Lieutenant-General presented no program either of constitutional revision or of legislation. He reported the abdication of Charles X and the Dauphin but

---

[58] Dupin, *Mémoires*, ii, 160; Bérard, *Souvenirs*, p. 180; *Moniteur*, Aug. 4, 1830, pp. 841, 842; *National*, Aug. 4, 1830; *Courrier français* (Paris), Aug. 4, 1830.

[59] *Moniteur*, Aug. 4, 1830, p. 841.

said nothing of the Duc de Bordeaux nor made any suggestion of how the present interregnum might be ended. The negative emphasis of the speech appealed to the majority of deputies and peers, who, like Guizot and Dupin, would limit the consequences of the revolution, and they gave their loudest applause to the Duke's reference to the preservation of the Charter. At the conclusion of the address the Lieutenant-General and his party withdrew, and the chambers in the leisurely manner of untroubled times adjourned until the next day.[60]

Some deputies feared that delay in establishing a definitive government favored the cause of extreme factions on both Right and Left. The Duc de Bordeaux still had many partisans, and a long interregnum might enable them to induce a majority of the conservative Chamber of Deputies to call the young duke to the throne. On the other hand, failure to give satisfaction to popular aspirations expressed in the revolution might drive support to republicans. In the evening a group of deputies and journalists who had gathered at Laffitte's house agreed that the circumstances demanded a quick end to the provisional and the establishment of a definitive government capable of rallying the country behind it. The Orléanists had a solution—the Duc d'Orléans as a constitutional monarch bound by contract to respect popular rights and liberties, and the *National* kept it before deputies and public. Bérard now suggested it to the group gathered at Laffitte's. He urged the presentation to the chamber of a proposal to call Orléans to the throne subject to his acceptance of specific conditions laid down by the chamber. Encouraged by the response to his suggestion Bérard went home and wrote out a definitive text; its essence was concentrated in three paragraphs.[61]

A solemn pact united the French people with its monarch; that pact has just been broken. The rights which

[60] *Ibid.*, pp. 841, 842; Bérard, *Souvenirs*, p. 184.

[61] Bérard, *Souvenirs*, pp. 186-89; Achille de Broglie, *Souvenirs, 1785-1870* (Paris, 1886), III, 390; Duvergier de Hauranne, *Histoire*, x, 644-45; *National*, July 31, Aug. 2, 3, 1830.

derived from it have ceased to exist. He who breaks the contract cannot, under any pretext, require its enforcement.

.   .   .   .

The instability of the present government encourages the fomentors of discord; let us put an end to that. A supreme law, that of necessity, placed arms in the hands of the people of Paris to repulse aggression. That law has moved us to name as provisional chief and as a means of salvation, a Prince who is a sincere friend of constitutional institutions. The same law requires that we install that Prince as the definitive head of our government.

But whatever the confidence that he inspires in us, the rights that we are called to defend demand that we fix the conditions by which he will receive power. Odiously deceived on many occasions we are justified in insisting on firm guarantees.[62]

He proposed as conditions the "necessary guarantees" promised by the deputies in their declaration of July 30 and a number of others, some that made the deputies' proposals more specific—abolition of the double vote, reduction of age and tax qualifications of voters and deputies—others that went well beyond them—complete equality before the law for all religions and the abolition of the hereditary nobility.[63]

The next morning Bérard deleted from his text the demand for abolition of the nobility, having decided that it would arouse unnecessary opposition to his project. He discussed the whole proposal with Dupont de l'Eure, the commissioner of justice in the provisional government, and with a number of deputies and concluded that the support for it justified his taking it to the chamber. About one o'clock that afternoon the commissioners arriving at the Palais-Bourbon sought out Bérard to tell him that the Lieutenant-General had learned of his proposition and wholly approved

[62] Bérard, *Souvenirs*, pp. 189-92.   [63] *Ibid.*, p. 191.

it, but he favored adding further guarantees of the public liberties, and he thought that instead of simply prescribing principles to guide future revision of the Charter the chamber should revise it immediately. Would Bérard delay presentation of his project, they asked, until they could discuss these changes? They wanted his help, and they would send for him that evening to join their discussions. The ministers had at the outset found Bérard's project too radical, and they flattered him into delaying his presentation of it to gain time for preparation of a more moderate substitute. The Lieutenant-General appointed Broglie and Guizot, two of his most conservative advisers, to draw up the government's project.[64]

The two men, in frequent consultation with the ministers, worked at their assignment through August 4 and 5 never finding time to call in Bérard, although they did have a long consultation with Lafayette. The next morning, August 6, Guizot handed to Bérard a draft of the government's project. It differed from his proposition in three significant ways. First, discarding the argument that Charles X had broken his contract with the French people, Guizot and Broglie stated simply that owing to the abdications of Charles and his son and the departure of the royal family from France the throne was vacant and must be filled. Second, the ministers proposed specific and immediate changes in a third of the articles of the Charter. Third, they wrote into the constitutional project itself the matters on which the chambers would promise legislation. The ministers, having failed to find an amenable deputy to bring their project before the chambers as his own, wanted Bérard to present it. He had three hours in which to revise it into form acceptable to him.

Bérard made few changes in the government's proposals. He first removed from the preamble the reference to the abdications lest one infer from it that Orléans as a Bourbon had a legitimate right to the crown. Bérard wanted to make

[64] *Ibid.*, pp. 193-95, 198-99, 202-4; Broglie, *Souvenirs*, III, 390-91.

clear that the chamber was freely granting the crown to the man of its choice. He eliminated mention of the royal family's departure, not wishing to place the new dynasty on a foundation that the Bourbons could undermine by remaining in France. He did not, however, restore the argument of the broken contract. In the ministers' revisions of particular articles of the Charter he made but four alterations, all of them intended to appease his democratic friends without real concession. After the revised articles Guizot and Broglie added, "The Chamber of Deputies declares . . . that it is necessary to provide successively and by separate laws" for seven reforms, which they specified, including in their list all but one of the laws promised by the deputies in their declaration of July 30. The one omission, reform of the electoral law, Bérard restored, and he proposed other changes intended to make these commitments more binding and precise.[65]

In the afternoon Bérard presented the Guizot-Broglie project with his revisions to the chamber. He gave no hint that it had not come entirely from his own hand. He was, as Rémusat observed, "a very useful instrument . . . of Doctrinaire policy." The principal changes this triumvirate proposed in the Charter began with the suppression of the Preamble, which made the Charter a gift from the crown not a right of the nation. They would also suppress Article 6, which declared "the Catholic, Apostolic, and Roman religion" the religion of the state. The power to issue ordinances for "the execution of laws and the security of the State," granted by Article 14, they would limit to enforcement of laws, precluding, they hoped, a repetition of Charles X's use of this power. Other changes included the granting of legislative initiative, hitherto the sole prerogative of the crown, to each house; the ending of the secrecy of debates of the Chamber of Peers; the reduction of the minimum age of deputies from forty to thirty years and of electors from

[65] Bérard, *Souvenirs*, pp. 209-33, facsimile reproduction of the project prepared by Guizot and Broglie appended opposite page 508; Broglie, *Souvenirs*, III, 390-96, 400.

thirty to twenty-five; and the banning of extraordinary ju-dicial courts or commissions—the allusion was to the *cours prévôtales* of 1815 and 1816—"under any designation what-soever." The third part of the project committed the Cham-ber of Deputies to the prompt passage of laws to achieve nine prescribed reforms:

1. Extension of trial by jury to minor offenses and notably to those of the press.
2. The responsibility of ministers and secondary agents of power.
3. Reelection of deputies appointed to public office.
4. Annual vote of the army appropriation.
5. Organization of the National Guard with the partici-pation of guardsmen in the choice of their officers.
6. A military code assuring the determination of officers' pay and promotions by law.
7. Election of departmental and municipal officials.
8. Public schools and freedom of education.
9. Abolition of the double vote and a new law govern-ing elections.

With a few exceptions these premises were concessions to "the party of the Hôtel de Ville" and to their supporters in the chamber and in the country. To these concessions Guizot and Broglie had added and Bérard had retained another, this to appease the mounting clamor against the hereditary peerage. They proposed that "all the nominations and new creations of peers made under the reign of King Charles X be declared null and void." Bérard's announce-ment of this brought a particularly lively burst of applause from the listening deputies.[66]

When the applause had subsided, Bérard read his two most momentous paragraphs, paragraphs that would create a new dynasty of French kings under contract to the French people.

[66] *Moniteur*, Aug. 7, 1830, pp. 860-61.

On condition of the acceptance of these requirements and propositions the Chamber of Deputies declares finally that the interest of the French people calls to the throne H.R.H. Louis-Philippe d'Orléans, Duc d'Orléans, lieutenant-general of the kingdom, and his descendants in perpetuity, from male to male by order of primogeniture to the perpetual exclusion of women and their descendants.

In consequence, H.R.H. Louis-Philippe d'Orléans, lieutenant-general of the kingdom, will be invited to accept and to swear to the clauses and engagements stated above, the observation of the constitutional charter and the changes indicated; and, after having done so, to take the title of King of the French.[67]

Some voices from the Right of the chamber charged Bérard with destroying the Charter, but most of his auditors applauded. When he had finished his presentation, the deputies agreed to refer the project to committee, and at 3 P.M. the assembly adjourned. The president announced that the session would resume at 8 P.M. to hear the committee's report.[68]

A crowd of demonstrators around the Palais-Bourbon that afternoon had reminded the deputies of the need for haste in ending the uncertainties of the interregnum. In the week of indecision since the appointment of the Lieutenant-General republicans had taken heart again. They had no illusions about their ability to establish a French republic, but they did aspire to give substance to Lafayette's avowed ideal of "a popular throne surrounded by republican institutions." Some of them denied the chamber's right to revise the constitution or to bestow the crown, and others talked of throwing the deputies into the Seine, but they fixed primarily upon one issue—the abolition of the hereditary peerage. A hereditary legislative house seemed among the

---

[67] *Ibid.*, p. 861. The title "King of the French," which had more democratic overtones than "King of France and of Navarre," used by Louis XVIII and Charles X, was no revolutionary innovation in 1830. Guizot and Broglie took it from the Constitution of 1791.

[68] *Moniteur*, Aug. 7, 1830, p. 861.

least republican of institutions, and by editorials, petitions, and demonstrations they pressed the deputies to abolish it. The movement drew its support chiefly from students and young journalists and lawyers; in the afternoon of August 6 many of them assembled in the gardens, courts, and adjoining streets of the Palais-Bourbon threatening to rekindle the revolution if the deputies failed to end the hereditary peerage. Another group, on the Place de l'Odéon, signed a declaration protesting the chamber's assumption of constituent power; they planned to march on the Palais-Bourbon that evening to present their statement to the assembly. At eight o'clock, when the deputies returned for the evening session they had to push their way through menacing crowds, and even within the palace they could hear the angry shouts of demonstrators. Several deputies, Lafayette and Constant among them, went to the steps on the river side of the palace and spoke to the young men gathered there, urging them to withdraw. Lafayette promised that the case for an end to the peerage would have its advocates in the chamber. The demonstrators did depart but not without first threatening to return the next day if the deputies failed to satisfy their demands.[69]

Quiet had settled over the precincts of the Palais-Bourbon when Dupin, reporter for the committee appointed to examine Bérard's project, mounted the tribune to deliver his report. He brought no surprises to the assembly; the committee returned the project almost unchanged. They had inserted a phrase, borrowed from the Napoleonic Concordat of 1801 stating that Catholicism was "the religion of the majority of Frenchmen." Bérard had objected to this in committee, arguing first that statistical data had no place in a constitution, and, second that the statement was false. If the committee must retain it, they should alter it to read, "indifferentism is the religion of the majority of French-

[69] Bérard, *Souvenirs*, pp. 264-65; Duvergier de Hauranne, *Histoire*, x, 651-52, 654-55, 659-62; Guizot, *Mémoires*, II, 30-33; Claude de Rambuteau, *Mémoires* (Paris, 1905), pp. 185-86; Rémusat, *Mémoires*, II, 360.

men." Over the ordinance power the committee placed an additional safeguard, prescribing in Article 14 that the King never use ordinances to suspend laws. After the paragraph nullifying Charles X's creation of peers, the deputies added, "and to prevent the return of the grave abuses which have altered the principle of the peerage, Article 27 of the Charter, which grants to the king unlimited power to name peers, shall be submitted to a new examination in the session of 1831." In appearance a further assault upon the peerage, the proposal might serve a conservative purpose of postponing consideration of abolition to less troubled times.[70]

The ministry could be well pleased with the accomplishments of the day. Bérard had presented their proposals on the future government of France as his own, and they had moved through the chamber and its committee substantially unchanged. No commissioner took any part in the deliberations, and so skillfully—and apparently unwittingly—did Bérard play his role that not a single deputy charged the government with forcing its decisions on the chamber. The commissioners did grow concerned during the day over the rising threat of renewed violence. They would have preferred to leave the hereditary peerage untouched, but not at the cost of reviving disorder in the streets, possibly compromising the entire Orléanist settlement. In the evening, when Dupin completed presentation of his report and debate over procedures in considering it grew acrimonious, Guizot proposed adjournment until the next morning, nominally to allow time for printing and distributing the committee's report. Actually Guizot and his colleagues sought time to assess the danger of violence and to negotiate with the republicans before they took a stand on the hereditary peerage. After adjournment of the session Guizot charged two of his friends, Rémusat and Duvergier de Hauranne, to go to the Hôtel de Ville the next morning and to discover if the republicans would resort to violence if the

[70] *Moniteur*, Aug. 7, 1830, p. 852; Aug. 8, pp. 854-65; Bérard, *Souvenirs*, pp. 236-45.

chamber retained the hereditary peerage. They arrived when Lafayette was engaged in discussion with a number of the most active members of the "Aide-toi." They learned that Lafayette had already called on his followers to abandon their projects for intimidating the chamber, and he reiterated this advice to the "Aide-toi" and sent the members out to prevent any resort to arms. Rémusat and Duvergier dispatched this reassuring news to Guizot, and the commissioners on hearing it at first decided to resist attacks on the peerage, but vivid recollections of the popular resort to violence only ten days earlier apparently aroused some doubts of Lafayette's ability to control his undisciplined followers. "If, contrary to all probability, a revolt took place," Guizot asked, "would the lieutenant-general be resolved to dissipate it by force of arms?" The Duke replied promptly and unequivocally, "No." His answer precluded resistance, and the ministers resolved to press for a compromise that would postpone discussion of the peerage to the next session of the chamber but still keep open the road to its abolition. Bérard agreed to propose to the chamber the referral of Article 27 in its entirety, not merely the clause on unlimited creation of peers, to the session of 1831.[71]

Shortly before ten o'clock on the morning of August 7 the chamber began its discussion of the proposed changes in the Charter and the dynasty. Six hours later it had completed its work, and France had, except for some formalities, a new constitution and a new king. At the outset of the debate a handful of legitimist deputies denounced their colleagues for violating their oaths and for assuming powers not rightfully theirs, but at no time did they or the opposite side of the chamber pose a serious threat to the government's project. Reference to the King's and his family's departure from the country was restored to the text. Anticlerical deputies tried to eliminate from Article 7 the phrase affirming

---

[71] *Moniteur*, Aug. 7, 1830, p. 862; Duvergier de Hauranne, *Histoire*, x, 665-67; Charles H. Pouthas, *Guizot pendant la Restauration: préparation de l'homme d'état, 1814-1830* (Paris, 1923), pp. 470-71; Lafayette, *Mémoires*, vi, 419.

Roman Catholicism as the religion of the majority of Frenchmen but were unsuccessful. Unpopularity of the Swiss Guard inspired an addition to Article 14, ". . . no foreign troop may be admitted to the service of the State except by law." Proposals to remove the inviolability of magistrates and to purge the courts of undesirable appointees of the preceding regime failed to win a majority of votes. When the debate reached the proposal on the Chamber of Peers, Bérard arose and presented as his own the government's compromise. Lafayette, faithful to his promise to the demonstrators of the preceding evening, spoke in favor of abolishing the hereditary peerage but implied his acceptance of Bérard's compromise, and when Sébastiani, close adviser of Orléans endorsed it, the deputies could surmise that Bérard's proposal was not his alone. Another deputy suggested a simpler version, "Article 27 shall be submitted to a new examination in the session of 1831," and the chamber adopted it by a large majority, both opponents and proponents of the hereditary peerage seeing in the compromise a triumph for their views. Against the revised charter's last paragraph, which named the new king, a single deputy raised his voice, and his protest went unheeded. While the deputies filed one by one to the voting urn to cast their secret votes on the entire project, Dupin proposed a final article to the Charter, adopted by acclamation, "France resumes her colors. In the future no other cockade than the tricolor shall be worn." The president announced the result of the balloting—219 deputies voted for the constitutional revision and the new dynasty, thirty-three against. More than 150 had failed to attend the session.[72]

Immediately after the completion of the vote the chamber marched in a body to the Palais-Royal. Here the Duke, surrounded by his family, received the deputies and listened to Laffitte read the chamber's declaration—the pronouncement of the vacancy of the throne, the constitutional amendments, the list of promised legislation, and finally the invi-

[72] *Moniteur*, Aug. 8, 1830, pp. 865-72.

192

tation to the throne. The Duke, much moved, replied, "I receive with deep emotion the declaration that you present to me; I regard it as the expression of the national will, and it appears to me in conformity with the political principles that I have professed all my life." He had never aspired to the throne, he added, and wanted only to continue his peaceful life amid his family, but love of country now required him to accept the crown, he embraced Laffitte as deputies and other onlookers filled the room with shouts of "Vive le Roi!" "Vive la Reine!" "Vive la Famille royale!" The Duke, accompanied by Lafayette, appeared on a balcony of the palace to receive the acclamations of the crowds in the courtyard. Even louder cheering greeted the appearance of the Duchess and the children. That evening all Paris was illuminated; fireworks lighted the sky; tricolors floated in the night breeze, and in the streets people of all classes mixed together celebrating the end of revolution and of uncertainty.[73]

Across the Seine the Chamber of Peers met in lugubrious session to consider the deputies' declaration. But the change of dynasty and the revision of the Charter were already accomplished; the declaration came before the peers only as a gesture of courtesy by the Chamber of Deputies, and the peers had no choice but to accept it. They did decline to approve the provision annulling Charles X's creation of peers and referred decision on this matter to "the high prudence of the prince lieutenant-general." In the final, secret vote eighty-nine peers cast ballots for the declaration, ten against; fourteen abstained; more than 200 were absent.[74]

The next day the Duke and his advisers decided that he should assume the title of Louis-Philippe I, not Louis XIX or Philippe VII, to indicate that he began a new dynasty and to affirm that he did not rule because he was a Bourbon. From the formula of royal acts they struck the survivals of

[73] *Ibid.*, pp. 863-64; Bérard, *Souvenirs*, pp. 382-91; Duvergier de Hauranne, *Histoire*, x, 675-76.
[74] *Moniteur*, Aug. 11, 1830, pp. 883-84; Barante, *Souvenirs*, III, 575.

divine right monarchy—the phrases "by the grace of God" and "the year of grace," and they drew up a simple, civil oath for the Duke to take in assuming the crown.[75]

On Monday, August 9, Orléans, accompanied by his ministers, appeared before the deputies and peers meeting together in royal session. Seated on a stool before the empty throne and between his two eldest sons he listened to Périer read the declaration of the Chamber of Deputies and to the newly appointed Chancellor Pasquier announce the adherence of the peers. He then declared, "I accept, without restriction or reserve, the clauses and engagements embodied in this declaration and the title of *King of the French* that it confers upon me, and I am ready to swear to observe it." The Duke arose; the Keeper of the Seals handed him the text of the oath. All the deputies and peers stood as the Duke swore to observe the Charter as modified by the declaration, "to govern only by the laws and according to the laws," and to render justice to all. When he finished the final words, the assembled deputies and peers broke into shouts of "Vive le Roi!" and "Vive Louis-Philippe I!" (The less well informed among them cried "Vive Philippe VII!" or "Vive Philippe I!") Four marshals of France, heroes of the Empire— Tarente, Reggio, Trévise, and Molitor—presented to the new king the symbols of his office—the crown, the scepter, the sword, and the hand of justice. He signed the declarations of the chambers and the oath—in triplicate, for France was already in a bureaucratic age—and mounted the throne as King of the French.[76]

The contrast between this simple ceremony and the elaborate medieval coronation of Charles X in the Cathedral of Reims only five years earlier emphasized the break from the old regime. The Duke had come to the Palais-Bourbon on horseback escorted only by the National Guard. He wore no ceremonial robes but the uniform of a lieutenant-general, and all of the deputies and most of the peers wore street

[75] Dupin, *Mémoires*, pp. 166-68; Bérard, *Souvenirs*, p. 408.
[76] *Moniteur*, Aug. 10, 1830, p. 878; Duvergier de Hauranne, *Histoire*, x, 684-86; Bérard, *Souvenirs*, p. 402; Broglie, *Souvenirs*, III, 409-12.

dress. Except for the phrase "before God" in the oath the ceremony was entirely civil. No clergyman anointed the new king nor administered the oath nor offered a prayer. The Bible and the crucifix had no place among the symbols. The mystery of the coronation had given way to the signing of a contract between ruler and ruled sanctioned only by law and, although few present would openly admit it, by violence.[77]

With Orléans' taking of the crown the revolution had reached the end of its second stage. The Bourbons were vanishing over the horizon into exile, their supporters disdainful of the new King but most of them relieved to accept him as a bulwark against the republic. The Bonapartists had rallied to Orléans and eagerly took appointments in his service. The republicans had overtly accepted "the best of republics" that they could achieve in 1830. The sovereign power had come to rest in the hands of the Duc d'Orléans— now King of the French—and the Chamber of Deputies.[78]

[77] Barante, *Souvenirs*, III, 577; Rodolphe Apponyi, *Vingt-cinq ans à Paris, 1826-1850: journal du comte Rodolphe Apponyi, attaché de l'ambassade d'Autriche-Hongrie à Paris*, 2d ed. (Paris, 1913-26), I, 299-300; Duvergier de Hauranne, *Histoire*, x, 683-85; Bérard, *Souvenirs*, pp. 401-2; *National*, Aug. 10, 1830.

[78] The often-advanced explanation of the Revolution of 1830 as a conflict between the *grande bourgeoisie* and the aristocracy (see Ch. IX) separates men who actually worked together for the same political end. As this chapter shows, the Orléanist solution to the crisis of July and August 1830 was the work of a handful of men: Laffitte, Périer, Dupin, Bérard, Guizot, Constant, Thiers, Broglie, Lafayette, Sébastiani, Laborde, Delessert. It was they who made the critical decisions or induced others to make them. They rejected Charles X's overtures to withdraw the offending ordinances and to appoint a new ministry, persuaded the deputies to designate the Duc d'Orléans Lieutenant-General of the Kingdom, refused to accept the Duc de Bordeaux as Henry V, and induced the deputies to offer the crown to Orléans. This cluster of men included two bankers, two lawyers, one professor, two writers and journalists, and five nobles, all united for a political objective.

VI

The Revolution in the
Provinces

ON MONDAY, July 26, stage coaches left Paris as usual, carrying to provincial subscribers copies of the *Moniteur* and other Parisian dailies, and from them citizens throughout France learned of the King's Four Ordinances. During the next several days interruption of communications between the capital and the departments—both by official ban and by the fighting in the streets—left provincials without dependable information on the momentous developments in Paris. On July 27 papers lacking official authorization or courage to defy the royal ban did not appear. The *Moniteur* went out as on any other day, but its issue of July 27 gave no hint of any hostile reaction to the ordinances. The four opposition papers printed in defiance of the first ordinance carried the protest of the journalists and their appeal for resistance to the government's illegal actions; the Prefect of Police ordered his agents to seize copies deposited in stage coach offices for delivery to the provinces. That night and the next morning the erection of barricades prevented the movement of coaches or any other vehicles through the streets, and for five days stage coaches could neither reach nor leave their stations in the center of the city. Some coaches apparently resumed limited service from the periphery of the city on July 31 or August 1, but Lady Aylmer, who had arrived on the twenty-seventh and was determined to continue on to England at the earliest possible moment, could not get a coach to Boulogne until August 3.[1]

[1] AN, F⁹ 1156, Combattants de Juillet, Monténicourt to Ministre de l'Intérieur, Dec. 6, 1831; F⁷ 6777, Rapports de Gendarmerie, Capitain de la Gendarmerie royale, Chateauroux to Ministre de l'Intérieur,

In the provinces as in Paris news of the ordinances, the long-expected royal coup d'état, stirred consternation among opponents of the Polignac Ministry and a mixture of satisfaction and anxiety among its supporters. The reactions in the capital concerned them all, and they waited impatiently for news. Isolated travelers who managed to leave the city in the first days of insurrection brought fragmentary information to some towns, and rumors spread with amazing speed along the highways. The Austrian diplomat, Count Apponyi, vacationing at Dieppe, attributed to two English travelers reports that street fighters had killed all the gendarmes who had fallen into their hands, that National Guards had recruited men in the streets and killed those who resisted impressment, and that the King had withdrawn his troops in order to stop bloodshed but planned to starve the city into submission. The next day, July 31, two hundred miles to the south Amable de Barante, traveling from his country seat to Paris, heard that 1000 people had been killed and that the King had fled to Compiègne. Apponyi entered in his diary for July 31 that fighting in Paris had claimed 6000 victims, among them Marshal Marmont, assassinated by a student of the Ecole polytechnique. He probably took comfort in a report that Marshal Bourmont, miraculously back from Algeria, was leading an army of 25,000 men on the capital.[2]

Resumption of stage coach services began to lighten the uncertainty. The arrival of the coach from Paris with its royal markings removed or effaced, tricolor ribbons flying, and carrying Parisian mail and newspapers frequently set

Aug. 2, 1830; Amable de Barante, *Souvenirs . . . 1782-1866* (Paris, 1890-91), III, 562, 564; Henri Vienne, "Dix jours à Paris du dimanche 25 juillet au mardi 3 août 1830," *Memoires* de la Société bourguignonne de géographie et d'histoire, VIII (1892), 113; R. Anchel, ed., "Un Témoinage anglais sur les journées de Juillet: souvenirs de Lady Aylmer," *Revue d'histoire moderne*, VI (1931), 366-68.

2 Rodolphe Apponyi, *Vingt-cinq ans à Paris, 1826-1850: journal du comte Rodolphe Apponyi . . .*, 2d ed. (Paris, 1913-26), I, 286-87, 290-91; Barante, *Souvenirs*, III, 561-62.

off demonstrations against the Bourbons and their local officials and usually gave the signal to opposition leaders to raise the tricolor on the city hall or church tower, to call out the National Guard, and to choose a new municipal council and mayor. A number of towns in Normandy dispatched volunteers to aid Parisians in their fight against the Bourbons.[3]

Almost everywhere throughout the country Frenchmen accepted the Parisian revolution and generally welcomed it. Nowhere except in Nîmes and the Department of the Gard in the Midi did royalists offer any prolonged resistance, and this opposition drew its sustenance more from deep-seated hostility to local Protestants and fear of religious persecution than from political loyalty to the Bourbons. The Vendée and Brittany, strongholds of royalism and traditionally anti-revolutionary, accepted the change in regime with surprising calm. In some cities royalist officials—prefects and commanders of military districts—resisted local pressures to fly the tricolor or to surrender their powers to new officers, and a few used armed forces to support their resistance, but none held out after learning of the establishment of the new government under the Duc d'Orléans and the arrival of orders from the provisional ministers. In one town in central France the order to troops to wear the tricolor cockade came while the court of assizes was in session, and members of the court noticed that the gendarmes first on duty in the court room that day wore the white cockade; their relief had none; the next relief wore the tricolor.[4]

The clergy alone among the elite of the Restoration per-

[3] AN, F[1d] III 81, Commission des Récompenses nationales [hereafter cited as CRN], Seine-Inférieure, "Liste des citoyens presentés au Roi pour la Medaille de Juillet," Dec. 29, 1831, "Liste des citoyens presentés au Roi pour la Croix de Juillet," Dec. 29, 1831; Jean Vidalenc, *Le Département de l'Eure sous la monarchie constitutionelle, 1814-1848* (Paris, 1952), p. 274.

[4] Georges Weill, "La Révolution de Juillet dans les départements (août-septembre 1830)," *Revue d'histoire moderne*, 6 (1931), 291, 293; S. Posener, "La Révolution de Juillet et le Département du Gard," *Mercure de France*, 221 (1930), 607-36; AN, F[1d] III 80, CRN citing *Gazette des Tribunaux* (Paris), Aug. 9-10, 1830.

sisted in their commitment to the fallen regime and in their hostility to Orléans. The bishops typically took no strong stand for either side but advised their priests to avoid provocation of the new government and its partisans. Some priests, however, refused permission to fly the tricolor from their church towers, declined to sing the *Domine, salvum fac Philippum*, and warned the faithful that the new government, like the revolutionary governments of the 1790s, threatened the Catholic religion. Their opposition, possibly exaggerated by local anticlericals who had been exasperated by the ecclesiastical policies and the ostentatious piety of Charles X, remained passive, and it little influenced popular attitudes toward the new regime.[5]

In some areas peasants, freed briefly from the restraints of local authorities, protested against the loss of traditional rights as they had done for centuries when the opportunity offered. They cut wood in forbidden forests, broke down enclosures of former common lands, and grazed their animals on stubble of newly harvested fields. In the Department of the Ariège on the Spanish frontier peasants revived memories of 1789 by devastating two chateaux, and in many towns tax records and toll houses fell victim of popular resentment released by the revolution. All these isolated acts committed in the name of liberty ended as new authorities took over, and they posed no serious threat to the Orléanist government.[6]

In Rouen local journalists and notables reacted to the ordinances much as did their counterparts in Paris, and they

---

[5] Weill, "Révolution dans les départements," pp. 291-92; Gabriel Perreux, "L'Esprit public dans les départements au lendemain de la Révolution de 1830," *Révolution de 1848*, xxx (1933-34), 230, 233, 234; René Durand, "La Révolution de 1830 en Côte d'Or," *Revue d'histoire moderne*, 6 (1931), 172; AN, F⁷ 6784, Rapports de Gend., Brig., Gend. at Saint-Florent (Vendée), Oct. 31, 1831.

[6] Weill, "Révolution dans les départements," p. 292; Albert Soboul, "The French Rural Community in the Eighteenth and Nineteenth Centuries," *Past and Present*, No. 10 (Nov. 1956), p. 91; AHMG, E⁵ 1, Administrateurs provisoires du Dépt. de l'Ariège to Ministre de la Guerre, Aug. 21, 1830, Lt.-gén. Cmdt., 10ᵉ Div. milit. to Ministre de la Guerre, Aug. 21, 1830.

organized resistance without waiting for news from the capital. A messenger bearing official copies of the ordinances arrived in Rouen at dawn on July 27. Later in the morning the prefect forbade the proprietors of the liberal *Journal de Rouen* to publish their paper, and he dispatched a similar order to the *Journal du Havre*. Advised by legal counsel that the first ordinance was illegal, the proprietors of the former paper decided to continue publication and warned the police of their intention. They called a meeting of the city's liberals and informed them that the *Journal* was at the disposal of patriots who would join them in opposing the ordinances. The meeting agreed to support the paper in its fight against the authorities. The next day a scene took place at the newspaper office similar to that in the courtyard of the *Temps* in Paris on the preceding day. At 5:30 A.M. a police commissioner arrived to seize the presses. Refused admittance, he departed but shortly returned with a picket of foot gendarmes, and a detachment of mounted gendarmes soon joined them. One of the editors, stationed before the office, refused to unlock the door and, like Baude of the *Temps*, persuaded three locksmiths whom the police had successively summoned to the scene to leave without touching the lock. A crowd openly sympathetic with the journalists had gathered, and the prefect, fearing a clash, ordered the police and gendarmes to withdraw. Later in the day liberals heard that the government planned to use units of the Royal Guard garrisoned in Rouen to force entry into the press room that night. In the evening a number of them with weapons in their hands assembled at the *Journal* office, barricaded the door, and prepared to defend the presses. Others, including some deputies and National Guardsmen, gathered nearby at the house of a liberal lawyer to lend their support. Both groups awaited an attack that never came.[7]

7 AN, F1c III 81, CRN, Seine-Inférieure, "Liste des citoyens . . . Croix de Juillet," Dec. 29, 1831, "Liste des citoyens . . . Medaille de Juillet," Dec. 29, 1831; H. Barbet, *et al.*, to Prés., Conseil des Ministres [Mar. 1832]; F1b I 16626, A. Barbet, "Précis des événemens qui ont lieu à Rouen depuis le 27 Juillet jusqu'au 5 Août . . . ," Aug. 6, 1830.

The next day, the twenty-ninth, the arrival of news of the fighting in Paris on the preceding day stirred popular excitement in Rouen. Groups of men gathered in the streets. Many National Guardsmen appeared with their arms. Men talked of going to the aid of the insurgents in Paris, and a few bolder spirits urged an attack on the barracks of the Royal Guard. The liberal leaders met again, this time at the house of a deputy, and discussed the dispatch of volunteers to Paris. They decided to send two of their number, both merchants in Rouen, to the capital to establish relations with the revolutionary movement there, and they made plans for a public appeal for funds to support volunteers. The local authorities, apparently awaiting the arrival of three squadrons of cavalry ordered to the city from Amiens, made no counter moves. That evening some three hundred National Guardsmen patrolled the city. On the thirtieth the crowds in the streets increased and so, too, did the clamor for a march on Paris. About three o'clock in the afternoon word arrived of the popular victory in the capital, and the mayor of the city, standing on a balcony of the Hôtel de Ville announced the news to the cheering throng that overflowed the *place* in front of the building.[8]

Cut off from Paris and Saint-Cloud, left without direction, the royal administration of the city and the department quickly withered away. Early in the morning of July 31 the mayor and most of his assistants resigned, and a provisional commission headed by Henri Barbet, a businessman of Rouen, took over the administration of the city. The next morning the Prefect of the Department of the Seine-Inférieure peacefully surrendered his powers to a departmental commission and ordered his subordinates to cooperate with it. The commission replaced the four subprefects of the department, ordered the tricolor displayed on all public buildings and churches, and provided for the establishment

---

[8] AN, F[1b] I 166[26], Barbet, "Précis"; F[1d] III 81, CRN, "Liste . . . Medaille de Juillet," Dec. 29, 1831; CRN, "Liste . . . Croix de Juillet," Dec. 29, 1831; AHMG, D[8] 131, Maréchal-de-Camp Cmdt., 3e Subdiv., 16e Div. milit. to Lt.-gén. Cmdt., 16e Div. milit., July 29, 1830.

and supply of the National Guard. The commissioners—all of them substantial businessmen, lawyers, or proprietors—feared an excess of popular involvement as much as did the deputies in Paris, and on August 2 they issued an appeal to manufacturers throughout the department to put idle employees back to work.[9]

Not even the Royal Guard resisted the swift-flowing tide. On August 3 the lieutenant-colonel of the one company remaining in the city reported to the Departmental Commission that the commanding officer had abandoned his command and that all but a dozen of the guardsmen wanted to accept the new government. That evening a banquet given by the commission in honor of the rallied officers of the Royal Guard, attended by notables of Rouen and twenty-six officers, marked the end of the city's bloodless revolution.[10]

The column of volunteers to aid the insurgents of Paris had a brief, inglorious history. On the afternoon of July 30 volunteers quickly filled the newly opened register with their names, and the first detachment—some one hundred men, most of them National Guardsmen—left the city that evening. The next day more than five hundred untrained and undisciplined volunteers from the streets of Rouen and from surrounding milltowns joined them at Pont l'Arche about thirteen miles from Rouen. Sent off without adequate supplies of food, the band stole what it needed along the way, and later when supply wagons did arrive from Rouen, only with difficulty did National Guardsmen save them from pillage by the unruly volunteers. Some of the Rouennais eventually joined with the Parisian column marching on Rambouillet, and although they never fought anyone but their National Guard officers, they could claim to have helped force the Bourbons out of France.[11]

[9] AN, F^{1b} I 166^{26}, Barbet, "Précis"; F^{1d} III 81, CRN, "Liste . . . Croix de Juillet," Dec. 29, 1831.

[10] AN, F^{1b} I 166^{26}, Barbet, "Précis."

[11] AN, F^{1d} III 81, CRN, "Liste . . . Medaille de Juillet," Dec. 29,

Two battalions of the National Guard of Rouen marched directly on Paris. The advance units entered the city on August 3 and the main body the next day. Others who had been with the Rambouillet column joined them there. Their presence may have been reassuring to Parisians as a token of provincial support, but they proved to be more a trial than a support to the already overburdened authorities. The provisional Municipal Commission had to provide them with quarters and food, and the official in charge of this operation complained on August 5 that the colonel and all the officers of the Guard had abandoned their men and that he was obliged to serve as their military chief. He urgently requested Lafayette to order the officers to join their troops, and he pressed the Municipal Commission to support his plea. On August 8 the Guards from Rouen and some from Le Havre paraded on the Place Vendôme, and the Lieutenant-General, accompanied by his two eldest sons, passed them in review, possibly in the hope that such recognition might move them to go home.[12]

The Norman department adjoining the Seine-Inférieure in the south—the Department of the Eure—accepted the revolution as readily as did its neighbor. Liberal strength had been growing there, especially since the formation of the Polignac Ministry, and both the economic depression and the unresolved epidemic of fires in the winter and spring of 1830 undermined popular confidence in the government. The voters expressed their disapproval in the general elections by reelecting the incumbent liberal deputies of the arrondissement electoral colleges and by choosing liberal candidates for the three seats filled by the departmental

1831; F. Dupont to Roi, Sept. 9, 1831; Deposition of A. Lecomte, Aug. 12, 1832; Deposition of J. Chevallet, Aug. 4, 1832; Deposition of Monthelier, May 14, 1831.

[12] Marie de Lafayette, *Mémoires, correspondance et manuscrits* (Paris, 1837-38), VI, 415, 418; AN, F⁹ 682, Gardes nats., Flotard to Commission municipale de Paris, Aug. 5, 1830; *Moniteur universel* (Paris), Aug. 9, 1830, p. 873.

college. Rejoicing in their victories the liberals contemplated no further exertions until the meeting of the chambers later in the summer.[13]

The King's Four Ordinances took them by surprise. For several days the department had no dependable news from Paris. The Guard regiments that had been there to hunt down incendiaries hurriedly departed, marching as in enemy territory with advance, rear, and flank guards, a precaution that suggested expectation of serious trouble. The nervous prefect asked the commanding general in Rouen to send a company of soldiers to Evreux, the departmental capital, but none had arrived on July 31, when three lawyers and a retired army officer organized the National Guard in Evreux, occupied the mayor's office, forced the mayor to withdraw, raised the tricolor over the city hall, and invited contributions to a fund to aid the victims of the fighting in Paris. Citizens of other towns in the department followed their example, and some went farther by sending their National Guards off to Paris to join the battle against the King. The Royal Guards remaining in the department did nothing to protect the crumbling regime of Charles X, the royalist nobles made no move, the Gendarmerie cooperated with the National Guard in maintaining order, and the prefect on August 4 abandoned his almost completely passive rôle of the preceding days by resigning and urging citizens of every commune to raise the tricolor. The revolution claimed but a single casualty among the department's residents—a retired army officer who happened to be in Paris at the time organized a group of combatants and was accidentally wounded by one of his own men![14]

Charles X and his party crossed the southern extremity of the department on August 5 and 6 and spent a night in the town of Verneuil. A number of the local gentry came to pay their respects, and the aged Bishop of Evreux, an ex-émigré, traveled down to say goodbye to his onetime protector, but the ordinary men and women who looked up

---

[13] Vidalenc, *Département de l'Eure*, pp. 248-71.
[14] *Ibid.*, pp. 271-77.

from their work or stood at the roadside to watch the strange procession pass seemed to be moved by no more than respectful curiosity. In a few remote communes local royalist officials delayed flying the tricolor—one mayor was still holding out on August 28, but the moderation of the Orléanist regime and the conciliatory skill of the new prefect won almost unanimous support for the new government.[15]

The rich agricultural Department of the Calvados had been pro-Bourbon during the Restoration, usually returning ministerial royalists to the Chamber of Deputies. The appointment of the Polignac Ministry had, however, displeased many electors, for it seemed to presage some reactionary adventure certain to endanger the order and stability that these rich proprietors cherished above abstract devotion to the Bourbons. In November 1829 the parliamentary seat of the district of Pont L'Evêque-Lisieux fell vacant, and Guizot, leader of the "Aide-toi," decided to contest it. He entered the race with a number of formidable handicaps. Most seriously he was not a Norman; he was by birth a southerner from wine-raising country (which nominally alienated him from cider-producing Normandy) and by residence a Parisian. He was a Protestant, and his principal supporters in the department were on the extreme Left. Nonetheless, a majority of the electors saw in his candidacy an opportunity to protest against the Polignac Ministry, and they elected him on the first ballot, giving him three times as many votes as his nearest competitor, a resident of the department.[16]

During the succeeding winter and spring the epidemic of fires in Normandy aroused widespread concern in the Calvados, and in May the government ordered units of the Royal Guard to the department in part as a gesture intended to restore popular confidence in the administration's ability to cope with the problem. The general elections of June and July 1830 gave the government a measure of its failure; the

15 *Ibid.*, pp. 277-83.
16 Henri Prentout, "Caen en 1830," *Revue d'histoire moderne*, VI, 102-4, 106-7 (1931); Charles H. Pouthas, *Guizot pendant la Restauration; préparation de l'homme d'état, 1814-1830* (Paris, 1923), pp. 404-17.

electors rejected all of Polignac's candidates, including one of his own ministers, Guernon-Ranville.[17]

Citizens of Caen learned of the royal coup d'état on July 28, when the *Pilote*, the liberal newspaper of the city, published the ordinances without comment. The failure of any mail or stage coach to arrive from Paris either that day or the next stirred fear of serious troubles in the capital. In the evening of the thirtieth five or six hundred people gathered on the Place Royale and shouted "A bas Charles X!" and "Vive la Charte constitutionnelle!" The next day demonstrators put tricolor flags on church towers, rang church bells, and tried to topple the statue of Louis XIV near the Abbaye aux Hommes. The mayor called a number of leading citizens of the Hôtel de Ville to advise him, and they, together with others whom they selected, constituted themselves a provisional municipal commission. The commission immediately established the National Guard, and on August 2 the guard began to patrol the streets. The commanding general of the military district, anxious to avoid a conflict with citizens, had at the first sign of trouble withdrawn his troops to the chateau on the north side of the city. After the National Guard had assured the maintenance of order, the troops returned peacefully to their barracks, and a few days later a new general took command of the district. On August 5 the city learned of the appointment of the Duc d'Orléans as Lieutenant-General of the Kingdom, and on the twenty-second it celebrated the formal proclamation of the new King. When in September all government officials and employees had to take the oath of allegiance to the new regime, only a few magistrates and some professors in the university refused it.[18]

In the city of Metz on the eastern frontier of France news of the ordinances set off a movement of protest independent of the events in Paris. Metz had a long tradition of Bona-

[17] Martial de Guernon-Ranville, *Journal d'un ministre* (Caen, 1873), pp. 85-86, 91; Prentout, "Caen en 1830," p. 107.

[18] Prentout, "Caen en 1830," pp. 109-13; *Moniteur*, Aug. 2, 1830, p. 835; Aug. 4, p. 843; Aug. 6, p. 851.

partist and liberal sympathies, and in 1830 it had a well-organized opposition movement. The army's *Ecole d'Application* and the arsenals brought to the city many army engineers who retained liberal sympathies acquired as students of the Ecole polytechnique. The Constitutional Committee founded in Metz in 1827 included most of the lawyers of the city, and it had correspondents in the neighboring towns of Thionville and Sarreguemines. A liberal newspaper, the *Courrier de la Moselle*, established in 1829 and influential, the prefect believed, among manufacturers in Metz, attacked the Polignac government and harried local authorities until the courts finally silenced it in June 1830. The elections of that month and the next returned five opposition candidates among the department's seven deputies.[19]

Copies of the Four Ordinances reached Metz on July 28. The next morning a sign posted on a wall of the Hôtel de Ville proclaimed, "Charles X was king by virtue of the Charter, which he swore to uphold. He has violated his oath. Payment of taxes should be refused. Long live the Nation." On the thirtieth the prefect, the mayor, and the commanding general of the military district, as a gesture of appeasement toward the opposition, called out the National Guard. This gave the liberals the opportunity they wanted, for they controlled the guard, and with its sanction the Constitutional Committee established itself as a virtual municipal government. The next day the tricolor floated over the cathedral, and the prefect and the procurer-general surrendered their powers and left the city. The commanding-general, whose 10,000 troops gave him power to speak, declined to approve the display of the tricolor without orders from Paris, and on August 1 he insisted that the flag on the cathedral tower come down. The National Guard placed sentries at the entrance to the tower to prevent execution of the general's orders, and a crowd of National Guardsmen and civilians massed on the *place* beside the cathedral and

19 Henry Contamine, "La Révolution de 1830 à Metz," *Revue d'histoire moderne*, 6 (1931), 115-18.

remained there through the night, deaf to the pleas of the mayor and the general, even though the leaders of the Constitutional Committee agreed to the removal of the flag. The next morning, August 2, four Polytechnicians arrived from Paris bringing news of the popular victory in the capital and a dispatch from Lafayette. Then the general acquiesced to the new flag, the mayor resigned, and the Constitutional Committee became the undisputed master of the city. Working through the deputies whom it had helped to put into the chamber it prevailed upon the new government to purge departmental offices of legitimists and to replace them with men of the committee's choice.[20]

The purge of the army at Metz and in the department went less smoothly. On August 1 officers of the garrison signed an address to the Minister of War beginning, "The heroic population of Paris has reconquered our liberties; we will all die to defend them" and went on to call for the expulsion of the Bourbons. A number of royalist officers voluntarily gave up their commands in the first days of August, but some of them, taking second thought, returned to their posts. On August 26 noncommissioned officers of the 6th Artillery Regiment came to the new commanding-general of the military district and asked him to remove their commanding officer, who had been a gentleman-in-waiting to Charles X. The general, after consulting with the higher officers of the regiment, agreed to replace the colonel the next day, but that evening impatient artillerymen decided to seize the regimental standard from the unpopular colonel by force. They marched to his residence and pillaged his quarters and all the other apartments in the building while the prefect looked on, powerless to restrain the excited soldiers. On the twenty-seventh many of them still roamed the streets, two other regiments talked of ousting their officers, and rumor spread of an impending attack on the Palais de Justice, the mayor's house, the Catholic seminary, and the houses of grain merchants. The alarmed local

[20] *Ibid.*, pp. 118-21.

authorities called the National Guard, which managed to prevent further violence, and the government in Paris soon sent a general untainted by service under the Restoration to remove royalist officers and to reestablish discipline.[21]

As the provisional government and the Orléanists assumed power in Paris they watched with particular concern the news from traditionally royalist areas in the south and west. On July 31, Mauguin proposed to the Municipal Commission the sending of "extraordinary commissioners," reminiscent of the deputies on mission of 1793-94, to all parts of the country where "the national spirit" needed guidance. He expressed particular concern over Brittany, but the adjoining district of the Vendée at the mouth of the Loire River posed at least an equally ominous threat. It had been the scene of prolonged and bloody resistance to revolutionary Paris in the 1790s, and in 1815 it joined Brittany in a revolt against the restored Empire that forced Napoleon to send 20,000 men to the area to establish his government's authority. In 1830 royalist sympathies remained strong, and the first thought of Marmont and the ministers as they contemplated the loss of Paris was to withdraw into the west and set up the government amid a sympathetic population.[22]

Nantes, the largest city in the west, had the outward appearance of a sure rampart of royalism. Uncompromising ultraroyalists held the office of mayor, most of the seats in the municipal council, and almost all the administrative posts. The commanding-general of the military district, General Despinois, shared the reactionary views of the King and his ministers. Opposition did, nonetheless, exist in the city. Liberals and a few republicans and Bonapartists disputed the royalists' ideas and their hold on political power. The newspaper, the *Ami de la Charte* defended constitutional government, attacked official abuses of authority, and

21 *Ibid.*, pp. 121-22.

22 Hippolyte Bonnelier, *Mémorial de l'Hôtel de Ville de Paris, 1830* (Paris, 1835), p. 133; Auguste de Marmont, *Mémoires du maréchal Marmont, duc de Raguse, de 1792 à 1841*, 3d ed. (Paris, 1857), VIII, 317-18; Guernon-Ranville, *Journal*, pp. 192, 202.

denounced excesses of the church with a vigor that brought its editor frequent fines and jail sentences. His campaign against an official candidate in the election of 1830 cost him a fine of 2000 francs and six months in prison, punishments from which the revolution saved him. The *Ami de la Charte* also spoke out for the working class of Nantes, suffering in 1830 from the effects of the nationwide depression and mounting food costs, aggravated here by unemployment resulting from increasing mechanization of local industry. In 1830, 14,000 Nantais among a total of 80,000 depended on public or private relief, a formidable force of potential opposition against a government that had showed little interest in their plight.[23]

Copies of the Four Ordinances were posted in Nantes in the morning of July 29. They attracted some crowds during the day, and liberals gravitated to the office of the *Ami de la Charte* and to their usual cafés to discuss them. In the evening, a warm summer night, people were on the streets in large numbers, especially after the closing of the theaters. On the Place Graslin in the center of the city a mixed crowd of workers, clerks, and young bourgeois began to shout, "Vive la Charte!" "Vive la liberté!" and "A bas les ministres!" In anticipation of trouble General Despinois had ordered out a detachment of mounted gendarmes and a unit of infantrymen. They surrounded the Place Graslin, and the gendarmes charged the crowd and arrested sixteen of the demonstrators. In Nantes as in Paris the presence of gendarmes invited stone-throwing, and six victims had to be sent to the hospital.[24]

The next morning the mayor ordered the closing of all stores and cafés by 8 P.M. and forbade public gatherings, but during the day many curious citizens did assemble at the

---

[23] M. Giraud-Mangin, "Nantes en 1830 et les journées de juillet," *Revue d'histoire moderne*, 6 (1931), 457-61.

[24] *Ibid.*, p. 461; René Blanchard, "Le 10ᵉ Leger et la Révolution de Juillet 1830 à Nantes," *Revue de Bretagne*, 29 (1903), 15-16; AN, F¹⁴ III 80, C. Pelletier to Préfet de la Loire-Inférieure, Aug. 1, 1831.

post office hoping for news from Paris. Eventually a coach arrived, and one traveler told the crowd of the fighting he had witnessed in the city. Young men, anxious to free their friends arrested the night before and to emulate their fellows in Paris, took up the cry, "Aux armes!" In the afternoon some of them broke into the shop of an arms dealer and took more than 600 muskets and a smaller number of side arms. Others raised barricades on the bridges and streets leading into Nantes from the south to block troops reportedly coming from La Rochelle. A number of businessmen fearful of increasing disorder appealed to the mayor to reorganize the National Guard at once, but the ultraroyalist magistrate, backed by the prefect and by General Despinois, refused to revive this liberal-tainted organization.[25]

In late afternoon two groups of about 150 armed men each converged on the general's headquarters on the Place Louis XVI to seek the release of the sixteen demonstrators. One hundred eighty men of the 10th Light Infantry, their bayonets fixed, guarded the general's residence. Neither citizens nor soldiers showed any hostility toward the other. The crowd shouted, "Vive le 10e Léger!" and the troops answered, "Vive le Charte!" and they were beginning to mix together when someone fired a shot. Both sides thought themselves attacked. The troops opened fire on the crowd; the demonstrators fired back, and when the purposeless exchange stopped, seven civilians and six soldiers lay dead or dying in the square and more than fifty others were wounded. Apparently shocked by this tragic clash General Despinois ordered the prisoners released and confined all troops, save a guard around his headquarters, to their bar-

[25] Giraud-Mangin, "Nantes en 1830," pp. 461-63; Blanchard, "10e Leger," pp. 17-18, 144-52; AN, F¹ᵈ III 80, Mairie de Nantes, "Récompenses nationales demandées pour les citoyens qui ont pris part aux événemens de Juillet 1830 dans cette ville," Jan. 25, 1831; C. Pelletier to Préfet de la Loire-Inférieure, Aug. 1, 1831; AN, F⁹ 1157, Extrait des minutes du Greffe de la justice de paix du Sixième Arrond. de Nantes, Aug. 2, 1830; Minutes de la Commission des Dommages, Nantes, April 30, May 6, 1833.

racks. Insurgents organized by a stone-cutter occupied all police posts in the city, and civilian patrols assured public order.[26]

During the next day, the thirty-first, a tacit truce between the ultras and the liberals permitted the organization of a provisional municipal commission and a volunteer urban guard, and the city passed two days in a tenuous peace awaiting news from the capital. In the night of August 1 a courier brought a report of the formation of a provisional government in Paris and of the King's abandonment of the city. On August 2 Despinois led his troops with all their baggage out of Nantes and headed south toward the Vendée. The prefect and the mayor left within the day. Thereafter the future lay with the liberals. On August 4 the tricolor flew on all public buildings. The Municipal Commission found a commander for the revived National Guard in Pierre Dumoustier, a Napoleonic general who had spurned service under the Bourbons. On learning of the proclamation of Louis-Philippe as King of the French, the commission sent a delegation to the new ruler to affirm the city's support of the new regime.[27]

Nantes held the distinction of being the only provincial city to resist the government of Charles X at the cost of citizens' lives, and the Commission des Récompenses nationales awarded more decorations there than in any other city except Paris—sixty-eight Crosses of July and sixty-five Medals of July. Possibly the Nantais' relatively spectacular demonstration of their sympathies had far-reaching consequences. It may have discouraged royalist counteraction in the Vendée and Brittany, and possibly it influenced Charles

[26] Giraud-Mangin, "Nantes en 1830," pp. 463-64; Blanchard, "10ᵉ Leger," pp. 154, 220-22, 295-300; AN, F¹ᵈ III 80, Mairie de Nantes, "Récompenses nationales," June 25, 1831; A. Bremens to Ministre de l'Intérieur, Dec. 5, 1831; Ch. Bosset to Ministre de l'Intérieur, Aug. 30, 1830.

[27] Giraud-Mangin, "Nantes en 1830," pp. 464-65; Blanchard, "10ᵉ Leger," pp. 395, 398, 399, 402; AN, F⁹ 1157, M. Varsavaux to Ministre de l'Intérieur, April 27, 1831; Déclaration de MM les membres de la commission provisoire, Nantes, Aug. 25, 1830; AN, F¹ᵈ III 80, Ch. Bosset to Ministre de l'Intérieur, Aug. 30, 1830.

X's decision to direct his retreat not into the west but to Cherbourg and exile.[28]

Events in the Vendée and Brittany never fulfilled the new government's apprehensions of serious troubles. Early in August the provisional commissioner of war gave to General Maximilien Lamarque, who had skillfully pacified the Vendée during the One Hundred Days in 1815, the command of the military districts stretching from Brittany southward to the Pyrenees. Reports came to him and to Paris of provocative acts by intransigent royalists. The Bourbon Prefect of the Department of Maine-et-Loire publicly announced in the first week of August that Charles X was marching on Paris at the head of 30,000 men and that "the 221" opposition deputies were under arrest. Rumors spread of a foreign army about to restore Charles, of persecution of priests, of suppression of the pensions granted by the Bourbons to former Vendéan rebels, and of bands of Chouans about to descend on the Breton coast. The commander of the Gendarmerie in three western departments reported on August 9, however, that although incitement of hotheads on either side could bring an explosion of violence, his district seemed disposed to calm.[29] Two days later Lamarque, installed in headquarters at Bourbon-Vendée (now La Roche-sur-Yon) declared in a proclamation to the people of the Vendée, "It was with a deep sense of sadness that, for the second time, I came to fight against you; it is with inexpressible happiness that I learn that you have rejected criminal projects [to rekindle civil war]."[30]

In Angers, which lay on the edge of the Vendée, liberal opponents of the Polignac Ministry gathered with their arms when they learned of Charles's ordinances and talked of

28 Giraud-Mangin, "Nantes en 1830," p. 466; AN, F⁹ 1157, Préfet de la Loire-Inférieure to Ministre de l'Intérieur, Aug. 25, 1830.
29 Charles Lesur, *Annuaire historique universel pour 1830* (Paris, 1832), pp. 261-62, 271; AHMG, D³ 131, Lt.-gén. Cmdt., 4ᵉ Div. milit. to Ministre de la Guerre, Aug. 6, 1830; Weill, "Révolution dans les départements," p. 145; AN, F⁷ 6777, Col., 9ᵉ Légion, Gend. roy. to Ministre de l'Intérieur, Aug. 9, 180.
30 *Moniteur*, Aug. 15, 1830, p. 904.

resisting their application by force if necessary, a necessity that never arose. At La Rochelle a rumor spread on July 31 that a battalion of the garrison had been ordered to Nantes for use against the insurgents of that city. A group of liberals, hoping to prevent departure of the troops, sent a deputation to both civil and military authorities with a demand that the battalion remain in La Rochelle. A crowd shouting, "Vive la Charte!" backed them up. Their démarche came too late, however, for the troops had already departed, but the next day troops of the Line remaining in the city rallied to the opposition, and the threat of violence vanished. At Rennes, the capital of Brittany a number of citizens prepared to resist enforcement of the ordinances, but as in Angers, they found no determined royalist partisans to combat, and at Brest, although the commanding officer held out against the arming of the National Guard and the procurergeneral blocked the administration of justice, the population demonstrated overwhelming support for the new regime, and the officials' resistance soon ended.[31]

Royalists looked to the south of France as well as to the west for support in time of crisis. The Department of the Gard on the lower Rhône and its *chef-lieu*, Nîmes, stood as bastions of ultraroyalism made more intense by attachment to a fanatical Catholicism in conflict with a scarcely less fanatical Protestantism. The city of Toulouse and the Department of the Haute-Garonne appeared almost untainted by liberalism. Lyon, the second largest city of France, had among its residents few sympathizers for the ultraroyalist cause, but it occupied a key position on the main route between Paris and the Midi. Should Charles X attempt to withdraw into friendly territory in the south he might pass through Lyon or, liberals in the city feared, he might try to

[31] AN, F^{1d} III 80, Préfet de Maine-et-Loire to Ministre de l'Intérieur, July 22, 1831; CRN citing *Gazette des tribunaux*, Aug. 9-10, 1830; F^{1d} III 79. Commission municipale des Récompenses nationales, Rennes, to Préfet d'Ille-et-Vilaine, Dec. 9, 1831; Dépt. du Finistère, Commission formée en execution de l'Ordonnance du Roi du 10 Nov. 1831, Procès-verbal, séance du 15 Décembre 1831; AHMG, D^3 131, SousPréfet, Brest, to Ministre de l'Intérieur, Aug. 4, 1830.

establish his government there, maintaining connections with his partisans in the Midi while fomenting troubles in the north. From this threat the Lyonnais believed that they saved France.[32]

Lyon learned of the Four Ordinances on July 27, and the next day the royal coup became the subject of discussion in cafés and on the streets, but not until the afternoon of July 29 was there a demonstration against them. That evening a large crowd gathered at the headquarters of a Masonic lodge in Brotteaux, a suburb across the Rhône from the administrative center of the city, and out of that meeting emerged a committee charged with organizing the National Guard. The next morning armed men appeared in the streets in large numbers, and the committee began forming them into four battalions of guards. In the afternoon seventy-five to eighty notable citizens, including at least one member of the committee appointed the preceding evening, met in the offices of the opposition newspaper, the *Précurseur*, and designated seven of their number to negotiate with the municipal authorities and twelve others to assume responsibility for the organization of the National Guard. Concerned by the growing ferment, the military command in the city took the precaution of closing the doors of the Hôtel de Ville, a move which blocked a passage always open to pedestrians. An exasperated crowd quickly gathered in the Place des Terreaux adjoining the building. Newly formed units of the National Guard, many of them veterans oddly arrayed in the uniforms of half a dozen services, came to the scene, followed by both infantry and cavalry from the garrison. The troops soon found themselves completely hemmed in by the dense crowd and unable to move. A single shot by an excited soldier or guardsman might have set off a bloody clash like that in Nantes, but before it happened negotiations between officials and the opposition leaders achieved an amicable agreement by which National Guardsmen and

32 AN, F1d III 81, "Seconde délibération motivée de la Comon" [municipale des récompenses, Lyon], Feb. 20, 1832; Chèze, Dupasquier, Tissot to Ministre de l'Intérieur, Sept. 2, 1832.

troops of the Line shared the guard posts of the Hôtel de Ville. The doors were reopened, and the new guards took their places to shouts from the crowd of "Vive la Charte!" and "Bravo, la garnison de Lyon!" The next day the National Guard joined the Line at posts throughout the city and patrolled the streets.[33]

On August 1 news arrived of the flight of Charles X, the establishment of a provisional government in Paris, and the reappearance of the tricolor. A delegation set off at once for Mâcon to offer the command of the National Guard to Jean Verdier, a general of the republican and imperial armies, living in retirement since 1815. He arrived in the city the next day wearing his Imperial uniform and he reviewed five to six thousand guardsmen on the Place des Terreaux. Unpracticed in riding during his long retirement, he fell from his horse during the review and had to be carried from the scene, but the accident proved no omen of disaster for the cause he represented. The commanding-general of the military district, the aging Paultre de Lamothe, who had begun his military service before the Revolution of 1789, on August 3 ordered his troops to wear the tricolor and gave up his post. The garrison passed to the command of Verdier until the arrival of the new commanding-general whom the provisional minister of war in Paris quickly dispatched to the city.[34]

The revolution in Lyon had been accomplished without violence and seemingly with little concern for the issues and little of the passion that inspired the struggle in Paris. Royal officials made no serious effort to defend their powers. The population generally welcomed the fall of the Bourbons

[33] Perreux, "L'Esprit public dans les départements," *Révolution de 1848*, 31 (1936), 98-100; AN, F[1d] III 81, "Rapport du Préfet du Rhône au commission des récompenses nationales à Lyon," Jan. 22, 1832; Olivier to Ministre de l'Intérieur, Feb. 29, 1832; AHMG, D[3] 131, Lt.-gén. Bachelu, 19e Div. milit. to Ministre de la Guerre, Aug. 5, 1830.

[34] Perreux, "L'Esprit public dans les départements," pp. 100-101; AHMG, D[3] 131, Bachelu to Ministre de la Guerre, Aug. 5, 1830; Lt.-gén. Verdier to Ministre de la Guerre, Aug. 4, 1830; Germain Bapst, *Le Maréchal Canrobert: souvenirs d'un siècle*, 2d ed. (Paris, 1898), I, 125-28.

but without apparent enthusiasm for their successor. For the time, nonetheless, Lyon in August 1830 had aligned reassuringly with the Orléanist regime and gave no encouragement to opposition on the Right or the Left.

Nowhere in France did the hold of the Bourbons seem more secure than in Toulouse and the Department of the Haute-Garonne. Throughout the twenties the electoral colleges of the department returned ministerial candidates; in the decade only two opposition candidates won seats. The department's voters, however, numbered but 1500 in a population of 390,000, and popular hostility to the regime could wax strong without being reflected in elections. In August 1830 it found brief expression in demonstrations against the local representatives of Bourbon authority.[35]

On August 2 the prefect of the department sent a subordinate, protected by a military escort, into all quarters of the city to read a proclamation defending the government in Paris. It elicited cries of "Vive la Charte!" and that evening some three thousand persons marched through the streets to the same cry. The next morning a rumor spread that Charles X had abdicated and that the provisional government had adopted the tricolor. Large crowds formed, paraded behind the revolutionary flag, and pulled down *fleurs de lis*. In the afternoon the authorities called out the entire garrison. Part of it occupied the Place Royale, the old city's principal public square and the site of the Capitale or Hôtel de Ville. A cluster of young men carried a tricolor through the troops, into the Capitale, and displayed it from a window. Then demonstrators from a western suburb came on the *place* following a tricolor flag, and this time troops surrounded the flag-bearer and a few defenders in the middle of the square. A brigade of gendarmes arrived, greeted by hostile shouts from the crowd; the commander, saber drawn, spurred his horse into the crowd toward the flag, apparently

---

[35] Jean Fourcassié, *Une Ville à l'époque romantique: Toulouse; trente ans de vie française* (Paris, 1953), pp. 113-16; AN F^{1d} III 79, Commission municipale [des récompenses nationales, Toulouse] Procès-verbal, Séance du 23 décembre 1831.

217

attempting to seize it. The demonstrators fell back, the gendarmes in pursuit, to the cafés around the *place,* where they broke up chairs and tables and threw the pieces at their assailants. Some shots were fired, but the infantry and artillery on the square took no part in the melee even when the gendarmes had to flee into their ranks for protection. The crowd dispersed, some to seek arms, others to pull up paving stones, still others to roof-tops to dislodge tiles, which could be rained on gendarmes and troops if the conflict should be renewed. Up to this time—about 5 P.M.—no one had been killed, but a more serious clash seemed imminent.[36]

Providentially into this tense situation arrived a courier from Paris carrying the Duc d'Orléans' first proclamation as Lieutenant-General of the Kingdom. The prefect and the commanding-general on learning of it ordered all troops back to their barracks. Until midnight crowds roamed the streets unrestrained, shouting "Vive la Charte!" In the early hours of August 4 a group of citizens led by liberals associated with the opposition newspaper, *France méridionale,* formed a provisional municipal council, and during the succeeding day the city resumed its usual calm as new military and civil officials replaced the old. In their proclamation to the citizens of Toulouse the new municipal councillors revealed themselves to be less than revolutionary. They based their claim to authority on the sanction of Charles X's prefect, and their interpretation of the revolution must have delighted Périer and Broglie. "The movement that has just been effected in France," they informed the *Toulousains,* "is destined to close the revolution that our fathers began more than fifty years ago." Six of the department's seven deputies subsequently resigned or were expelled from the chamber, but the legitimist sympathies of the majority of electors remained unshaken for another decade.[37]

[36] AN, F[1d] III, 79, Maire de Toulouse to Préfet de la Haute-Garonne, Feb. 14, 1831; *Moniteur,* Aug. 10, 1830, p. 880.
[37] *Ibid.*

The city of Bordeaux the Bourbons had honored by giving its name to the heir to the throne, Charles X's only grandson, the Duc de Bordeaux, but in 1830 its citizens showed no disposition to return the compliment by defending the young prince's inheritance. When the text of the ordinances reached the city, the loading of ships in the port was suspended, wine warehouses were closed, and shops were deserted. On July 28 local officials seized the presses of opposition newspapers in the city. The next day a band of young men replied by breaking the presses of the ministerial journal, the *Défenseur de la Monarchie*. They seized the prefect, who had tried to defend himself sword in hand, and were threatening to drag him through the streets when a leader of the opposition managed to rescue him. Early in the morning of July 31 armed men again roamed the streets. They destroyed several *octroi* collection posts and threatened another tax office, which probably escaped pillage only owing to the timely arrival of troops of the Line. About noon a crowd attempted to force its way into the Hôtel de Ville; its defenders repulsed the attack, and cavalry broke up the crowd. That evening hastily organized companies of the National Guard joined with the troops in restoring order in the city. News of the formation of a provisional authority in Paris reached the city in the evening of August 1 and was enthusiastically received. On August 3 the prefect sanctioned the formation of a provisional municipal government. The transition to the new regime then moved forward without serious disorder. By August 4 the tricolor flew from all public buildings.[38]

In the other large city of the south, Marseille, so uneventful was the passage from Bourbon to Orléanist government that not a single claim for an award of damages came from the city. Not many miles away in the neighboring Department of the Vaucluse the republic came close to a momen-

---

[38] AHMG, D³ 131, Lt.-gén. Cmdt., 11ᵉ Div. milit. to Ministre de la Guerre, July 31, Aug. 3, 4, 1830; Cmdt., 1ᵉ Subdiv., 11ᵉ Div. milit. to Lt.-gén. Cmdt., 11ᵉ Div. milit., Aug. 1, 2, 1830; *Moniteur*, Aug. 2, 1830, pp. 835, 836; Aug. 4, pp. 843-44; Aug. 5, p. 845; Aug. 8, p. 851.

tary local revival. Three officers in command of a vessel carrying troops from Lyon to the Department of the Gard in August persuaded their men to follow them in proclaiming the republic and forcing the mayor of Avignon to recognize it. Their colonel heard of the plan in time to recall the officers and place them under arrest before they could intimidate the mayor.[39]

In Nîmes and the Department of the Gard the revolution kindled deep-seated religious passions that kept the city and the surrounding countryside in constant tension and frequent turmoil for weeks after calm had returned to most of the nation. The population of the city fell into two hostile camps, the one Protestant and liberal, the other Catholic and royalist, and the two rarely met except in conflict. Protestant workers found jobs only with Protestant employers, Catholic workers with Catholic employers. On Sundays the Protestants strolled on one boulevard, the Catholics on another. Each group had its own cafés. Baron Haussez, Prefect of the department from 1820 to 1823, tried to mix both parties at his official receptions but found to his dismay that they kept rigidly apart, and soon, he noticed, the Protestants alone came one week, the Catholics alone the next week. This hostility was the bitter fruit of the wars of religion in the sixteenth century, of the persecution of Protestants after the revocation of the Edict of Nantes, and of the anticlericalism of the First Republic. Only fifteen years earlier hostility erupted into violence after the second defeat of Napoleon and the second restoration of Louis XVIII. Bands of royalists abetted by the governmental authorities assassinated one hundred or more persons, most of them Protestants of Nîmes, attacked and damaged three hundred houses of Protestants in the Department of the Gard, extorted money from as many as two thousand, and obliged hundreds to flee the city. During the Restoration a few reasonable leaders willing to compromise in the public

[39] AN, F[14] III, 79, Commission municipale [de Marseille] pour l'execution de l'Ordonnance royal du 10 novembre 1831; Bapst, *Canrobert*, I, 139.

interest emerged on both sides, but the old antagonism survived.[40]

Nîmes received the news of the overthrow of Charles X with remarkable restraint. Leaders of both parties exhorted their followers to remain calm, and Protestants warned fanatical coreligionists in the nearby Cevennes to stay out of the city. On August 6 the tricolor flew over the principal monuments, and with the consent of the prefect several municipal officers, including the mayor, were replaced, and a local lawyer took over the office of procurer-general, but in the succeeding days the partially purged administration, unsupported by a National Guard, could not control the growing effervescence of the royalists. They spread rumors of the imminent arrival of the Army of Africa to overthrow Orléans and of the landing of Charles X on the nearby Mediterranean coast. Royalist activists of 1815 and 1816 fomented trouble in workers' quarters and made it unsafe for a liberal wearing a tricolor cockade to venture into those areas.[41]

On Sunday, August 15, a ceremony staged to proclaim the Orléanist monarchy brought the two groups into open conflict. Cries of "Vive Charles X!" greeted the official procession, and in the evening crowds gathered in the cafés and streets of the populous workers' quarters shouted the same slogan. About nine o'clock some of their number attacked a group of young men, supposedly liberals, killed one of them and injured four others. A band of liberals came from the center of the city singing the "Marseillaise" got involved in a clash in which a partisan of the Bourbons suffered knife wounds. The next day officials cleared the boulevards but failed to prevent a renewal of isolated violence that killed

---

[40] S. Posener, "La Révolution de Juillet et le Département du Gard," *Mercure de France,* 221 (1930), 507-10; Charles d'Haussez, *Mémoires du Baron Haussez, dernier Ministre de la Marine sous la Restauration* (Paris, 1896, 1897), I, 280-81; Daniel P. Resnick, *The White Terror and the Political Reaction after Waterloo* (Cambridge, 1966), pp. 51, 53-55, 80, 81, 86.

[41] Posener, "Révolution de Juillet," pp. 610-14; *Moniteur,* Aug. 15, 1830, p. 904.

two more. Royalists called on their supporters in the nearby countryside to arm themselves. Liberals vainly demanded the organization of the National Guard.[42]

The government in Paris ordered a regiment of infantry to Nîmes, and for about two weeks after its arrival the two factions lived together in uneasy peace, until August 29, when the last battalion of a regiment of Swiss Guards that had been billeted in Nîmes awaiting dissolution departed for Besançon. Some two hundred royalists, all of them wearing white cockades and following a white flag, accompanied the Swiss to the city's gate shouting "Vive Charles X!" and "Les Bourbons ou la mort!" They marched back into the city and attacked suspected liberals whom they encountered in the streets, and a rumor spread that they had killed a liberal deputy of the department. Several hundred young men from the opposing camp found such weapons as they could—hunting pieces, pitch forks, and spades—and went into the streets to defend the lives and property of their fellow Protestants. The next day liberals, having no faith in the municipal authorities, organized a bourgeois militia and set up headquarters in a Catholic working-class quarter. This provoked the local population, and a band of them attacked the militia headquarters. The sound of gunfire brought more people to the scene, and the news of the battle there excited the whole city. Royalists sent agents into the countryside to seek the aid of the Catholic peasantry; they spread stories that the Protestants of Nîmes were pulling down crosses, massacring Catholics, and preparing to kill all the priests in the city. By dawn of the thirty-first 1700 to 1800 peasants had assembled on the outskirts of the blasphemous city prepared to rescue their fellow Catholics. Meanwhile, the Protestants appealed to their coreligionists in the Cevennes, and in the morning of the thirty-first men from nearby communes began to arrive in Nîmes.[43]

The outbreak of bloody civil war between parties divided

---

[42] Posener, "Révolution de Juillet," pp. 614-16.

[43] *Ibid.*, pp. 616-22; AN, F⁹ 1157, Charles Baillet to Ministre de l'Intérieur, Mar. 23, 1831; F¹ᵈ III, 79, CRN, Dossiers of claimants [1831].

more by religion than by politics seemed imminent. The government ordered troops from as far away as Lyon to hurry to the scene, but none arrived until September 1. In the course of the day and evening of August 31 the Bishop of Nîmes, to whom the municipal government had appealed, induced the Catholic peasants to withdraw before they confronted the Protestant militants. The next day another band of peasants approaching from the direction of Arles fled on encountering troops sent out to stop them. When army units arrived in force, the commanding-general placed the city under martial law, forbade meetings of more than five persons, and ordered all citizens to wear the tricolor cockade under pain of arrest. Before the army enforced this peace the three days of disorder in the city had taken a toll of seven killed—five of them Protestants—and fifteen wounded —all of them Protestants save two. The government undertook to prosecute 1200 persons involved in the rioting, but only twenty-four cases actually reached the courts. Judicial investigations revealed no political conspiracy; the peasants had been without leaders, they admitted no disloyalty to the new government, and had moved only because they saw their religion threatened.[44]

In the months of superficial peace that followed, the Protestants and liberals remained apprehensive. Royalists in Nîmes still openly wore the white cockade, insulted National Guardsmen in the streets, posted seditious signs, and spread rumors of imminent arrival of foreign armies to restore the Bourbons. Villagers in one hamlet near Nîmes hauled down the tricolor and raised the white flag; in another supporters of the fallen monarch paraded a donkey through the streets with a tricolor cockade on its ears. The procurer-general estimated in November that two-thirds of the population of the department were Carlists, and a month later the Minister of War issued special instructions to the commanding-general in the area on measures to be taken in the event of a Carlist insurrection. Nowhere else in

44 Posener, "Révolution de Juillet," pp. 622-26.

France did the partisans of the old regime display so active and sustained a hostility to the new order, but here the bitterness of centuries of strife confused the issues that other Frenchmen saw in the revolution. The peasants who furnished mass support for the Carlists were moved less by their love of Charles X and his ministers—no one shouted, "Vive Polignac!"—than by fears of religious persecution. Royalists could easily excite these apprehensions and give them political direction, but the feared Carlist insurrection never occurred.[45]

Across the Mediterranean in Algeria the Army of Africa, which rumors repeatedly had disembarking in France to save the Bourbon monarchy, waited in uncertainty and inaction for a fortnight until definite word of the events in Paris arrived. Then without incident it transferred its allegiance to the new regime. In an order of the day dated August 11 Marshal Bourmont informed his command that no official report coming to him confirmed the rumors then circulating in the army, but three days later in a new order of the day he announced the abdication of Charles X. The white flag continued to fly over the ships and encampments of the expedition until the sixteenth, when tricolors were raised to the thunder of twenty-one gun salutes. The newly appointed commander of the expedition, General Bertrand Clauzel, and his staff disembarked in Algiers on September 1; Bourmont turned over his command and on September 3 departed into exile, the last of the Bourbon marshals.[46]

The long-established view of the revolution as a Parisian event, accomplished in the capital and carried to the provinces cannot be discarded, but it is misleading insofar as it implies passive acceptance of the revolution. It leaves unexplained, moreover, the sudden and universal collapse of the royal administration throughout the country. It must be tempered by the realization that most of the conditions that produced a revolution in Paris and caused Parisians to

45 *Ibid.*, pp. 626-33.
46 BN, MSS. Fr. 7988, Papiers relatifs à expédition des armées françaises en Afrique et à la prise d'Alger (1830).

welcome a change in government existed in the provinces, too. The Polignac Ministry had undermined the popularity of the regime among the electors. In the elections of June and July 1830, which had posed a clear option between the parliamentary opposition and the ministry and King, the provinces' choice had clearly emerged—they added some fifty deputies to the opposition majority in the preceding chamber. Throughout the country the opposition had organized to contest the elections, and their local committees offered the nuclei of revolutionary committees, ready to protest and perhaps to resist the royal coup d'état, or of provisional municipal governments willing to follow the lead of like-minded men in Paris. To the liberal journalists in the provinces, well-practiced in disrespect for the Bourbon regime, the first ordinance appeared no less vital a threat than it did to Parisian journalists, and in provincial cities they reacted no differently—they defied the ordinance and tried to continue publication of their journals and to excite opposition against the government.

The depression beginning in 1827 ended the Restoration's long years of prosperity in the provinces as well as in Paris. The decline of industrial activity and the drop in wages brought unemployment and distress to urban workers, and the rise in the price of bread hurt urban and rural workers alike. Businessmen suffered from dwindling markets and pressure on profits for the first time in more than a decade. Food riots, violent protests against taxes, and labor disturbances reached a high point in 1829. Conditions had improved by the spring and summer of 1830, but the price of bread remained above the levels of the earlier prosperous years of the Restoration. Everywhere the lingering economic malaise probably disposed men of all classes to accept an attack on the established authorities and undermined the inclination to stand in their defense. The government compounded its weakness in the provinces and failed to utilize its strength by offering no guidance to its partisans. The coup d'état took them by surprise as much as it did the opposition. Unprepared, already shaken by the results of

225

the recent elections, and left without instructions from Saint-Cloud, they allowed their liberal opponents to seize the initiative, win popular support, and install themselves in power almost unopposed.[47]

[47] In an article to be published in the *Journal of Social Issues* in 1972 James Rule and Charles Tilly maintain that popular resistance to the establishment of the authority of the new central government continued for many months after July 1830. The opposition came not from partisans of the Bourbons but from the urban and rural poor protesting taxes and high food prices.

VII

The Little Things: Liquidation
of a Revolution

A REVOLUTION fought in the streets of a great city inevitably disrupts the fragile complex of functions and services upon which its denizens depend. Interference with provisioning, suspension of sanitary services, and disruption of police protection menace health, even life itself. The environment of disorder and uncertainty disturbs the conduct of every business. Death and injury of breadwinners drastically alters the lives of dependents as well as of victims themselves and imposes new obligations on the community. The new government must at once concern itself with the restoration of the conditions of normal life within the city and with the care of the injured and dependents.

In the final days of July 1830 and the succeeding days of August in Paris the struggle for political power, constitutional reform, the threat of disorders in the provinces, and the menace of foreign war preoccupied the leading actors of the revolution, and these matters have commanded the first attention, often the exclusive attention, of historians. But in those days the municipal administration and most of the population of Paris were more concerned with restoring the mundane machinery of daily existence. The "little things," now almost forgotten, then loomed large indeed. Streets had to be reopened and repaired, food supplies assured, street lighting restored, garbage and sewage removal resumed, police services reestablished. The dead of the revolution had to be buried, the wounded nursed back to health, and their dependents provided for. Citizens who had lost property by theft or damage in the course of the fighting expected compensation. The resumption of the administration of justice, the settlement of commercial accounts, even the control of newly "liberated" prostitutes demanded immediate attention.

Once the fighting in the streets came to an end life in Paris superficially resumed its accustomed patterns. On Saturday, July 31, peaceful citizens again appeared on the streets. Shops reopened. Workers returned to their jobs. Men and women again strolled in the Tuileries Garden, and gardeners were busy with their endless watering and pruning. In the evening the garden of the Palais-Royal attracted its usual crowds. Even the city's pigeons, which had fluttered about continuously during the fighting, disturbed by musket fire, had resumed their accustomed places. Lady Aylmer, who had not stirred from her hotel on the Rue Saint-Honoré since Wednesday morning, the twenty-eighth, ventured out Saturday evening; she found the streets peaceful, well lighted by lamps and candles placed in windows of abutting houses. Barricades still obstructed traffic, but their guards had opened passages for pedestrians, and Lady Aylmer was impressed by the courtesy of the National Guardsmen who helped her and her maid pass them.[1] On Sunday, August 1, churches held their customary services. Holiday crowds thronged the Tuileries Garden, promenading and reading newspapers just as they had done a week earlier. The chance of seeing the Duc d'Orléans and his family attracted hundreds to the garden of the Palais-Royal throughout the day. On the east side of the Louvre a continuous procession filed past the mass graves of some thirty victims of the fighting; National Guardsmen at the scene displayed a large plate in

---

[1] R. Anchel, "Un Témoinage anglais sur les journées de Juillet: souvenirs de Lady Aylmer," *Revue d'histoire moderne*, 6 (1931), 363; Henri Vienne, "Dix jours à Paris du dimanche 25 juillet au mardi 3 août 1830," *Mémoires* de la Société bourguignonne de géographie et d'histoire, 8 (1892), 110; Herbert P. Gambrell, "Three Letters on the Revolution of 1830," *Journal of Modern History*, 1 (1929), 605; BHVP, NA 153, Papiers Odilon Barrot, Folio 345, Gouverneur du Chateau des Tuileries to Gen. Dubourg, July 31, 1830.

which they solicited contributions "pour le veuves et les orphelins des braves."[2]

The authorities on August 1 ordered the partial dismantling of barricades, asking that they be restricted to one side of the street, and this operation permitted limited resumption of traffic the next day. Stage coaches reached the center of the city that day for the first time since the twenty-eighth. Theaters, dark for almost a week, resumed performances. The Bibliothèque du Roi on the Rue de Richelieu reopened its doors on August 2, and a number of readers took places in the reading room. On August 5 trading resumed on the stock exchange; 5 percent government bonds opened 2.50 francs above the closing price at the last preceding session on July 27. Prostitutes, ordered off the streets four months earlier by Charles X's Prefect of Police, flooded back on the public way, apparently assuming that the revolution restored their liberties, too.[3]

The resumption of traffic required not merely the removal of barricades but also the repaving of streets. Citizens in areas of fighting had pulled up cobblestones and carried them to top floors of houses to hurl down on soldiers; police found more than two hundred in a single house on the Rue Saint-Martin. Now citizens cooperated in dismantling barricades and in returning, even roughly relaying, the paving stones, but normal traffic demanded a smooth surface that only skilled pavers could lay. The Prefect of Police on July

[2] Emmanuel Viollet le Duc, "Lettres d'Emmanuel Viollet le Duc à sa femme," *Revue de Paris*, 69th year (June 1962), p. 100; Vienne, "Dix jours," pp. 110-11; Anchel, "Témoinage anglais," pp. 363-66; BHVP, NA 153, Cmdt. du Poste des Tuileries to Lafayette, rapport du 1-2 Août 1830.

[3] Anchel, "Témoinage anglais," p. 366; Vienne, "Dix jours," p. 113; *Globe* (Paris), Aug. 2, 3, 1830; *Moniteur universel* (Paris), July 28, p. 824, Aug. 6, 1830, p. 856; *National* (Paris), Aug. 4, 1830; Suzanne d'Huart, "Le Dernier Préfet de Police de Charles X; Claude Mangin," *Actes* du quatre-vingt quatrième Congrès national des sociétés savantes, Dijon (1959); Section d'histoire moderne et contemporaine, p. 607; A. J. de Marnay, *Mémoires secrèts et témoinages authentiques: chute de Charles X, Royauté de Juillet; 24 février 1848* (Paris, 1875), p. 67.

31 appealed to all paving workers to report at once to con-
tractors charged with repaving streets. Their number fell
far short of the need, and at least one police commissioner
employed jobless citizens to do the work in his quarter, but
unskilled workers could accomplish little. In the middle of
August pavers were still busily engaged in restoring streets
in all parts of the city. The national commission set up in
December 1830 to determine compensation for losses suffered as a consequence of the revolution awarded the city
135,000 francs for damages to its streets.[4]

Barricades and breaks in pavements created a sanitary
problem that required even more immediate attention than
the movement of traffic. Most Parisian streets in 1830 lacked
underground sewers. Residents ordinarily dumped household waste waters into street gutters that carried them to the
nearest underground drain. Normally sweepers came
through the streets daily, opened water taps installed at
intervals along the streets and flushed and swept down the
gutters. During the final days of July waste waters backed
up behind barricades and accumulated in holes in the pave-
ment. In the exceptionally hot weather these fetid liquids
and accumulations of garbage and other debris in the streets
—garbage and refuse collection being interrupted—stank to
heaven and created a menace to public health. The Prefect
of Police, acting on the advice of the Conseil de Salubrité,
called on residents to remove waste water accumulated in
holes, to replace paving stones, and to sweep down gutters at
least once daily with fresh water, and, until the flow in
gutters was reestablished, to carry household waste waters to
the nearest underground sewer. On August 2 he ordered

---

[4] AP, A A/420, Commissaire, Qtr. du Marché Saint-Jean to Préfet de
Police, July 31, Aug. 1, 1830; Comm., Qtr. des Lombards to Préfet de
Police, Aug. 3; Comm., Qtr. de Popincourt to Préfet de Police, Aug. 3;
Comm., Qtr. de la Banque de France to Préfet de Police, Aug. 4;
Comm., Qtr. de la Porte Saint-Martin to Préfet de Police, Aug. 4;
Comm., Qtr. du Faubourg Saint-Denis to Préfet de Police, Aug. 5;
"Avis du Préfet de Police," July 31, AN, F7 3884, "Bulletin de Paris,"
Aug. 13; F7 12329, "Bulletin de Paris," Aug. 15, 21; F9 1157, Dom-
mages de Juillet, "Etat de situation des indemnités . . . ," Sept. 25, 1832.

resumption of street cleaning and refuse collection, and he authorized the municipal inspector in charge of the service to obtain additional wagons and carts if necessary and to hire extra hands for street sweeping. The cleaning of sewers and the removal of sanitary sewage—a manual operation, for the city had no sanitary sewers—were resumed at the same time. On August 4 a police commissioner in the Faubourg Saint-Antoine complained that piles of garbage and debris still remained on several streets in his quarter; they smelled badly, and he urged the prefect to order their immediate removal.[5]

After the rioting of July 26 and 27 and the fighting of the two succeeding days scarcely a single street lamp remained unbroken in the central quarters of Paris. The Municipal Commission in one of its first proclamations appealed to Parisians to place lamps in their windows to light the streets. Some had already done this, and most apparently joined in, for observers remarked on the unusual illumination of the streets in the early days of August. The police placed lanterns at points where broken pavements presented special hazards to pedestrians or carriages. Municipal officials soon began replacing the broken lamps, and by the close of the third week of August, the Prefect of Police reported, most of them were again in service.[6]

Even amid the pressing demands of restoring streets the

---

[5] AP, A A/420, Préfecture de Police, Conseil de Salubrité, "Avis," July 31, 1830; Préfet de Police, "Avis," July 31; Comm. de Police, Qtr. de Saint-Eustache to Préfet de Police, July 30; Comm., Qtr. des Marchés to Préfet de Police, July 31; Comm. Qtr. des Champs Elysées to Préfet de Police, Aug. 1; Préfet de Police to Comm. de Police, Aug. 2; Préfecture de Police, Inspection gén. de la Salubrité to Chef de la 3ᵉ Div., Préfecture de Police, Aug. 1; Préfet de Police to [Inspection gén. de Salubrité], Aug. 2; Comm., Qtr. des Lombards to Préfet de Police, Aug. 3, Comm., Qtr. de Chaillot to Préfet de Police, Aug. 3; Comm., Qtr. des Quinze-Vingts to Préfet de Police, Aug. 4.

[6] *Moniteur universel* (Paris), July 31, 1830, p. 828, Aug. 1, p. 831, Aug. 8, p. 864; Anchel, "Témoinage anglais," pp. 364-65; Vienne, "Dix jours," p. 110; BHVP, Série 23, Carton 1830, Guelle to Onazine [Aug. 3]; AP, A A/420, Comm. de Police, Qtr. du Marché Saint-Jean to Préfet de Police, July 31; AN, F⁷ 3884, "Bulletin de Paris," Aug. 13, 1830; F⁷ 12329, "Bulletin de Paris," Aug. 15, 21, 1830.

municipal authorities found time to rechristen streets and bridges whose names recalled the fallen regime. The Rue Charles X became the Rue Lafayette, a name it still carries. The Rue du Duc de Bordeaux, running between the Rue de Rivoli and the Rue Saint-Honoré, became the Rue du 29 Juillet. The Place Louis Seize, the Pont du Jardin du Roi, and the Pont des Invalides regained their Revolutionary or Imperial names—Concorde, Austerlitz, and Jena. The provisional commissioner of the navy, similarly moved, ordered the maritime prefects to change the names of a number of ships, the "Comte d'Artois" to "Ville de Paris," the "Royal Charles" to "Jemmapes," the "Duc de Bordeaux" to "Friedland," "Le Douze Avril," which commemorated the date of the recall of the Bourbons in 1814, to "La Charte." In a similar breaking with the past an ordinance of August 13 prescribed that the King's ministers no longer be addressed as "Monseigneur" but simply as "Monsieur le Ministre."[7]

The deputies who on July 29 appointed the provisional Municipal Commission had two principal motives. One was to provide for the maintenance of order in the city, the other to assure the food supply. The fighting and the barricading of streets had interrupted the daily movement of supplies to the city's markets, and no one could be sure that it would automatically recover. Conceivably, too, royal troops might surround the capital and attempt to starve it into submission. Soon after the commission established itself at the Hôtel de Ville it charged Jean Baude, an editor of the *Temps* and a former subprefect under the Empire, with assuring the provisioning of the city. Happily the threat of starvation proved ephemeral. Supplies of flour in the city on July 30, a survey revealed, would meet the population's need for six weeks. Grain dealers at the central grain markets organized an emergency service to supply wheat to millers at any hour of the day or night. Farmers could not

[7] *Globe*, Aug. 3, 4, 1830; *Moniteur*, Aug. 10, 1830, p. 878, Aug. 14, p. 899; Jacques Hillairet, *Dictionnaire historique des rues de Paris* (Paris, 1962), I, 120, 375, 654, II, 11, 650.

drive their wagons to the markets, but they came to the city's gates and merchants went there to make their purchases, and they met with no serious shortages. The clearing of streets after August 1 permitted resumption of trading in the markets.[8]

The Parisian press in its ecstasy over the "heroes of July" scarcely mentioned the mundane matter of the disposal of the bodies of the dead. Yet it was a serious problem made especially pressing by the extreme heat and complicated by the city's normal procedures of burial. In 1804 the Napoleonic government, concerned by the growing menace to public health of continued burial in the ancient and crowded cemeteries of Paris, opened the first of three new burial grounds on the outskirts and forbade internments within the city. The blocking of streets during the July Days cut off access to these cemeteries, but the rapid decomposition of bodies in the hot weather precluded long delay in burial. On July 28 the fire station on the Rue de la Poterie became a morgue for bodies of victims of fighting around the Market of the Innocents. By the next day the stench was unbearable, and the mayor of the arrondissement and several other citizens decided, despite the law, to inter the bodies in the Place des Innocents. They dug two graves, and into one placed some fifty bodies of civilian fighters, in the other the remains of thirty-five soldiers. Similar emergency burials were made in the cellars of the nearby church of Saint-Eustache, which received forty-three bodies, and in two mass graves near the Louvre, which received thirty-two. More than 150 bodies lay in the morgue on the Ile de la Cité and on the lower level of the Quai Pelletier near the Hôtel de Ville, and on July 30 the Prefect of Police had them loaded on boats and carried to the Champ de Mars for burial. A number of bodies cast into the Seine were retrieved and buried here, too. At least seventy other victims were buried

8 Marie de Lafayette, *Mémoires, correspondance et manuscrits* (Paris, 1837-38), VI, 389; Odilon Barrot, *Mémoires posthumes*, 3d ed. (Paris, 1875-76), I, 113; *Moniteur*, July 31, 1830, p. 827, Aug. 2, p. 855; *Globe*, Aug. 1, 3, 1830.

singly or in small groups near where they fell in a dozen spots scattered across the city.[9]

Even when under ground the dead continued to pose problems. Scarcely a week had passed before the *curé* of Saint-Eustache complained to the local police commissioner of the odor rising from the bodies under his church and expressed fear of the detrimental effect on the health of the neighborhood. The commissioner reported to the Prefect of Police that the remains had not been buried deeply enough nor the vault adequately sealed. He recommended their removal, and in the night of August 16-17 they were exhumed and reburied in the Cemetery of Montmartre beyond the city's limits. In September municipal authorities ordered the area over the soldiers' graves in the Place des Innocents repaved, a process that required the removal of considerable earth, and the remaining cover, even when topped with paving stone, did not suffice to prevent the escape of unpleasant odors. In damp weather odors above the grave of the fifty "patriots" reminded passersby of its contents, too. The latter tomb presented other inconveniences. Covered with flags, flowers, and epitaphs it took up space needed for market stalls, and the crowds attracted by it obstructed traffic. In October 1830 the police commissioner of the district urged the removal of the bodies to the Cemetery of Montmartre, but they remained undisturbed for almost ten years.[10]

[9] BHVP, Série 23, FGms 443, "Précis des Evénemens de Juillet 1830, . . . par Sr. Duplessis . . ."; AP, A A/420, Comm., Qtr. des Marchés to Préfet de Police, Oct. 14, 1830; Préfecture de Police, Directeur de la Salubrité et de l'Eclairage to Préfet de Police, Sept. 11; Police de Paris, Qtr. des Invalides, "Procès verbal constatant . . . l'exhumation du cadavre . . . déposé sur la berge du port d'Orsay . . . ," May 24, 1833; Etat définitif des victimes de Juillet 1830 susceptible d'être exhumées [1840].

[10] AP, A A/420, Curé de Saint-Eustache to Comm. de Police, Qtr. de Saint-Eustache, Aug. 7, 1830; Comm. Qtr. de Saint-Eustache to Préfet de Police, Aug. 13; Police de Ville de Paris, Qtr. de Saint-Eustache, "Procès verbal de l'exhumation . . . des 43 cadavres . . . inhumés dans les caveaux de l'Eglise St. Eustache," Aug. 17; Comm., Qtr. des Marchés to Préfet de Police, Oct. 14, n.d. [Oct. 1830]; Etat définitif des victimes de Juillet 1830 susceptible d'être exhumées [1840].

A royal ordinance of July 6, 1831, prescribed that the remains of all citizens killed in the July Days should be exhumed and placed in the Panthéon, but not until 1840 were they moved and then not to the Panthéon but to the cellars under the newly completed Column of July on the site of the Bastille.[11]

On July 28 the army had taken over responsibility for maintenance of order in Paris. The Prefect of Police fled, leaving his agents to their own initiative and with uncertain authority. The next day the withdrawal of troops and the Gendarmerie left the city without any organized peace-keeping force. The vision of thousands of armed workers, intoxicated by victory and wine, in an unpoliced city raised the gravest apprehensions among citizens fearful for their property and even for their lives. As early as July 28 talk had begun of reestablishing the National Guard of Paris to protect life and property. A few guardsmen appeared on the streets in uniform that day, most of them intending only to stand guard over their own homes and shops. The next day Lafayette accepted command of the National Guard and immediately set about reviving its legions and putting pa-trols on the streets, despite the handicaps inevitable in re-viving an organization three years disbanded. From the Hôtel de Ville, where he established his headquarters that afternoon, he issued a proclamation calling on colonels and other officers of the Guard to form their legions and on noncommissioned officers and guardsmen to prepare to join their units at the first roll of the drums. Pending this sum-mons they should, he advised, go to the homes of their officers and sign the muster rolls. He further asked the colonels or their battalion commanders to come immediately to the Hôtel de Ville for conferences and instructions. The Guard quickly took on the policing of the city. The Barrot

[11] *Moniteur*, July 7, 1831, p. 1183; France, *Bulletin des lois du Royaume de France*, 11th Series, Vol. 3, Part 2, p. 1; 11th Series, Vol. 19, p. 72; AP, A A/420, Comm., Qtr. du Faubourg Saint-Antoine, "Procès-verbal constatant le dépôt des dépouilles mortelle des victimes de Juillet 1830 dans les caveaux de la Colonne de la Place de la Bastille," July 29, 1840.

papers in the Bibliothèque historique de la Ville de Paris include some fifty reports dated July 30 alone addressed to Lafayette from guard posts and patrols, attesting at least to the administrative industry of the new defenders of order. At the Palais-Bourbon one hundred Guards protected the meetings of the deputies. Sixty guarded the Ecole militaire, thirty the Ministry of Finance. Still others manned posts at the Hôtel de Ville, the Louvre, the Tuileries, and the Invalides, and pickets patrolled the streets. A captain on duty at the post at the Hôtel de Ville in the night of August 1-2 recorded sixty-six patrols reporting there in three hours between 11 P.M. and 2 A.M.[12]

These heavy demands required more men than the National Guard of the Restoration, reduced to some 12,000 men in Paris by 1827, could furnish. At the first royal review—on August 28—some 50,000 men paraded before the King, and each day this small army furnished 3700 men for guard and patrol duty. This Guard was less a revival of the old than a newly recruited force organized by experienced officers of the old Guard. The high cost of uniforms and equipment, about 250 francs, which guardsmen had to pay for themselves, had been before 1827 an obstacle to expansion and had limited membership to the well-to-do. In 1830, however, so high stood the esteem for "the good working-man" who had fought and routed the royal troops, that the Parisian legions took in some hundreds of the combatants of July and equipped them at the expense of other members or by the use of funds raised by public subscription. At the time of the dissolution of the Guard in 1827 the government had permitted the officers and men to retain their weapons, but scores of new recruits in 1830 lacked arms, and Lafayette was beseiged with requests for muskets and cartridges. At

<hr />

[12] *Moniteur*, July 31, 1830, p. 827; BHVP, NA 153, Papiers Odilon Barrot, Folios 99, 101, 104, 253-75, 277, 279, 281-90, 292-95, 297, 302, 303, 305-24; Emmanuel Viollet le Duc, "Lettres," p. 99; Hippolyte Bonnelier, *Mémorial de l'Hôtel de Ville de Paris* (Paris, 1835), pp. 247-48.

the end of November the muster rolls still listed a fourth of the men as unarmed.[13]

The National Guard had to perform almost all peace-keeping duties in the city from containing rioters to chasing street peddlers and aiding in the collection of the *octroi*, the municipal tax on certain commodities entering the city. In the first weeks guardsmen showed great zeal for their duties and basked in an atmosphere of public respect and even enthusiasm for this citizen force. Police agents, whose rôle in the July Days had done nothing to reduce popular distrust of them, ordinarily required support of the Guard. Troops of the Line would attempt patrols only if accompanied by a picket of National Guards. Popular exasperation with the Gendarmerie precluded its use in the city, and in mid-August the government formally dissolved the Gendarmerie de Paris and created in its place the Garde municipale de Paris. The force received new and distinctive uniforms, but its close similarity in organization and in strength to the Gendarmerie de Paris suggested that its name and uniform were a disguise for the old organization. The disguise did not apparently make it palatable to Parisians or dependable in the eyes of the authorities, for police and military archives reveal no instance of its being used except in routine guard duty at the time of the disorders and threatened disorders of October and December 1830.[14]

The loss of equipment and the destruction of guard posts posed yet another obstacle to the resumption of routine police services. Many stretchers, hundreds of emergency lanterns and torches, and fire buckets stored at the police

13 Louis Girard, *La Garde nationale* (Paris, 1964), pp. 12, 137, 167-68; BHVP, NA 153, Folios 117, 137, 141, 143, 149, 155, 165, 169, 231, 239, 291, 377; AN, F⁹ 682, Chef d'Etat major, Garde nat. de Paris, "Situation générale au 30 Novembre 1830"; *Moniteur*, Aug. 26, 1830, p. 965.

14 Girard, *Garde nationale*, pp. 167-68; Paul Thureau-Dangin, *Histoire de la Monarchie de Juillet* (Paris, 1888-1900), I, 104; AHMG, E⁵ 1, Maréchal-de-Camp Cmdt., Place de Paris, to Cmdt., 1ᵉ Div. milit., Aug. 9, 1830; Ministre de la Guerre to Cmdt., 1ᵉ milit., Aug. 11; Lt.-gén. Cmdt., 1ᵉ Div. milit. to Ministre de la Guerre, Aug. 18; *Moniteur*, Aug. 19, 1830, p. 922.

commissariats throughout the city were missing after the July Days. On August 2 the Prefect of Police instructed all commissioners to send him reports of equipment they lacked, and the next few days he received reports of dismayingly large needs. The commissioner of the Quartier des Lombards asked for two hundred lanterns; the commissioner of the Quartier de la Porte Saint-Martin wanted two to three hundred. The Quartier de la Banque de France had no lanterns whatsoever, and stretchers had disappeared from two guard posts in the quarter. The Prefect of the Seine ordered the mayors of the arrondissements to see to the most urgent repairs of guard posts such as the replacement of damaged or broken doors and windows and installation of new camp beds. Many of the posts had to be completely rebuilt, and the city eventually presented to the Commission of Damages a bill of nearly a quarter of a million francs for the repair and reconstruction of guard posts.[15]

Financial problems born of the revolution beset both the municipal government and private business. The Provisional Municipal Commission from its first meeting faced financial obligations that could be ignored or postponed only at the risk of upsetting the tenuous peace—relief for thousands thrown out of work by the revolutionary disorders, support for the victims of the fighting and their dependents, feeding and shelter of National Guards from Rouen, Le Havre, and elsewhere, pay for the ephemeral salaried Garde nationale mobile authorized by a decree of July 31.[16] The enforced closing of business establishments during the fighting and the interruption of communications made difficult the settlement of commercial accounts and threatened a rash of damaging legal actions against delin-

[15] AP, A A/420, Préfet de Police to Comm. de Police, Aug. 2, 1830; Comm., Qtr. des Lombards to Préfet de Police, Aug. 3; Comm., Qtr. de la Porte Saint-Martin to Préfet de Police, Aug. 4; Comm., Qtr. de la Banque de France to Préfet de Police, Aug. 4; AS, D³ 1-2, Préfet de la Seine to Maire, 8ᵉ Arrond., Aug. 16; AN, F⁹ 1157, "Etat de Situation des Indemnités . . . ," Sept. 25, 1832.

[16] AN, F⁹ 1152, Préfet de la Seine to Ministre de l'Intérieur, Jan. 27, 1832.

quent debtors. On July 31 the Municipal Commission extended by ten days the maturity of commercial bills coming due between July 26 and August 15, and on the same day the Tribunal de Commerce of the department sanctioned this action and declared that it would entertain protests against nonpayments only eleven days after settlement dates falling within the prescribed three-week period.[17]

The government's abandonment of the capital and the subsequent uncertainty over the legal seat of power caused an extended interruption in the orderly administration of justice in Paris. Members of the bar refused to appear before the courts until certain that judgments would not be nullified. On Monday, August 2, the judges of both the first and second chambers of the Royal Court of Paris took their places on the bench, intending to resume the court's sessions. A number of barristers and solicitors were present, but they sat in the visitors' gallery and were dressed in civilian clothes or in National Guard uniforms instead of in the robes of their offices. When the presiding judge remonstrated with them, they replied that they would not plead before the court until they knew in whose name it administered justice. To the Court of Cassation members of the bar presented the same refusal. The next day the Duc d'Orléans signed an ordinance prescribing that all courts administer justice in the name of "Louis-Philippe d'Orléans, lieutenant-général du Royaume." The bar of Paris still refused to appear before the courts, and not until August 12, after the judges had taken the oath of fidelity to the new king, did the courts resume their routine sittings.[18]

The Municipal Commission ordered the preparation of an official history of the July Days. The commissioners had in mind not a critical examination of its origins and consequences but a narration of the heroic deeds of the com-

17 *Moniteur*, Aug. 1, 1830, p. 857.
18 *Moniteur*, Aug. 4, 1830, pp. 841-42; Aug. 13, p. 896; Georges-Denis Weil, "La Magistrature inamovible et la Révolution de 1830," *La Droit, journaux des tribunaux*, 53rd year (1889), 541; Marcel Rousselet, *La Magistrature sous la Monarchie de Juillet* (Paris, 1937), pp. 22-23.

batants on the winning side. "There will be published," the commission's resolution declared, "an official account of the acts of heroism and humanity that gave lustre to the last days of July." To write the history it tapped a barrister of the Royal Court of Paris who also served as a secretary of the Municipal Commission, Plougoulm by name, and it instructed the mayor of each arrondissement to appoint two men to collect data in his district and deliver it to the chief historian. In September Plougoulm complained that he had received from these assistants very little of the documentation that he needed, and he himself undertook to collect all the data he could. He wrote to persons mentioned in newspaper or other printed accounts of the July Days and sought information directly from them, and he solicited reports from other individuals who had played active rôles in the fighting. In the spring of 1831 he obtained an assistant, and during the summer the Minister of the Interior received a proposal that the ministry subscribe for one hundred copies of his book in order to provide a subsidy for its preparation. Here unfortunately Plougoulm's history drops from the record. No book under his name appears in the catalogues of the Bibliothèque nationale nor in the *Bibliographie de la France*, reasonable proof that it never was published, and no trace of his collected materials exists in the Archives nationales nor in the archives of the city of Paris. In the troubled and disorderly years after 1830 the government, dominated by conservatives, had no desire to extol the virtues of street fighters, and they perhaps allowed the history to die an unrecorded death.[19]

Historians of revolutions preoccupied with political power, social structure, and economic change commonly ignore a question that surely looms large to the contem-

[19] *Moniteur*, Aug. 6, 1830, p. 849; AS, VK³ 17, Vice-Prés., CRN, to Maire, 11ᵉ Arrond., Sept. 9; AN, F¹ᵈ III 33, Plougoulm to Ministre de l'Intérieur, Mar. 23, 1831; F¹ᵈ III 82, Chef, Div. des Gardes nat., to Ministre de l'Intérieur, March 31, July 16, 1831; Ministre de l'Intérieur, March 31, July 16, 1831; Ministre de l'Intérieur to Sous-Préfet de Rambouillet, July 5, 1831; *Bibliographie de la France*, 20ᵉ-24ᵉ Années (1831-35).

poraries of any revolution—who pays the costs? Who settles
the bill for the repair of buildings damaged by gunfire? Who
pays for the replacement of street lamps and the repaving of
streets? Who bears the cost of food and beverages stolen or
requisitioned without payment? Who covers the losses of
looted arms shops? In 1830 the revolutionary chamber of
deputies recognized these costs as obligations of the national
government. In the chamber's second session after the installation of the new king, Benjamin Delessert, one of the
signers of the declaration of the deputies on July 27, introduced a proposal for awards to the participants and aids to
the victims of the July Days. The second article of his bill
declared, "All persons whose property suffered as a consequence of these events [the July Days] will be indemnified at
the expense of the state."[20]

The parliamentary committee on the bill recommended
the adoption of this provision without change, and the
entire project passed the chamber with only six dissenting
votes. In the upper house one lone peer cast a negative vote.
In each arrondissement of Paris a local committee received
and investigated claims and passed on its recommendations
to a central Commission of Damages created in December
1830 and presided over by the Prefect of the Seine. The
commissioners examined business records, listened to testimony of public officials, and sought the advice of independent experts in their efforts to determine the validity of
claims and to establish fair compensation. They received
3700 claims seeking damages totaling 6,600,000 francs. Of
these, 2057 came from private individuals and another 1220
from former members of the Gendarmerie of Paris, and the
remainder from the city of Paris. The largest single category
of claims was for "loss of movable objects by removal, pillage, or accidental destruction." A retailer of tobacco and
brandy on the Place de Grève asked for 3334 francs for
"considerable losses" in his shop. An employee of a wine
seller on the Rue du Temple asked compensation for the

20 *Moniteur,* Aug. 12, 1830, p. 891.

loss of his watch, stolen by men who invaded his employer's shop in the night of July 28. A modest shopkeeper near the Rochechouart Gate reported that the crowd that had destroyed the *octroi* booth there had consumed a cask of wine and all the food in her shop and failed to pay her. A gardener of the Tuileries Gardens who lived on the premises declared that on July 30 men found their way into his wine cellar and drank or wasted two casks of wine and broke one hundred bottles. A M. Soupe, purveyor of wines to the royal household, informed the commission that his contract required him to keep a month's supply of wine on hand in the cellars of the royal palaces; the Civil List paid him for the bottles used, but until they were used title remained with the supplier. The "heroes" who broke into the wine cellar of the Tuileries on July 29 and drank themselves into a stupor had not consumed the wine of "Charles le Sot," as they assumed, but the wine of the unhappy M. Soupe. He asked indemnification for 668 bottles of wine, beer, and liqueur broken or carried away from the Tuileries and for 2600 empty bottles broken, and he presented even larger claims for his losses at Saint-Cloud, the Grand Trianon, and Rambouillet. The commission reimbursed him for his losses at the Tuileries, but twelve years later he was still trying to collect 15,000 francs for his cellars at the other royal residences. One ingenious claimant, a barber, avowed that he had given free shaves to wounded combatants of July at the Hôpital de la Charité and at the Ambulance Saint-Sulpice and had hired an assistant to help him. In November 1830, with creditors pressing him, he asked to be paid for the shaves. Another claimant declared that when on July 29 the doors of Saint-Pélagie Prison were forced and all the prisoners escaped, among the escapees was a foreigner who owed him 22,000 francs. The debtor had fled the country, and the creditor had lost all chance of recovering his money. He regarded this as a loss resulting from the events of July, and he asked an indemnity.[21]

[21] *Moniteur*, Aug. 18, 1830, p. 918; Aug. 19, p. 926, Aug. 28, p. 979; Dec. 6, p. 1627; AN, F⁹ 1157, Dommages de Juillet, "Note relative au

Nearly a year and a half after the revolution the Commission of Damages was still receiving new claims, and not until November 1832 did it finally complete its work. In more than fifty sessions spread over a two-year period it approved 3370 claims and authorized payment of 4,029,000 francs in damages. More than 2,500,000 went to the city of Paris, the largest single beneficiary. For the repair and reconstruction of public buildings alone it received in excess of 800,000 francs. The commission at first borrowed a modest sum from the city to pay the most pressing individual claims, but in January 1831 the Minister of the Interior put at its disposal 1,000,000 francs and later in the year a second 1,000,000, and from these appropriations the commission paid all approved claims of amounts less than 1000 francs, larger claims that required immediate payment, and half of the other private claims. At the end of December 1832 the government asked the chamber for more than 2,000,000 francs to settle its remaining obligations. The Chamber of Deputies balked at appropriating funds to pay some 415,000 francs to former gendarmes for loss of equipment, furniture, and personal effects and 8100 francs to former employees of the Civil List. The government's spokesman argued that the law prescribed payment to all who had suffered loss of property and made no distinction among them based on political affiliations or sympathies, but the majority voted to reduce the appropriation to 1,665,000 francs. A provincial deputy introduced an amendment to eliminate the damages payable to the city of Paris. The state was poorer than the city of Paris, he held, and provincial taxpayers should not be forced to pay the city's expenses, but this appeal to anti-Parisian sentiment did not win enough support to pass amendment. The ap-

---

projet de loi des dommages de Juillet" [n.d.]; "Etat de situation des indemnités dues en execution de la loi du 30 août, 1830 . . . ," Dec. 3, 1831; "Etat de Situation des Indemnités réglés pour pertes aprouvées [*sic*] par suite des événemens de Juillet 1830 . . . ," Sept. 25, 1832; F⁹ 1158, Mme. Dhiet to Roi, May 30, 1831; Dossier Cautrel, Nov.-Dec. 1831; Dossier Bechet, Sept. 6, 1831; Dossier Gaudet, Sept. 7, 1831; Dossier Ranc, Feb.-Sept. 1831; F⁹ 1159, Dossier A. Soupe, [1830]-1842; AS, Vᵇˡˢ 153, P. Martin to Ministre de l'Intérieur [Nov. 1830].

propriations bill as finally approved prescribed that no more claims for damages would be entertained, but it did grant to the Ministry of the Interior 60,000 francs for compensation of property losses in the provinces, which had not yet been considered.[22]

The Ministry of the Interior had received claims totaling nearly 95,000 francs from the provinces, and it now turned them over to local committees for investigation and recommendation. The committees recommended payment of 134 claims for 44,000 francs. The minister approved awards of 27,605 francs. The largest number of claims came from the Department of the Eure-et-Loir for damage to property and other losses resulting from the passage of Charles X's party on the road to Cherbourg. Claimants asked compensation for losses of wine, brandy, bread, eggs, soap, candles, grain, forage, firewood, even kitchen utensils, and still others reported that their growing crops had been damaged by troops bivouacking in their fields. The individual awards in the department varied from 1.15 francs to 400 francs; most of them did not exceed 50 francs. In Nantes two arms merchants received compensation for weapons stolen from their shops, and a contractor was reimbursed for missing tools. The director of the Theater of Nantes claimed that revolutionary disturbances discouraged attendance at the theater and cost him 15,000 francs in revenues; the local committee, pointing out that the law covered only property losses, rejected his claim for damages.[23]

[22] AN, F⁹ 1157, Exposé des motifs de la Loi sur les Dommages de Juillet," [n.d.]; "Etat de Situation des Indemnités reglées pour pertes . . . de Juillet 1830 . . . ," Sept. 25, 1832; "Note relative au projet de lois des dommages de Juillet"; F⁹ 1158, Ministre de l'Intérieur, to Roi [Dec. 1831]; Ministre de l'Intérieur to Ministre des Finances, Nov. 23, 1833; *Moniteur*, Feb. 19, 1833, pp. 436-38, Feb. 20, p. 440; *Bulletin des lois*, 9th Series, Vol. 5, Part 1, pp. 58-59.

[23] AN, F⁹ 1157, Ministre de l'Intérieur, "Rapport au Roi . . . aux dommages causés aux propriétés dans les départements en Juillet 1830," Apr. 18, 1834; Commission des Dommages, Eure-et-Loir, Dossier, 1833; Comm. du Roi auprès la Commission des Dommages to Ministre de l'Intérieur, Sept. 17, 1831; Conseiller de Préfecture, Loire-Inférieure to Ministre de l'Intérieur, May 11, 1833.

Two disappointed claimants had remarkable persistence. The Revolution of 1848 and the establishment of a new government inspired one to revive his claim, dormant since 1842, of 12,000 francs in payment for food, wine, and cash distributed to combatants of the preceding revolution. He neglected to provide any firm evidence of his extraordinary generosity. Late in 1849 another hopeful man asked compensation for loss of personal property in the July Days. The rejection of his claim in December 1849 finally closed the story of the "Damages of July" more than nineteen years after the events that began it.[24]

In the days and weeks immediately after the Revolution Parisians hailed the combatants of July as heroes. Gratitude for deliverance from threatening despotism, relief that the street fighters had stopped with the expulsion of Marmont, and the apprehension that they might, if not treated respectfully, renew the battle against other authorities, combined to produce a paean of immoderate praise. No story of bravery, disinterested sacrifice, or restraint before the temptations of loot was too extravagant for the sympathetic press to recount.[25] This enthusiasm found expression, too, in the outpouring of contributions for care of the wounded and for relief of distress of combatants and their dependents. Liberal newspapers in Paris established funds in their offices and invited contributions. The *Constitutionnel* alone collected more than 1,000,000 francs, and other papers an additional quarter of a million. The Municipal Commission on July 31 invited the mayors of the city's twelve arrondissements to appoint committees to receive contributions. The mayor of the Ninth Arrondissement, who was probably typical, followed this instruction and also posted bills inviting gifts, placed collection boxes at frequented points in his district, and organized a door-to-door canvas. National

---

[24] AN, F⁹ 1158, Dossier Moglia, June 3, 1842—Apr. 22, 1848; Dossier Vauthier, Dec. 3, 19, 1849.

[25] John E. Talbott, "The Good Workingman; Image and Reality in the Revolutions of 1830 and 1848," *Missouri Honors Review* (Univ. of Missouri, 1964), I, 51-55.

Guardsmen joined in soliciting contributions; Lady Aylmer encountered two of them in a china shop in the Rue de l'Arbre-Sec when she went shopping on August 2. Each day the press reported the names of individual contributors. The Lieutenant-General of the Kingdom led the list with a gift of 100,000 francs, and hundreds of others followed his example, some of them in unusual ways: two barbers offered the proceeds from all shaves in their shop during the month of August, artists contributed paintings to a benefit exhibition, and Victor Hugo offered the royalties from two performances of "Hernani." The proceeds of this generosity rose within a year to more than 3,000,000 francs, most of it from Paris, but the departments contributed 900,000 and foreign countries 210,000. England alone sent 156,000 to the fund, and the United States, the second largest foreign contributor, 49,000.[26]

In the first days the newspapers and the local committees in the arrondissements undertook to distribute relief directly to those who applied for it or were reported to them, a system that led to many abuses. On August 12 delegates from the arrondissements organized the Commission de la Souscription nationale, and it supervised expenditures until early October, when the Commission des Récompenses nationales, established by a law of August 30 to administer all aids, indemnities, and awards connected with the revolution, assumed the task. In these two months some 15,000 widows, orphans, wounded, and other combatants in need received more than 700,000 francs from the fund of public contributions.[27]

[26] AN, F^{1d} III 33, Commission des Récompenses nationales (hereafter cited as CRN) to Prés. du Conseil [des ministres], [n.d., rec'd. Nov. 27, 1830]; "Rapport dressé par le Maire du Neuvième Arrondissement," Sept. 25, 1830; F^{1d} III 82, Commission de la Souscription nationale (hereafter cited as CSN), *Compte rendu*, pp. 3-4, 40; AS, VK^3 11, report headed "Mairie du XIe Arrondissement," Sept. 25, 1830; D^3 1-2, "Concert au bénéfice des Blessés"; Anchel, "Témoinage anglais," p. 366; *Journal des débats* (Paris), Aug. 2-5, 8-11, 1830; *National* (Paris), Aug. 10, 1830; *Moniteur*, Aug. 4, 1830, pp. 842-43; *Courrier français* (Paris), Aug. 14, 1830.

[27] AN, F^{1d} III 33, CRN to Prés. du Conseil [n.d., received Nov. 27,

Care of the hundreds of wounded required space that the capital's hospitals lacked and expenditures that their budgets could not meet. In the public hospitals the city assumed the costs of treatment, but the wounded overflowed these institutions. During the July Days doctors and other citizens organized twenty-one field hospitals near the scenes of the fighting, and they received some 1500 victims. These improvised hospitals were intended to provide only temporary, emergency care, but because no place could be found in the hospitals for all their patients, some remained in operation for several weeks. The last to close its doors did not release its last patient until October 8. Voluntary and unofficial organizations, these hospitals depended for financial support on gifts from citizens in their neighborhoods, public collections in the streets, and, in a number of cases, grants by the local mayors' offices, probably from funds of the Commission de la Souscription nationale. The commission also organized and financed a convalescent home for recuperating wounded in the former barracks of the Garde du Corps at Saint-Cloud, which during its three months' existence cared for more than 400 men. In the spring of 1830 the commission paid the cost of sending some four score convalescents to watering places reputed for the healing of wounds. The Law of December 23, 1830, on aids and awards to participants in the revolution authorized the admission to the Hôtel des Invalides of victims whose wounds qualified them for pensions, but only three among them applied for the privilege.[28]

1830]; "Rapport dressé par le Maire du Neuvième Arrondissement," Sept. 25, 1830; Ministre de l'Intérieur to Roi [1831, report on Récompenses nationales]; F^{1d} III 47, CRN, Dossier Ch. Brunet; F^{1d} III 82, CSN, *Compte rendu*, pp. 8-13, 15-16; BHVP, Révolution de 1830, Carton 23, "Observations sur l'emploi des fonds de la souscription pour les blessés des memorables Journées de Juillet," [n.d.].

[28] AN, F^{1d} III 82, CSN, *Compte rendu*, pp. 13-15, 19-23; F^9 1154, Jourdan and Desportes to Ministre de l'Intérieur, May 24, 1831; Ministre de l'Intérieur to Roi, Aug. 1831; AS, V^{bis} 153, CRN, 11ᵉ Arrond., Dossier Mallet; AN, F^{1d} III 33. Ministre de l'Intérieur to Roi [1831, report on Récompenses nationales]; F^9 1156, Ministre de l'Intérieur to Ministre de la Guerre, Jan. 10, 1832.

As the wounded recovered and as the Commission des Récompenses nationales assumed responsibility for the support of the disabled and of widows and orphans, the Commission de la Souscription nationale had fewer and fewer legitimate outlets for the still very large sums of money in its possession. In 1830 it decided to use most of its remaining funds to grant modest endowments in government bonds to the permanently disabled among the wounded, to widows and orphans, and to dependent parents. Smaller cash grants went to combatants whose wounds had been only temporarily disabling. By the time it closed its books in 1832 the commission had made nearly 4000 individual grants. After the completion of this principal distribution of its assets the commission had about 100,000 francs in uncommitted funds. The commissioners decided to use this sum and any awards unclaimed by January 1, 1834, for grants to orphans of the revolution when, on reaching the age of eighteen, they ceased to receive allowances from the government.[29]

Another philanthropic effort initiated in the spring of 1831 undertook to aid the children of surviving combatants. A sense of indebtedness to the vanquishers of Marmont and an anxiety to divert potential revolutionaries to peaceful paths inspired a group of liberal deputies and peers, including Lafayette and Odilon Barrot, to provide scholarships for needy sons of combatants who received the Cross or the Medal of July. In its appeal for funds the committee carefully explained that it had no intention of financing advanced education that might make children dissatisfied with their stations in life. Vocational training in keeping with the position of each child's parents was its highest aspiration, and in pursuit of that end the committee used its funds to grant scholarships in a vocational school newly established in the Faubourg Saint-Antoine.[30]

[29] AN, F¹ᵈ III 82, CSN, *Compte rendu*, pp. 29-32; F¹ᵈ III 40, Préfet de la Seine to Ministre du Commerce et des Travaux publics, May 8, 1832; Préfet de la Seine to Ministre de l'Intérieur, "Espèce de Tontine crées en faveur des Orphelins de Juillet sur un fond provenant de la Souscription nationale," Aug. 1840.

[30] AN, F¹ᵈ III 39, "Souscription nationale au profit des enfans des

A royal ordinance of August 26, 1830, made the first hesitant step toward what became an elaborate governmental system of awards, pensions, and indemnities paid to participants and victims of the revolutionary days. This ordinance created a commission headed by General Charles Fabvier, commander of the "Place de Paris," to receive claims from citizens who distinguished themselves by their devotion to "the national cause" on July 27, 28, and 29. Three days after the publication of this ordinance the King signed a law authorizing government pensions for widows, orphans, and parents of those killed in the fighting of July and for the permanently disabled and interim support for the temporarily disabled. The law provided, too, that a medal be struck to commemorate the events of July. A subsequent law prescribed that in addition to the medal, which would be distributed to participants designated by the commission, a special decoration, later known as the "Cross of July," be created for those who had particularly distinguished themselves. The commission later ruled that the cross was especially intended for those who had played such a rôle that they would have paid with their lives had the revolution failed and the Bourbons prevailed, but this prescription was generously interpreted.[31]

The commission functioned through the winter and spring and summer and finally completed its work in October 1831. It received more than 20,000 claims, and its existence was rarely serene. In May it had to call for guards to protect it against the crowds of claimants for the cross who swarmed to its offices and interfered with its work. Guards were still there in late August, when the commission protested a proposal to remove them.[32]

Combatants de Juillet, Séance du lundi 2 Mai 1831"; Ministère de l'Intérieur, Chef, Div. des Gardes nats., to Ministère de l'Intérieur, May 9, 1831; F⁹ 1156, Ministre de l'Intérieur to Veuve Landion, May 24, 1832; Archives dépts. de Seine-et-Oise, IV.M.1³², Choiseul to Préfet [n.d.]; Hillairet, *Dictionnaire*, I, 325.

31 *Moniteur*, Aug. 27, 1830, p. 971, Sept. 2, p. 1009, Dec. 17, p. 1725, July 26, 1831, p. 1262.

32 AN, F¹ᵈ III 33, Ministre de l'Intérieur to Prés., CRN, Mar. 2, 1831;

Its investigations completed, the commission recommended the granting of life-time pensions to 271 widows, 331 parents, and 506 wounded. Three hundred eighty-one orphans received aid until they completed their eighteenth years. On the commission's recommendation 274 combatants of July were appointed sublieutenants in the army and 590 were offered noncommissioned officerships.[33]

The Law of December 13, 1830, authorized the formation of local commissions of reward in the provinces, and commissions were established in thirty-nine departments, but only two—the Gard and the Gironde—recommended the granting of pensions, only three—the same two and the Seine-Inférieure—asked indemnities for wounded, and two —the Seine-Inférieure and Seine-et-Oise—recommended men for commissions in the army.[34]

The Commission des Récompenses nationales, after completing careful investigations both of the claimants' rôles in the revolution and of their respectability and loyalty to the new regime recommended the award of the 3831 Medals of July and 1830 Crosses of July. The provincial commissions were especially generous in their recommendations for the cross. Ten commissions proposed the awarding of 145 crosses—110 in Lyon alone—and fifty-nine medals, but the government approved only thirty-seven crosses—none in Lyon—and fifty-eight medals.[35]

The Law of December 13, 1830, prescribed the erection of

Gran de Saint-Vincent to Ministre de l'Intérieur, May 6, 1831; Ministre de l'Intérieur to Préfet de Police, May 7, 1831; Comm. du Gouvernement, CRN, to Prés. du Conseil, Aug. 30, 1831; Ministre de l'Intérieur to Lt.-gén. Cmdt., 1er Div. milit., Aug. 31, 1831; Comm. du Gouvernement, CRN, to Prés. du Conseil, Nov. 1, 1831; Ministre de l'Intérieur to Prés., CRN, Mar. 2, 1831.

[33] AN, F1d III 33, Ministre de l'Intérieur to Roi [1831]; F1d III 40, Royal Ordinance of Aug. 23, 1831; Ministère de l'Intérieur, Sous-Sécrétaire d'Etat, to Ministre de l'Intérieur, Dec. 18, 1840.

[34] AN, F1d III 81, Ministère de l'Intérieur, Chef, Div. des Gardes nat. et des Affaires milit., to Ministre de l'Intérieur, Feb. 11, 1833.

[35] AN F1d III 33, Ministre de l'Intérieur to Roi [1831]; F1d III 81, Ministère de l'Intérieur, Chef, Div. des Gardes nat., to Ministre de l'Intérieur, Feb. 11, 1833.

a monument to the events of July, and in mid-1831 a royal ordinance provided that the monument—then redefined as a memorial to the victims of the fighting—would be built on the site of the Bastille. The first stone was laid on July 27, 1831, the anniversary of the revolution, but funds for construction were not appropriated until 1833, and a supplemental appropriation to complete it was necessary in 1839. The finished structure is the "Column of July," which still stands on the Place de la Bastille. The names of 504 dead are inscribed on the bronze plates that cover the column, and the remains of the dead, exhumed from earlier burial places, are buried in the crypt below. The King dedicated the monument on July 28, 1840, the tenth anniversary of the revolution.[36]

[36] *Moniteur,* July 7, 1831, p. 1183, July 29, 1840, p. 1769; *Bulletin des lois,* 9th Series, Vol. 1, Part 1, p. 127, Vol. 19, p. 72; F^{1d} III 82, Ministère de l'Intérieur, Sécrétaire-gén., to Ministre de l'Intérieur, Sept. 9, 1839; Ministre de l'Intérieur to Ministre des Travaux publics, Sept. 12, 1839.

VIII

The Crowd in the Revolution

THE KEY rôle of the crowd in the Revolution of 1830 no historian has disputed, but for decades none sought to determine the interests and aspirations that motivated its participation. Historians commonly saw the crowd as a unit with a single set of motives that were usually only a reflection of those of the opposition deputies and journalists. In the mid-twentieth century historians, particularly Ernest Labrousse and Louis Chevalier, established that thousands of Parisian workingmen and women in 1830 had specific grievances—lack of work, low wages, the high price of bread, wretched housing, rejection by an aristocrat- and bourgeois-dominated society—that had nothing to do with the constitutional quarrel between deputies and crown or with the dispute over censorship that alienated journalists and printers from the Polignac Ministry. Labrousse and Chevalier suggested that the crowds in 1830 were recruited from these economically distressed and rejected citizens, but only an examination of the composition of the crowd and the motives of its individual members can determine who actually fought and why they fought.[1]

The crowd in 1830—like the crowds in the Revolution of 1789—was not made up of the desperately poor and the dispossessed, nor did the substantial middle class of business, the professions, and public office have more than a small part in it. Among the 211 dead on the surviving list of the Commission des Récompenses nationales and the 1327 wounded and other combatants who received compensation

---

[1] Ernest Labrousse, *Le Mouvement ouvrier et les idées sociales en France de 1815 à la fin du XIXᵉ siècle* (Paris, 1948), pp. 30-39, 90-94; Louis Chevalier, *Classes laborieuses et classes dangereuses à Paris pendant la première moitié du XIXᵉ siècle* (Paris, 1958).

from the commission, fewer than 300 were laborers and servants, and but 85 came from the professions. Fifty-four were shopkeepers. Nearly 1000 were artisans and skilled workers: 126 carpenters, joiners, and cabinetmakers, 118 stonemasons, 94 shoemakers, 57 locksmiths, 31 jewelry-makers, 28 printers, and 27 tailors.[2] The numerical prominence of some of these occupations in the crowd merely reflected their large numbers in the population of the city. No occupational census exists for 1830, but a record of the occupations of persons who died in Paris in 1831 and the Chamber of Commerce's industrial census in 1846 give some clue to the occupational structure of the city's population. The percentage of printers, shoemakers, jewelrymakers, and tailors among the adult combatants is approximately the

2 AN, F¹ᵈ III 33, Ministère de l'Intérieur, Commission des Récompenses nationales (hereafter cited as CRN), 2ᵉ Etat des citoyens tués. . . ; F¹ᵈ III 34-37, Etats des sommes payées aux combattants blessés et non blessés. . . . The CRN compiled the names of the dead together with their dates and places of birth, residence, and occupations in two *états*, the first of which is missing from the archives. The "2ᵉ Etat" includes 211 of the 496 names on the two *états*. In 1840 the names of the dead were inscribed on the Column of July on the Place de la Bastille; these names, 504 in all, are printed in the *Bulletin des lois du Royaume de France*, 9th Series, Vol. 21, pp. 79-86. The acceptability of the dead, wounded, and other combatants who received compensation as a representative sample of the whole body of combatants may be questioned. The well-to-do are probably underrepresented in the latter two categories. Financial assistance was intended for those in need, and some, even among the wounded did not apply for it; others who applied did not qualify. At the opposite end of the social scale men with police records and fugitives from justice may have feared to ask for assistance, and some illiterates perhaps did not even know how to apply, although the government made a conscientious effort to find all those deserving of help. The dead are subject to fewer reservations as a sample, for no compelling reasons existed to induce either the government or relatives to keep names off the list. The occupational distribution in the two lists—the dead, on the one hand, and the wounded and other combatants, on the other—are strikingly similar, which suggests that the latter was not seriously affected by omissions. Both compilations may have been distorted by the reluctance of combatants to report themselves, and of survivors and government agents to report others, under any but respectable occupational rubrics even though their connections with them were perhaps remote.

same in each case as their percentage in the adult, employed, male population. The percentage of masons among the adult dead and wounded, however, was more than double, of locksmiths approximately double, and of carpenters, joiners, and cabinetmakers at least a third larger than their percentages in the total population of employed, adult men.[3] Members of these same old, established crafts so conspicuously active in 1830, had usually occupied a large place in the revolutionary crowds in Paris of 1789 to 1795.[4] Their *esprit de corps* and their *frondeur* tradition perhaps encouraged collective violence in 1830.

The records include no category of the unemployed. The rubric of lowest economic status is that of the laborer, and but only a little above it are the clerks and *garçons* in a variety of enterprises. All of these contributed to the combatants—126 laborers, 79 clerks, 52 *garçons*—although not out of proportion to their large numbers in the city, and even these must not be equated with the scum and the barbarians of Paris.[5] An official of one of the dressing stations set up during the fighting to care for the wounded reported that almost all the combatants whom he saw were honest, laborious workmen, well thought of by their employers,[6] and the report of a committee organized to aid the wounded in the Third Arrondissement stated pointedly that anyone who thought that the revolution was made by "the last class" of the people would be mistaken. The combatants from that district, which included the quarter of Montmartre and the area around the central markets, were crafts-

[3] Dépt. de la Seine, *Recherches statistiques sur la ville de Paris et le Département de la Seine* (Paris, 1826-60), v, Tableau 120; vi, 34, 256, 626; Chambre de Commerce de Paris, *Statistique de l'industrie à Paris . . . pour les années 1847-1848* (Paris, 1950), Partie 1, p. 38, Partie 2, Tableaux gén. 2C, 2D, 2E, 2G, 2H, 2I, 2K.

[4] George Rudé, *The Crowd in the French Revolution* (Oxford, 1959), pp. 185, 246-48.

[5] AN, F^{1d} III 33, 2e Etat des citoyens tués; F^{1d} III 34-37, Etats des sommes payées aux combattants; Seine, *Recherches statistiques*, v, Tableau 120.

[6] Victor Crochon, "Souvenirs," MS in BHVP, Série 23, FGms 320-22, II, 881.

men who owned their own shops, well-paid workers with jobs, and former soldiers.[7] A police report to the Commission des Récompenses nationales on the morality of thirty-three claimants for widows' pensions who were not legally married showed among them only three "exceptions" to good morals; most of the widows were orderly women who had lived with their men for many years.[8]

Independent compilations of the dead and wounded in two arrondissements confirm the important place of skilled craftsmen in the crowd. A registry of payments made to dependents in the Eighth Arrondissement, which included the Faubourg Saint-Antoine and the Marais, listed fifty-four men killed in combat. Among them were three laborers. The largest occupational groups were six cabinetmakers and joiners, four sawyers, three locksmiths, and two masons.[9] On an early list of fifty-two dead and wounded in the Second Arrondissement identified by occupation were seven masons and six locksmiths.[10]

In the so-called Bourgeois Revolution of 1830 the middle and upper bourgeoisie were either immune to bullets or absent from the firing line. Immunity is improbable, however, for some bourgeois met their ends as uninvolved bystanders like that *négociant filateur* who, the record says, was killed while "out on business" or like the merchant killed "at his window."[11] On the commission's list of dead were one doctor and one teacher but no bankers, no lawyers, no deputies, no publishers or journalists, although one source listed one journalist dead.[12] A few from this class do figure among the wounded and other combatants—four doctors, one lawyer, and eight teachers but no journalists, no publishers, no

---

[7] AS, V^{b1s} 287, Commission des Secours pours les Blessés de Juillet, 3ᵉ Arrond., Compte rendu.

[8] AN, F^{1d} III 33, Préfet de Police to Prés., CRN, June 20, 1831.

[9] AS, D³ 1-2, "Morts. Ancien 8ᵉ Arr^t."

[10] BHVP, Série 23, FGms 784, "Rapport de M. Sensier . . . commissaire de 2ᵉ Arrondissement, chargé de constater le nombre de victimes . . . des glorieuses journées des 27, 28 et 29 Juillet 1830."

[11] AS, D³ 1-2, "Morts. Ancien 8ᵉ Arr^t."

[12] AN, F^{1d} III 33, 2ᵉ Etat des citoyens tués; AS, V^{b1s} 3, CRN, 4ᵉ Arrond., Dossier Thonux.

deputies—and all combined their numbers do not even approach the number of masons or of cabinetmakers alone.[13] The top-hatted bourgeois on the barricade in Ferdinand Delacroix's "Liberty Leading the People" scarcely deserves his conspicuous place, certainly not as a symbol of his kind in this perilous spot.

Delacroix would mislead us, too, if we should assume from his painting that women and gamins played a considerable rôle in the fighting of July. The commission recorded no women dead on its list. At least two were killed, not, however, as combatants but apparently as unlucky spectators.[14] The names of fifty-two women appear on the commission's list of wounded. One was reported to have fought the Royal Guard with a kitchen knife, but more commonly the rôle of women, if they were actively engaged, was in pulling up pavements, throwing stones, and caring for the wounded.[15]

A prefect of police wrote in 1832 that the gamins of the capital, those homeless, lawless urchins of the streets, always carried the first stones to the barricades and were always in the forefront of resistance in revolutionary movements, a statement that would seem to justify the prominence that Delacroix gave to his gamin mounting the barricade, a pistol in each hand, side by side with Liberty herself.[16] Yet the presence of the gamin there is as misleading as that of the cravated bourgeois or the bosomy female. Among the recorded dead were three boys of fourteen years and one of twelve. The twelve-year-old was killed while passing cartridges to his father, a relationship that rules him out of the abandoned youth.[17] On the tables of the wounded and other

[13] AN, F[1d] III 34-37, Etat des sommes payées aux combattants.

[14] "Rapport de M. Sensier"; AS, D[8] 1-2, "Morts. Ancien 8e Arr[t]."

[15] "Rapport de M. Sensier"; AS, V[bis] 1, CRN, 4e Arrond., Dossiers A. Antoine and M. Gabriel; AN, F[9] 1155, Combattants de Juillet, Dossier Haeberlet; Raymond Lecuyer, *La Révolution de Juillet . . . impressions et récits contemporains: Mémoires de Alex. Mazas-Chronique de Rozet* (Paris, n.d.), pp. 62, 63, 77, 96, 105.

[16] Chevalier, *Classes laborieuses*, p. 120.

[17] AN, F[1d] III 33, 2e Etat des citoyens tués.

fighters who received financial assistance were two eight-year-old boys, one of ten years, and sixteen between the ages of twelve and fifteen, a total of nineteen among more than 1500 combatants.[18] Some of these were probably accidental casualties—the two eight-year-olds, almost certainly. Not all the remainder were waifs and urchins. One thirteen-year-old was the son of a building contractor and elector. His brother, just a year older, won the Medal of July for his part in the fighting.[19]

Of the dead and wounded whose ages were recorded, 54 percent were between the ages of twenty and thirty-five. All of these were born after 1789 and could not have remembered the great days of the Revolution or been moved by a personal experience in it. Indeed, fewer than 5 percent were old enough to have any meaningful personal recollections of the Revolution. On the other hand, more than half were of an age to remember the Empire and to have served in the imperial armies.[20]

The theory that the crowd in the revolution was recruited from the nomadic, rejected part of the population is not sustained by a comparison between the proportion of immigrants to Paris among the activists and their proportion among the total adult population. The difference between the two figures is slight if, indeed, there is any difference at all. About 67 percent of the city's population in 1833 were born outside the capital department. Seventy-six percent of the dead and 71 percent of the wounded on whom this information is available (two-thirds of the total) were born outside the Department of the Seine. The first figure, 67 percent, should probably be revised upward before it is compared with the latter two, for the dead and wounded were almost exclusively adults. The total population, on the

18 AN, F^{1d} III 34-37, Etats des sommes payées aux blessés pensionnés . . . ; Etats des sommes payées aux blessés pensionnés temporairement.

19 AN, F^{1d} III 43, CRN, Dossier Barbier.

20 AN, F^{1d} III 33, 2ᵉ Etat des citoyens tués; AN, F^{1d} III 34-37, Etats des sommes payées aux blessés pensionnés; Etats des sommes payées aux blessés pensionnés temporairement.

other hand, included children, of whom a higher proportion is likely to be native born, and the adult population alone would have a higher proportion of those born outside the department.[21]

Knowing that the crowd was composed largely of men from skilled crafts, reasonably mature in years, makes the question of their taking up arms not less but more puzzling. Charles X's last Minister of the Navy, Haussez, believed that the anti-Bourbon conspiracy had organized the combatants and paid them to fight. Most of the prisoners taken by royal troops on July 27 and 28, he claimed, carried blue or yellow triangular cards showing the amount of their pay and where they could collect it.[22] An officer of the 3d Regiment of the Guard reported that poorly dressed combatants taken prisoner near the Pont Neuf on July 28 had in their pockets twenty franc pieces that they could not satisfactorily explain.[23] Guernon-Ranville, Minister of Public Instruction, and Montbel, Minister of Finance, had heard the story of the triangular cards, too, probably from the same source as did their colleague, Haussez, but no other source offers confirmation of these charges.[24]

The crowds on July 26, the day on which the four ordinances appeared in the *Moniteur*, were simply random strollers and idle spectators around the Palais-Royal and the offices of the opposition newspapers. Paris was a city of apartment dwellers, and to escape their cramped and hot quarters Parisians spent much of their leisure time in parks and on the streets. July 26 was a Monday, a holiday for many, and the crowds that day scarcely differed from those

Louis Chevalier, *La Formation de la population parisienne au XIXe siècle* (Paris, 1950), pp. 284-85; AN, F^{1d} III 33, Etat des citoyens tués; Etats des sommes payées aux blessés pensionnés; Etats des sommes payées aux blessés pensionnés temporairement.

[22] Charles d'Haussez, *Mémoires du Baron d'Haussez, dernier Ministre de la Marine sous la Restauration* (Paris, 1896, 1897), II, 232-33.

[23] AS, D 4 AZ 1181, "Précis des événemens aux quels à pris part la troisième regiment d'infanterie de la garde royale . . . ," p. 14.

[24] Martial de Guernon-Ranville, *Journal d'un ministre* (Caen, 1873), p. 175; Guillaume de Montbel, *1787-1831; souvenirs du comte de Montbel, ministre de Charles X* (Paris, 1913), pp. 244-45.

that gathered in the center of the city on any hot, summer holiday. They showed little interest in the newly published ordinances. The King and Polignac were confident that the people would be indifferent, and on the twenty-sixth and the morning of the twenty-seventh the temper of the city sustained their judgment.[25] Armand Carrel of the *National* remarked bitterly to Charles de Rémusat on the peaceful appearance of the streets on the afternoon of the twenty-sixth.[26] At a meeting of journalists in the offices of the *National* those who had just come across the city reported that the people were not moving.[27] The next day the Vicomte de Saint-Chamans, an officer of the Royal Guard, happened to pass newspaper offices where editors and publishers were defying efforts of police to seize their presses because of their violation of the new press ordinance; a large crowd had assembled, and he heard some threatening words, but he had seen such crowds in Paris before, and he recalled that they had shouted but not acted. He expected nothing different this time.[28]

The unconcerned gatherings even on the twenty-sixth did include some groups of men who had well-established connections among themselves and were not simply random concourses of individuals thrown together that day by chance. One such group was the printers, probably the most coherent and articulate body of skilled workers in the city, and they had just acquired a new and common grievance. To them alone among the craftsmen and workers of Paris, the ordinances posed a direct and immediate threat. The first ordinance placed heavy censorship on the publication of newspapers and magazines, and enforcement of it would

---

[25] AN, 115 AP, Archives des familles Montholon et Semonville, "Recit detaillé des entrevues qui eut le duc de Semonville avec Charles X du 25 juillet au 7 août"; CC 546, Chambre et Cour des Pairs, Testimony of Vte. Foucauld, Col., Gendarmerie royale de Paris, Nov. 28, 1830; Achille de Vaulabelle, *Histoire des deux restaurations* (5th ed., Paris, 1860), VIII, 164-65; Louis de Viel-Castel, *Histoire de la Restauration* (Paris, 1860-78), XX, 539.

[26] Charles de Rémusat, *Mémoires de ma vie* (Paris, 1958-67), II, 316.

[27] Louis Blanc, *Histoire de dix ans*, 12th ed. (Paris, 1877), I, 181.

[28] Alfred de Saint-Chamans, *Mémoires* (Paris, 1896), pp. 489-90.

close many printing establishments and throw hundreds of printers out of jobs.[29] Printers did not work on Mondays, and on Monday, July 26, as they often did on holidays, they went out beyond the *octroi* wall to the rustic cafés, where the price of food and wine, free of municipal taxes, was lower than in the city. Here on this day they talked about the ordinances, denounced Charles X, and the majority of them agreed that they would protest the new censorship by staying away from work the next day. They tried to stir up the masons, the carpenters, and other workers gathered in the cafés but with no apparent success. The succeeding morning a few of the printers reported for work, but they soon joined their striking colleagues after publishers cancelled printing orders and heads of printing establishments closed their shops. Some five thousand aggrieved printing workers now roamed the streets looking for allies in their protest.[30]

Throughout that day, July 27, the printers mixed in the thick of the increasingly threatening crowds around the Palais-Royal. They alone among all the occupational groups in Paris appeared repeatedly in police reports and other testimony of eyewitnesses. About noon some thirty of them provoked a squad of mounted gendarmes on the Place du Palais-Royal into charging up a narrow street where they were assailed by stones and flower pots. Rémusat's friend, Pierre Leroux, one of the publishers of the *Globe*, encountered a band of printers roaming the streets that afternoon, and he was alarmed by their threatening appearance. A similar group, probably, ambushed a detachment of cavalry on the Rue de Rohan and pelted it with rocks. A police summary of the growing violence that evening declared that everywhere the leaders of the crowd were heads of printing

[29] *Moniteur universel* (Paris), July 26, 1830, p. 814.

[30] Ladvocat, "Note pour Monsieur le Ministre de l'Intérieur sur les ouvriers imprimeurs," Sept. 4, 1830, reprinted in Paul Chauvet, *Ouvriers du livre en France de 1789 à la constitution de la Fédération du Livre* (Paris, 1956), pp. 645-46; Vaulabelle, *Histoire*, VIII, 204-5; Marie de Lafayette, *Mémoires, correspondance et manuscrits* (Paris, 1837-38), VI, 384.

shops, journalists and unemployed lawyers and that their followers were their workers.[31]

The printers' rôle seems to have been principally one of provocation. They did not figure prominently in the serious fighting of the succeeding days. Twenty-eight appear in the Commission des Récompenses nationales' record of dead, wounded, and other combatants—a small showing compared with the 118 stonemasons or the 126 carpenters, cabinetmakers, and joiners.[32]

The liberal journalists were another coherent group among the early aimless crowds. The ordinances at once assaulted their principles and threatened their livelihoods. A number of them met on July 26 in the offices of the *National* and signed an inflammatory protest drawn up by Thiers against the King's violation of the Charter.[33] The next morning the *Globe*, the *Journal du commerce*, the *National*, and the *Temps*, appearing in defiance of the law, carried the protest, and the last two also printed it on posters. Journalists, printers, and the employees of at least one newsdealer distributed copies to cafés, restaurants, and reading rooms in all quarters of Paris, and some of them went about reading the protest aloud to all who would listen and adding their own comments and exhortations.[34]

[31] AN, 149 AP 1, Papers of Jean-Claude Mangin, Préfet de Police, Rapports de Police, July 27, 28, 1830; CC 547, Chambre et Cour des Pairs, Commission de la Chambre des Députés, Enquête, Sept. 16, 1830; CC 550, Chambre et Cour des Pairs, Mondar, Officier de Paix, Rapport, July 27, 1830, 1:00 P.M., Sous-chef de la Police municipale, Report to Préfet de Police, July 27, 1830; AS, VK⁸ 17, Report of "un attaché à la rédaction du Figaro"; AS, Vᵇⁱˢ 3, CRN, 4ᵉ Arrond., Dossier Melien; Rémusat, *Mémoires*, II, 322.

[32] AN, F¹ᵈ III 33, 2ᵉ Etat des citoyens tués; F¹ᵈ III 34-37, Etat des sommes payées aux combattants.

[33] Rémusat, *Mémoires*, II, 316; Crochon, *Souvenirs*, II, 30-32; Viel-Castel, *Histoire*, XX, 562-66.

[34] Blanc, *Histoire*, I, 188; Viel-Castel, *Histoire*, VIII, 205; Anaïs de Raucon Bazin to J. F. Michaud, Aug. 10, 1830, in A. J. de Marnay, *Mémoires sécrets et témoinages authentiques: chute de Charles X . . .* (Paris, 1875), pp. 12-13; Alexandre Mazas, *Mémoires* in Lecuyer, *Révolution de Juillet*, p. 27; AN, CC 549, Chambre et Cour des Pairs, Mangin to Polignac, July 27, 1830; AS, DM¹⁸ 1, Administration gén., Venard to CRN, Feb. 7, 1831; Vᵇⁱˢ 1, CRN, 4ᵉ Arrond., Dossier De-

Except for the journalists' printed protest we do not know what they and the printers said in their incitement of the crowd. The published protest was purely political—a denunciation of the ministry for violation of the Charter and an appeal to the Chamber of Deputies to resist the government's illegal actions. The crowds first heard it with surprise and incomprehension. Defense of a charter under which they had neither the right to hold office nor the right to vote was no affair of theirs. One captured combatant, questioned about the Charter, identified it as a piece of state-owned property whose revenue the King was trying to appropriate![35] Yet by evening of that day the crowd was hurling bricks and stones at police and soldiers and pillaging arms shops and the next day was in pitched battle with the King's best troops.

The journalists' call for defiance, although couched in political terms, may have been understood as an invitation to protest economic distress, both present and past, that was easily blamed on the government. In the depression that had afflicted France since 1828 wage rates had fallen generally throughout the country, and unemployment had reached serious proportions.[36] The price of bread in Paris, forced up by poor harvests in 1827 and 1828, reached an ominous high of twenty-one sous for a four-pound loaf in May and June 1829.[37] The price had by February 1830 receded to fifteen sous, an amount that the police judged still to be excessive for a workingman's budget.[38] In June

---

lavier; *Globe* (Paris), July 27, 1830; Henri Vienne, "Dix jours à Paris du dimanche 25 juillet au mardi 3 août 1830," *Mémoires* de la Société bourguignonne de géographie et d'histoire, VIII (1892), 79.

[35] Blanc, *Histoire*, I, 188, 202-3; Paul Mantoux, "Patrons et ouvriers en juillet 1830," *Revue d'histoire moderne et contemporaine*, III (1901-1902), 292.

[36] Labrousse, *Mouvement ouvrier*, pp. 30, 37, 90-95; Louis Girard, *Etude comparée des mouvements révolutionnaires en France en 1830, 1848, 1870-71 (1830-1848)* (Paris, 1960), pp. 55-56.

[37] Girard, *Etude comparée*, p. 91; AN, F 3883, Préfecture de Police, "Bulletin de Paris," 1829.

[38] AN, F⁷ 3884, "Bulletin de Paris," Feb. 27, 1830; Chevalier, *Classes laborieuses*, p. 314.

1830 the price of flour on the Paris market again began to rise. On July 16 the price of bread was increased for the first time in eight months, and the police were apprehensive of the popular reaction to the increase.[39] The closing of printing shops and a number of other businesses on July 27 and 28, either for lack of orders or deliberately to add to popular resentment against the government, aggravated existing troubles.[40]

In the July Days some Parisians were unquestionably on the streets to protest against economic distress. A police officer on duty in the gardens of the Palais-Royal on the afternoon of July 27 reported that men there complained of having no jobs.[41] Foucauld, commander of the Gendarmerie in the fighting, heard complaints from combatants of lack of bread.[42] When Saint-Chamans, commander of the column sent across Paris on July 28 to pacify the Faubourg Saint-Antoine, exhorted the crowd in the Rue du Faubourg Saint-Antoine to be calm and to go back to work, a woman shouted that one could not be calm when one lacked money to buy bread or go back to work when shops were closed. Saint-Chamans gave her a five-franc piece, and she began to shout "Vive le Roi!" a cry that those around her took up while holding out their hands. Had he been given a treasury van loaded with coins instead of artillery pieces to head his column, Saint-Chamans claimed, he could have pacified the Faubourg Saint-Antoine without firing a shot.[43] The people whom he encountered in the street were not, however,

---

[39] AN, F⁷ 3883, "Bulletin de Paris," Nov.-Dec. 1829; F⁷ 3884, "Bulletin de Paris," Jan.-July 1830.

[40] AN, CC 550, "Troubles du Palais-Royal," July 27, 1830; Police report, July 27, 1830, 8:30 P.M.; AS, V^bis 322, CRN, 1er Arrond., Dossier Marie; Mantoux, "Patrons et ouvriers," pp. 293-95; Jean-Pierre Aguet, Les Grèves sous la Monarchie de Juillet (Geneva, 1954), p. 3.

[41] AN, CC 550, Monnet, Officier de Paix, Rapport, July 27, 1830, 1 P.M.

[42] Jacques-Jean Foucauld, Mémoires sur les événements de juillet 1830 (Paris, 1851), p. 43.

[43] Saint-Chamans, Mémoires, pp. 495-97; AN, CC 546, Juge d'instruction, Tribune de 1e Instance, Epernay, Testimony of Saint-Chamans, Nov. 16, 1830.

combatants, and the willingness to shout "Vive le Roi!" in the hope of receiving five francs did not mean that the shouters were all hungry and about to resort to violence if they did not get it.

Among the known combatants economic grievances certainly did exist, but for only a minority did they provide an acknowledged motive to take up arms. In 1142 individual dossiers in the archives of the Commission des Récompenses nationales and its local committees are but fifty-eight acknowledgments of personal motives for joining the combat of the July Days. Of these fifty-eight only seven persons mentioned economic grievances. Six said they were unemployed. One of them added that he owed three quarters of rent, another that he had had no work "for a long time." One spoke of the "state of misery" to which unemployment had reduced him. One was a printing worker thrown out of his job by the events of July 26 and 27.[44]

Had economic distress been the principal force driving men to revolution, one might logically expect that those in most dire misery would have been in the forefront of the insurrection. The combatants were not in fact from the poorest levels of Parisian society but chiefly from skilled and settled occupations not at this time particularly affected by unemployment.

One man seems to have been moved by a desire to escape his family responsibilities. The "Widow" Andro reported to the commission that her husband left their lodgings on July 27 and never returned. Three witnesses testified to having seen his body among the dead on the Pont Notre Dame, the scene of heavy fighting on July 28. Two months later the commission learned that this particular "mort pour la liberté" was living in Pacy-sur-Eure in good health.[45]

The secondary place of economic distress in the discernible motivation of the combatants may have been owing to the considerable recovery of the Parisian economy between

[44] AN, F^{1d} III 42-47, Individual dossiers AS, V^{bis} 1, 3, 153, 285, 322, CRN, 1er, 4^{e}, 11^{e} Arronds., Individual dossiers.
[45] AN, F^{1d} III 42, Dossier Andro.

the nadir of the depression of 1829 and the summer of 1830. Deep misery was not uncommon in the winter of 1829-1830, but the cold was neither so intense nor so prolonged as in the preceding year, and a higher level of employment left fewer persons destitute. The price of bread, although still high, was 30 percent below its top of the preceding year. The building trades, one of the city's largest industries, revived early in the spring, and both resident and migrant workers found jobs. Martin Nadaud, who went to Paris in March 1830 to begin his career as a mason, recorded in his memoirs no shortage of work during that spring and summer. Daily police reports reflected a relaxation of the apprehensions of the preceding year; in the late winter and early spring they occasionally remarked on the tranquillity of the population, and in the succeeding weeks the reports carried scarcely an allusion to the possibility of public disorders. The modest rise in the price of bread in mid-July, which did arouse some official apprehension, actually stirred no popular protest.[46]

Georges Lefebvre, drawing on his knowledge of the behavior of crowds in the Revolution of 1789, suggested that a dramatic event can change an innocent gathering of individuals into a revolutionary crowd. A revolutionary mentality may lie latent below the surface of an apparently random assembly of men and women; then some happening may quickly call it to the surface, giving all a common cause and galvanizing them into a revolutionary force.[47] Louis Blanc and Achille de Vaulabelle, writing a hundred years before Lefebvre, discerned this pattern in the changing complexion of the Parisian crowd of July 1830. The men and women gathered in the garden of the Palais-Royal and the nearby streets had at first heard the incitement of the printers and journalists and a few interested bourgeois with

[46] AN, F⁷ 3884, "Bulletin de Paris," Jan.-July 1830; F⁷ 6777, Col., 1ᵉʳᵉ Légion, Gend. roy. to Ministre de l'Intérieur, Feb. 5, Mar. 5, Apr. 5, 1830.
[47] Georges Lefebvre, "Foules révolutionnaires," Etudes sur la Révolution française (Paris, 1954), pp. 277-78.

indifference. The concentration of gendarmes and troops in the area stirred some resentment, but it found outlet in the throwing of stones, the breaking of street lamps, and one or two isolated attacks on police posts.[48] Crowds formed easily in the confined central quarters of the city, and they were not unusual, especially on warm summer nights. On the evening of July 23 the police reported four hundred to five hundred persons gathered in the Rue du Champ des Capucins near the hospital of the Val-de-Grâce and another group about half as large on the Rue de Lourcine in the same poor district. The police dispersed both without incident except half a dozen arrests and did not bother to report, if, indeed, they knew, what had caused them.[49] Seven weeks earlier on the evening of May 31 police agents, gendarmes, and the Royal Guard had to join forces to clear the garden of the Palais-Royal of a large disorderly crowd, and they arrested thirty-seven of its apparent leaders.[50] The mere presence of crowds, even disorderly crowds, did not presage revolution. Two occurrences, Blanc and Vaulabelle suggested, opened up the vast storehouse of accumulated resentments against the Bourbons and awakened revolutionary and imperial memories of resistance to them. The first was the appointment to the command of troops charged with maintaining order in Paris of Marshal Marmont, Duc de Raguse. This man, whose surrender had precipitated the fall of France in 1814, was associated with national humiliation and shame. News of his appointment, declared Blanc, discredited the

[48] AN, CC 550, Préfecture de Police, "Rondes du soir," 2ᵉ Arrond., July 26, 1830; Gronfier, Officier de Paix, Rapport, July 26, 1830; Carton, Officier de Paix, to Chef de la Police municipale, July 26, 1830; Police report, July 27, 1830, 8:30 P.M.; Comm. de Police, Qtr. Sainte-Eustache, to Préfet de Police, July 27, 1830, 9:00 P.M.; ibid., CC 548, Chambre et Cour des Pairs, Rapport de l'Etat-major de la 1ᵉʳ Div. milit. du 26 au 27 Juillet, 1830; ibid., 149 AP 1, Papiers de Mangin, Rapports de police, July 28, 1830; ibid., F⁷ 4174, Gend. roy. de Paris, "Rapport général du 23 au 24 [sic; deals with the evening of July 26] Juillet 1830"; AD, Seine, 4 AZ 1181, "Précis des événemens . . . ," pp. 6-7.

[49] AN, F⁷ 4174, Gend. roy. de Paris, "Rapport gén. du 23 au 24 Juillet 1830."

[50] AN, F⁷ 3884, "Bulletin de Paris," June 1, 1830.

government and turned a printers', journalists', and politicians' quarrel into a popular cause.[51]

On the succeeding morning came a second provocative event. The tricolor appeared atop one of the towers of Notre Dame, and the ringing of the cathedral's great bell, seldom heard in the capital, at once attracted attention to it. For fifteen years this proscribed revolutionary flag had been seen only surreptitiously in Paris. Now it flew above the city—a popular symbol of the revolution and the Empire and of successful resistance to the Bourbons and their foreign allies.[52] The appointment of Marmont had recalled the resentments, the anger, both personal and national, against the Bourbons that had accumulated over a decade and a half. The tricolor recalled the possibility of defiance and national triumph over the unpopular house. Now mixed with earlier cries of "Vive la Charte!" "A bas Polignac!" and "A bas les ministres!" were shouts of "A bas les Bourbons!" and "A bas la Royauté!" Bands of men roamed the streets destroying the royal arms on shop signs and defacing the royal adjective on public buildings.[53] Rémusat was amazed to discover in those days "the fund of black, patriotic passion that a good part of the population harbored against the Bourbons," and even the contemporary royalist historian, Alfred Nettement, conceded that patriotic resentment against the Bourbons, albeit misguided, was a potent force behind the popular rising.[54]

[51] Blanc, *Histoire*, I, 188-89, Viel-Castel, *Histoire*, xx, 577; Vaulabelle, *Histoire*, VIII, 209-11.

[52] Blanc, *Histoire*, I, 202; Vaulabelle, *Histoire*, VIII, 225; Odilon Barrot, *Mémoires posthumes*, 3d ed. (Paris, 1875), I, 104; Alphonse de Herbelot, *La Jeunesse libérale de 1830: lettres à Charles de Montalembert et à Léon Cornudet, 1828-1830* (Paris, 1908), p. 267.

[53] Vaulabelle, *Histoire*, VIII, 224, 245-46; AS, VD³ 3, Bala to Prés., CRN, 12ᵉ Arrond., Jan. 25, 1830 [sic]; CRN, 4ᵉ Arrond., Dossier Méline; BHVP, Révolution de 1830, Carton 23, "Les Trois Glorieuses vues par De Creuze, peintre," MS; Louis Rozet, *Chronique de Juillet 1830* (Paris, 1832), I, 161-62; Vienne, "Dix jours à Paris," p. 86; François Guizot, *Mémoires pour servir à l'histoire de mon temps, 1807-1848*, New ed. (Paris, 1872), II, 3; Barrot, *Mémoires*, I, 104.

[54] Rémusat, *Mémoires*, II, 337; Alfred Nettement, *Histoire de la Restauration* (Paris, 1860-72), VIII, 618.

In the records of combatants' professed motives, hostility to the Bourbons occupied the most prominent place. Almost half of those who stated why they took up arms said that they were moved by personal grievances against the governments of Louis XVIII and Charles X. Fourteen of them had been dismissed from the army, the navy, or the civil service or retired on small pensions. Four charged that they were the victims of political persecution, two that the government had discriminated against their families, and two that they had been refused jobs in the civil service. Two mentioned resentment against actions of the King's troops on July 27. The second largest category of motives fell within the revolutionary sentiments that Blanc and Vaulabelle saw aroused by the display of the tricolor. Eight men affirmed that they fought for their rights and liberty, and five others professed other ideological motives: to defend the *patrie*, to repulse "assassins of the nation," or to fulfill the duties of a citizen. One said he was a former Carbonaro.[55]

Anticlericalism seems to have had no distinct part in moving men to violence until the last day of the fighting, July 29. That morning a rumor spread that priests were firing on the people from windows of the archbishop's palace; stirred by this report and perhaps by the rumor that the archbishop had urged adoption of the Four Ordinances, a crowd of men, women, and children broke into the palace and ransacked it.[56] Early in the afternoon a group of National Guardsmen invaded the Jesuit house at Montrouge, an establishment that had been popularly associated with the alleged occult power of that order in the government of Charles X. They found the place deserted except for a few frightened servants; the priests had hastily fled, leaving behind their dinner on the stove, their places set at the refectory table, and an "excellent wine," which the invaders

---

[55] AN, F^{1d} III 42-47, CRN, Individual dossiers; AS, V^{bis} 1, 3, 153, 285, 322, CRN, 1er, 4e, 11e Arronds., Individual dossiers.

[56] Vaulabelle, *Histoire*, VIII, 295; Nettement, *Histoire*, VIII, 662; BHVP, Révolution de 1830, Carton 23, Guelle to Onzine, [Aug. 3, 1830]; Vienne, "Dix jours à Paris," p. 100.

used, one of them reported, to drink "to the health of Saint-Ignatius."[57]

These anticlerical outbursts were peripheral actions that had no influence on the outcome of the insurrection. Elsewhere, however, the crowd had within two days so harassed, unnerved, and finally routed its opponents that on the afternoon of the twenty-ninth the government ordered all its forces out of the capital city.

How was this chance assemblage of Parisians able to sustain a prolonged resistance and eventually to defeat the royal army and make itself the master of Paris? Clearly the street fighters were skillfully led. This leadership has been attributed to the National Guard and to students of the Ecole polytechnique, but they did little until near the end of the struggle. Many guardsmen donned their uniforms, banned since the disbandment of the Guard in 1827, but with few exceptions they took no part in the fighting, being concerned chiefly with guarding their own property.[58] Had the combatants depended on the students of the Ecole polytechnique for leadership they surely would have been defeated, for few if any of the students appeared on the scene until the twenty-ninth. A delegation from the school called on Odilon Barrot and Lafayette in the night of the twenty-seventh and twenty-eighth to offer the services of the students, but for their trouble they received only the avuncular advice to stay in their classrooms.[59] The next day the royal authorities closed the school, and the students dispersed to the homes of families and relatives, and there most of them remained until the fighting was almost over.[60]

57 "Rapport de M. Martinet," MS in BHVP, Rév. de 1830, Carton 23.

58 Barrot, Mémoires, pp. 102-3, 106; Blanc, Histoire, I, 203, 204, 212, 244; Vaulabelle. Histoire, VIII, 223, 284; AS, V^{bis} 3, CRN, 4e Arrond., Dossiers Piochelle, Risler, Raveneau; V^{bis} 285, CRN, 1er Arrond., Dossier Rouget.

59 AS, VK^3 17, Laubespin to President, CRN, 12e Arrond., [n.d.]; Vaulabelle, Histoire, VIII, 291, n. 1.

60 Vaulabelle, Histoire, VIII, 291, n. 1, 291-92; Blanc, Histoire, I, 204-5; AS, VK^3 17, letters of Polytechniciens to CRN, 12e Arrond., Mar.-Apr. 1831; AP, A A/420, Événemens divers, 1830, Chef d'Etat-major de la Garde nat. de Paris, Ordre No. 2, July 30, 1830.

One ingenuous student reported to a local committee of the Commission des Récompenses nationales that on July 28 he had gone to his parents' house in the Faubourg du Roule on the west side of the city; here all was calm and not until the thirtieth did he learn that a revolution had occurred in Paris. Another declared that he had been unable to get away from his parents' house on the Rue d'Anjou Saint-Honoré on the twenty-eighth, and he did not reach the center of the city until the next day, when the combat had almost ended.[61] Of the 250 or more Polytechnicians who sympathized with the opposition to Charles X only sixty-one actually fought in the July Days and those only on the final day after the outcome was largely decided.[62]

Equally dubious is the leadership attributed to students from other schools in Paris and to former Carbonari. Law students did appear among the disorderly gatherings around the Palais-Royal on July 26 and 27. Some of them later claimed that they had excited the crowds to resistance, and one even testified that he led a group of youths in attacks on a barracks of the Gendarmerie, the Hôtel de Ville, and the Tuileries. The casualties among students indicated, however, that few were on the firing line; three student dead appeared on the list of the Commission des Récompenses nationales and but seven wounded.[63] Both Blanc and Vaulabelle mentioned former Carbonari among the activists, but the archives yield but one vague allusion to any of them acting within their organization to resist the ordinances. A clerk named Raveneau, who had been a Carbonaro in 1821-1822, told a district committee of the Commission des Récompenses nationales that on July 27 and 28 a "loge" to

---

[61] AS, VK³ 17, Récompenses nationales, Rejon to Commission des Récompenses, 12ᵉ Arrond., Apr. 13, 1831, Laubespin to Prés., Commission des Récompenses, 12ᵉ Arrond. n.d.

[62] Blanc, *Histoire*, I, 204-5; AS, VK³ 17, CRN, 12ᵉ Arrond., Rapport, Feb. 15, 1831.

[63] AS, Vᵇⁱˢ 3 CRN, 4ᵉ Arrond., Dossiers Marlhiou, Pesguy; Vᵇⁱˢ 153, CRN, 11ᵉ Arrond., Dossier Lagond; Vᵇⁱˢ 285, 1ᵉʳ Arrond., Dossier Guyanie; AN, F¹ᵈ III 33, 2ᵉ Etat des citoyens tués; F¹ᵈ III 34-37, Etat des sommes payées aux combattants.

which he belonged had met and decided to excite workers to take up arms against the government. Even though he was seeking a decoration he claimed no part in the actual fighting for himself or his associates. On the government's final compilation of 504 dead are but two known to have belonged to the Carbonari in 1821-1822, and one other was among the wounded.[64]

The principal source of leadership was probably the armies of the republic and the Empire. The Revolution of 1789 had made warfare a citizen's business, and among Parisians of 1830 were hundreds of veterans of revolutionary and Napoleonic armies. A report prepared for the mayor of the Second Arrondissement listed, among forty-three persons who had distinguished themselves in the fighting in that district, five former officers and soldiers cited particularly for their leadership. It mentioned, too, a sergeant on leave from the 8th Infantry Regiment of the Line who took command of men in the streets and showed them how to cope with the fire of the soldiers. The records of the Commission des Récompenses nationales reveal the similar role of veterans in other districts of Paris. A doctor who cared for wounded during the days of combat reported that two-thirds of those he treated were verterans.[65]

In Nantes, the only provincial city in which a crowd became involved in even brief combat with government troops, the composition of the crowd was similar to that of Paris. Among about 250 men identified by local committees of the Commission des Récompenses nationales as participants were fifteen businessmen and proprietors, an equal number of professional men, about twenty clerks, and approximately 200 workers. Among the last category most of

[64] Vaulabelle, *Histoire*, VIII, 219-20, 281-82, 288; Blanc, *Histoire*, I, 261; AS, V^{bis} 3, CRN, 4^e Arrond., Dossier Raveneau; *Bulletin des lois*, 9th Series, Vol. 3, Part 2, pp. 70-78; Vol. 21, pp. 79-86; list of Carbonari in 1821-22, compiled by Alan Spitzer, State University of Iowa.

[65] "Rapport de M. Sensier"; AS, V^{bis} 1, CRN, 4e Arrond., Dossiers Chauvin, Des Pommiers des Baumes, Meline; V^{bis} 153, CRN, 11e Arrond., Dossiers Leger, Lemière, Trepaud, Lejouz, Pieraggi; Crochon, "Souvenirs," II, 883-84.

those identified were members of old skilled crafts—cabinet-makers, locksmiths, shoemakers, blacksmiths, hatmakers. The age distribution of the few for whom ages were recorded was almost exclusively, as in Paris, between twenty and thirty-five years.[66]

Historians and sociologists attempting to assign causes to violent popular movements of the late eighteenth and nineteenth centuries, have usually associated public disorder with social change. Industrialization and urbanization undermined the authority of traditional elites, created miserable conditions of material existence for large parts of the population, uprooted people from familiar environments, and placed them in strange surroundings where they found no honorable places. Along with these developments came new aspirations for reform or revolution and new alignments of those who shared these aspirations and of those who feared them.

Study of the crowd in the Revolution of 1830 confirms some of these generalizations but raises significant reservations about others. The issue of an elite discredited by recent social change is scarcely involved because for Parisians in 1830 the discredit of the Bourbons and their aristocratic adherents was part of the political heritage of the Revolution of 1789, not a recent social development. Miserable conditions of existence and rejection by society appear to be less important in this case than the generalizations would make them. The combatants of 1830 were not men bowed down by the weight of misery. They were largely artisans from the city's established and respected crafts, shopkeepers, and employees. In July 1830 no sudden affliction of misery had touched them. The printers perhaps foresaw a rapid decline into poverty if the first ordinance were enforced, but most of the combatants were not directly hurt by the ordinances. No more were those who took up arms the up-

[66] René Blanchard, "Le 10ᵉ Leger et la Révolution de Juillet 1830 à Nantes," *Revue de Bretagne*, 29 (1903), 223-28, 302-3; M. Giraud-Mangin, "Nantes en 1830 et les journées de Juillet," *Revue d'histoire moderne*, 6 (1931), 467.

rooted and the outcasts of Paris. The structure of Parisian society had not yet been seriously disturbed by industrialization; the factory system had effected few new alignments among the working population. Loyalties were still to traditional crafts, and the record of the many strikes and labor demonstrations in the months after July 1830 shows that it was within them that Parisian workers ordinarily took collective action.[67] The rôle of the printers in the revolution and the large numbers of men from the other old, established crafts—masons, cabinetmakers, and locksmiths, for example—suggest that these traditional occupational affinities had a part in inducing men to resort to force. The aspirations for reform, too, were traditional, not the products of new industrialization. They came from the Revolution of 1789. In taking up arms the combatants of 1830 expressed personal and public grievances against the Bourbons and struck a blow, they hoped, for the restoration of vaguely conceived liberties and national prestige popularly associated with the Revolution and the Empire.

The activists and the public disorders that they created were not, then, products of massive social changes of the nineteenth century. Rather they were an expression of timeless economic complaints, of loyalties within traditional crafts, of popular resentment against symbols of the old regime, and of eighteenth century ideas of liberty, equality, and fraternity.

[67] Edouard Dolléans, *Histoire du mouvement ouvrier, 1830-1871*, 3d ed. (Paris, 1947), pp. 45-47, 52-55; Aguet, *Grèves sous la Monarchie de Juillet*, pp. 14-25.

See p. 195 for 78

IX

Purge and Replacement*

AMONG THE commonly accepted patterns that historians have imposed upon the past is the conception that the years 1830-1832 mark the beginning of a new era in Western Europe. The Revolution in France and the passage of the Reform Act in Britain were the climactic events that consummated the change and set off the two great liberal powers of the West from the aristocratic and autocratic states of the center and east. In the history of France the key piece in this pattern is the view of the Revolution of 1830 as the Bourgeois Revolution, a revolution in which the rising bourgeoisie wrested control of the state from the landed aristocracy.[1] The Revolution of 1789 also has been seen as a bourgeois revolution because of the benefits that revolutionary legislation brought to the bourgeoisie, but on that revolution there are many rival and conflicting judgments. The stereotype of *the* Bourgeois Revolution has been fixed almost uncontested on the events of 1830.

This judgment has been difficult to challenge because of the ambiguity of its terms. "Bourgeois" and "bourgeoisie" lack precise meaning. They may indicate a man's status in society, as they ordinarily did in eighteenth century France, where everyone except noblemen, peasants, and

* This chapter was originally published in somewhat different form as "The Myth of the French Revolution of 1830" in *A Festschrift for Frederick B. Artz*, David H. Pinkney and Theodore Ropp, eds. (Duke University Press, Durham, N.C., 1964), pp. 52-71. It is used here with permission of the Duke University Press.

[1] See for examples Louis Blanc, *Histoire des dix ans, 1830-1840*, 6th ed. (Paris, 1846), I, 350, II, 31-32; Alexis de Tocqueville, *The Recollections* (New York, 1949), pp. 2-3; Felix Ponteil, *L'Eveil des nationalités et le mouvement libéral, 1815-1848*, New ed. (Paris, 1968), pp. 300-301; Jean Lucas-Dubreton, *La Royauté bourgeoise, 1830* (Paris, 1930), Ch. I, "La Révolution bourgeoise."

274

manual laborers might come within varying definitions of "bourgeois." They may designate, as they did for Karl Marx, a man's function in the economy, indicating that he obtains his income through ownership of means of production other than land. Either broad definition included in France of 1830 men whose situations and interests were widely and significantly different—wealthy bankers and small shopkeepers, industrialists and artisans, professional men, and the large official class of civil servants.[2] Clearly not all of these won control of the state in 1830 nor even had the same political convictions and aims. The phrase "control of the state" is equally ambiguous. What constitutes "control"? How can it be measured historically? These questions have no generally accepted answers. Without some answers, however, and without a definition of "bourgeois" any discussion of a bourgeois revolution is doomed to futility.

Among students of social classes and of the French Revolution of 1830 "bourgeois" has been more precisely defined than it ordinarily is in general context. It is used to mean only the *grande bourgeoisie*—the wealthy businessmen. The Revolution of 1830 is then seen as an event in which the rising class of bankers and manufacturers and wholesale merchants displaced the landed aristocracy in the control of the French state.[3] This more carefully delineated con-

---

[2] Cf. Alfred Cobban, "The Vocabulary of Social History," *Political Science Quarterly*, 71 (1956), 1-17; Halvedan Koht, "The Class Struggle in Modern History," *Journal of Modern History*, 1 (1929), 353-60; M. Vovelle and D. Roche, "Bourgeois, rentiers, propriétaires; éléments pour la définition d'une catégorie sociale à la fin du XVIII⁰ siècle," *Actes* du 80⁰ Congrès nationale des sociétés savants, Dijon (1959), Section d'histoire moderne et contemporaine, pp. 419-21; René Rémond, *La Droite en France de 1815 à nos jours* (Paris, 1954), pp. 77-78.

[3] For a sophisticated statement and defense of this thesis see Jean Lhomme, *La Grande Bourgeoisie au pouvoir, 1830-1880* (Paris, 1960). E. de Beau de Loménie, *Les Responsabilités des dynasties bourgeoises*, Vol. I, *De Bonaparte à MacMahon* (Paris, 1943), is concerned not with a class but with certain bourgeois families; the Revolution of 1830 brought a significant increase to their economic and political power, but in Beau de Loménie's view they achieved their power on the occasion of Napoleon's coup d'état of 18 Brumaire in 1799 and never lost

ception of the Bourgeois Revolution enjoys a firm place in the historiography of France and in the literature of revolutions.

The validity of this historical judgment can, nonetheless, be challenged. The nature of the challenge depends on the challenger's assumptions about the meaning of that still difficult term "control of the state." The American historian Sherman Kent, assuming that control rested with the electorate, challenged the conception of the regime of Louis-Philippe as a bourgeois monarchy by showing that the electorate was overwhelmingly composed of the landed gentry, not of the *grande bourgeoisie*.[4] On equally defensible methodological grounds one may assume that control lies in the hands of members of parliament and high administrative officials. Starting from that assumption one may dispute the validity of the conception of the Revolution of 1830 as a bourgeois revolution by demonstrating that the revolution did not give the *grande bourgeoisie* any significantly increased hold on public offices. After the violence of July was passed and the new King firmly installed upon the throne, the number of bankers, manufacturers, and *négociants* in parliament and the key offices of state was small, scarcely more than before the revolution.

The Revolution of 1830 did bring new men into public office. The change of men was probably the most revolutionary aspect of the revolution. The replacement of officeholders began at the top with the King and ministers and quickly spread down through both houses of parliament, the administration, the courts, and the army to obscure subprefects, mayors, and junior officers. The Chamber of

---

it, not even during the Restoration. He does not, moreover, distinguish between the *grande bourgeoisie*, on the one hand, and the official class and the professional men, on the other. Rémond, *La Droite en France*, pp. 74-79, sees an "Orléanist right" triumphant in 1830, but he differentiates it from Lhomme's *grand bourgeoisie*; it was, he maintains, "only very partially a business bourgeoisie"; its principal source of wealth was still the land.

[4] Sherman Kent, *Electoral Procedure under Louis-Philippe* (New Haven, 1937).

Peers and the Chamber of Deputies purged their own ranks. In the Ministry of the Interior Guizot in a month swept out all but seven of the old prefects. Before the year's end Dupont de l'Eure in the Ministry of Justice replaced more than four hundred members of the magistracy. All the commanding generals of the nineteen military districts under Charles X lost their commands. Probably at no other time did France experience so thorough a purge of the higher offices of state so rapidly. In December 1830 the men who governed France were not the same men who had governed the country six months earlier. Conventionally one would here conclude that the old were the landed aristocracy, the new, the *grande bourgeoisie*. In fact, the social composition of the new group of officeholders was little different from that of the old.

Louis-Philippe, the first of the new men, has gone down in history as the "Bourgeois King," but socially he was as far removed from the bourgeoisie as Charles X. A prince of the royal blood and one of the great landed proprietors of France, he can be classified only with the aristocracy. In 1825 he was among the former émigrés who applied for indemnification for property confiscated during the Revolution, and he and his sister received some twelve million francs, by far the largest sum awarded to any family.[5] His much-publicized decision to send his elder sons to public school in Paris was less than democratic in practice. In royal style each son had his private tutor, and at the school they took their lunches apart from the other students and were served special dishes. On the playground they associated only with boys selected by their father.[6] In the 1820s the Duke entertained in the Palais-Royal in a manner more regal than did the King himself in the Tuileries. The ball he gave for his brother-in-law and sister-in-law, the

[5] André Gain, *La Restauration et des biens des émigrés* (Paris, 1929), II, 192, 223-31.

[6] M.D.R. Leys, *Between Two Empires* (London, 1955), p. 180; T.E.B. Howarth, *Citizen-King: the Life of Louis-Philippe, King of the French* (London, 1961), p. 136; Agnes de Stoeckl, *King of the French: A Portrait of Louis-Philippe, 1773-1850* (London, 1961), pp. 101-2.

King and Queen of Sicily, on the occasion of their visit to Paris in the spring of 1830 astounded those who saw it by its extravagant display of wealth. "We are dancing on a volcano," declared an anxious guest, and looking out at the unruly crowd of spectators gathered in the palace gardens, he might well have been concerned with the consequences of his host's display of extravagance.[7] Later, when Louis-Philippe was safely on the throne his behavior corresponded more closely to bourgeois standards, but his liberal bourgeois supporters learned to their dismay that he did not share their ideas on parliamentary government. No Bourbon was more unwilling than he to become a mere reigning figurehead.

Change in the membership of the Chamber of Deputies began when the revolutionary days were scarcely past. All during August 1830 and into September letters of resignation flowed to the desk of the chamber's president from deputies who concluded that they could not or should not serve under the new King.[8] Late in the month the chamber speeded the process by requiring all public officeholders, including the deputies and peers, to take an oath of fidelity to the new King and of obedience to the revised Charter. The law gave deputies two weeks, peers one month, in which to take the oath, and failure to do so was considered equivalent to resignation.[9] Twenty-one deputies refused to take the oath and were treated as having resigned; some fifty resigned outright; and others were excluded by the annulment of their elections.[10] In all, some eighty deputies, approximately 20 percent of the membership, left the

[7] *Moniteur universel* (Paris), June 2, 1830, p. 598; Rodolphe Apponyi, *Vingt-cinq ans à Paris (1826-1850); journal du Comte Rodolphe Apponyi* . . . , 2d ed. (Paris, 1913-26), I, 1-4, 243-44, 260-62; AN, F⁷ 3884, Préfecture de Police de Paris, "Bulletin de Paris," June 1, 1830; Howarth, *Citizen-King*, p. 140.

[8] *Moniteur*, Aug. 11–Sept. 5, 1830, pp. 881-1032.

[9] *Bulletin des lois du Royaume de France*, 9th Series, Vol. 1, Part 1, pp. 66-67.

[10] *Ibid.*, Part 2, pp. 138-42, 169, 170, 171, 255, 495, 547, 671; *Moniteur*, Aug. 6, 1830, pp. 852-55, Aug. 18, pp. 915-16.

PURGE AND REPLACEMENT

chamber before the year's end and were replaced by new men.[11]

To fit the stereotype of the revolution's dislodging the landed aristocracy and enthroning the businessmen, most of the retiring deputies should have been proprietors; their successors, merchants, bankers, and manufacturers. An actual count shows among the retiring deputies five businessmen and twenty-one proprietors; among the newcomers, eleven businessmen and twelve proprietors. The shift was in the expected direction but very small and far from sufficient in the total composition of the chamber to move control of parliament from one social category to another. A comparison of the composition by social classes of the Chamber of Deputies in 1829 and of the chamber at the beginning of 1831, after the purge and replacement had been completed, shows that the revolution for all its reshuffling of deputies had made surprisingly little change in the chamber.[12] Proprietors dropped from slightly less than

COMPOSITION OF THE CHAMBER OF DEPUTIES
(*in percent*)

	1829	1831
Businessmen (*grande bourgeoisie*)	14	17
Professional men	5	12
Public officeholders	40	38
Proprietors	31	23
Unidentified	10	10

[11] *Almanach royal pour l'an MDCCCXXIX* (Paris, 1829), pp. 117-30.
[12] The names of the retiring and new deputies were obtained from the *Bulletin des lois* and the *Moniteur*. The membership rolls of the Chamber of Deputies in 1829 and in 1830 were taken from the *Almanach royal, MDCCCXXIX*, pp. 117-30, and the *Almanach royal et national pour l'an MDCCCXXXI* (Paris, 1831), pp. 86-94. The social and economic identification of the deputies is based on information from Adolphe Robert *et al.*, *Dictionnaire des parlementaires français* (Paris, 1891), I-V, *passim*; Gustave Vapereau, *Dictionnaire universel des contemporaines* (Paris, 1858), *passim*; and *Almanach royal, MDCCCXXIX*, pp. 117-30.

279

one-third of the membership to about one-fourth, but in 1831 they still enjoyed a margin of some thirty seats over the businessmen.[13]

The chamber of 1830 can be made to appear predominantly bourgeois in composition by combining the wealthy businessmen, the professional men, and the civil servants in a single category. So, too, can the chamber of 1829. But in neither case does this sustain the thesis of the *grande bourgeoisie au pouvoir* because neither the official class nor the professional men in France of the eighteenth and early nineteenth centuries can properly be identified with the wealthy business class. The public officeholders of 1830, like the royal officials of the eighteenth century, are a group that does not fit into the Marxian categories, based on English experience, of aristocracy, bourgeoisie, and proletariat. Their values, in-

[13] Patrick Higonnet's computer studies of the composition of the Chamber of Deputies confirmed that the by-elections of the fall and winter 1830-31 scarcely changed the number of businessmen in the chamber, nor did the elections of 1831-34 under the new electoral law of April 19, 1831, which nearly doubled the electorate by reducing the tax qualification for voters from 300 francs to 200 francs and reducing the age requirement from thirty to twenty-five. Moreover, after the postrevolutionary elections businessmen were no longer the numerically predominant group within the body of the bourgeois deputies, as they had been from 1827 to 1830, their place being taken by lawyers. Higonnet goes on, however, to maintain that the membership of the chamber of 1831, both after the by-elections and after the general election of July 1831, did differ significantly from that of its predecessor of 1827-30; it was younger, less rich, and more bourgeois, bourgeois being by his definition all who were not noble. The chamber might, he suggests, have served as the base for a new policy of reform and reconciliation had the right leadership been forthcoming. Patrick-Bernard Higonnet, "La Composition de la Chambre des Députés de 1827 à 1831," *Revue historique*, 239 (1968), 354, 361-64, 371.

Adeline Daumard in her *La Bourgeoisie parisienne de 1815 à 1848* (Paris, 1963), pp. 479-84, holds that the Revolution of 1830 and its immediate aftermath brought about a birth of political consciousness among the mass of the Parisian bourgeoisie heretofore not politically active. This political consciousness was expressed first in service in the National Guard and later, after the passage of the new electoral law, in voting in parliamentary elections. This development was not confined to Paris, and it was a step in the direction of later bourgeois regimes in France, but in 1830-31 it did not establish the *grande bourgeoisie* in power.

terests, aims were not the same as those of the *grande bour-geoisie*.[14] The professional class, chiefly lawyers, which made up an eighth of the chamber in 1831, was more akin to the official class than to the businessmen, for their careers, too, were in considerable degree dependent on favors from the state. Few of the lawyer deputies had not been on the public payroll at one time or another.[15] Professorships in the state schools were plums dangled before physicians and scholars. Public funds or public prosecution could make or break the careers of journalists and writers. Once in office and in favor themselves these men found their interests bound up with those of the great block of officeholders that dominated the chamber and that became the parliamentary foundation of Louis-Philippe's and Guizot's achievement in the 1840s of a rule more personal than any Charles X ever achieved. Almost certainly, moreover, almost all these men were substantial proprietors, their eligibility to sit as deputies being based on payment of taxes levied on real property.

The change in ministers after the revolution accurately reflected the alteration of the class composition of the chamber. Here, too, was no clear-cut shift from landed proprietors to businessmen. Polignac's ministry of eight members had included no businessmen and two proprietors, but it was heavily weighted with men who had made their careers in the civil and military services. Among their successors—the twenty men appointed to cabinet posts between July 1830 and the middle of March 1831—the predominance of officeholders remained essentially unchanged. None among them is identifiable as a proprietor.[16] Marshal

---

14 Cf. Alfred Cobban, *The Myth of the French Revolution* (London, 1955), pp. 14-19; Marcel Reinhard, "Sur l'histoire de la Révolution française," *Annales: économies-sociétés-civilisations,* 14th year (1959), 553-62.

15 Robert, *Dictionnaire des parlementaires,* I-V, *passim.*

16 *Almanach royal, MDCCCXXXI,* pp. 65-66; Robert, *Dictionnaire des parlementaires,* I-V, *passim*; *Biographie universelle et portative des contemporaines* (Paris, 1836), I-IV and Supplément, *passim*; Vapereau, *Dictionnaire, passim*; C. Mullié, *Biographie des célébrités militaires des armées de terre et de mer de 1789 à 1850* (Paris, 1851), I, 96-99, II, 528-30; Marcel Rousselet, *La Magistrature sous la Monarchie de*

Soult, who became Minister of War in November 1830, was a general turned businessman. He had made his name and his fortune in the Imperial armies, but during the Restoration he turned his energies and his money to industry, and in 1830 he was actively involved in mining, smelting, and transportation enterprises in the Midi. Two others were prominent bankers, and their rôle in the revolution and their entry into the ministry, disproportionately magnified, are perhaps a principal source of the myth of the Bourgeois Revolution of 1830. Jacques Laffitte was the head of a leading banking house of Paris and a former regent of the Bank of France, and Casimir Périer owned a family business that had widespread interests in industry, shipping, and real estate as well as finance. Laffitte and Périer were ministers without portfolio in Louis-Philippe's first government, and in November 1830 Laffitte was named to the Ministry of Finance and to the presidency of the council of ministers.[17]

In most of the key posts—Interior, Justice, Finance, Foreign Affairs—were men of different origins and attachments, officeholders and professional men like their predecessors. Baron Louis, the first Minister of Finance, had managed to serve almost all regimes during his lifetime. He began his public career in a purchased office of the Parlement de Paris ten years before the Revolution of 1789, filled a number of diplomatic missions for Louis XVI in the early 1790s, and under the Empire rose through the ranks of the civil service to high place in the Ministry of Finance. On three occasions before 1820 he served Louis XVIII as Minister of Finance, and in August 1830, enjoying a reputation as an expert in public finance, he was again called to head the same ministry.[18] Guizot, the Minister of the Interior, the

Juillet (Paris, 1937), p. 452; Etienne Léon Lamothe-Langnon, *Biographie des préfets depuis l'organisation des préfectures (3 mars 1800) jusqu'à ce jour* (Paris, 1826), pp. 324-25.

[17] Robert, *Dictionnaire des parlementaires*, III, 518, IV, 584-85; Bertrand Gille, *Recherches sur la formation de la grande entreprise capitaliste, 1815-1848* (Paris, 1959), pp. 98-101.

[18] Robert, *Dictionnaire des parlementaires*, IV, 182-84.

son of a lawyer and himself trained as a lawyer, had made his career and his reputation as a professor and historian, although in the early years of the Restoration he was briefly secretary-general of two ministries and an officer of the Council of State.[19] The new Minister of Justice, Dupont de l'Eure, was a career judge; he had entered the magistracy during the Revolution and under the Empire rose to the presidency of the Imperial Court of Rouen, where he remained until dismissed in 1817.[20] Molé, the Minister of Foreign Affairs, was a son of a president of the Parlement de Paris. He entered the Imperial civil service as an *auditeur* of the Council of State in 1806, became a prefect two years later and Minister of Finance in 1813, and he continued in public service under the moderate royalist governments of the early years of the Restoration.[21] Among the remaining thirteen men called to the ministerial posts in the months immediately after the revolution, ten had made their careers and reputations in the civil service or the military service.[22]

France was not, of course, governed by king, ministers, and parliament alone. The councillors of state, the prefects, the *procureurs-généraux* of the royal courts, the top-ranking military commanders were as influential in determining the present situation of the country and its future course. Through their ranks the Revolution of 1830 swept like a great broom, and after it came swarming into office a multitude of new men. The purge was intended in part to remove the unreliable and to install dependable officials. "Authority," proclaimed the new king in the first week of his reign, "should be in the hands of men firmly attached to the national cause."[23] Out went the still devoted supporters of

---

19 *Ibid.*, III, 291-92.

20 *Ibid.*, II, 498-99; Rousselet, *Magistrature*, p. 23.

21 Robert, *Dictionnaire des parlementaires*, IV, 385.

22 *Ibid.*, I-V, *passim*. Among the entire body of ministers in the eighteen years of the July Monarchy essentially the same pattern of class affiliation is apparent. Of the sixty men who held portfolios under Louis-Philippe, thirty-six were civil servants, and only seven were businessmen. Charles H. Pouthas, "Les Ministères de Louis-Philippe," *Revue d'histoire moderne et contemporaine*, I (1954), 108.

23 *Bulletin des lois*, 9th Series, Vol. 1, Part 2, pp. 27-28.

the old regime, out went those no longer devoted but suspected of having served the Bourbons too zealously in the past, and out, too, went still others who had showed insufficient enthusiasm during the "Three Glorious Days" of revolution in July. But at least an equally powerful motive behind the purge was the need to find jobs for thousands of Frenchmen who saw in the revolution an opportunity to achieve that common French ambition of getting on the public payroll. The "Revolution of the Job-Seekers" brought thousands into the streets, not to man the barricades but to besiege the ministries and the Commission des Récompenses nationales demanding rewards for real or fancied services during the revolution or for opposition to the Bourbons during the Restoration. The old and ailing Benjamin Constant complained that in a single week in August six to seven thousand persons called at his house to bespeak his support of their quests for government jobs.[24] Lafayette was said to have endorsed 70,000 job applications.[25] Jules Michelet wrote an urgent letter to his friend Edgar Quinet pressing him to hurry to Paris to claim a place before all were taken.[26] The opposition newspaper, the *Globe*, had to suspend publication a few weeks after the revolution because most of its staff and contributors resigned to take jobs with the new government.[27]

The Council of State, that Napoleonic creation that survived all the revolutions of the nineteenth and twentieth centuries, was not immune from revolutionary housecleaning. Of the thirty-four members in 1829 twenty-four were out by the end of 1830. To the ten councillors retained the new regime added fifteen of its own appointees.[28] All who can be identified were, like most of their predecessors,

[24] Constant to C.J.B. Hochet, Aug. 19, 1830, BN, Dépt. des MSS, NA Fr. 11909.

[25] C. J. Gignoux, *La Vie du Baron Louis*, 2d ed. (Paris, 1928), p. 230.

[26] Richard H. Powers, *Edgar Quinet: A Study in French Patriotism* (Dallas, 1957), p. 60.

[27] Charles de Rémusat, *Mémoires de ma vie* (Paris, 1958-67), II, 366-67.

[28] *Almanach royal MDCCCXXIX*, pp. 88-89; *Almanach royal MDCCCXXXI*, p. 68.

lawyers or civil servants.[29] The purge of individuals did not deliver this potent instrument into the hands of the businessmen. It remained a stronghold of the professional civil servants.

Since the time of Cardinal Richelieu most French governments have operated at the local level through the intendants and their Napoleonic successors, the prefects, and since the First Empire each new regime has filled the prefectoral posts with its own supporters.[30] In 1830 Guizot took charge of the reconstitution of the service, a task for which he had been prepared by his term as secretary-general of the Ministry of the Interior during the purge that followed the fall of Napoleon in 1814. In an article published in 1828 he had expressed his dismay that after the liberal victory in the elections of 1827 the same old prefects continued in office as though nothing had happened.[31] Now he had his chance to carry out a purge. Appointed commissioner of the Ministry of the Interior on August 1, 1830, he at once began to fill the pages of the *Bulletin des lois* with ordinances dismissing old prefects and naming their successors. Before the month was out only three of Charles X's eighty-six prefects remained in their posts; four others stayed on in the service but were transferred to new positions. The remaining seventy-nine were dismissed.[32] For replacements the new regime drew on former prefects of the Empire, dismissed prefects and subprefects of the Restoration, other civil servants, journalists, deputies, and army officers. The num-

29 Robert, *Dictionnaire des parlementaires*, I-V, *passim*.
30 Brian Chapman, *The Prefects of Provincial France* (London, 1955), p. 32.
31 Charles H. Pouthas, *Guizot pendant la Restauration; préparation de l'homme d'état, 1814-1830* (Paris, 1923), p. 8; François Guizot, "De la session de 1828," in *Mélanges politiques et historiques* (Paris, 1859), pp. 469-70. This article was originally published in the *Revue française*, September 1828.
32 Charles Lesur, *Annuaire historique universel pour 1830* (Paris, 1832), Appendix, p. 145; *Bulletin des lois*, 9th Series, Vol. 1, Part 2, pp. 25, 32, 33-34; Part 2, pp. 5-6, 15-18, 26-27, 29-30, 46-48, 58-60, 67-68; Charles H. Pouthas, "Réorganisation du Ministère de l'Intérieur et la reconstitution de l'administration préfectorale par Guizot en 1830," *Revue d'histoire moderne et contemporaine*, 9 (1962), 246.

ber of nobles among the prefects dropped from sixty-four to thirty, and the number designated especially as members of "old" or "illustrious" families dropped from nine to one. But there was no influx of businessmen or sons of business families. Perhaps seven of the new prefects could be classified as coming from the *grande bourgeoisie* and among the retiring prefects only three, but the majority of the corps after the revolution was composed of men whose careers and social positions were made in employment of the state.[33]

The purge of local officials reached down to the mayors of cities. The revolution brought new mayors to forty-seven of the fifty largest cities of France.[34] Biographical information on these local figures is difficult to find, but data on about a fifth of them suggest that in municipal government the business class may have experienced a modest increase in influence as a consequence of the revolution. Among the mayors who were replaced nobles and proprietors predominated. Among the new, businessmen outnumbered both the proprietors and the professional men. Here is a step, perhaps in the slow rise of the *grande bourgeoisie* to political power, but it is at most a very small one. The evidence is so limited and the offices clothed with so little power that the larger picture of continuity in the balance of class influence is not altered.[35]

In Paris the barricades were scarcely down when the press began an attack on the law courts. The judges, the prosecu-

[33] *Annuaire historique 1830*, Appendix, pp. 145-46; Lamothe-Langnon, *Biographie des préfets*, *passim*; Robert, *Dictionnaire des parlementaires*, I-V, *passim*; *Nouvelle biographie générale depuis les temps le plus reculés jusqu'à nos jours* (Paris, 1855-70), XVIII, 381-83, XX, 726-27; Pouthas, "Réorganisation," p. 249; Nicholas Richardson, *The French Prefectoral Corps 1814-1830* (Cambridge, Eng., 1966), pp. 205, 211. Pouthas classified ten of the new prefects as businessmen, still a small percentage ("Réorganisation," p. 255).

[34] *Almanach royal MDCCCXXIX*, pp. 543-46; *Almanach royal MDCCCXXXI*, pp. 555-58.

[35] Robert, *Dictionnaire des parlementaires*, I-V, *passim*; Vapereau, *Dictionnaire*, *passim*; *Biographie universelle*, I-IV and Supplément, *passim*; A. Kleinclausz, *Histoire de Lyon* (Lyon, 1952), III, 77; Franklin L. Ford, *Strasbourg in Transition, 1648-1789* (Cambridge, 1958), p. 250.

tors, and their assistants were only flatterers of the Bourbon government, and most of them deserved dismissal. "Almost the entire bench," stormed the *Constitutionnel* on August 7, 1830, "must be renewed." Louis Bernard, the new procurer-general of the Royal Court of Paris, gave the attack official sanction in declaring early in August that henceforth the laws should be applied by magistrates "without reproach."[36] The task of eliminating those unfit to serve the new regime fell to Minister of Justice Dupont de l'Eure, who had been ousted from the presidency of the Royal Court of Rouen in 1817, and to Joseph Mérilhou, secretary-general of the ministry, who had lost his place in the Royal Court of Paris in purges after the Hundred Days. In four months this dedicated pair, often working eighteen or nineteen hours a day, replaced 426 members of magistracy.[37] The judges of the highest court, the Court of Cassation, were untouched, but a new procurer-general of the court was appointed. Thirteen of the twenty-seven royal courts throughout the country received new presiding judges. The key figures in the administration of justice were procurers-general of the royal courts, the approximate equivalents of the federal district attorneys in the United States, although more powerful in highly centralized France. They were responsible for the enforcement of laws, for bringing violators to justice, and for keeping the Minister of Justice informed of threats to order in their districts. Of the twenty-seven in office in July 1830 only seven continued to hold their places at the end of August.[38] The new procurers not only exercised the usual important powers of their offices but had a rôle in shaping the new regime in the courts; Dupont de l'Eure appointed most of them within a few days of his taking office, and he depended on them for advice on the purge of judges and other court officials.[39] One may

[36] Rousselet, *Magistrature*, p. 32.

[37] *Ibid.*, pp. 33, 452; *Bulletin des lois*, 9th Series, Vol. 1, Part 1, pp. 7, 10, 20; Robert, *Dictionnaire des parlementaires*, IV, 344-45.

[38] *Almanach royal MDCCCXXX*, pp. 368-405; *Almanach royal MDCCCXXXI*, pp. 281-319.

[39] Rousselet, *Magistrature*, pp. 34-36.

search their biographical records in vain, however, for evidence that the new procurers represented the business community any more than did their predecessors. The duties of their offices required that they have legal training, and all of them on whom information is available were lawyers, magistrates, or former magistrates. If they may be said to represent any class, it was the professional class and the kindred official class, the same groups that had occupied pre-eminent place in the parliaments and administration since the first years of the Revolution of 1789.[40]

Pursuit of evidence of change in the class structure of the officeholding elite becomes increasingly unrewarding as one moves further into the ranks of professional officials. Although the Revolution of 1830 here, too, brought extensive changes in persons holding office, both the dismissed and the newly appointed were necessarily professional men or civil servants. The case of the procurers-general proves the point. The same necessity prevailed in the army. To assure its control over the armed forces the new government dissolved the Royal Guard, dismissed the Swiss Guard and repatriated its officers and men, hurried off a new general to Algeria to win the loyalty of Charles X's newly victorious Army of Africa, abolished the post of governor in the nineteen military districts, and replaced every one of the commanding generals in these districts and most of the corps and divisional commanders.[41] All of the commanders, new and old alike, were professional soldiers. A clue to class distinctions among them is in their titles of nobility, but it proves unrewarding. All of the thirty-three top-ranking officers dismissed from commands held noble titles—eight of them granted by Napoleon; thirty-three among thirty-nine newly appointed top commanders were also nobles. The latter included a few more parvenus—fifteen of them had been ennobled by

[40] *Ibid.*, pp. 38, 77, 85-86, 89, 453-54, 456, 492; *Biographie universelle*, I-IV and Supplément, *passim*; Vapereau, *Dictionnaire*, *passim*; Robert, *Dictionnaire des parlementaires*, I-V, *passim*.

[41] Lesur, *Annuaire historique 1830*, pp. 261-62; *Moniteur*, Aug. 15, 1830, p. 903; *Almanach royal MDCCCXXXI*, pp. 587-603.

Napoleon—but not enough to distort the similarity of the two essentially professional groups.[42]

After the smoke had blown away, the barricades disappeared, and the scramble for jobs subsided, one might see hundreds of new faces in the places of political, administrative, judicial, and military authority, but socially they looked so much like their predecessors that no significant change is discernible. In terms of classes the elite of the officeholders was essentially unchanged by the revolution.

Men are not differentiated by class alone, nor does class affiliation necessarily determine the behavior of legislators and government officials. Political ideas and political loyalties are at least equally important in influencing men in their exercise of official power, and one should ask, therefore, if the "Revolution of the Job-Seekers" brought to office men whose political loyalties were significantly different from those of their predecessors.

Biographical records do not ordinarily offer clear-cut definitions of their subjects' politics, nor, indeed, could they be expected to in a time of such political fluidity as the years between 1780 and 1850, wherein fall the political careers of the men who are the subject of this chapter. Occasionally a victim of the purge of 1830 is designated as an "ultra" or "very pious," a newcomer as a "Carbonaro" or ambiguously as a "liberal." A number of the retiring officials had been émigrés during the Revolution of 1789, which at first would seem to identify them politically, but most of them had returned and accepted appointments under Napoleon.

Among the scores of biographies of the new deputies and officials in 1830 one item of political interest does persistently recur; that is the holding of public office under the Empire. Among the twenty men who were appointed to ministerial posts in the first seven months of the new regime eighteen had been officials of the Empire and twelve

---

[42] *Biographie universelle,* I-IV and Supplément, *passim;* Mullié *Biographie,* I-II, *passim;* Vapereau, *Dictionnaire, passim; Almanach royal MDCCCXXX,* pp. 586-94; *Almanach royal MDCCCXXXI,* pp. 587-603.

had been loyal to Napoleon even in the critical One Hundred Days of 1815. One was the son of an imperial minister. Of the six who survived to see the revival of the Empire in 1852, five again became servants of the Emperor.[43] The Chamber of Deputies at the beginning of 1831 included among its 430 members eighty-two former officials of the Empire, sixty veterans of Napoleonic armies, and sixty-six deputies who held Napoleonic titles of nobility. Eleven lived on to assume the dignity of senator of the Second Empire.[44]

When Louis-Napoleon appeared before the Chamber of Peers in September 1840 on trial for his life after his attempted coup at Boulogne, he declared, ". . . finding myself within these Senate walls, filled with memories of my childhood, among you whom I knew, gentlemen, I cannot believe that I can justify myself here or that you can be my judges." He reminded his listeners that they had served the Empire, that like him they would avenge the defeat at Waterloo. "No," he concluded, "there is no quarrel between you and me. . . ."[45] He spoke as though he were addressing a Bonapartist assembly and with some justification.[46] He might have spoken in similar terms to the Chamber of Peers of 1831. Its membership, fallen from three hundred in 1829 to 191 two years later, included 112 peers who had held public office under Napoleon, and eighty-eight of its members bore titles granted by the Emperor.[47]

In the civil and military services the ratio of men with imperial connections was similarly high. Among the ninety-three men named to prefectures in the six weeks after the Revolution of 1830 thirty-six were former imperial officials,

---

[43] Robert, *Dictionnaire des parlementaires*, I-V, *passim*; *Biographie universelle*, I-IV and Supplément, *passim*; Vapereau, *Dictionnaire*, *passim*; Mullié, *Biographie*, I, 96-99; Lamothe-Langnon, *Biographie des préfets*, pp. 324-25.

[44] Robert, *Dictionnaire des parlementaires*, I-V, *passim*.

[45] *Moniteur*, Sept. 29, 1840, p. 2033.

[46] *Ibid.*, Oct. 7, 1840, p. 2082.

[47] *Almanach royal MDCCCXXIX*, pp. 107-14; *Almanach royal MDCCCXXXI*, pp. 78-84; Robert, *Dictionnaire des parlementaires*, I-V, *passim*.

and twenty-three of these had either refused to serve under the Bourbons or been rejected by them.[48] Twelve among thirty new procurers-general had been in public office during the Empire.[49] All of the army officers named to the top military posts in 1830 had held commands in the armies of Napoleon, and all but two had rallied to his cause when he returned from Elba in 1815.[50] The new Minister of War, Gérard, was a man of humble origin who rose to the rank of lieutenant-general in the imperial armies and became a count of the Empire. In 1815 Napoleon was about to make him a marshal of France when the fall of the Empire ended his military career for the next fifteen years. On July 31 he was named commissioner of the Ministry of War and on August 11, Minister of War, and the next week he received his long-delayed marshal's baton, not from the Emperor but from Louis-Philippe. He commanded the French army in Belgium in 1831, and three years later he was president of the council of ministers. In 1852 Napoleon III named him a senator of the revived empire.[51] His successor as minister of war in November 1830 was another imperial count and Napoleonic general, Nicolas Soult.[52] One might object that no army officers could be found who were not Napoleonic veterans, but there were a few—and more who had chosen to side with the Bourbons during the Hundred Days; eleven of the latter group held high commands under Charles X and were removed in 1830.[53]

The mere fact of having held public office under the Empire or even of having an imperial title of nobility was no proof of Bonapartism. Yet these men must have had a

[48] Lamothe-Langnon, *Biographie des préfets, passim*; Vapereau, *Dictionnaire, passim*; *Biographie universelle*, I-IV and Supplément, *passim*; Robert, *Dictionnaire des parlementaires*, I-V, *passim*.

[49] Rousselet, *Magistrature*, pp. 38, 77, 85-86, 89, 453-54, 456, 460, 492; *Biographie universelle*, I-IV and Supplément, *passim*; Vapereau, *Dictionnaire, passim*; Robert, *Dictionnaire des parlementaires*, I-V, *passim*.

[50] Mullié, *Biographie*, I-II, *passim*.

[51] *Ibid.*, I, 563-66; Robert, *Dictionnaire des parlementaires*, III, 157-58; *Bulletin des lois*, 9th Series, Vol. 1, Part 2, p. 9; *Biographie des membres du Sénat* (Paris, 1852), p. 121.

[52] Mullié, *Biographie*, II, 537.   [53] *Ibid.*, I-II, *passim*.

potent, even though covert attachment to the Empire. For many it was the Empire that had launched them in successful public or military careers. Before the Revolution of 1789 few among them could have aspired to the eminence that the Empire offered. They were indebted to Napoleon for keeping careers open to talents and indebted to his conquering armies for the opportunities they offered to military officers and to civil officials who administered the conquered lands. In 1814 and 1815 scores of them saw their careers ended by the return of the Bourbons. The Empire in retrospect must have looked like a golden age of unlimited horizons. The new prefect of the Department of the Seine-Inférieure in 1830, for example, began his public career as an *auditeur* of the Council of State; two years later at the age of twenty-five he became Prefect of the Ariège; in 1810 he moved to a prefecture in Italy and remained there until the French were driven out in 1814. Appointed imperial prefect of the Nord during the One Hundred Days, he was dismissed by the returning King, his career apparently ended at the early age of thirty-two. He held no public office again until 1830, when the revolution restored him to his administrative calling.[54]

The new Procurer-General of the Royal Court of Paris in August 1830, Louis Bernard, had his career as magistrate cut off by the Second Restoration, and from 1815 to 1830 he engaged in the private practice of law. The Revolution of 1830 enabled him to resume his career, and he finally fulfilled it as a member of the Court of Cassation under Louis-Napoleon.[55] At Toulouse the new Procurer-General was the Imperial procurer originally appointed in 1813 and recalled by Dupont de l'Eure in August 1830 after a fifteen-year interruption in his career.[56]

Many of the officers appointed to high military commands

---

[54] Lamothe-Langnon, *Biographie des préfets*, p. 198; Charles Durand, *Les Auditeurs au Conseil d'Etat de 1803 à 1814* (Aix-en-Provence, 1958), pp. 9-10, 20-22; Robert, *Dictionnaire des parlementaires*, II, 503.

[55] Vapereau, *Dictionnaire*, p. 177.

[56] Robert, *Dictionnaire des parlementaires*, II, 178.

in 1830 had spent the fifteen years after Waterloo in exile, and all had spent at least part of the period in retirement.[57] Certainly the decade and a half of the Restoration were frustrating years for ambitious military men accustomed to the boundless opportunities of the Empire. For them the Revolution of 1830 renewed careers, revived hopes, awakened old ambitions. Not without good reason did Louis-Napoleon make special efforts to cultivate army officers when in the 1830s he sought to build a following in France.[58]

Indeed, the Revolution of 1830 may have come close to being a Bonapartist revolution. Until the fourth day of the revolution a revival of the Empire was a more likely prospect than the establishment of an Orléanist monarchy. In Paris during the revolutionary days of July crowds in the streets mixed cries of "Vive l'Empereur!" with "A bas les Bourbons!" and "Vive la Charte!"[59] and Napoleonic veterans fought in the front ranks of the insurrectionary forces.[60]

The faithful Gaspard Gourgaud, Napoleon's aide-de-camp during the One Hundred Days and his companion on Saint-Helena, went on July 29 to Laffitte's house and protested against the candidacy of the Duc d'Orléans, and a number of army officers supported him.[61] Had he been prepared with a substitute he might have had some success, for Orléans was far from being a popular candidate in Paris. Crowds had defaced or destroyed signs bearing the Orléans

[57] Mullié, *Biographie*, I-II, *passim*.

[58] F. A. Simpson, *The Rise of Louis-Napoleon*, 3d ed. (London, 1960), pp. 90-91.

[59] AN, CC 550 Chambre et Cour des Pairs, Carton, Officier de Paix, to Chef de la Police municipale, July 26, 1830; Report of Boussiron, Officier de Paix, July 26, 1830; CC 551, Chambre et Cour des Pairs, Bosche to Prés., Chambre de Pairs, Oct. 22, 1830; AN, F^{1d} III 81 Vendée, Commission de Récompenses nationales (hereafter CRN), J. B. Baudry to Baudry père, Aug. 11, 1830.

[60] AS, V^{bis} 1 & 2, CRN, 4e Arrond., Individual dossiers; V^{bis} 153, CRN, 11e Arrond., Individual dossiers; AN, F^{1d} III 45, CRN, Dossier Bonnecasse; AN, F^9 1155, Ministère de l'Intérieur, Combattants de Juillet, Affaires particulières, Dossier Brivois.

[61] Blanc, *Histoire de dix ans*, I, 325-26; *Procès-verbal de la réunion préparatoire des électeurs du deuxième arrondissement . . . offert à messieurs les électeurs par M. Jacques Lefebvre* (Paris, n.d.), pp. 6-7.

arms, and a crowd had tried to sack the Orléans estate office on the Rue Saint-Honoré.[62] Orléans' eldest son, the Duc de Chartres, was seized by revolutionaries in Montrouge just outside Paris and narrowly escaped with his life.[63] Louis-Philippe's first proclamation as Lieutenant-General of the Kingdom was torn from the wall, and even on his reputedly triumphant visit to the Hôtel de Ville on July 31 he was greeted with shouts of "Plus de Bourbons!" from men who saw him as just another Bourbon.[64]

But supporters of the Empire were unprepared. Napoleon II was far away and scarcely known in France. No old general whose name would stir the populace mounted his horse or drew his sword for the Empire. Probably avid for new careers and new honors the generals preferred the promise of the better organized Orléanist solution to a gamble on the dubious cause of a distant and little known new Napoleon. The one man who tried to organize a Bonapartist coup, the virtually unknown Evariste Dumoulin, was easily diverted at the critical moment.[65]

Who, then, did rule France after the Revolution of 1830? Different men, certainly, filled public offices. Bonapartists or ex-Bonapartists, or at least men indebted to the Bonapartes, took over scores of high posts. It cannot be said, however, that they formed a Bonapartist party or that in important matters of policy they followed a distinctively Bonapartist line or behaved in any way that set them apart from their fellows who had no close imperial connections. They and the other new officeholders of 1830 and 1831, elected and appointed, represented essentially the same social classes as their predecessors. "There has been

[62] AN, F¹ᵈ III 45, Dossier Bonneau; F¹ᵈ III 46, Dossier Boyaud.

[63] Paul Thureau-Dangin, *Histoire de la Monarchie de Juillet* (Paris, 1888-1900), I, 10.

[64] BHVP, Série 23, Carton 1830, Armand Marrast, "Document pour l'histoire de France," MS; Blanc, *Histoire de dix ans*, I, 343, 348; Thureau-Dangin, *Histoire*, I, 19; Armand Marrast, *Programme de l'Hôtel de Ville ou récit de ce qui est passé depuis le 31 juillet jusqu'au 6 août 1830* (Paris, 1831), p. 5.

[65] See Ch. IV.

no revolution," declared Casimir Périer in 1830. "There has been only a change in the person of the king."[66] Had he added, "and a change in the persons of public officials," he would have expressed the essence of the revolution as it affected the balance of social classes in public office in France. After the revolution the landed proprietors, the official class, and the professional men continued to predominate in key offices of state as they had under the Empire and under the Bourbon Restoration. Here the revolution had introduced no new regime of the *grande bourgeoisie.*

[66] Quoted in S. Charléty, *La Monarchie de Juillet, 1830-1848,* in *Histoire de France contemporaine,* ed. F. Lavisse (Paris, 1921), v, 5.

X

Revolution Unresolved,
August–November 1830

THE Duc d'Orléans' formal acceptance of the crown from the Chamber of Deputies in the modest ceremony of August 9 proclaimed the Orléanists' victory in the second stage of the revolution over their legitimist, Bonapartist, and republican rivals. It did not, however, assure the future of their resolution of the upheaval of July. Even as their victory celebrations spread across the land, enemies old and new conspired against them, preparing to challenge their hold on power. The great problem confronting the Orléanists suddenly changed from the revolutionary seizure of a throne to the defense of an acquired position. Historians have commonly seen in the first months of the new regime's life the beginnings of a dramatic split over principle within the leadership of the victorious party—even within the ministry itself—between a conservative "party of resistance" and a liberal "party of movement," but on the basic problem that autumn there was no disagreement. All were anxious to retain power, and the threats to their hold upon it from rivals at home and enemies abroad precluded the luxury of division on principle. They divided only on methods of defending their new-found position.

Immediately after the ceremony of August 9 Louis-Philippe had begun consultations on the selection of a definitive ministry to replace the provisional government that he had named ten days earlier.[1] The *Moniteur* of August 12 announced his appointment of seven ministers, each heading a department in the traditional manner, and four ministers without portfolio, who had neither prescribed functions nor

[1] Achille de Broglie, *Souvenirs, 1785-1870* (Paris, 1886), III, 414-25.

salaries.[2] It was a hastily improvised combination of the King's friends and of men active in the second stage of the revolution. All had achieved prominence as opponents of Charles X and of Polignac in electoral and parliamentary conflicts or in the law courts. All were deputies and members of "the 221" save Molé and Broglie, who sat in the Chamber of Peers. Four of the seven new ministers with portfolio had been members of the provisional government and continued in the places they already occupied. Guizot remained in the key post of the Ministry of the Interior, which controlled the police and the internal civil administration of France. A leader of the "Aide-toi, le ciel t'aidera" in the electoral campaigns of 1827 and 1830, he was in July 1830 identified with the left wing of the liberal party. Louis-Philippe probably gave him his original appointment and retained him in the ministry of August 11 to appease the young liberals grouped around the "Aide-toi" and to forestall its being turned against the new regime. To the office Guizot brought the administrative experience of service as secretary-general of the Ministry of the Interior during the first Restoration and in 1815-1816 as secretary-general of the Ministry of Justice.[3]

The seals remained in the hands of Dupont de l'Eure, deputy from Paris; he was a friend of Lafayette, and with him, in the forefront of the liberal cause for more than a decade, he had become a popular symbol of uncompromising opposition to the Bourbons. On August 1, 1830, Louis-Philippe picked him for the Ministry of Justice over André Dupin, his personal lawyer and close friend, lest Dupin's appointment to so critical a post offend the journalists whom he had ordered out of his office on July 26 when they proposed to draw up a protest against the new ordinance on the press.[4]

2 *Moniteur universel* (Paris), August 12, 1830, p. 887.
3 Charles H. Pouthas, *Guizot pendant la Restauration; préparation de l'homme d'état, 1814-1830* (Paris, 1923), pp. 2, 102, 326-29, 360-61, 371-80, 423-24, 432, 464.
4 Gustave Vapereau, *Dictionnaire universel des contemporaines* (Paris, 1858), p. 593; Charles de Rémusat, *Mémoires de ma vie* (Paris,

To the new regime the loyalty of the army was no less essential than the support of the prefects, the police, and the magistracy. For the Ministry of War Louis-Philippe chose Etienne Gérard, and he could scarcely have imagined a man better qualified by his antecedents to appeal to both army and public. A volunteer in the revolutionary armies of 1791, he advanced through the ranks to become a lieutenant-general under the Empire. Forced into exile for two years after 1815, he remained in retirement until 1822, when he won a seat in the chamber; he sat with the opposition throughout the remainder of the decade. Louis-Philippe bound him to the new regime by granting him a marshal's baton a few days after his joining the ministry.[5]

Baron Louis, called to the Ministry of Finance by the Provisional Municipal Commission on July 30, combined the assets of ministerial experience and long service as an opposition deputy. He had been Minister of Finance during the first Restoration and again in 1815 and from 1818 to 1819. Louis-Philippe probably retained him in the ministry both for his specialized knowledge and as a gesture of reassurance to the financial community and to investors.[6]

Both Molé and Horace Sébastiani coveted the portfolio of foreign affairs. The King chose Molé over his friend and adviser because he feared the appointment of Sébastiani might alienate Pozzo di Borgo, the Russian ambassador, who had a deep personal animosity against his fellow Corsican. Molé did have a particular qualification for the office. A noble of the old regime, he had personal ties with the heads of the principal foreign missions in France, and during the July Days he had used his influence with them to

1958-67), 55 n., 203 n.; François Guizot, *Mémoires pour servir à l'histoire de mon temps 1807-1848*, New ed. (Paris, 1872), II, 43-44; Broglie, *Souvenirs*, III, 418; Pouthas, *Guizot*, p. 463.

[5] C. Mullié, *Biographie des célébrites militaires des armées de terre et de mer de 1789 à 1850* (Paris, 1851), I, 563-66; Broglie, *Souvenirs*, III, 416; Guizot, *Mémoires*, II, 42; France, *Bulletin des lois*, 9th Series, Vol. 1, Part 2, p. 30.

[6] *Biographie universelle et portative des contemporaines* (Paris, 1836), II, 351; Broglie, *Souvenirs*, III, 415; Guizot, *Mémoires*, II, 45.

prevent their taking a public stand with the Bourbons and to encourage their benevolence toward the Duc d'Orléans. He, too, had been a minister of Louis XVIII, but through the twenties he had been a spokesman of the opposition in the Chamber of Peers. Sébastiani, a Napoleonic general unsullied by appointed office under the Restoration and among the first deputies to declare for Orléans, was consoled with the Ministry of the Navy.[7]

The last portfolio—Public Instruction and Religion—went to the Duc de Broglie. Its provisional holder, Baron Bignon, Louis-Philippe believed, had no competence for the delicate task of reconciling the clergy to the new regime. As Lieutenant-General he had moved him to that place only to get him out of the Ministry of Foreign Affairs, to which the Municipal Commission had named him and where his imperial past—he had been a high official under the Empire and had rallied to Napoleon during the Hundred Days—might alarm foreign courts. Broglie had deep family and personal roots in the liberal cause. On July 31 he had refused appointment as commissioner of the interior, offered by the Provisional Municipal Commission, not wishing, he declared, to be an instrument of "the headquarters of insurrection," but through Sébastiani he had offered his services to the Duc d'Orléans, and since August 1 he had been one of the Lieutenant-General's small circle of intimate advisers.[8]

When Orléans named the provisional commissioners to the various ministries on August 1 and 3, he charged them with the administration of their respective departments, but for advice on high policy he relied on an unofficial privy council composed of Laffitte, Périer, Dupin, Sébastiani, and Broglie. They were in fact, though not in name, ministers without portfolio. After Louis-Philippe mounted the throne

[7] Pouthas, *Guizot*, pp. 457, 463; Broglie, *Souvenirs*, III, 417; Etienne Audriffret-Pasquier, *Histoire de mon temps; mémoires du Chancelier Pasquier*, 3d ed. (Paris, 1895), VI, 316; Vapereau, *Dictionnaire*, p. 1231; Rémusat, *Mémoires*, II, 341; *Biographie universelle*, IV, 1297, 1298.

[8] Broglie, *Souvenirs*, III, 334-36, 359; *Moniteur*, Aug. 1, 1830, p. 829, Aug. 2, p. 833; *Biographie universelle*, I, 392-93.

on August 9 Broglie declined to continue in a rôle that he regarded as irreconcilable with parliamentary government, and to retain his services Louis-Philippe gave him a portfolio. Sébastiani took the Ministry of the Navy on his way to the Ministry of Foreign Affairs. Laffitte and Périer—too eminent in the opposition movement to be omitted from the new government—Dupin, Orléans' personal lawyer and adviser and popular as a defender of liberal causes in the courts, and Bignon became members of the ministry but without assignment to any department.[9]

This hastily formed combination, representing the Left and the Left-Center of the Chamber of Deputies, the coalition that in March 1830 had challenged Polignac, was united by a common desire to establish the constitutional monarchy on firm foundations and to consolidate the hold of the coalition on political power. But an effective team they were not. Accustomed to working together only in the politics of opposition, they found themselves, on assuming the responsibilities of power, divided by conflicting ambitions, clashing personalities, and differences over methods of day-to-day government. The strong personalities in the ministry were Laffitte, Périer, Dupont, Guizot, and Dupin. Both Laffitte and Périer aspired to head the ministry. Laffitte, outgoing, optimistic, flexible, delighting in popular adulation, found little to his liking in the aloof, high-principled, pessimistic Périer, and Périer returned his disdain. Guizot, alarmed by the outbreak of violence in July, by the "popular flood rising to the stairs of the palace," shared Périer's suspicion of the popular Laffitte, and he suspected that Dupont de l'Eure also valued popular acclaim above the interests of the country. But he could not completely trust Périer either; Périer's ambition to head a ministry of his own, Guizot thought, precluded his full commitment to the present government. Laffitte resented the aristocratic condescension of Guizot and of his closest adherent in the

[9] Broglie, *Souvenirs*, III, 359, 413-14, 425; André Dupin, *Mémoires de M. Dupin* (Paris, 1855-61), II, 178-79; *Moniteur*, Aug. 12, 1830, p. 887.

ministry, the Duc de Broglie. Dupin recalled that the Duke, who was near-sighted, used a lorgnette and one day directed it on Laffitte when the minister without portfolio was in an ill-humor. "Monsieur le Duc," he snapped, "I beg you not to look at me that way."[10] Dupin thought of himself as the government's chief spokesman and defender, but his colleagues did not share his view. A brusque and imperious man, he took pride in his independence and was seemingly incapable of the joint endeavor required of a minister. He complained that he and the other ministers without portfolio were not kept informed of the government's actions, although the press and the public held them all responsible. Broglie accused Laffitte and Dupont de l'Eure of revealing the secrets of the ministers' deliberations to their friends on the Bourse and in the law courts.[11]

The King himself acted as president of the council of ministers and participated in all its decisions, but he did not, except in foreign policy, attempt to impose his views upon it. He thought of himself as the embodiment of the state, above parties and factions, and in the first months of his reign he optimistically sought to shelter all Frenchmen under his "vast sentimental umbrella." Moreover, the precariousness of the new regime, beset by enemies at home and abroad, and of his own position dictated the utmost caution. A single mistake could prove fatal—a move to appease the activists of July might revive the European anti-Napoleonic coalition and plunge the nation into war for which it was unprepared; a strong stand against some popular demand might precipitate a renewal of the insurrection. For Louis-Philippe the stakes were high. Failure would at best leave open only the bitter road of exile and expropriation for

10 Dupin, *Mémoires*, II, 216.

11 Guizot, *Mémoires*, II, 40-47; Broglie, *Souvenirs*, III, 418, IV, 18; Dupin, *Mémoires*, II, 180, 216-17; Rémusat, *Mémoires*, II, 268; BN, Dépt. des MSS, NA Fr. 20601, Correspondance et papiers d'Adolphe Thiers, "Sur la situation au 30 Septembre 1830—appréciation du caractère de M. Périer; Note dictée par M. Thiers"; Charles H. Pouthas, "Les Ministères de Louis-Philippe," *Revue d'histoire moderne et contemporaine*, 1 (1954), 104.

himself and for all his family. Both expedience and principle dictated a policy of compromise and reconciliation. Within the ministry, as outside, he sought to reconcile all his diverse supporters. Guizot thought he lavished most attention on his ministers with the largest popular following—Laffitte, whom he treated with almost eager familiarity, and Dupont de l'Eure, but he paid particular attention to Périer, too; and Guizot, Molé, and Broglie were made to feel that he held them in special esteem.[12]

Despite its internal stresses and strains the ministry agreed on its first and most important objective—to keep the new monarchy in power, and all agreed, too, that this was a defensive operation. They must defend the King and the revised Charter against their enemies. They saw four principal sources of dangerous opposition to the regime—the conservative powers of Europe, the Bourbons and their agents, the Catholic clergy in France, and popular discontent, especially in Paris. These threats preoccupied the thoughts, deliberations, and energies of the King and his first two ministries.

In the weeks after the revolution the menace of war hung heavily over France. A few enthusiasts among the men of July would have "la Grande Nation" resume her crusading rôle of 1792 and carry the blessings of French liberty to all oppressed peoples of Europe. A delegation of republicans who called on the Duc d'Orléans on July 31 queried him on his view of the treaties of 1815 and warned him that the revolution was national, not liberal, that it would be easier "to push Paris to the Rhine than to Saint-Cloud." A few days later a young republican whom Guizot characterized as "distinguished" and "sincere" handed to Guizot as he entered the Palais-Royal a petition asking, among other demands, that "France march boldly to the Rhine; that the frontier be established there and that the national movement be continued by war." Less ardent Frenchmen who

---

[12] Rémusat, *Mémoires*, II, 392; Guizot, *Mémoires*, II, 47-50; T.E.B. Howarth, *Citizen-King; the Life of Louis-Philippe, King of the French* (London, 1961), pp. 160, 181-82.

urged no revival of the revolutionary crusade foresaw renewal of the war by a revitalized anti-French coalition. The great powers that had restored the Bourbons after long and costly struggles would not, they feared, stand by while revolutionaries undid their work.[13]

On the other side of the frontier the revolution raised grave apprehensions of renewed French aggression. The adoption of the tricolor as the national flag, the revival of the "Marseillaise," the association of Orléans with the revolutionary victory at Jemappes, the hurried reorganization of the National Guard raised the specter of French armies again on the march across the continent. Although few men on either side wanted war, fears and suspicions of the other's intentions made it a very real threat. But war would have been a disaster for the new regime in France. Rarely had a government been less well prepared for a major conflict. The two elite units of the army were in dissolution; the government had abolished the Swiss Guard and ordered its men back to Switzerland, and the Royal Guard, a force of 25,000 men, was being broken up, its officers dismissed, and the guardsmen who wished to remain in the service incorporated into the Line. Nearly 40,000 troops were in Algeria, and more than 2000 in Greece. The threat of royalist revolt pinned down others in the west and the south. The Ministry of War could put fewer than 40,000 in the field to meet a foreign attack, and their effectiveness as a fighting force had been seriously impaired by the resignation of officers unsympathetic with the new regime, by the dismissal of others, and by desertions and the breakdown of discipline.[14] In six weeks after the revolution the Minister of War dismissed or reassigned more than seventy general officers and appointed new colonels to sixty-five regiments. Reports of desertions flowed into the Ministry of War, and on August 16 the

---

[13] Paul Thureau-Dangin, *Histoire de la monarchie de Juillet* (Paris, 1888-1900), I, 47, 50, 51; Guizot, *Mémoires*, II, 30-32.

[14] Thureau-Dangin, *Histoire*, I, 54-55; *Moniteur*, Nov. 7, 1830, pp. 1400-1401; Odilon Barrot, *Mémoires posthumes*, 3d ed. (Paris, 1875), I, 606; Guizot, *Mémoires*, II, 375.

Gendarmerie advised the Commanding General of the First Military District that deserters filled the roads around Paris. Insubordination spread so widely and so ominously that the Minister of War in early September issued a proclamation to the army calling on men to maintain discipline and promising that devotion to the King would be rewarded. He ordered that the proclamation not merely be posted in barracks but also be read to all ranks. With such an army and with its grasp on power at home still precarious the new monarchy could scarcely expect to survive a war. The most pressing obligation upon the ministry was to reassure the chancelleries of Europe that it threatened no nation and that it wanted only to live in peace with its neighbors.[15]

Unanimous in their determination to pursue the most conciliatory course, the ministers at once dispatched emissaries to the principal foreign courts with personal letters from the King explaining the recent events in Paris and requesting recognition of the new ruling house. These missives contained none of the revolutionary phraseology of the government's pronouncements to its own citizens. In the letters that General Augustin Belliard carried to Vienna and General Louis Athalin to Saint-Petersburg the glorious revolution became "a catastrophe," and Louis-Philippe depicted himself not as the king of the best of republics but as the last bulwark against the perils of continuing revolution.[16] The ministry especially hoped for prompt recognition from Great Britain, which would smooth the road to acceptance by the conservative powers of central and eastern

[15] Guizot, *Mémoires*, II, 375; AHMG, D³ 131, Lt.-gén. Cmdt., 4ᵉ Div. milit. to Gén. Gérard, Aug. 4, 1830; O.C. à Beauvais to Ministre de la Guerre, Aug. 4, 1830; O.C. Gendarmerie, Cie. d'Eure-et-Loir, 9ᵉ Légion, to Ministre de la Guerre, Aug. 6, 1830; Lt.-gén. Cmdt., 1ᵉ Div. milit. to Comm. au Dépt. de la Guerre, Aug. 8, 1830; Col., 1ᵉ Légion de la Gend. to Lt.-gén. Cmdt., 1ᵉ Div. milit., Aug. 16, 1830; Comm. du Dépt. de la Guerre to Lt.-gén. Cmdt., 1ᵉ Div. milit., Aug. 19, 1830; Ministre de la Guerre to Lts.-gén. Cmdts., Div. milit., Sept. 6, 1830.

[16] Clemens von Metternich-Winneburg, *Mémoires, documents, et écrits divers* (Paris, 1880-84), V, 26-28; Victor de Nouvion, *Histoire du règne de Louis-Philippe Iᵉʳ, roi des français, 1830-1848* (Paris, 1858-61), II, 14-16.

Europe. The King's emissary, General Marie Baudran, received a warm welcome in London from the public, enthusiastic over the revolution. The Tory Government of the Duke of Wellington could not but deplore a break in the settlement of 1815, but the Algerian expedition and the Polignac government's persistent refusal to pledge French withdrawal from Africa once the expedition's nominal objectives had been attained ended any disposition the government might have had to defend its protégés of 1814 and 1815. Before the month was out Wellington informed Molé that Britain would recognize the new government, and on August 31 the British ambassador presented his credentials to Louis-Philippe.[17]

General Belliard in handing the King's letter to Metternich on August 27 declared that his government pledged itself to respect all treaties, that it sought no extension of its territories, that it eschewed all interference in the affairs of other nations. On September 5, after consulting Berlin and Saint-Petersburg, the Emperor received Belliard, thereby formally recognizing the new regime. That day dispatches went out from Vienna to all its diplomatic missions announcing the reestablishment of diplomatic relations with France.[18] Metternich explained to Belliard that this action did not imply approval of the revolution or confidence in the new government's ability to survive, but in a choice between the Orléanist government and anarchy His Imperial Majesty would not give his support to anarchy. Prussia soon granted its recognition. Tsar Nicholas of Russia, who had threatened armed intervention to keep the Bourbons on the throne, also followed the Austrian lead and consoled his conservative conscience by omitting from his letter to Louis-Philippe the customary salutation of fellow monarchs, "Monsieur mon frère."[19]

17 Broglie, *Souvenirs*, IV, 22-33; Thureau-Dangin, *Histoire*, I, 60-62; Joseph d'Haussonville, *Histoire de la politique extérieure du gouvernement français, 1830-1848*, New ed. (Paris, 1850), I, 16.

18 Metternich, *Mémoires*, V, 17-20, 24-25, 28-30.

19 Nouvion, *Histoire*, II, 12-13, 18-20; Thureau-Dangin, *Histoire*, I, 66-68.

When the Spanish government openly encouraged the plots of the French royalist émigrés on its territories and King Ferdinand continued to treat with Charles X's ambassador as the representative of France, the French allowed Spanish refugees in France to make preparations to raise a revolt in Spain. Few in number, divided among themselves, the Spanish patriots without official French support posed no serious threat, but they alarmed Ferdinand, and he soon informed Paris that he would recognize Louis-Philippe, if the French government would remove the Spanish refugees from his frontiers. The bargain was struck, and on October 13 the Spanish ambassador in Paris delivered his credentials to the King. By the end of October the new French government had established diplomatic relations with every state in Europe save the tiny Duchy of Modena, which withheld its recognition. In 1831 the Duke of Modena had second thoughts and offered to recognize Louis-Philippe. The French government did not respond, and throughout the July Monarchy the duchy had no diplomatic representative at the French court.[20]

Parallel with its diplomatic campaign of reassurance the new government had sought to avoid any military provocation of its neighbors. On August 23 the Minister of War ordered the dispatch of urgent instructions to the commanding generals of frontier military districts to cease all military preparations or movements that could cause anxiety among the powers, and the next day a letter to these commanders advised them that the government intended to remain on friendly terms with all countries. No extraordinary defenses were to be undertaken, and artillery pieces and crews that had been moved to frontier positions in the early days of August should be returned to depots.[21]

These orders had scarcely left Paris when the outbreak

---

[20] Nouvion, *Histoire*, II, 21-28; Thureau-Dangin, *Histoire*, I, 68-69; Broglie, *Souvenirs*, IV, 28-30.

[21] AHMG D³ 131, note signed Brahaut, Aug. 23, 1830; Ministre de la Guerre to Lts.-gén. Cmdts. 2ᵉ, 3ᵉ, 5ᵉ, 6ᵉ, 7ᵉ, 11ᵉ, 16ᵉ Divs. milits., Aug. 24, 1830.

of revolution in Brussels on August 25 threatened to precipitate the war that the ministry eagerly sought to avoid. Long-accumulating resentments of both Catholic and liberal Belgian nationalists against Dutch rule erupted into street riots that forced the withdrawal of the Dutch garrison. When King William rebuffed demands for parliamentary and administrative autonomy for the Belgian provinces and tried to reoccupy Brussels, his troops were repulsed, and nationalist leaders on October 4 proclaimed the independence of Belgium. The revolt at once became an international issue more grave than the replacement of the Bourbons in France. In 1815 the Congress of Vienna had given the Belgian provinces to the House of Orange to strengthen the Dutch buffer against revolutionary France. The Belgians in their bid for independence defied the political settlement that made them subjects of the House of Orange, but more ominously they made the first breach in the territorial settlement of 1815.

The events in Brussels alarmed all beneficiaries of the Vienna settlement and, together with the appeal at the end of September from The Hague for assistance in reestablishing Dutch rule in the south, raised the question of intervention of the powers to protect that settlement as they had done in Italy and Spain in the preceding decade. Tsar Nicholas offered to send 60,000 men, and Prussia massed an army corps near the Dutch frontier. Prussia had a special reason for concern; a successful Belgian revolt would place a second revolutionary state on the frontiers of the Prussian Rhine Province. The Belgian nationalists were in part inspired by the revolution in Paris, and some of them at least looked to France for encouragement and support. Within France the Belgian cause won enthusiastic popular backing, and the government found itself under pressure to aid its brother revolutionaries across the frontier. Belgium had been part of France from 1793 to 1814, and as recently as September 1829 a French government had proposed annexation of Belgium to France, this being part of Polignac's grand plan for redrawing the map of Europe and partitioning the Ottoman Empire. In 1830 the conservative powers immediately suspected French collusion in the revolt and feared open French intervention, even annexation. For the English, Belgian independence raised no specter of doom, but they could be expected to join in any allied effort to prevent the reestablishment of the French on the Scheldt River. On the other hand, the French government, fearful of allied intervention in France, would not tolerate Prussian or Russian troops in Belgium lest it become a staging area for a descent on Paris. The ministry, confronted in its first weeks with this explosive problem, sought to reassure the powers of its pacific intentions, but with a boldness that belied its military weakness it threatened to use force to prevent the installation of foreign troops in Belgium. On August 31 Molé called the Prussian ambassador to his residence and informed him that the French government did not intend to intervene in support of the Belgians but, he warned, if Prussian troops crossed the Belgian frontier, French forces would immediately move in to expel them. Molé justified this policy as the application of the "principle of nonintervention"; Belgium should be allowed to settle her own affairs without foreign interference. The same day the Minister of War instructed commanders of military districts along the northeastern frontier to maintain strict neutrality.[22]

The King of Prussia hesitated to risk war with France unsupported by allies, and he made his intervention conditional upon joint action by the guaranteeing powers. The immediate danger of Prussian invasion of France's neighbor passed, but the threat of union of the victors of 1815 to

[22] Thureau-Dangin, *Histoire*, I, 67-70; Pierre Renouvin, *Histoire des relations internationales* (Paris, 1953-58), v, Part 1, pp. 64-65; Broglie, *Souvenirs*, IV, 36-42; AHMG, D³ 131, Ministre de la Guerre to Lts.-gén. Cmdts., 2ᵉ, 3ᵉ, 16ᵉ Divs. milits., Aug. 31, 1830; R. Demoulin, "L'Influence française sur la naissance de l'état belge," *Revue historique*, 223 (1960), 14, 19-23. See Demoulin's article for a discussion of the historians' dispute over the rôle of Frenchmen in the Belgian revolt. French volunteers did go to aid the Belgians but not until after September and then not in large numbers.

reverse France's bold pretension to substitute—by her own unilateral action—the principle of nonintervention for the principle of legitimacy remained. When Louis-Philippe told the Russian ambassador in September, "If the Prussians enter Belgium, there will be war, because we will not permit it," Pozzo di Borgo replied that intervention, if it came, would be by all Europe, not by Prussia alone. Talleyrand, friend and adviser of Louis-Philippe, believed that the coalition would never revive without the support of Britain, and he convinced the King that peace and security lay in France's winning the British government's support of the principle of nonintervention. Despite the opposition of Molé, who feared that so eminent an ambassador would bypass the foreign minister, Louis-Philippe induced his ministers to approve Talleyrand's appointment to the Court of Saint-James's.[23]

The Tory Government of the Duke of Wellington deplored the Belgian revolt—"Devilish bad affair!" said the Duke, and it would reluctantly sanction dismemberment of the Dutch barrier that the British had helped to create in 1815. But Belgian nationalism could not be conjured away. Any attempt to reestablish Dutch rule might force the Belgians into the arms of the French, and French annexation of Belgium would be more inimical to British interests than an independent Belgium. Talleyrand acted quickly to reassure the British on France's intentions. Immediately upon his arrival in London on September 25 he informed the British government that France had no thought of annexing Belgium or of placing a French prince on a Belgian throne. The future of the country, he declared, should be settled diplomatically by the powers of Europe. He was even prepared to offer French withdrawal from Algeria as the price of English support in Belgium, but Molé objected, and Louis-Philippe instructed Talleyrand to avoid any

[23] Thureau-Dangin, *Histoire*, I, 70-71; Broglie, *Souvenirs*, IV, 57-58; Raymond Guyot, "La Dernière Négociation de Talleyrand: l'indépendance de la Belgique," *Revue d'histoire moderne et contemporaine*, 2 (1900-1901), 580-82, 584.

commitment on that matter. The English cabinet found Talleyrand's assurances acceptable and proposed that the Belgian problem be referred to a conference of the five great powers then meeting in London to deal with issues of the recent Greek War of Independence. Talleyrand quickly agreed, and on October 6, just eleven days after his arrival in London, when he was received by King William, he was able to speak of nonintervention as the joint policy of the two countries.[24]

The Catholic Church had been closely identified with the Bourbons during the Restoration, and many of the clergy regarded the defeat of the Bourbons in 1830 as a defeat for the church. Potentially it was a dangerous source of opposition for the new regime, for it had an organization covering the whole country. More than 28,000 priests throughout the nation had tribunes from which to speak and confessionals in which to influence consciences, and a bishop was well-placed in every department. Although some of its supporters engaged in anticlerical activities, the ministry adopted a conciliatory policy of adhering strictly to the Concordat, which regulated relations between church and state, and of asking of the clergy only that it include in its services the customary prayer for the King. On August 9 the Archbishop of Paris, Louis de Quélen, in a secret meeting with Louis-Philippe, agreed to send a confidential emissary to Rome to get the Pope's advice on the attitude the clergy should assume toward the new government, especially on the taking of the oath of fidelity to the King of the French. On September 25 the Pope formally recognized Louis-Philippe and gave him the traditional title of "Very Christian King," and in a letter to Archbishop Quélen he authorized the taking of the oath and the inclusion of prayers for Louis-Philippe. When the Duc de Broglie left office as Minister of Public Instruction and Religion in early November, he reported that only 300 priests had been the subject of any

[24] Thureau-Dangin, *Histoire*, I, 71-72; Broglie, *Souvenirs*, IV, 41; Renouvin, *Histoire*, Vol. IV, Part 1, p. 65; Nouvion, *Histoire*, II, 57-58; Guyot, "Dernière Négociation de Talleyrand," p. 585.

complaint and only nine of the eighty-three bishops had failed to order the customary prayers for the new King or to announce their intention to do so. Not until January, however, did the Archbishop of Paris, who had been obliged to go into hiding during the revolution and had been living outside the city, pay a public call on the King and adjudge Paris sufficiently calm for him to resume residence there.[25]

The church aroused the apprehensions of the government chiefly because of the aid it might give to the supporters of a new Bourbon restoration, and it was from this side of the political spectrum that the principal threat to Louis-Philippe still came. If the Orléanist solution were to be only a temporary expedient, as many believed, the most likely replacement was a restored monarchy under Henry V. He was favored by foreign powers, and he enjoyed widespread support in France. Within a month of the revolution Ferdinand de Bertier, the trusted adviser of Charles X before the revolution, assembled a group of about thirty peers, deputies, former officials, and friends to discuss means of restoring the Bourbons. A few days later an emissary brought him a request from Charles X for a report on the strength and prospects of the legitimists, and on September 25 Bertier sent a long reply to Lulworth. The majority of Frenchmen, he assured Charles, would welcome the return of Henry V; preparations should be made for an internal uprising in his favor to coincide with or to precede invasion of France by foreign powers. Once the young king and his mother, the popular Duchesse de Berry, showed themselves in the west—Brittany and the Vendée—they could count on the support of 150,000 armed men, of which 60,000 would be ready to march on Paris. Bertier suggested that Marshal Bourmont, who had rejoined Charles after his replacement as the commander of the Army of Africa, be given command

---

[25] Broglie, *Souvenirs*, IV, 111-15; Roger Limouzin-Lamothe, *Monseigneur de Quélen, Archévêque de Paris; son rôle dans l'Eglise de France de 1815 à 1839 d'après des archives privées* (Paris, 1955, 1957), II, 11-14, 22-28, 41; Paul Droulers, *Action pastorale et problèmes sociaux sous la Monarchie de Juillet chez Mgr. d'Astros, Archévêque de Toulouse, censeur de La Mennais* (Paris, 1954), p. 49.

of these forces and that Charles obtain from the powers an advance of funds or their guarantee of a loan to provide the royalists with arms. The young king could also count on support from sixteen departments in the south, Bertier continued, but the rising there would serve only as a diversion to the powerful effort in the west; mobile forces from the south could, however, protect the right flank of the expedition against Paris. Foreign war, Bertier declared, was inevitable either through the intervention of the powers in France or by French aggression, and Charles, he advised, should take steps to assure that foreign troops not treat France as a defeated enemy. The best way to assure this was to have important royalist forces under arms when the invasion began; Charles should devote his chief attention to preparing these forces. About two weeks later Charles authorized Bertier to take charge of preparations in France.[26]

He established a central committee and assigned each of its members to head a subcommittee responsible for a particular part of the preparations, including the press, paramilitary organizations in Paris, and relations with the Chamber of Deputies. In keeping with his conspiratorial experience under the Empire he also organized a secret society, the Société des Amis de l'Ordre, through which he hoped to rally to the support of the legitimists all men anxious to maintain public order. Affiliated with it were two other organizations, one to raise funds for the royalist cause and the other to bring together the most faithful partisans of the Bourbons. The whole effort was almost fatally handicapped by lack of money and equipment, increasing defections to the government, and especially by the failure of Charles X to offer resolute leadership; in November Bertier himself was growing discouraged. At the time, however, this was not

[26] Guillaume de Bertier de Sauvigny, *Le Comte Ferdinand de Bertier (1782-1864) et l'énigme de la Congrégation* (Paris, 1948), pp. 468-73; Guillaume de Bertier de Sauvigny, "La Conspiration des légitimistes et de la duchesse de Berry contre Louis-Philippe 1830-1832 (correspondance et documents inédits)," *Etudes d'histoire moderne et contemporaine*, 3 (1950), 1, 4-5.

apparent to the government, and it remained justifiably and deeply concerned with the legitimist threat to its existence.[27]

A second pressing anxiety stemmed from unrest among the working class, especially in Paris. Itself sprung from a popular revolution, the Orléanist regime was peculiarly sensitive to workers' demonstrations and disorders in the streets. The revolution had occurred when the long depression dating from the middle twenties was just beginning to lift, and it set back the recovery. The Paris money market suffered from a crisis of confidence; values on the stock market declined. Credit for the transaction of routine business was in short supply, and in the early autumn occurred a number of alarming bankruptcies among Parisian commercial houses. As early as August 21 the government became sufficiently concerned to appoint a commission to study "the commercial and industrial situations of the country" and to propose to the King measures to restore business to its "habitual regularity." The working class found that the revolution, far from bringing them an amelioration of their lot, as they expected, only worsened it, and hundreds of them publicly, and often violently, expressed their discontent. Beginning in mid-August Paris was racked by a series of strikes and labor demonstrations aimed at winning jobs and achieving higher wages and better working conditions.[28]

On August 15 some four hundred carriage and saddle workers marched from the Barrière des Martyrs on the

[27] Bertier de Sauvigny, *Ferdinand de Bertier*, pp. 478-79; Bertier de Sauvigny, "Conspiration," pp. 16-22, 30, 32, 35; AN, F⁷ 12329, Ministère de l'Intérieur, Préfecture de Police, "Bulletin de Paris," Oct. 11, 12, 1830.

[28] Georges Bourgin, "La Crise ouvrière à Paris dans la seconde moitié de 1830," *Revue historique*, 198 (1947), 203-14; Thomas Raikes, *Private Correspondence of Thomas Raikes with the Duke of Wellington and Other Distinguished Contemporaries* (London, 1861), pp. 38-40; Octave Festy, *Le Mouvement ouvrier au début de la Monarchie de Juillet* (Paris, 1908), pp. 38, 67; AN, F⁷ 12329, "Bulletin de Paris," Sept. 15, 16, 20, 27, 28, 29, Oct. 4, 8, 13, 1830; France, *Bulletin des lois*, 9th Series, Vol. 1, Part 2, p. 286.

northern limits of Paris to the Prefecture of Police, where they presented to the prefect a petition asking for the expulsion of foreign workers in order to make more jobs available for Frenchmen.[29] That evening butchers demonstrated in favor of ending governmental regulation of butcher shops. The next day cab drivers publicly protested against the competition of omnibuses, which were a fairly recent innovation in Paris.[30] A few days later, on August 21, four hundred carpenters asked the Prefect of Police to issue a regulation fixing their wages at a higher level.[31] On the twenty-third the police reported a new gathering of protesting carriage workers and carpenters in the Faubourg Montmartre, and on the same day four or five thousand locksmiths and machinists came to the Prefecture of Police to ask the prefect for an ordinance cutting their work day by one hour. The latter group had been stirred to action, the prefect believed, by provocateurs seeking to undermine public order and confidence. On the twenty-fifth a crowd of six hundred locksmiths went from shop to shop to induce their fellow workers to walk off their jobs in support of demands for higher wages and an eleven-hour day; the next day a crowd of two thousand of them was pressing employers to agree to these changes, and the authorities called out the National Guard to assure order.[32] On the twenty-fourth groups of saddle and carriage workers in two widely separated quarters of Paris revived their call for the expulsion of foreigners; some of them threatened to set fire to shops of employers who resisted their demands, and the National Guard was summoned to the scene. That same day port workers struck in protest against working conditions at the Port de la Grève, and stone masons marched to the Prefecture of Police with flags flying and drums beating to ask the prefect for higher wages and shorter hours. The preceding

[29] Festy, *Mouvement ouvrier*, p. 38; AN, F⁷ 12329, "Bulletin de Paris," Aug. 15, 1830.

[30] Festy, *Mouvement ouvrier*, pp. 38-39.

[31] AN, F⁷ 12329, "Bulletin de Paris," Aug. 22, 1830.

[32] *Ibid.*, Aug. 23, 25, 26, 1830.

evening 150 bakery workers gathered on the boulevards near the Barrière de Montparnasse to express demands for higher wages.[33] Similar strikes and demonstrations continued on into the months of September and October.[34]

The government was nominally committed to a policy of noninterference in these disputes and to assuring a free labor market by forbidding coalitions of workers or employers. In practice, however, the Prefect of Police, with the sanction of the government, tolerated coalitions on both sides and frequently intervened to mediate disputes between workers and their employers. The overriding concern of the government in these matters was with their effect on public order. Fearing a renewal of street disturbances, which enemies of Right and Left might exploit to threaten the stability of the new government, the prefect actively encouraged efforts to achieve peaceful resolution of differences.[35]

The police kept careful watch over all threats to public order, and in the weeks after the July Days they reported a ferment among Parisians that from time to time inspired serious anxiety. On August 15 the National Guard was called to disperse a crowd intent on driving gendarmes from their barracks near the present Place des Vosges. The next day police broke up a gathering on the nearby Place de la Bastille and arrested six of its leaders. These crowds, the prefect reported, were made up largely of vagabonds and n'er-do-wells interested in assault and theft, but many of them, he feared, were being paid by the government's enemies to stir up civil disorders. The next week ominous crowds were reported in many parts of the city, and the

[33] *Ibid.*, Aug. 24, 1830.

[34] *Ibid.*, Sept. 1-5, 8-10, 12, 14-18, 22-25, 28, 30, 1830; Oct. 3, 4, 7, 9, 1830; Festy, *Mouvement ouvrier*, p. 41; BHVP, Papiers Odilon Barrot, Folio 34, Col., 1ᵉ Légion, Gend. nat., to Préfet de la Seine, Sept. 8, 1830; Jean-Pierre Aguet, *Les Grèves sous la Monarchie de Juillet (1830-1847)* (Geneva, 1954), p. 3.

[35] David H. Pinkney, "Laissez-faire or Intervention? Labor Policy in the First Months of the July Monarchy," *French Historical Studies*, 8 (1963), 125-28.

prefect advised the Minister of the Interior that National Guard posts had been reinforced, the number of night patrols increased, and reserve detachments organized. About 11 P.M. on August 23 a column of men carrying torches, and most of them armed with sabers, marched through streets to the Palais-Royal, where they sang patriotic songs until they dispersed on orders from the commander of the National Guard post at the palace. A few days later a crowd in Vincennes, seeking to force the resignation of the mayor, marched to the city hall, destroyed a bust of Louis XVIII, and later sought to search houses, where, they claimed, Jesuits were hiding. The National Guard intervened and made four arrests. Public appeals by the Prefect of Police and by Lafayette for the maintenance of public order, issued on August 25, were followed by a week of relative calm within the city, but on September 3 the prefect advised the Minister of the Interior that workers had gathered at several points that morning and that he had issued new orders to his police commissioners to keep careful watch over them and especially to seek out the agitators responsible for the gatherings.[36]

Fearing that the many unemployed were potential recruits for these dangerous crowds, the city government sought to occupy the jobless and to relieve distress by opening *ateliers de secours*, public works projects offering employment to the needy. On August 20 the Municipal Council appropriated 150,000 francs for a project of leveling and filling on the Champ de Mars, and the Prefect of the Seine, Barrot, immediately organized the operation. The chambers authorized the advance of funds to the city to finance the enterprise, and in the latter half of September six thousand persons were drawing wages from it. Early in October the Municipal Council concluded that threats to public order made the workshops a necessity, and it authorized their continuation for another month, but it hoped gradually to

[36] AN, F⁷ 12329, "Bulletin de Paris," Aug. 16-18, 24, 26-31, Sept. 1-3, 1830; AN, F⁷ 6777, Ministère de l'Intérieur, Police gén., Col., 1ᵉ Légion, Gend. nat., to Ministre de l'Intérieur, Aug. 27, 1830.

reduce the numbers on the rolls and to discontinue them after the end of the month, a decision that was reversed before it was carried out.[37]

While the government kept an uneasy eye on the streets in Paris they received reports of unrest and defiance in the provinces. Demonstrations against taxes and the high price of bread occurred in Issoudun, Soissons, Limoges, Tours, Saint-Quentin, and several other provincial towns in August and September. At the end of August the Prefect of the Indre asked for four hundred soldiers to restore order in Issoudun after rioters had destroyed records of the *octroi* and of indirect taxes, forcing the suspension of the collection of these levies, and had threatened to massacre grain merchants. The local National Guard had refused to intervene.[38] In Soissons on August 28 rioters demanded substantial reduction in the price of bread, threw stones at grain farmers, demolished the interior of the grain market, and would have burned it to the ground had not the National Guard stopped them. The local military commander forwarded to Paris a report that the rioting crowd included many unemployed from Paris.[39] On August 27 textile workers in Rouen marched on the city hall to demand reduction in working hours and changes in shop regulations. The mayor promised that a committee of employers would hear their complaints, but demonstrators remained on the streets for several days, and both National Guard and regular army troops were called in to maintain order, which at times seemed to be hanging precariously in the balance.[40] In Meaux a quick doubling of the National Guard posts was credited with forestalling a planned demonstration by three

[37] David H. Pinkney, "Les Ateliers de secours à Paris (1830-1831); précurseurs des Ateliers nationaux de 1848," *Revue d'histoire moderne et contemporaine*, 12 (1965), 66-67.

[38] AHMG, E⁵ 1, Préfet de l'Indre to Lt.-gén. Cmdt., 15ᵉ Div. milit., Aug. 24, 1830.

[39] AHMG, E⁵ 1, Gend. roy., Cie. de l'Aisne, Rapport du 29 août, O.C., Place de Soissons, to Lt.-gén. Cmdt., 1ᵉ Div. milit., Aug. 29, 1830.

[40] Festy, *Mouvement ouvrier*, pp. 47-50; BHVP, NA 154, Folio 29-31, Duhanzel to Vinaiyun, Sept. 6, 1830.

or four hundred workers to force the mayor to reduce the official price of bread.[41] In the third week of September wine merchants in Saint-Denis and Passy refused to pay certain taxes, and others in Sèvres, Saint-Cloud, and Bas Meudon threatened to follow their example.[42]

In the latter half of September and early October the issue of the trial and punishment of the ministers of Charles X who had signed the ordinances of July became the focal point of popular opposition to the government. The ministry had hoped that the ex-ministers would escape, but four of them had been captured, and the public demanded their punishment. The Chamber of Deputies had referred to a committee the question of bringing the ex-ministers to trial, and on September 23 the committee had made its report, recommending that the men be charged with treason under Article 56 of the Charter and be tried before the Chamber of Peers. Their treasonable acts were specifically defined as abuse of power in corrupting elections and depriving citizens of the free exercise of their civic rights, arbitrary and violent change of the institutions of the monarchy, plotting against the internal security of the state, exciting civil war by arming or causing citizens to arm themselves against each other, and bringing devastation and massacre to Paris and several other communes. These were, the commission's resolution continued, crimes recognized by certain articles of the Penal Code, and two of these articles prescribed the death penalty. The deputies discussed the commission's recommendation on September 27 and approved the charges against Polignac by a vote of 244 to 44, and the next day gave its approval to the indictments of the other ministers. The present ministers and a majority of the deputies wanted to avoid the death penalty, which would tarnish the new

[41] AN, F⁷ 6777, Col., 1ᵉ Légion, Gend. nat., to Ministre de l'Intérieur, Aug. 17, 1830.
[42] BHVP, NA 154, Folio 55, Chef, 1ᵉ Légion, Garde nat. to Préfet de la Seine, Sept. 22, 1830; Folio 56, Sous-Préfet, Saint-Denis, to Préfet de la Seine, Sept. 22, 1830; Folio 57, Maire adjoint, Passy, to Préfet de la Seine, Sept. 23, 1830; Folio 59, Col., 1ᵉ Légion, Gend. nat. to Préfet de la Seine, Sept. 24, 1830; AN, F⁷ 12329, "Bulletin de Paris," Sept. 24, 1830.

regime's admirable record of moderation in dealing with its opponents, invite bloodshed without foreseeable limit, and further embroil the government with the courts of Europe. The chamber already had before it a proposal to abolish capital punishment, and before adjournment on October 10 it took up its committee's report on this project. Sentiment favored an end to the death penalty in political cases and the tempering of other punishments proscribed by the law code, but the chamber lacked time to deal adequately with so complex a reform before adjournment. The majority wished, nonetheless, to put its opinion on record, and on October 8 it adopted an address to the King, proposed by the Minister of Justice, declaring its wish to end the death penalty especially for political crimes and petitioning the King to propose the appropriate legislation. An official delegation, supported by a large number of other deputies, presented the address to the King the next day, and he endorsed its recommendations and promised to act upon them.[43]

For several days preceding the adoption of the resolution the police had noted the great interest of Parisians in the punishment of the ex-ministers. On October 1 the Prefect of Police reported a notice posted on the Rue Saint-Denis that called for their deaths and threatened popular justice if the court should spare them; a police agent watched as a man read it aloud to some two hundred applauding spectators. Three days later a sign beginning "Mort aux Ministres" appeared on a doorway at the corner of the Rue Saint-Denis and the Boulevard Bonne Nouvelle, and the next day the Prefect of Police informed the Minister of Interior that among crowds in the streets, at cafés, and in theaters words threatening to the ex-ministers were regularly heard. The chamber's address to the King on October 8 was popularly interpreted as a move to save the ministers and as another frustration of the revolution, and it set off more widespread and vehement protests against the government and the

[43] *Moniteur*, Aug. 21, 1830, pp. 936-40; Sept. 24, pp. 1146-50; Sept. 28, pp. 1174-80; Sept. 29, pp. 1184-86; Oct. 9, pp. 1274-76; Oct. 10, p. 1277; Thureau-Dangin, *Histoire*, I, 111-14; Guizot, *Mémoires*, II, 118-22.

chamber. On the evening of October 9 a National Guards-man on duty at the Palais-Royal reported that his unit had almost been obliged to fire on a large crowd that was dem-onstrating its hostility to the ending of the death penalty. In succeeding days the populous quarters of the center and east were inundated by handwritten signs demanding death for the ex-ministers. The police were unable to destroy them all. Even the attempt to do so was likely to stir up trouble, and the police got little help from the National Guard, who seemed to be in sympathy with their messages. Some signs threatened the judges; one began with the words, "Death to the Ministers. We consider as accomplices in high treason every individual who attempts to save them from the pun-ishment that our fathers, our brothers killed on July 27, 28, and 29, 1830, demand."[44]

In daylight crowds gathered around the Luxembourg Palace, seat of the Chamber of Peers, and chalked on the garden fence, "Mort aux ex-ministres et à ceux qui les pro-tègent." At night the focal points of the protests were the Palais-Royal and the city gates. On the evening of Sunday, October 17, the King on returning from a review of the National Guard at Versailles found his palace almost be-sieged by a crowd that shouted for the heads of the ex-ministers. When the palace gardens were closed, the demon-strators, three to four hundred in number, marched through the neighboring streets and then returned to the Palais-Royal shouting "Vive le Roi! Mort aux Ministres!" From here they proceeded across the river to the Luxembourg Palace, where they tried unsuccessfully to break down the principal gate. The same evening a crowd of almost the same size gathered at the tomb of victims of the fighting in July on the Place des Innocents and marched off to shouts of "A Vincennes!" where the ex-ministers were being held.[45]

The most ominous disorders occurred the next day, Octo-

---

[44] AN, F⁷ 12329, "Bulletin de Paris," Oct. 1, 4, 5, 9, 10, 11, 13, 14, 15, 16, 1830.

[45] Ibid., Oct. 14, 18, 1830; AHMG, E⁵ 3, Col., 1ᵉ Légion, Gend. dépt. to Ministre de la Guerre, Oct. 18, 1830; Broglie, Souvenirs, IV, 84.

ber 18. At noon a crowd larger than that of the preceding evening appeared at the Palais-Royal behind a flag bearing the inscription, "Desir du peuple: Mort aux ministres." The demonstrators were dispersed without incident, but in the evening the garden and courts of the palace again filled with a noisy crowd that shouted insults to the King and the Chamber of Deputies as well as demanding death to the ex-ministers. Only with difficulty did the National Guard clear the gardens and courts and close the gates, and as they completed the task, the crowd was taking up the cry, "To Vincennes!" The ministers, called into an emergency session at the Ministry of Justice, decided that the disorders must be forcibly suppressed, and Guizot at once dispatched a request to the commander of the military division to assure the defense of Vincennes and to aid the National Guard in breaking up demonstrations. Balancing this vigorous stand and reflecting division within the ministry was a concession to the protesters—an announcement published in the press that morning declaring that the time and study required to prepare a finished proposal on abolition of the death penalty would prevent any early action on the matter by the chambers. This was in effect a declaration that the government would take no action on the death penalty before the trial of the ex-ministers.[46]

As the ministers deliberated, the crowd moved on Vincennes, and about 11 P.M., armed with a few muskets and swords and many clubs and sticks, it gathered before the main gate of the chateau and demanded of the governor, the one-legged General Pierre Daumesnil, who hobbled out to confront them, that he produce his prisoners, the four ministers of Charles X. Daumesnil replied that before surrendering them he would blow up the chateau's powder magazine. This apparently intimidated the crowd, for they moved off shouting, "Vive la jambe de bois!" Two or three hours later, about two o'clock in the morning, fatigued by the long march to Vincennes and inflamed by wine con-

---

[46] Guizot, *Mémoires*, II, 124-27; Broglie, *Souvenirs*, IV, 84-85; *Moniteur*, Oct. 19, 1830, p. 1321, Oct. 20, p. 1325.

sumed along the way, they reappeared before the Palais-Royal shouting the same threats against the ex-ministers and their protectors and demanding to see the King. The National Guard units on duty there earlier in the evening had been withdrawn, and the remaining guard posts were insufficient to restrain the demonstrators. Some of them had broken into the palace and reached the grand staircase before hastily summoned National Guards, supported by troops from the 31st Regiment of the Line, dispersed the crowd, sparing Louis-Philippe another June 20, and made more than one hundred arrests.[47]

The next day, while tensely awaiting renewal of disorders, the government, with memories of the July Revolution still fresh in their minds, took precautions to keep the capital under their control. A royalist paper of October 19, the *Quotidienne*, carried a report that the King and his family had withdrawn to Neuilly, and the government held up copies being mailed to the provinces until a denial could be added lest it start a rumor outside Paris that the city was out of the government's control. The Prefect of the Seine issued a proclamation to the people of the city reassuring them that the ex-ministers would be brought to justice and urging them to remain calm, to spurn incitements to violence. At the same time he instructed mayors of the arrondissements of Paris to remain in their offices throughout the day, to wear their insignia of office, and to be prepared to go in person if necessary to break up crowds. He asked that they send him hourly reports of developments in their districts. The Minister of War ordered the commander of the First Military Division to send, under the command of a colonel, six to seven hundred men from one of the infantry regiments in Paris to the Palais-Royal to aid the National Guard should there be a recurrence of the

---

[47] Ministère de la Justice, Div. des Affaires criminelles et des Graces, BB²¹ 370, Notice sur Charles Levieux, Mar. 21, 1831; Guizot, *Mémoires*, II, 127-28; Broglie, *Souvenirs*, IV, 85-86; *Moniteur*, Oct. 20, 1830, p. 1325, Oct. 21, p. 1328.

disorders of the preceding day.[48] The mayor of the Second
Arrondissement, which included the Palais-Royal, appealed
to the Prefect of the Seine for five hundred additional National Guards, and Lafayette set up a reserve of one hundred
guardsmen at the mayor's office of the adjoining Fourth
Arrondissement to be at the disposal of any public officer
who might need them to maintain order. The hourly reports of the mayors to the prefect reveal extraordinary precautions in the form of strengthened and extra National
Guard patrols and concentration of forces at key points.
Some turbulence was reported in the Faubourg Saint-Antoine, and a few people were arrested there for shouting
insults at the National Guard, but most of the capital remained calm, and the disorders around the Palais-Royal
were not renewed. For the next several days the police and
the military continued to keep a close watch over the city,
but they had no serious threat to the peace to report. The
Prefect of Police did note a continuing anxiety among the
populace over the trial of the ex-ministers and also over
the stagnation of commerce and the high cost of bread as
winter approached.[49]

The disorders of mid-October widened a split within the
ministry over how best to defend the new regime against

[48] *Moniteur,* Oct. 20, 1830, p. 1326; AS, VD³ 3, Préfet de la Seine to
Maire, 8ᵉ Arrond., Oct. 19, 1830; BHVP, NA 154, Folio 113, Proclama-
tion du Préfet de la Seine, Oct. 19, 1830; AHMG, E⁵ 3, Ministre de la
Guerre to Lt.-gén. Cmdt., 1ᵉ Div. milit., Oct. 19, 1830.

[49] BHVP, NA 154, Folio 120, Maire, 2ᵉ Arrond., to Préfet de la Seine,
Oct. 19, 1830; Folio 123, G. W. Lafayette to Chef, 4ᵉ Légion, Garde
nat. de Paris, Oct. 19, 1830; Folio 124, Maire, 4ᵉ Arrond., to Préfet de
la Seine, Oct. 19, 1830; Folio 125, Maire, 5ᵉ Arrond., to Préfet de la
Seine, Oct. 19, 1830; Folios 126, 127, Maire, 8ᵉ Arrond., to Préfet de la
Seine, Oct. 19, 1830; Folios 128, 129, Maire, 10ᵉ Arrond., to Préfet de
la Seine, Oct. 19, 1830; 3 P.M., 8:15 P.M.; Folio 132, Maire, 11ᵉ Arrond.,
to Préfet de la Seine, Oct. 19, 1830; Folio 134, Maire, 12ᵉ Arrond., to
Préfet de la Seine, Oct. 19, 1830; AN, F⁷ 12329, "Bulletin de Paris,"
Oct. 20, 21, 22, 23, 28, 1830; AHMG, E⁵ 3, Major Chatry de la Fosse
to Lt.-gén. Cmdt., 1ᵉ Div. milit., Oct. 19, 1830; Lt.-gén. Cmdt., 1ᵉ Div.
milit. to Ministre de la Guerre, Oct. 20, 1830; AS, VD³ 3, Préfet de la
Seine to Maire, 11ᵉ Arrond., Oct. 20, 1830.

threats from the street. The lines of disagreement on this question had emerged a month earlier when the ministry had sought to evolve a policy on the treatment of the political clubs that sprang up and flourished in Paris in the weeks after the revolution. Guizot, Périer, and Broglie wanted to close them and advocated new legislation to strengthen the ministry's hand in dealing with them. Dupont and Laffitte, on the other hand, thought that they should be tolerated, fearing the alienation of the government's friends on the left if their colleagues' hard line were followed. At the time the King had asked Laffitte to explore the possibilities of forming a new council of ministers, but some of the present ministers whom he wished to retain declined to serve in a more left-oriented council, and the matter was dropped.[50]

The disturbances of October 17, 18, and 19 rekindled the dispute within the ministry. Differences then centered on the proclamation issued by the Prefect of the Seine, Odilon Barrot, on October 19 in which he seemed to be placing the blame for the disorders on the ministers and the Chamber of Deputies. Apparently seeking to appease the populace he declared that the people of Paris were the bravest and most generous in the world and that they sought not vengeance but justice. "An inopportune démarche," the proclamation continued, "made it possible to conclude that there was a collusion to interrupt the ordinary course of justice in regard to the former ministers; delays that have no other purpose than the accomplishment of the forms that give justice a more solemn character supported and accredited that opinion." The proclamation went on to assure the populace that "the course of justice has been neither suspended nor interrupted and it will not be." "An inopportune démarche" could be only a reference to the address to the King from the majority in the Chamber of Deputies asking for abolition of the death penalty, an address welcomed by the King and the ministry. To Guizot, Broglie,

[50] BN, Dépt. des MSS, NA Fr. 20601, Correspondance de Thiers, "Sur la situation au 30 septembre 1830."

and Périer it was intolerable that an appointed official should carry popular appeasement to the point of publicly condemning an action of the chamber and of the King and his ministers. Guizot as Barrot's superior in the Ministry of the Interior blocked the publication of the proclamation in the *Moniteur* but did not prevent its circulation in the city in both manuscript and printed form.[51]

Broglie and Guizot wanted Barrot disavowed and dismissed; Dupont refused to agree, and Broglie and Guizot offered their resignations to the King. The formation of a new ministry seemed to be inevitable, but Laffitte proposed to substitute a reshuffling of the present council and the creation of the office of president of the council to give it greater unity. Louis-Philippe, anxious to avoid the complications of forming a new ministry, welcomed this proposal. Guizot and Broglie, however, opposed it, the latter arguing that the government must choose between resistance and appeasement and that the new president of the council must be free to select men of his own persuasion; continuation of the present divisions, he added, simply rendered the government impotent. The King then accepted the resignations of Broglie and Guizot and charged Laffitte, still a minister without portfolio, with the presidency and with the task of organizing a new government. Negotiations went on during the next two weeks. From day to day the press reported the imminent appointment of numerous men and the intervention of Lafayette into the discussions. Louis-Philippe prevailed upon Gérard and Sébastiani to remain in the ministry, but he failed in his efforts to persuade Louis and Molé. The final composition of the new ministry was hammered out in two midnight meetings at the end of October, the King signed the necessary orders on November 2, and the *Moniteur* published the new cabinet list the next day.[52]

[51] Broglie, *Souvenirs*, IV, 87-89; Guizot, *Mémoires*, II, 129; BHVP, NA 154, Folio 113, Proclamation du Préfet de la Seine, Oct. 19, 1830; AS, VD³ 3, Préfet de la Seine to Maire, 8ᵉ Arrond., Oct. 19, 1830.
[52] Broglie, *Souvenirs*, IV, 89-91; Guizot, *Mémoires*, II, 132-33; Jacques

Laffitte was formally designated president of the council of ministers, and he took the Ministry of Finance, vacated by Louis. The three other ministers without portfolio—Périer, Dupin, and Bignon—resigned, and that office was allowed to lapse. Gérard remained at the Ministry of War, Dupont de l'Eure at the Ministry of Justice, and Sébastiani at the Ministry of the Navy. A young peer and son of a Napoleonic minister, the Comte Marthe de Montalivet, took the Ministry of the Interior. Marshal Maison became the Minister of Foreign Affairs, the post coveted by Sébastiani. Broglie's position at the head of the Ministry of Public Instruction and Religion was assumed by Joseph Mérilhou. Two weeks later a slight reshuffling took place, occasioned by the resignation of Gérard for reasons of health. Marshal Soult succeeded him in the Ministry of War. Lafayette complained that he had not been consulted on this appointment, implying that he had had a voice in earlier appointments, although Rémusat, who was close to Lafayette, declared in his memoirs that he did not. Maison accepted an ambassadorship, and Sébastiani realized his ambition to move up to the Ministry of Foreign Affairs. The Ministry of the Navy was taken by the Comte d'Argout.[53]

All save one of the new appointees were members of the Chamber of Peers, but all had been active in the left opposition during the last years of the Restoration. Montalivet had been a member of the "Aide-toi, le ciel t'aidera" during the elections of 1827 and had assisted in the campaign to defeat Peyronnet in the Department of the Cher

---

Laffitte, "Mes deux ministres (1830-1831)," *Revue des deux mondes*, 100th year, 58 (1930), 664. A. Fortier, "Dupont (de l'Eure); la Révolution de Juillet 1830," *Révolution de 1848*, XII (1916), 145-48; *Journal des débats*, Oct. 26, 27, 28, 30, 31, Nov. 1, 1830; *Gazette de France* (Paris), Oct. 25, 30, 31, Nov. 2-3, 4, 1830; *National*, Oct. 28, 1830; *Moniteur*, Nov. 3, 1830, p. 381.

[53] *Moniteur*, Nov. 3, 1830, p. 1381, Nov. 18, p. 1487; Broglie, *Souvenirs*, IV, 125-26; Marie de Lafayette, *Mémoires, correspondance et manuscrits* (Paris, 1837-38), VI, 473; Marthe de Montalivet, *Fragments et souvenirs* (Paris, 1899, 1900), 1, viii.

that year. Soult had been Louis XVIII's Minister of War in 1814, but in 1827 he was under surveillance, along with Laffitte, Lafayette, Sébastiani, and others prominent in 1830 as a possible partisan of the Duc d'Orléans. Argout was one of the two peers who had on July 29, 1830 prevailed upon Charles X to withdraw the four offending ordinances and to appoint a new ministry, and he had subsequently attempted to act as a mediator between Charles and the liberal deputies in Paris. In the twenties he had been a member of the philanthropic society, the Société de la Morale chrétienne, which included on its rolls most of the prominent left opposition. Mérilhou was a lawyer who had made his reputation as a defender of civil rights against the government. In the early twenties he belonged to the Carbonari, and in 1827 he stood in good liberal company as a member of the Société des Amis de la Liberté de la Presse. Since August 1, 1830, he had been secretary-general of the Ministry of Justice.[54]

Although the proclamation of Barrot provided the occasion for the changes in the cabinet, the issue that most seriously concerned the ministers old and new and that largely determined the choice of the new ministers was the approaching trial of the ministers of Charles X. All were united in the determination to prevent the trial's turning into an act of popular vengeance that would sully the reputation of the new regime and perhaps trigger new acts of violence and bloodshed. The question was how and by whom could the popular demand for the death penalty for the ex-ministers be allayed. Guizot, Broglie, and the other ministers who stepped down in November advocated firm resistance to the popular demands and vigorous suppression of disorders. Laffitte, Dupont, and their partisans were no less opposed to disorders in the streets, no less determined to assure the ministers a fair trial, but they were more flexible in dealing with the public, more given to persua-

---

[54] Pouthas, *Guizot*, pp. 68, 284, 342-43, 348, 367, 370, 377, 383; Rémusat, *Mémoires*, II, 67 n.

sion and cajolery, more kindly disposed toward the program of the Hôtel de Ville, more sympathetic, as Laffitte
put it in his opening speech before the Chamber of Deputies, with the revolution, and they were more popular with
Parisians. Freed of ministerial alliance with their more
conservative colleagues and the consequent suspicion that
they were themselves tainted by conservatism, they would
be in a stronger position, it was believed, to guide Paris
and the country through the difficult days ahead.[55]

On November 3 the Chamber of Deputies reassembled
after a three-and-a-half week recess. Sitting in it were 113
newly elected members chosen in the by-elections to replace deputies resigned or purged for failure to take the
required oath of fidelity to the new regime or forced to
stand for reelection by accepting public office. They were
elected under the electoral laws of the Restoration only
slightly altered, and in taking their seats they changed
neither the social composition of the chamber nor its political sympathies. The liberal monarchism of "the 221"
still dominated the house, and it was sympathetic with the
moderate Orléanism of the outgoing government. In its
early sessions the chamber listened politely to the spokesmen of the Laffitte ministry but reserved its warmest reception for Guizot, who spoke for the retiring ministers,
and it spelled out its sympathies by overwhelmingly rejecting
the ministry's candidates for the presidency and vice-presi-
dency of the chamber and electing the more conservative
Casimir Périer and André Dupin. In its short life before it
was dissolved in May 1831 this chamber was to pass three key
laws of the new regime—the electoral law, the law on the
organization of the National Guard, and the law on local
government, acts that set the tone for the management of
three very important areas throughout the July Monarchy.
In November 1830, however, the primary concern of deputies and ministers alike was the trial of the ex-ministers. The

[55] Guizot, *Mémoires*, II, 132-33, 141; *Journal des débats*, Nov. 7, 1830;
Moniteur, Nov. 11, 1830, pp. 1436-38, 1441; Rémusat, *Mémoires*, II, 406.

328

King had appointed the new ministry because he thought it better qualified than the old to handle the crisis, and until that crisis was passed the chamber was not likely to make difficulties for the government and its supporters.[56]

[56] *Moniteur*, Sept. 15, 1830, pp. 1089-90; Nov. 11, pp. 1436-44; Nov. 12, p. 1447; Rémusat, *Mémoires*, II, 405-7; Guizot, *Mémoires*, II, 142-43.

XI

The Close of the Revolution, November–December 1830

THE CHAMBER of Peers had begun preparations for the trial of Charles X's ministers early in October. On the first a message from the president of the Chamber of Deputies formally notified the Chamber of Peers of the former body's accusation of the ministers of treason. The peers immediately constituted themselves a court of justice, and on October 4 a commission of the court began the preliminary investigation of the case, a process that occupied the next eight weeks. The commission studied the documentary evidence, heard about one hundred witnesses, and questioned the accused. After the disorders of mid-October the King seriously considered postponement of the trial for six months and insisted that it should not start earlier than mid-January, when, he hoped, passions would have subsided. The National Guard of Paris, however, composed largely of merchants and shopkeepers, was anxious that the trial be completed before Christmas, lest the threats and uncertainties that it imposed upon the city ruin the year-end trade connected with the traditional celebration of New Year's Day, the equivalent of American Christmas shopping. Since the government was dependent on the Guard for the maintenance of order, the authorities listened to its wishes and moved the trial forward. On November 29 the court met in secret session to receive its commission's report and after hearing it accepted the accused for trial and affirmed its own competence in the case. The next day the president of the peers set the opening of the public trial for Wednesday, December 15.[1]

[1] Paul Bastid, "Le Procès des ministres de Charles X," *Revue d'histoire*

While the investigation was still in progress the government began to take extraordinary measures to maintain the security of the court and to assure public order in the turbulent days that they saw ahead. The trial was to be held in the seat of the Chamber of Peers, the Luxembourg Palace, and on October 25 the commissioner of police of the Luxembourg Quarter, an architect of the prefecture, and an engineer of the quarries of Paris inspected the quarries under the Luxembourg Garden to make sure that they offered no escape route from the palace to the catacombs. The investigators reported that no connection between the two quarry systems existed, but the Prefect of Police was still apprehensive, and he warned the Grand Référendaire of the Chamber of Peers of the danger he saw there. A few days later the police investigated a report that barrels of gunpowder had been collected in houses near the Luxembourg Palace with the intent of exploding them and freeing the ex-ministers in the resulting confusion.[2] On November 15 the Commanding General of the National Guard, Lafayette, issued new instructions for the rapid call-up and deployment of the Guard in an emergency. His concern was to be able to assemble an imposing force of guards without beating the general alarm, which in itself might be disturbing to the peace. One battalion of each of the twelve legions was to be on immediate call for a period of fifteen days, and one sergeant or corporal was to be on twenty-four hour duty at the mayor's office in each arrondissement. In case of a summons to arms this man was to inform the officers of the battalion on call and to warn the sergeants and corporals to assemble their men. Each battalion was then to proceed to one of twelve key points for the control of the city, including the Palais-

moderne et contemporaine, 4 (1957), 188-93; Moniteur universel (Paris), Oct. 2, 1830, pp. 1205-6, Supplément A, Dec. 4, pp. 7-8; Etienne d'Audiffret-Pasquier, Histoire de mon temps; mémoires du Chancelier Pasquier, 3d ed. (Paris, 1895), VI, 410-11.

2 AN, F⁷ 12329, Ministère de l'Intérieur, Préfecture de Police de Paris, "Bulletin de Paris," Oct. 26, 30, 1830.

Royal, the Hôtel de Ville, the Place de la Bastille, the Place de l'Odéon near the Luxembourg Palace, and several bridges. The general call was to be beaten only on written orders from the Commanding General or the Chief of the General Staff of the National Guard. Early in December the King gave to Lafayette the command of the troops of the Line in Paris, concentrating under his charge all the armed forces of the capital.[3]

During the anxious weeks before the trial the government achieved some success in reducing the threat from the legitimists, who were anxious to replace Louis-Philippe with the young Henry V. Ferdinand de Bertier, the royalist leader, reported to the Duchesse de Berry in mid-November that the government's persuasions and threats had cut the number of army officers on whom the royalists could depend from 1500 to about 450. The number of men prepared to take up arms in the west and march on Paris had dwindled from early estimates of 60,000 to fewer than half that number. Everywhere royalist partisans were weakened by shortages of arms and money and by the absence of firm leadership from the royal family. In the first weeks after the revolution, when the situation of the government was precarious, bold action by a few officers, Bertier thought, might have raised revolt in Brittany, roused support in other royalist areas, and within a month returned a Bourbon ruler to Paris or at least set up a rival government in Brittany and the Vendée that would in time have won over the rest of France. By November this possibility had vanished. Uprisings in the west and in the Midi, if they were to be more than local outbreaks, would have to be accompanied by a foreign invasion or at least the threat of invasion. Bertier reported that the Minister of War had advised the government that the army would not be prepared for foreign war before the end of April and that he was

[3] AN, F⁹ 682, Ministère de l'Intérieur, Affaires milit., Gardes nat., Arrêté du Gén. Cmdt. en Chef, Garde nat. de Paris, Nov. 15, 1830; BHVP, Révolution de 1830, Carton 23, Lafayette, Ordre du jour du 8 décembre 1830.

fearful of the consequences should France be attacked before that time. The royalists' diminishing prospects could be saved, Bertier warned, only by their taking advantage of this grace period, by substituting vigorous leadership for the irresolution of the preceding months. Time was running out, and no later than February the partisans of Henry V must launch revolt in France and arrange for simultaneous foreign intervention. Bertier suggested negotiations for Spanish support; he had word that the Spanish king was prepared to furnish an army of 60,000 men to restore his French relatives to their throne, and he proposed a marriage between Henry V and a grand duchess of Russia as a means of assuring the Tsar's assistance. The outbreak of revolution in Poland at the end of November fixed Nicholas's attention closer to home, but Bertier thought that it would be easy to convince him that the seat of revolution was not in Warsaw but in Paris and that Russian troops should be on the Rhine by the first days of February.[4]

Although he wrote of grand plans that might assure success to the pretender, Bertier was losing confidence in his cause. On December 16, the day after the trial of the ministers opened, he informed the exiled court that the National Guard and the army had the departments around Paris and in the east and the northeast, and the royalist cities of the west and of the Midi firmly under their control. At the same time the Carlists had lost supporters. The men of the Royal Guard and the Gendarmerie, potential partisans when rejected by the new regime, had been recalled to service and even officers of the Guard were rejoining the army. Conscripts were answering their calls without delays or protests. The government had succeeded in filling the magistracy and the administration with men devoted to the revolution. Bertier still urged "une action forte et

---

[4] "Rapport du baron de Bordigne," [Oct.-Nov. 1830], F. de Bertier to Duchesse de Berry, Nov. 16, 1830, in Guillaume de Bertier de Sauvigny, "Le Conspiration des légitimistes et de la duchesse de Berry contre Louis-Philippe 1830-1832 (correspondance et documents inédits)," *Etudes d'histoire moderne et contemporaine*, 3 (1950), 20-42.

générale," but after three months of vain attempts to inspire it, three months utilized by the government to fortify itself in power, he revealed his discouragement when he bluntly warned the exiled court that if it did not quickly reverse its present policy of inaction, it must, in loyalty to its partisans, advise royalists of the interior of its intentions lest they further compromise themselves to no purpose.[5]

The war that Bertier hoped for was a continuing threat to the new Laffitte government as it had been to its predecessor. The conference of ambassadors, convened to find a peaceful solution to the problem posed by the revolt of the Belgians against their Dutch rulers, met in London on November 4, but the Russians took a belligerent stance, urging joint action of the powers to restore the rebellious provinces to their legitimate ruler and offering to contribute up to 200,000 men to the effort. The new French ministry professed a pacific policy, seeking to calm apprehension of war at home and to allay fears of French belligerence abroad. On November 6, Sébastiani, the new Minister of the Navy and a confidant of the King, told the Chamber of Deputies that "the policy of the government is peace at home and abroad." France would take up arms, he declared, only in defense of her own territory or to avenge an insult to the national honor, a declaration that could be interpreted as a retreat from Molé's threat of the preceding August that France would send troops into Belgium if Prussia intervened in support of the Dutch. A week later Marshal Maison, the Minister of Foreign Affairs, reassured the chamber that the government was confident that peace would be preserved and expressed his opinion that peace was "preferable even to victory," a pronouncement that brought approving shouts of "Très bien! Très bien" from his audience.[6]

[5] F. de Bertier to Emmanuel de Brissac, Dec. 16, 1830, in *ibid.*, pp. 42-45.

[6] J. A. Betley, *Belgium and Poland in International Relations, 1830-1831* (The Hague, 1960), pp. 23, 42, 43, 49, 50; *Moniteur*, Nov. 11, 1830, p. 1404, Nov. 14, p. 1463. One country in which the French Revolution stirred much sympathy was the United States, and the months of No-

Despite its public display of confidence the government was concerned by Russia's warlike moves, and on December 1 Sébastiani, who had moved to the Foreign Ministry, sent to Saint-Petersburg a blunt note that went beyond the policy enunciated by Molé three months earlier. Russia was in no way threatened by developments in France, he warned, and the French government could understand her military preparations only as a step toward the revival of an anti-French coalition. If Russian troops crossed the Polish frontier into Prussia, France would regard the peace as broken and would be guided only by her own interests. At the same time the government proposed to the chambers the calling up of an additional 80,000 men to the army, but when one deputy urged an even larger call-up and another advocated the annexation of Belgium, the Minister of Foreign Affairs felt obliged to intervene. He made no reference to his warning to Russia but reiterated his government's policy of nonintervention and declared that the government expected belligerent action by no nation.[7]

In December the outbreak of revolution in Poland cut Russia's power to act in the west, and the Belgian crisis cooled down. Talleyrand and Lord Palmerston, the British foreign minister, knowing that Russia's rôle in the London conference would henceforth be minimal, began to press for recognition of Belgian independence, and on December 20 the conference formally recognized the "future independence of the Belgian state." This left unresolved the vexing questions of the new state's boundaries and its

---

vember and December saw positive manifestations of it in Paris. On November 18 a delegation of Philadelphians, accompanied by Lafayette, came to the Hôtel de Ville and presented to the Prefect on behalf of a meeting held in Philadelphia an address of congratulation to the people of Paris. About a month later Lafayette personally delivered to the faculty and students of the Ecole polytechnique an address of the students of the United States Military Academy congratulating the Polytechnicians on their "noble conduct" during the July Days. AN, 271 AP 21, Odilon Barrot Papers, Report of Prefect [Nov. 18, 1830]; *Moniteur*, Dec. 15, 1830, p. 1708.

7 Betley, *Belgium and Poland*, pp. 53-54; *Moniteur*, Dec. 2, 1830, p. 1601; Dec. 5, p. 1626; Dec. 7, pp. 1638, 1639-41.

ruler, but it was a victory for the French, for the territorial settlement of 1815, oriented against France, had been breached. More important for the immediate security of the new French government the threat of war had been greatly reduced just at the time that the Laffitte Ministry faced a domestic crisis over the trial of Charles X's ministers.[8]

In the first weeks of the new ministry's tenure no repetition of the frightening disorders of mid-October recurred, and labor troubles had subsided from the peak of August and September; but unemployment was high, distress growing as the rains and cold of late autumn closed over Paris, and the authorities were fearful of renewed violence. On November 25, 560 men sought jobs on the Place de Grève and Place du Chatelet, and very few found them. Among the job-seekers police overheard complaints of hunger and grumbling that workingmen were worse off than before the revolution and that the present situation could not continue. Treilhard, the Prefect of Police, reporting an even greater surfeit of workers on December 1, warned the Minister of the Interior that something must be done quickly to forestall serious trouble. Employers lacked markets and encountered grave difficulties in obtaining credit, and they were forced to release more and more workers. The Prefect feared that enemies of the regime would exploit the growing distress. The *ateliers de secours*, the work-relief projects organized in the late summer, continued to function, but they provided jobs for only 3000 persons, and Treilhard urged on December 4 that the government immediately open new projects for at least 10,000 unemployed. He was particularly concerned over what the jobless thousands, already exasperated by economic distress, might do if provoked by an acquittal of the ex-ministers. Rumors were spreading that the Chamber of Peers had already decided on acquittal and that individual peers were preparing for hasty departure from the capital once the verdict was re-

[8] Betley, *Belgium and Poland*, pp. 25, 58, 60, 69-70, 74, 259-60.

turned. Parisians believed that Polignac and his colleagues were guilty, the Prefect warned, and they were likely to take justice into their own hands if the peers did not condemn at least Polignac to death.[9]

The government's anxiety was heightened by doubts of the reliability of the National Guard in a crisis provoked by the acquittal of the ministers. The government was dependent on the Guard because the use of the army, except in conjunction with the Guard, after its rôle in the July Days might only provoke trouble. On December 14 and 15 Treilhard called to his office the police commissioners from all forty-eight sections of Paris, and they agreed—and other sources confirmed their opinion—that the National Guard could not be counted upon to offer any real resistance to popular action directed against the former ministers. In his report to the Minister of the Interior on December 16, the Prefect of Police was even more convinced of the Guard's unreliability. Some of the party of the Hôtel de Ville, dissatisfied with the conservative record of the government since August, thought to accept the sparing of the ministers in return for a commitment from the government to carry out more of the program of the Hôtel de Ville, but even if such a bargain could be struck, it was doubtful that this faction would guarantee the loyalty of the National Guard in a crisis.[10]

On December 12 the funeral of Benjamin Constant threatened order in the capital. A procession composed of deputies, delegations of workers, of combatants of July, students of the schools of law and medicine, Polytechnicians, National Guardsmen, and other mourners extended over the whole length of the inner boulevards from the Madeleine to the Place de la Bastille, and the police re-

---

9 AN, F⁷ 12329, Préfecture de Police, "Bulletin de Paris," Nov. 25, Dec. 1, 4, 5, 6, 7, 8, 12, 13, 14, 15, 1830; F³ ɪɪ, Seine 44, Ministère de l'Intérieur, Administration communale, Extrait des procès-verbaux, Conseil gén., Nov. 4, 1830.

10 AN, F⁷ 12329, "Bulletin de Paris," Dec. 15, 16, 1830; Achille de Broglie, *Souvenirs, 1785-1870* (Paris, 1886), ɪᴠ, 143; Charles de Rémusat, *Mémoires de ma vie* (Paris, 1958-67), ɪɪ, 409.

ported most of the population of Paris on the boulevards to watch the procession. Authorities feared a popular demonstration and an attempt by students to take the body to the Panthéon. While the funeral service was in progress in the Protestant chapel on the Rue Saint-Antoine mourners in the church could hear the tumult of the crowd gathered outside. When the procession emerged on the street shouts arose, "Au Panthéon! Au Panthéon!" The Prefet of the Seine came forward and appealed to the crowd to respect the law and warned that it would be enforced. The throng parted and permitted the casket and mourners to move on to the Eastern Cemetery, where the burial took place as planned.[11]

Two days earlier the accused ministers had been moved from the chateau of Vincennes to the Luxembourg Palace. Early in the morning an impressive escort of mounted National Guard, a squadron of cavalry, and a detachment of artillery, all commanded by the Minister of the Interior himself, brought Polignac, Peyronnet, and Guernon-Ranville to the palace. Their route led through the Faubourg Saint-Antoine, where the procession attracted the hostile attention of some spectators, across the Austerlitz Bridge, and along the boulevards to the southern extremity of the Luxembourg Garden, and thence to the palace. Chante-lauze, who had been ill, was brought to the Luxembourg that evening in an unescorted carriage accompanied only by Daumesnil, the Governor of the chateau of Vincennes. The ministers were incarcerated in the Petit Luxembourg, a small building on the Rue de Vaugirard about one hundred yards to the west of the main palace. Semonville, the Grand Référendaire of the Chamber of Peers, had taken extraordinary precautions to make it secure against either escape or attack. Workmen had erected stout wooden fences around the building, enclosing the walk leading to the palace. The windows and the chimneys were barred; doors four to five inches thick reinforced with iron and equipped

---

[11] *Moniteur*, Dec. 13, 1830, p. 1689, Dec. 14, pp. 1699-1700; AN, F⁷ 12329, "Bulletin de Paris," Dec. 12, 1830; Rémusat, *Mémoires*, II, 423.

with heavy bolts were substituted for the existing doors; and the corridors were obstructed by successive gates. Sentry boxes were erected at every turn. The Municipal Guard took responsibility for the internal security of the building, and the National Guard manned guard posts on the outside. Despite the isolation of the prisoners their presence attracted the curious; about one hundred persons were constantly gathered in the adjoining sections of the Luxembourg Garden apparently hoping for a glimpse of the accused.[12]

Preparations went forward for defending the palace during the trial. On December 11 the Odéon Theater was closed for the duration of the proceedings and placed at the disposal of the National Guard for the concentration of reserves near the palace. Beginning on December 14, the day before the scheduled opening of the trial, all officers and men of the National Guard, numbering more than 50,000, were ordered to be in uniform at all times. One battalion of each legion remained constantly on call, and members of battalions in reserve had to leave word at their homes on where they could be reached. Lafayette specifically enjoined guards on duty at the Luxembourg Palace not to leave their posts save on written orders from a commanding officer. A police ordinance effective December 15 closed to traffic between 8 A.M. and 7 P.M. the Rue de Vaugirard in front of the palace and streets running into it from the north, prescribed approach routes for peers and others admitted to the trial, and closed the Luxembourg Garden to the public.[13]

12 *Moniteur*, Dec. 11, 1830, p. 1670, Dec. 12, p. 1682; Broglie, *Souvenirs*, IV, 145, 146; Pasquier, *Mémoires*, VI, 411-12; F⁷ 12329, "Bulletin de Paris," Dec. 10, 12, 1830.

13 *Moniteur*, Dec. 11, 1830, p. 1670; AN, F⁷ 12329, "Bulletin de Paris," Dec. 9, 1830; BHVP, Révolution de 1830, Carton 23, Lafayette, Ordre du jour, Dec. 8, 1830; AP, A/420, Préfecture de Police, Ordonnance concernant des mesures d'ordre à observer pendant le procès des ex-ministres, Dec. 13, 1830; AN, F⁹ 682, Chef d'Etat major, Garde nat. de Paris, Situation gén. au 30 novembre 1830, Inspection gén. des Gardes nat., "Situation sommaire de l'armement des légions de la banlieue," [Nov. 1830].

The opening of the trial attracted a crowd of spectators to the vicinity of the Luxembourg Palace, but they saw no more than the arrival of the peers and of ticket-holders, and no disorders occurred. Among the ticket-holders were forty deputies with tickets drawn by lot and newspapermen, each paper being permitted two reporters in the court room. All the ticket-holders were in their places by ten o'clock, when attendants closed the doors. The four accused ministers then entered the court, accompanied by their counsel, and took seats on the second row of benches immediately behind their lawyers. The peers, dressed in the uniform of their office, filed in; they had previously met in secret session to hear final instructions from their president, Pasquier. Last to enter came the commissioners of the Chamber of Deputies; they, too, were in uniform with the *fleurs de lis* conspicuously removed.[14]

The president declared the court in session, and the clerk called the roll. The peers had been under heavy pressure to be present at the trial, the president having warned them that excuses would be examined with the most careful scrutiny and unjustified absences regarded with great displeasure. One hundred sixty-three peers answered the roll call that morning; twenty-nine were absent, all of them excused. The clerk read the resolution of the Chamber of Deputies accusing all seven of Charles X's last ministers of high treason under Article 56 of the Charter of 1814 and of violation of certain articles of the Penal Code; he also read the order of the Chamber of Peers affirming the charge of high treason. As a court of justice the peers were to decide if the acts of the ex-ministers constituted the crime of treason and, if their decision were affirmative, to determine the appropriate punishment, which was not prescribed by law. Bérenger, one of the commissioners of the Chamber of Deputies, took the floor briefly, appealing to the peers to render impartial justice and to the populace of Paris to respect the court's

[14] *Moniteur*, Dec. 14, 1830, p. 1699, Dec. 16, p. 1716; *Journal des débats* (Paris), Dec. 16, 1830; AN, F⁷ 12329, "Bulletin de Paris," Dec. 15, 1830; Broglie, *Souvenirs*, IV, 147; Pasquier, *Mémoires*, VI, 425.

decision. The court's great act of justice, he declared, would terminate the revolution.[15]

The first three days of the trial, Wednesday, Thursday, and Friday, December 15, 16, and 17, were given over to the interrogation of the accused and of witnesses by the president of the court and by the commissioners of the lower house. On the streets no serious disorders marked these days, the public seemingly awaiting the outcome of the proceedings before expressing itself, but the Prefect of Police was concerned that on the coming weekend the crowds ordinarily at the cafés beyond the city's gates would swarm into the center of Paris and perhaps disrupt the fragile peace. The police took extra precautions to meet the threat, and the prefect urged the command of the National Guard to do so also, but it apparently thought existing arrangements adequate to any foreseeable trouble, for it took no additional measures.[16]

On the trial's fourth day, Saturday, December 18, Jean Persil, one of the commissioners of the Chamber of Deputies, presented the chamber's case against the ex-ministers. He reviewed the three principal charges and marshalled the evidence to support them—illegal activities in preparation for the elections of June and July, adoption of the Four Ordinances in violation of the Charter and justified by neither law nor necessity, and exciting civil war by a number of provocative acts. He emphasized the primary guilt of Polignac, who, he charged, made the essential decisions in concert with the King without consulting the other ministers. Yet all bore a heavy measure of guilt. All had engaged in the illegal electoral preparations, and all had approved and countersigned the ordinances. Persil argued that even though the law on punishment of treason by ministers prom-

15 AN, CC 551 Chambre et Cour des Pairs, Extrait du procès-verbal de la séance du 4 Octobre 1830; Prés., Cour des Pairs, to MM les pairs, Oct. 11, Dec. 8, 1830; Audience publique du mercredi, 15 décembre 1830; Pasquier, *Mémoires*, VI, 425; *Moniteur*, Dec. 16, 1830, p. 1717.

16 *Moniteur*, Dec. 16, 1830, pp. 1717-22, Dec. 17, pp. 1727-33, Dec. 18, pp. 1739-43, Dec. 19, pp. 1750-52; AN, F7 12329, "Bulletin de Paris," Dec. 16, 17, 1830.

ised by the Charter of 1814 had never been enacted, laws were on the books under which the ex-ministers could be punished. He cited particularly—and rather surprisingly—an article on responsibility of ministers in the Constitution of 1799, which he held to be applicable because it was in force when the Charter of 1814 was promulgated, and articles of the Penal Code that punished violation of constitutional laws, resort to civil war, and illegal use of armed force. He concluded by calling on the peers to return "a striking condemnation, equal to the enormity of the crime." He seemed, Pasquier thought, to be addressing himself more to the public than to the peers.[17]

Persil was followed at the tribune by the counsel for Polignac, Jean-Baptiste Martignac, Polignac's predecessor as Charles X's first minister. He spoke long and eloquently in defense of his client, arguing first that the accusation was inadmissible. It was based on a Charter that had been replaced; the composition of the Chamber of Peers had been so altered since the revolution that the guarantee of trial before one's peers was violated; and no written law prescribed any punishment for treason committed by ministers. Were the Chamber of Peers simply a court concerned with the application of the law, he avowed, the charges should be summarily dismissed, but, he conceded, it was also a political body concerned with national security, and consequently he went on to attempt to prove that the charges against his client were ill-founded. In attempting to influence elections the ministers had simply followed established practice, and Polignac himself was little involved even in that. Their use of Article 14 of the Charter was not treasonable; the ministers had seen the security of the state threatened, and in these circumstances the Charter authorized action by royal ordinance. The formation of the Ministry of August 8 had involved no plot nor had the recasting of the ministry in May 1830. The charge that the ministers had later plotted civil war was untenable. They had nothing

<hr>

[17] Bastid, "Procès des ministres," pp. 194-97; *Moniteur*, Dec. 19, 1830, pp. 1752-57; Pasquier, *Mémoires*, VI, 433.

to gain from disruption of the peace and expected no resistance to the ordinances; never in time of danger had fewer precautions been taken. Finally Martignac declared that since no law prescribed a punishment for acts of treason by ministers, the chamber, were it to avoid mixing inadmissibly its legislative and its judicial functions, might impose, not as a legal judgment but as an administrative act, only one punishment—banishment from French soil. In a moving peroration he urged the judges to shun the death penalty; it would bring only remorse, regret, and a desire for revenge. "The blood that you would shed today, do you think that it would be the last?" he asked. "In politics, as in religion, martyrdom breeds fanaticism and fanaticism in its turn breeds martyrdom."[18]

On Sunday, December 19, Peyronnet spoke in his own defense reading a prepared speech. He was followed by his attorney, Antoine Hennequin, and when Hennequin had finished his long and frequently repetitious plea, Paul Sauzet, the young counsel for Chantelauze took the floor. A skillful advocate and a facile speaker, he so impressed his auditors that the president had to remind them that regulations forbade overt expressions of approval. He had not finished his defense before the court reached its customary adjournment time, and he was obliged to postpone completion of his plea until the next day.[19]

Peers leaving the Luxembourg that evening noticed small but to them ominous gatherings in the adjacent streets. The Prefect of Police had received many reports of maturing plans among combatants of July to call upon workers to join them in an attack on the Chamber of Peers. He had instructed his commissioners in all the quarters of Paris to keep a careful watch on the workers in their districts, and in the late afternoon of December 19 he called them to his office. Their reports convinced him that no plot had yet

[18] *Moniteur*, Dec. 19, pp. 1758-70; Bastid, "Procès des ministres," pp. 197-201; Pasquier, *Mémoires*, VI, 433-34.

[19] *Moniteur*, Dec. 20, 1830, pp. 1772-74, Dec. 21, pp. 1779-83; Pasquier, *Mémoires*, VI, 436-38.

reached the factories and workshops but that if the ex-ministers were acquitted a spontaneous and unpredictable movement against them would break out. Almost all his agents agreed, moreover, that the National Guard would not resist this movement and that a large part of the Guard would join it. That same day only one among the twelve mayors of Paris reporting to the Minister of the Interior expressed any confidence in the dependability of his National Guard legion. Perhaps alarmed by these or similar reports Lafayette issued an order of the day to the National Guard in which he sought to appease opposition to Louis-Philippe and the government by stating his belief that the government had been the best possible in the circumstances in which it was founded and that it continued to be; he would continue to defend it, and he counted on the support of his "brothers in arms," the National Guard.[20]

The court resumed its sitting the next day, December 20, at 10:30 A.M. and heard the conclusion of Sauzet's defense of Chantelauze. Adolphe Crémieux, a young lawyer recently come to Paris from Nîmes, spoke in defense of Guernon-Ranville. He had completed his speech and had just launched into his peroration when he grew pale, fainted, and fell back on a bench and had to be carried from the room, his National Guard uniform appearing from below the folds of his robe. Guernon-Ranville declared that nothing remained to be added to his defense, and Pasquier gave the floor to commissioners of the Chamber of Deputies. While Crémieux and Alphonse Bérenger, the first of the commissioners, were speaking Pasquier received several notes from the press gallery informing him that large and menacing crowds were gathering in the streets outside the palace. He sent Semonville to investigate, and the Grand Référendaire returned to confirm the reports. The usual time for adjournment had not yet arrived when Bérenger

[20] Pasquier, *Mémoires*, VI, 438; AN, F⁷ 3884, Ministère de l'Intérieur, Préfecture de Police, "Bulletin de Paris," Dec. 19, 1830; BHVP, NA 154, Papiers Barrot, Folio 234, Maire, 9ᵉ Arrond. to Préfet de la Seine, Dec. 21, 1830; *Moniteur*, Dec. 20, 1830, p. 1771.

344

finished, and Martignac urged that Joseph Madier de Mont-jau, another commissioner of the Chamber of Deputies, be allowed to deliver his discourse, giving Martignac the night in which to prepare his reply to the prosecution. Pasquier was about to call on Madier, when the officer responsible for the safety of the prisoners insisted to him that they be moved as soon as possible to the security of the Petit Luxembourg. The president hastily terminated the session, announcing that public tranquillity would be served by adjournment before nightfall.[21]

Soon after noon that day crowds had gathered in the streets near the Luxembourg Palace, and by four o'clock the National Guard posts were hard pressed. Lafayette had positioned both National Guard and troops of the Line around the palace but had made no effort to block the approaches; people were allowed to move freely across the Pont Neuf and on to the Rue de Tournon, which led directly to the main gate of the palace. Monday was a holiday for many Parisians, and they came to swell the smaller crowds of the preceding days; in late afternoon all the streets between the palace and the river were filled with a milling throng of people. When the peers emerged from the palace about 4:30, the National Guard was holding the crowd on the Rue de Tournon about fifty paces from the palace gate, and the peers were greeted with shouts of "Mort aux ministres!" About 6 P.M. the reinforced National Guard pushed the head of the crowd back to the Place de l'Odéon and the Carrefour de Buci. For the next few hours the Guard remained under pressure as the throng grew even larger, but after nine o'clock the police and military reported that it was breaking up, and no more troubles occurred that night.[22]

---

[21] *Moniteur*, Dec. 21, 1830, pp. 1783-90; Pasquier, *Mémoires*, VI, 438-42.

[22] AN, F⁷, "Bulletin de Paris," Dec. 20, 1830; AHMG, E⁵, Maréchal-de-Camp Cmdt., Place de Paris to Lt.-gén. Cmdt., 1ᵉ Div. milit., Dec. 20, 1830, 7:30 P.M., 9 P.M., 11 P.M.; *Moniteur*, Dec. 21, 1830, p. 1775; Pasquier, *Mémoires*, VI, 442-43.

The evening had passed without serious incident, no firearms had been used, and the National Guard, despite ominous predictions, had shown no disposition to surrender or to join the demonstrators. Nonetheless, the authorities responsible for the security of the court and the prisoners and for the maintenance of public order were alarmed at what might occur after the court passed sentence on the accused. Within the ministry apprehensions arose that the peers, intimidated by the events of the evening, might not appear in sufficient numbers the next day to carry on the trial and that the proceedings might drag on for days as tensions built up intolerably in the streets. Pasquier, stopping at the Palais-Royal that evening, assured a meeting of the ministers that the peers would be in their places in the morning if given adequate protection. He urged that at dawn National Guard and troops of the Line occupy the approaches to the Luxembourg Palace in force and that strong detachments be posted to watch over the Faubourg Saint-Marceau, the working class district on the Left Bank. He further proposed that as soon as the prosecution had completed its case and the defense its pleas the four prisoners should immediately and in great secrecy be returned to the fortress of Vincennes. Here they would be safe from popular vengeance before the public even learned that the debates were closed. The ministers approved, and later that evening Pasquier and Montalivet met at the Luxembourg Palace with Lafayette, his son George, Sébastiani, Semonville, and Barrot to work out details of the transfer. They agreed that after the close of the court's public sessions the ex-ministers would be taken directly to the palace garden, which would be occupied by troops of the Line. Here they would be placed in a waiting carriage; a few cavalrymen would escort the carriage across the garden to the Observatory, where a squadron of regular cavalry, stationed there every day during the trial, would take up the escort and accompany the carriage to Vincennes. Lafayette objected to the exclusion of the National Guard from the operation, which reflected upon their loyalty, and he thought it reckless to attempt the transfer in full daylight. Nevertheless, he was won over to acceptance of the plan.[23]

The meeting broke up about 11:30. Pasquier, before retiring, ordered messages sent to all peers advising them that the court would convene the next morning at the usual hour. Montalivet went to the Ministry of War to inform Soult of the decisions of the conference that concerned him. On the way he visited two National Guard posts on the Left Bank, and although he found all peaceful, he did detect among the guardsmen at least a trace of the popular demand for vengeance on the ex-ministers.[24]

During the day both the Prefect of the Seine and the Prefect of Police had issued proclamations to the people of Paris. Barrot appealed to the public to accept the decision of the court that was soon to be handed down. Resort to violence would benefit only France's enemies, for it would lead to civil war and invite foreign attack. Seeing the present agitation directed not solely against the former ministers but also toward a liberalization of the regime, he expressed his sympathy with these demands but insisted that they could be achieved only by peaceful use of the press and elections. The Prefect of Police warned his "fellow citizens" that violent resistance to the court's decision would destroy the moral force of the revolution that had won it the support of peoples everywhere and would play into the hands of its enemies at home and abroad. That afternoon a speaker in the Chamber of Deputies citing these two proclamations and Lafayette's order of the day of December 19 as indications of ominous developments in the capital, called on the government for an explanation. Laffitte was ready with a reply. Partisans of the Bourbons and "anarchists" threatened the peace, he declared. The government did not credit all the rumors of disorders that circulated freely, but it was acting as if they were true so as to be prepared for any eventuality. Confident of the support of the National Guard,

23 Pasquier, *Mémoires*, VI, 449; Marthe de Montalivet, *Fragments et souvenirs* (Paris, 1899, 1900), I, 172.
24 Pasquier, *Mémoires*, VI, 449; Montalivet, *Souvenirs*, I, 172.

the army, and the population of Paris, it was ready to cope with whatever the coming days might bring. Laffitte's position was uncompromising, demonstrating how little he differed on the question of order from the reputed hard-liners who had left the ministry in November. Two of them, Dupin and Broglie, now endorsed his stand. Dupin spoke of a plot of an attack not only on the Chamber of Peers but on the lower chamber and the King as well, and he was not alone in his apprehensions. Many rumors of conspiracies were in the air. According to one, Carlists had formed a regency and were about to issue proclamations to the country. Another rumor had a committee of public safety about to be proclaimed by a combination of revolutionaries from the faubourgs, the suburbs, the newspapers, and the schools. Yet a third report put Napoleon's son, the Duc de Reichstadt, on the French frontier at the head of an Austrian army; a provisional Bonapartist government would be announced in Paris as soon as the verdict on the ex-ministers was revealed.[25]

Although Laffitte played down the threat of violence, everyone on December 21, according to Rémusat, feared an attack on the Chamber of Peers, and the government, belying its assurances, took extraordinary precautions. At dawn that day a massive concentration of troops numbering, one newspaper estimated, 30,000 men, occupied the Left Bank. National Guards reinforced by five battalions of the Line and a squadron of cavalry guarded the Luxembourg Palace. They blocked the approach streets at defensible points five or six hundred yards from the palace to keep access streets clear and to avoid being forced back to the walls of the palace as they had been on Monday afternoon. Additional troops occupied key points on the Right Bank. Since the preceding afternoon the commander of the "Place de Paris" had doubled the guards at the Ministry of War and at the minister's residence and posted sentries at eleven foreign embassies and legations. Police officers had visited

[25] *Moniteur*, Dec. 21, 1830, pp. 1775, 1777-78; *National* (Paris), Dec. 22, 1830.

gun and arms dealers and urged them to secure their stocks against violent seizure. Lafayette issued another order of the day to the National Guard calling on them to defend the capital against the violence and anarchy that threatened it. During the day orders went out from the Ministry of War to regiments of the Line in Versailles, Fontainebleau, Provins, Compiègne, and Chartres to proceed to points within easy marching distance of Paris and there to await further orders.[26]

The Court of Peers assembled in public session at 10:30 that morning, and 162 peers answered the roll call, only one short of the number in attendance the preceding day. They had met briefly in secret before proceeding to the chamber, and Pasquier informed them of the measures taken for the security of the court and urged them to expedite their business so as not to prolong the dangerous situation of the capital. After the roll call Pasquier gave the floor to Madier de Montjau, and he spoke for more than an hour reaffirming with vigor and often in inflammatory language the proofs already presented of the ex-ministers' guilt. He did not openly ask for the death penalty, but he spoke of a "great punishment" and urged that justice prevail over pity. Martignac returned to the defense of his client, speaking at some length, and he was followed briefly by the three other counsels for the defense. The accused declined the offer of the court to hear them further. The final word came from Bérenger, commissioner of the Chamber of Deputies, "Peers of France," he declared, "our mission is finished. The resolution of the Chamber of Deputies is before you and so, too, is the book of the law; it defines your duties; the country waits; it hopes for good and severe justice." As Bérenger returned

26 Rémusat, *Mémoires*, II, 412; Pasquier, *Mémoires*, VI, 449; *Journal des débats*, Dec. 22, 1830; *Moniteur*, Dec. 22, 1830, p. 1791; AHMG, E⁵ 5, Maréchal-de-Camp Cmdt., Place de Paris to Lt-gén. Cmdt., 1ᵉ Div. milit., Dec. 20, 1830; 11 P.M.; Ministre de la Guerre to Lt.-gén. Cmdt., 1ᵉ Div. milit., Dec. 21, 1830; Maréchal-de-Camp Cmdt., Place de Paris to Gén. xxx, Dec. 20, 1830; AHMG, D³ 131, Lt.-gén. Cmdt., 1ᵉ Div. milit. to Ministre de la Guerre, Dec. 20, 1830; AN, F⁷ 12329, "Bulletin de Paris," Dec. 20, 1830.

to his seat, Pasquier pronounced the debates closed. The hour was about 1:30 P.M.[27]

The time had come to put into execution the plans made the preceding night to spirit the accused away from the Luxembourg to the safety of the fortress of Vincennes. Unfortunately Lafayette had permitted National Guards of the suburbs to occupy the Luxembourg Garden, which was to be held by troops of the Line alone. The suburban guardsmen had wanted a place of honor, Lafayette explained, and he could not deny them. They were reported to be particularly incensed against Polignac, and Montalivet feared the consequences of any contact between them and the ex-ministers. This meant that he could not remove the prisoners by way of the garden as originally projected. Hastily improvising a new plan he brought his own carriage to a little known door of the Petit Luxembourg opening on the Rue de Vaugirard. Montalivet called together the National Guardsmen in the immediate area and told them that the accused ministers were going to be brought to the carriage for their return to Vincennes. He appealed to them to let the prisoners pass without hostile word or act. The commanding officer assured Montalivet that he could depend on these guardsmen. They formed in two ranks outside the door and stood in silence as the four ex-ministers emerged and walked to the waiting vehicle. Two National Guard officers of unquestioned loyalty took places beside them. The carriage moved westward down the Rue de Vaugirard to the corner of the Rue Madame, where mounted National Guards and a squadron of regular cavalry formed an escort, and, led by Montalivet and General Fabvier, commander of the "Place de Paris," the column proceeded by narrow streets to the Boulevard d'Enfer, out of the city by the Enfer Gate, and thence, as the shadows of this shortest day of the year lengthened into dusk, across the Plaine d'Ivry, the Pont de Charenton, and

[27] Pasquier, *Mémoires*, VI, 440, 450-53; AN, CC 551 Cour des Pairs, Audiences secrètes, Séance du Mardi, Dec. 21, 1830; Bastid, "Procès des ministres," pp. 203-04; *Moniteur*, Dec. 22, 1830, pp. 1792-94, Dec. 23, pp. 1796-99.

on to Vincennes. At 6 P.M. the prisoners were delivered safely into the hands of General Daumesnil. Montalivet had succeeded in removing the ex-ministers from Paris without attracting any significant attention. The National Guards at the main gate of the Luxembourg Palace had not even noticed the carriage and escort a few hundred feet down the Rue de Vaugirard, and with the approach streets all blocked no spectators were present to witness the column form and move off. The crowds in the streets knew nothing of the operation until long after it was completed, and the National Guard continued to believe that they were protecting both judges and prisoners in the Luxembourg Palace.[28]

While the accused were being spirited away, the court met in secret session, convening at 2 P.M. Pasquier informed the peers that, following precedent, two votes, both of them oral, would be taken on each question before them and that the second would be decisive. A five-eighths majority would be required to establish guilt and to impose the death penalty. The court would decide only on the charge of treason, not on the charges of violation of specific articles of the Penal Code included in the Chamber of Deputies's indictment, and consequently, Pasquier declared, it would not be bound by these articles in its choice of punishments. Before the trial had started Pasquier had held several conferences with his colleagues on the appropriate punishment for the ex-ministers should they be found guilty, and all had agreed to exclude the death penalty. Now Pasquier was inviting the entire court to avoid that penalty.[29]

The preliminaries accomplished, the court proceeded to the vote on the guilt of Polignac, a process that took considerable time, for many peers explained their votes as they

[28] Montalivet, *Souvenirs*, I, 176-203; Rémusat, *Mémoires*, II, 413; BHVP, NA 154, Folio 196, Chef, 1ᵉ Légion, Garde dépt. to Préfet de la Seine, Dec. 21, 1830, Folio 206, Proclamation du Préfet de la Seine, Dec. 21, 1830, AHMG, E⁵ 5, Col., 1ᵉ Légion, Gend. dépt. to Ministre de la Guerre, Dec. 21, 1830.

[29] Pasquier, *Mémoires*, VI, 419-22, 453-55; AN, CC 551, Cour des Pairs, Audiences secrètes, Séance du 21 décembre; Bastid, "Procès des ministres," pp. 204-5.

cast them. The final tally was 136 guilty, 20 not guilty. Separate votes on each of the three other ministers pronounced them guilty, too. These proceedings occupied nearly four hours, and at 6 P.M. the court took a half-hour recess. About this time a rumor spread among the National Guards on duty on the Left Bank that the ministers had been condemned to death. Rémusat, sent out by Lafayette to investigate the report, found guardsmen celebrating the news and preparing to return to their homes. Rémusat went from post to post telling them that the trial was not yet over and inducing them to remain on duty. The guards were annoyed, and Rémusat doubted they could be depended upon to defend the Chamber of Peers were it attacked.[30]

The court resumed its session to determine the punishment of the guilty ministers. On the first ballot on Polignac some of the peers cast votes for life imprisonment, some for life imprisonment with the accessory punishments of deportation, namely, "civil death," and some for banishment. Eight voted for death. In the second and definitive vote a clear majority of 128 peers favored the second of these punishments; the number wanting death dropped to four. For Peyronnet, Chantelauze, and Guernon-Ranville the court voted life imprisonment combined with loss of certain civil rights and of titles, ranks, and orders. Pasquier and six colleagues withdrew to an adjoining room to draw up the decree embracing the court's decisions. When it was ready half an hour later, the court voted its approval of the proposed text, and each peer signed it. Attendants then summoned the commissioners of the Chamber of Deputies and the counsel for the defense to the chamber. National Guards on duty at the palace filled the galleries. At 10 P.M. Pasquier read the court's decision. In a gesture of appeasement to those who demanded the death penalty the court specified that Polignac was condemned to "civil death," although this punishment was always included among the

---

[30] Pasquier, *Mémoires*, VI, 455-56, AN, CC 551, Cour des Pairs, Audiences secrètes, Séance du 21 décembre; Rémusat, *Mémoires*, II, 413-14.

accesssory punishments of deportation; it imposed the loss of all civil rights including the right to hold property.[31]

Crowds awaiting the court's decision had begun to gather about noon in the streets leading southward into the Place de l'Odéon and the Carrefour de Buci. They milled about, shouted, "Mort aux ministres!" and tried to push on to the Luxembourg Palace. The Sixth and Seventh Legions of the National Guard blocked the streets to the palace, but as the crowds grew they had difficulty in containing them. About 2:30 the Second Legion joined the other two, and together they pushed the demonstrators back to the quais and made many arrests. The crowds were confined to this area and on the adjoining Right Bank for the remainder of the afternoon and evening. Montalivet, returning in the early evening from Vincennes, encountered on the Pont Neuf an agitated crowd shouting the most savage threats against the ex-ministers and the Chamber of Peers, but its only overt violence was the breaking of lights on the bridge and on nearby streets. A mile away the Court of Peers deliberated in peace, and when the session terminated, the peers, some of whom had plotted escape routes through the garden, left the palace through the main gate unmolested by demonstrators. The only disturbance near the palace occurred when National Guards stationed in the courtyard learned that the lives of the ministers had been spared. They broke ranks, threw their weapons into the air, shouted their disapproval, and demanded to be relieved of further duty. Lafayette went out personally to speak to them and in time managed to return them to order, and he soon released most of them to return to their homes, for neither judges nor prisoners remained in the palace to be guarded.

---

31 Pasquier, *Mémoires*, VI, 459-63; AN, CC 551, Cour des Pairs, Audiences secrètes, Séance du 21 décembre; *Moniteur*, Dec. 22, 1830, p. 1794. The three ministers who escaped from France in August 1830—Capelle, Haussez, and Montbel—were pronounced guilty by default on April 11, 1831, and condemned to the same punishment as that imposed on Peyronnet, Chantelauze, and Guernon-Ranville. Bastid, "Procès des ministres," p. 207.

Late that evening the Prefect of the Seine issued a proclamation announcing the decision of the court and the removal of the prisoners to Vincennes, but by that time the crowds had dispersed, and the announcement produced no overt reaction that night.[32]

The threat to the regime was not passed, only postponed to the next day, when the punishment imposed on the ex-ministers would be generally known. Barrot warned of the existence of a powerful conspiracy to overthrow the government; one mayor foresaw attacks on the homes of peers and on the Palais-Royal, and Daumesnil feared a march on Vincennes. Crowds on the streets in the morning of December 22 were smaller than those of the preceding day, but they were excited by speakers denouncing the sentences on the ministers, and police reported many shouts of "Mort aux ministres!" One band of demonstrators from the Faubourg Saint-Marceau tried to invade the Luxembourg Palace; they were held off by the small guard post until the local legion of the National Guard could be alerted and brought to the scene to disperse them. About 11 A.M. the command of the National Guard of Paris ordered the beating of the general call, and the legions, despite the fatigue of several days of extraordinary duty and displeasure with the verdict of the Court of Peers, responded promptly and occupied their assigned posts in the city. They were reinforced by 2700 National Guards from the suburbs, and troops of the Line were sent to the Cham-

[32] AN, F⁷ 3884, "Bulletin de Paris," Dec. 21, 1830; Montalivet, *Souvenirs*, I, 206; *National*, Dec. 22, 1830; Broglie, *Souvenirs*, IV, 166-67; Pasquier, *Mémoires*, VI, 464; Rémusat, *Mémoires*, I, 414-15; *Moniteur*, Dec. 22, 1830, p. 1791; BHVP, NA 154, Folio 206, Proclamation du Préfet de la Seine, Dec. 21, 1830; Folio 221, Maire, 4ᵉ Arrond. to Préfet de la Seine, Dec. 21, 1830; 8:15 P.M.; Folio 240-41, Maire, 11ᵉ Arrond. to Préfet de la Seine, Dec. 21, 1830; Folio 242, Chef, Bat. de Service, 11ᵉ Légion, Garde nat., to Préfet de la Seine, Dec. 21, 1830; Folio 218, Maire, 3ᵉ Arrond., to Préfet de la Seine, Dec. 21, 1830, 11 P.M.; Folio 285, Maire adjoint, 7ᵉ Arrond., to Préfet de la Seine, Dec. 22, 1830, 1:30 A.M.; Folio 288, Maire, 8ᵉ Arrond. to Préfet de la Seine, Dec. 22, 1830; Folio 239, Maire, 10ᵉ Arrond. to Préfet de la Seine, Dec. 21, 1830, 11 P.M.; AHMG, E⁵ 5, Lt.-gén. Cmdt., 1ᵉ Div. milit., "Rapport du 21 au 22 Xᵇʳᵉ 1830."

ber of Deputies, to the Place Vendôme, to the Louvre to watch over the artillerymen of the National Guard, suspected of potent republican sympathies, and especially to the Palais-Royal, where more than 800 troops were deployed. The *ateliers de secours* provided jobs that day for 6000 persons, keeping that many unemployed off the streets. Two orders revealed how deeply apprehensive were the Prefect of the Seine and the Minister of the Interior. Barrot instructed mayors of all the arrondissements of Paris to report to him every three hours throughout the day on the situation of their districts. Montalivet personally ordered the mayors to be prepared to cut the bell ropes in all churches lest they be used to sound the dreaded tocsin. Messages from both the Left and Right Banks reported crowds forming to march on Vincennes, and the governor of the fortress urgently requested a battalion of troops of the Line to reinforce his guard. The Minister of War gave orders that the four prisoners should be moved from Vincennes that night if possible, and early the next morning at the latest, to the fortress of Ham in the Department of the Somme, a good eighty miles from the tumult of Paris.[33]

Some authorities were apprehensive that students from the Ecole polytechnique and the schools of law and medicine might join the demonstrators. One student proclamation demanded "a more republican base for our institutions" and threatened to join the people of Paris in conquering it. But another proclamation by students called on

[33] Broglie, *Souvenirs*, IV, 172; *Moniteur*, Dec. 23, 1830, p. 1795; BHVP, NA 154, Folio 226, Maire, 6ᵉ Arrond., to Préfet de la Seine, Dec. 22, 1830, noon; Folio 265, Etat des bataillons . . . à l'Hôtel de Ville, Dec. 23, 1830, 6 A.M.; Folio 274, Maire, 1ᵉ Arrond. to Préfet de la Seine, Dec. 22, 1830, 10 A.M., 3:30 P.M.; Folio 281, Maire, 6ᵉ Arrond. to Préfet de la Seine, Dec. 22, 1830; Folio 290, Maire, 8ᵉ Arrond. to Préfet de la Seine, Dec. 22, 1830; 4:30 P.M.; Folio 299-300, Maire, 11ᵉ Arrond. to Préfet de la Seine, Dec. 22, 1830, evening; AS VD⁴ 5886, Ministre de l'Intérieur to Maire, 1ᵉ Arrond., Dec. 22, 1830; AHMG, E⁵ 5, Lt.-gén.-Cmdt., 1ᵉ Div. milit. to Ministre de la Guerre, Dec. 22, 1830; Maréchal-de-Camp Cmdt., Place de Paris to Lt.-gén. Cmdt., 1ᵉ Div. milit., Dec. 22, 1830; Préfet de Police to Préfet de la Seine, Dec. 22, 1830; Gouverneur de Vincennes to Ministre de la Guerre, Dec. 22, 1830; Ministre de la Guerre to Général Pelet, Dec. 22, 1830.

the public to rally to the support of the National Guard, and a large body of students actually joined the guard in defense of order. About noon 500 to 600 students from the three principal schools—the Polytechnique, law, and medicine—gathered on the Place du Panthéon, the Polytechnicians in uniform, the others with their student cards or cards reading "Ordre public" or similar sentiments stuck in their hats. They aided the National Guard in dispersing a crowd of demonstrators that had come to the place shouting "Long live liberty!" and "Death to the ministers!" and then divided into small groups and marched about the city proclaiming their solidarity with the National Guard and the government. Most of them reassembled near the Louvre and proceeded to the Palais-Royal, where the King appeared on a balcony as the students shouted "Vive le Roi!" "Liberté et ordre public!"[34]

Tensions lessened in the afternoon as the loyalties of the National Guard and students became clear, and in the evening rain began to fall, driving demonstrators from the streets. Barrot wrote to the Prefect of Police, "I believe that we have emerged from the crisis." The next day the city was completely calm. The Prefect of Police could scarcely believe that Paris could be so different on successive days, and he declared that France could now really enjoy the benefits of "the revolution of three days." The King took advantage of fair weather on the twenty-third to review the National Guard units and troops of the Line throughout the city. Accompanied by his son, the Duc de Nemours, the ministers of war and the interior, high officers of the National Guard, and an escort of mounted National Guards he left the Palais-Royal at 1 P.M. and in the course of the

[34] BHVP, NA 154, Folio 208, Proclamation, "Au peuple de Paris; les Ecoles réunies"; Folio 209, Proclamation, "Les Ecoles polytechnique, de Droit et Medicine," Dec. 22, 1830; Folio 305, Maire, 12ᵉ Arrond. to Préfet de la Seine, Dec. 22, 1830, 4 P.M.; *Moniteur*, Dec. 23, 1830, p. 1795; Dec. 24, 1830, pp. 1807-8, Dec. 25, 1830, p. 1814; AN, Fᵍ 682, Ministère de l'Intérieur, Affaires milits., Gardes nats., Capt., 3ᵉ Cie., 2ᵉ Bat., 12ᵉ Légion, Garde nat. to Roi, Dec. 27, 1830; AHMG, E⁵ 5, Lt.-gén. Cmdt., 1ᵉ Div. milit. to Ministre de la Guerre, Dec. 22, 1830, 2 P.M.

afternoon visited every arrondissement of the city and completed his tour with a torchlit review of National Guards in the Place du Carrousel. To each unit of the Guard and the Line he expressed his gratitude for its devotion and service through the critical days just passed, and everywhere he was warmly received.[35]

On December 23 and 24 the center of interest shifted from the streets to the Chamber of Deputies and the Palais-Royal. Since the end of July the King, the ministers, and the chamber had been dependent on Lafayette, for only he could assure the loyalty of the National Guard, and since the army's ability to preserve order in Paris was uncertain, the very life of the regime might depend on the Guard's protection. In the crisis of December, when the threat to the regime seemed real and imminent, he was even more indispensable. During these days he was in frequent contact with hostile elements in the Guard and among students and workers, and he sought to appease them by deploring the reluctance of the government to carry out the program endorsed by Louis-Philippe on July 31, and he at least half-promised that once the crisis had passed, rapid progress would be made toward the realization of this program. In his order of the day of December 24 he declared that the National Guard's reward for having "done all for order" was to hope that "all will be done for liberty." His actions and public statements made him suspect to the conservative majority in the chamber and an embarrassment to the government, and the ministry took pains to make clear that it had made no deals to accelerate reforms in return for popular support during the crisis of December.[36]

[35] BHVP, NA 154, Folio 245, Préfet de la Seine to Préfet de Police, Dec. 22, 1830; Folio 291, Maire, 8e Arrond. to Préfet de la Seine, Dec. 22, 1830, 11 P.M.; Folio 295, Maire, 10e Arrond., to Préfet de la Seine, Dec. 22, 1830; 9:30 P.M.; Folio 296, Maire, 11e Arrond. to Préfet de la Seine, Dec. 22, 1830, 1:30 P.M., evening; Folio 305, Maire, 12e Arrond. to Préfet de la Seine, Dec. 22, 1830, 4 P.M.; AN, F7 12329. "Bulletin de Paris," Dec. 22, 23, 1830; AHMG, E5 5, Col., 1e Légion, Gend. dépt. to Gouverneur de Vincennes, Dec. 22, 1830; Montalivet, Souvenirs, I, 226; Moniteur, Dec. 24, 1830, pp. 1801-02, Dec. 25, p. 1809.
[36] Broglie, Souvenirs, IV, 168-69, 171-73; François Guizot, Mémoires

With the trial of Polignac and his colleagues safely passed and its outcome generally accepted and with the loyalty of the National Guard clearly established Lafayette lost his indispensability. The Chamber of Deputies moved to curtail his powers and at the same time by implication to repudiate the program that he advocated. On December 24 the chamber, which for several days had been discussing a law on the definitive organization of the National Guard, took up the text of Article 50, which forbade all commands over geographical areas larger than a commune. The article made no exception for Lafayette, who since August 16 had been Commanding-General of the National Guard of the Kingdom. The chamber had earlier decided to reduce the Guard from a national armed force as Lafayette conceived it, a veritable auxiliary army under a single command, to a collection of municipal forces for the maintenance of order and the protection of property on a local level. The application of that policy in Article 50 now enabled the chamber to deprive Lafayette of the power base that made him a veritable Constable of France, a potentially dangerous rival to the King himself, and a threat to the chambers. Several deputies proposed amendments to soften the blow to Lafayette, and the Minister of the Interior suggested that the general be permitted to continue in his post at the King's pleasure, but the chamber rejected this amendment along with all the others and approved its commission's text of Article 50. Laffitte then announced that the King would give Lafayette the title of Honorary Commanding-General of the National Guard of the Kingdom.[37]

Lafayette on learning of the action of the chamber and without waiting for the final enactment of the law wrote to the King expressing his intention to resign from the post

pour servir à l'histoire de mon temps, 1807-1848, New ed. (Paris, 1872), II, 152-53; *Moniteur*, Dec. 25, 1830, p. 1809.

[37] *Moniteur*, Aug. 18, 1830, p. 913, Dec. 26, pp. 1818-20; Montalivet, *Souvenirs*, I, 227-32; Louis Girard, *La Garde nationale, 1814-1871* (Paris, 1964), pp. 190-91.

that was about to be suppressed, and he added that he could not accept the decorative title of Honorary Commanding-General. Possibly he thought by threat of resignation to put himself in a position to bargain with the King and the Chamber of Deputies for the reforms he had been advocating and half-promising. Certainly he later did pose specific changes in the structure of the regime as the condition of his remaining in office. But in his letter to the King he suggested no compromise. The King immediately wrote to the general asking him to make no public announcement of his resignation until the two had had an opportunity to talk. Would he come to see him, Louis-Philippe asked, late that afternoon or evening after the meeting of the council of ministers? At the council meeting the King declared that he would not accept Lafayette's resignation, and the ministers agreed that every effort should be exerted to induce him not to resign. King and ministers alike apparently wanted to avoid the possibly inflammatory act of a well-publicized resignation and to substitute for it a simple transition from the potent commanding generalship to the powerless honorary post. A long conversation between the King and Lafayette that evening, however, brought no agreement, and the ministry shortly met again in emergency session. Although Lafayette had refused to commit himself not to resign, he had not submitted a formal resignation. Moreover, Dupont de l'Eure, who was closer to him than any other member of the ministry, reported that he was less upset by the vote of the chamber on the command of the National Guard than by more general developments, presumably the conservative orientation of the government and of the majority of the deputies. The ministry concluded that he was perhaps prepared to bargain, and it decided to offer him as a first concession the office of Honorary Commanding-General conferred not by royal ordinance but by law, thereby changing it from a consolation offered by the King to a positive legislative act. The ministers charged Laffitte and Montalivet to carry the proposal to Lafayette and to assure him that the entire government was anxious that he not resign.[38]

After ten o'clock Laffitte and Montalivet drove to the headquarters of the National Guard on the Rue de la Chaussée d'Antin. Lafayette received them cordially and listened patiently as Laffitte talked long and eloquently of the King's esteem for him, an esteem shared by the ministry and the public, and he urged the general to accept the honorary title as a token of the nation's gratitude and to continue his patriotic mission as the Commanding-General of the National Guard of Paris. Laffitte never touched Lafayette's presumed real grievance—his dissatisfaction with the government's conservatism—but, characteristically carried away by his own eloquence, he thought he had won over Lafayette to acceptance of the ministry's proposals. He terminated the interview with Lafayette having said very little. In the carriage returning to the Palais-Royal Montalivet protested that the interview had accomplished nothing, that they knew no more of the general's intentions than they did when they had set out earlier in the evening. Laffitte, still confident, advised the young minister to return to Lafayette and be reassured.[39]

Montalivet retraced his steps. Lafayette received him again, and this time the general spoke frankly. He had not yet resigned, he said, and he did not want to resign unless he were convinced that he could not accomplish the obligation that he felt he had to achieve the reforms promised by the Duc d'Orléans on July 31. He would retain command of the National Guard of Paris and even accept a lesser appointment if the government would meet three conditions: the replacement of the Chamber of Peers with an assembly composed of "sincere friends of the revolution," the election of a new Chamber of Deputies on a broad

[38] AN, 252 AP 2, Lafayette papers, Lafayette to Roi, Dec. 25, Roi to Lafayette, Dec. 25, A.M., 4:30 P.M.; Montalivet, Souvenirs, I, 237-41.
[39] Montalivet, Souvenirs, I, 241-46; Jacques Laffitte, Souvenirs de Jacques Laffitte raconté par lui-même (Paris, 1844-45), III, 43.

popular suffrage, and the formation of a new ministry that would include a minister of the interior and a minister of foreign affairs who enjoyed more public confidence than the present incumbents. He proposed Barrot as the minister of the interior. Montalivet could, of course, make no such commitments for the government. He simply asked Lafayette for assurances that he would not in any case give up the command of the National Guard of Paris on the next day, when it might be needed to preserve order. Lafayette would make no promises. The minister took his leave and returned at about 11:30 to the Palais-Royal. Here he reported to the King on his interview and confided his anxiety over the threat of the Parisian Guards being without a commander the next day.[40]

The King found Lafayette's conditions unacceptable, and, recalling the acclaim with which he had been received everywhere in the city when he reviewed the Guard and troops of the Line on December 23 and reassured by Montalivet's report that the news of the chamber's action of December 24 had been calmly received in Paris even by the National Guard, he concluded that he was in a strong enough position to rebuff Lafayette and in effect to dismiss him. He had just come to this conclusion when a letter arrived from Lafayette saying nothing of the conditions put to Montalivet but declaring that his objections to the government's proposals had not been met and that he now considered that he had resigned. His principal staff officers, he added, were leaving with him, and he urged that arrangements be made to transmit orders to the National Guard of Paris on the next day's assignments. The King dictated a short letter in reply, expressing his regret that he could not alter the general's resolution and accepting his resignation.[41]

In the early hours of December 26 the King and Montalivet had to act quickly to assure the continuity of the com-

40 Montalivet, *Souvenirs*, I, 247-57.

41 *Ibid.*, pp. 257-64; Marie de Lafayette, *Mémoires, correspondance et manuscrits* (Paris, 1837-38), VI, 501-3.

mand of the National Guard of Paris. No time remained to consult the full ministry, for the effectiveness of the Guard and the security of the regime itself might depend on the early issuance of orders by an acceptable commander. The two men hurriedly considered several possible successors to Lafayette and soon fixed on General Lobau, a Napoleonic general with impeccable liberal antecedents; he had fought at Waterloo, spent several years in exile after 1815, was elected an opposition deputy in 1828, and on July 29, 1830, became a member of the provisional Municipal Commission. Montalivet hurried to Lobau's residence on the Rue de Lille and routed him out of bed to summon him to the Palais-Royal. The minister had already called to the palace the colonels of the twelve legions of the Guard and the colonel of the Guard's artillery. All but two were quickly on the scene, and Montalivet informed them of Lafayette's resignation and of the government's efforts to dissuade him. Two colonels insisted that the general must have been misunderstood, that he could certainly be persuaded to change his mind. Montalivet suggested that they try, and they went off to Lafayette's headquarters only to return with confirmation of the minister's report. He then informed the colonels that until Lafayette's successor was named, he would assume personal command of the National Guard of Paris, and they agreed to accept his orders. He had already begun to draw up his first order of the day when Lobau arrived at the palace. He quickly accepted the King's appointment, and the King presented him to the assembled colonels, who received him warmly. He ordered them to return to their headquarters and await further instructions. After paying his respects to his predecessor he would, he announced, establish his headquarters at the Louvre.[42]

Lafayette's resignation became common knowledge in Paris only on Monday, December 27. The *Moniteur* that day printed Montalivet's report to the King of the general's

[42] Montalivet, *Souvenirs*, I, 258-59, 264-75; Girard, *Garde nationale*, p. 193.

determination to resign and the royal ordinance appointing Lobau Commanding-General of the National Guard of Paris. The same day a proclamation by the King appeared in the city's streets expressing the royal regret at the retirement of Lafayette and praising his services to France. Montalivet feared hostile reactions to the news, particularly a demonstration against the Chamber of Deputies for its action of December 24, and he ordered two battalions of the National Guard to the Palais-Bourbon to assure the protection of the deputies, and other battalions were held in reserve at the Tuileries and the Luxembourg palaces. But everywhere the announcement of the general's stepping down was received calmly, even among the National Guard. A few arrests were made among groups gathered near the Palais-Bourbon, but the prisoners were soon released for lack of serious charges against them. A band of some eight hundred students marched to Lafayette's house on the Rue d'Anjou Saint-Honoré to demonstrate their support for him and for Dupont de l'Eure and Barrot, but they caused no serious disorder.[43]

The retirement of Lafayette inspired other changes in high places. Dupont de l'Eure, Lafayette's closest associate in the ministry, resigned on December 27 as Minister of Justice, and his friend, Mérilhou, moved up from the Ministry of Public Instruction to take his place, and Félix Barthe, a president of the Royal Court of Paris succeeded Mérilhou. Barthe, a Parisian lawyer long associated with the opposition to the Bourbons and a former Carbonaro, had, in the by-elections in October, won a seat in the Chamber of Deputies. Treilhard, the Prefect of Police, resigned on December 26 and in his place the King appointed Jean-Jacques Baude, the former editor of the *Temps* who had defied police sent to seize his presses on July 27, and a

---

[43] *Moniteur*, Dec. 27, 1830, p. 1821, Dec. 28, p. 1825; BHVP, Série 23, Carton 1830, C. Périer to MM. les Questeurs de la Chambre des Députés, Dec. 27, 1830; Guizot, *Mémoires*, II, 160; Pasquier, *Mémoires*, VI, 473; AN, F⁷ 12329, "Bulletin de Paris," Dec. 28, 1830; *Gazette de France* (Paris), Dec. 28, 1830.

secretary of the provisional Municipal Commission. Since mid-November he had been Montalivet's undersecretary of the Minister of the Interior. Both these appointments could be taken as reassurance to the government's liberal supporters and so, too, was Barrot's decision to remain in the Prefecture of the Seine despite his close association with Lafayette. The Prefect satisfied his conscience by penning a memoir to the King urging him to press for a new, more democratic electoral law and for the reconstitution of the Chamber of Peers as a more representative house.[44]

On December 27 Lafayette issued his final order of the day to his "brothers in arms"; he thanked them for their loyalty and devotion and urged them to demonstrate their affection for him by redoubling their devotion to order and liberty. Later in the day he spoke to the Chamber of Deputies and to the large audience in the galleries. He declared that he had always intended to step down from his post of Commanding-General of the National Guard of the Kingdom when the position was no longer necessary. The action of the chamber on December 24 had forced his decision earlier than he would have reached it had he not been pressed, for, although he was satisfied that part of his mission was accomplished—the reestablishment of public order, part remained unachieved—the "popular throne surrounded by republican institutions." But this unfinished business did not demand his remaining in office, because it could be accomplished, he said, by the ballot, the press, and petition. The deputies, uncertain of what direction the general's appeal might take, were obviously relieved by his conciliatory order of the day and his speech and gave him a prolonged ovation as he took his seat. The next day the Prefect of Police reported public order undisturbed, and on the

[44] *Moniteur*, Nov. 11, 1830, p. 1435, Dec. 27, p. 1821, Dec. 28, p. 1825; A. Fortier, "Dupont (de l'Eure); la Révolution de Juillet 1830," *Révolution de 1848*, XII, 151-52 (1916); Gustave Vapereau, *Dictionnaire universel des contemporaines* (Paris, 1858), pp. 118, 127-28; Rémusat, *Mémoires*, II, 52, n. 1, 284, n. 3; AN, 271 AP 21, Papiers Barrot, Mémoire au Roi, Dec. 28, 1830.

twenty-ninth he observed that not for a long time had Paris enjoyed so peaceful a day.[45]

Laffitte spoke to the chamber on December 28 declaring, as a concession to the conservative majority, that the government would use the "most rigorous severity" to maintain order at home, and figuratively bowing to the Fayettists, he promised that in two days the government would introduce a new electoral law extending the right to vote, short of universal manhood suffrage but still enough to satisfy "the friends of liberty." Although committed to peace, France would continue to prepare for war, he added, as long as other powers armed against her, but the Belgian crisis had been largely resolved, and France's weathering of the crisis of December had had, he believed, a salutary effect on her former enemies. He was confident that peace would be preserved.[46]

The critical days of December had been passed, and the principal beneficiary was the King. His leading rival as a national leader had been eliminated. The ministry had been purged of the one member clearly identified with the left opposition, and only a single hawkish minister—Soult— remained in office. The National Guard of Paris had in the showdown proved loyal not merely to its commander but to the regime, and the one doubtful unit—the artillery— was dissolved on January 1, 1831. The trial of the ex-ministers had been concluded without a shot fired or a barricade raised. The republican threat, exaggerated by the Orléanists since the days of July, proved to be a paper tiger.[47]

On December 30 the *Journal des débats* declared that the revolution was ended. It had started as a protest against Charles X's Four Ordinances, which struck at the livelihoods of journalists and printers and would have broken the op-

[45] *Moniteur,* Dec. 28, 1830, pp. 1825, 1828-30; AN, F⁷ 12329, "Bulletin de Paris," Dec. 28, 29, 1830.

[46] *Moniteur,* Dec. 29, 1830, p. 1836.

[47] Guizot, *Mémoires,* II, 161; Rémusat, *Mémoires,* II, 417; AN, F⁷ 12329, "Bulletin de Paris," Dec. 26, 1830; Girard, *Garde nationale,* p. 195.

position. The intervention of the Parisian crowd, motivated by resentments against the Bourbons, by economic distress, and by vaguely conceived ideals of the earlier Revolution, changed protest to revolution and resulted in the expulsion of the royal forces from Paris. The ensuing struggle among rivals for power—legitimists pressing the cause of the young Duc de Bordeaux, Bonapartists dreaming of a revived Empire, republicans recalling 1792, and Orléanists intriguing for their duke—ended with the victory of the last, symbolized by the investiture of Orléans as Louis-Philippe I, king by contract with the Chamber of Deputies. In the provinces the same conditions that had weakened the Bourbons in Paris made them vulnerable there, too, and their partisans, outnumbered, discouraged by the results of the elections of 1830, and left without guidance from Charles and his ministers, allowed their opponents to seize the initiative and install the new Orléanist regime everywhere.

The new government had to cope with the hostility of the conservative powers of Europe and the possibility of their intervention to restore their former protégés, the Bourbons. At home it was threatened by legitimists, by the clergy sympathetic with the Bourbons, and by popular discontent in Paris, both economic and political. The last was the most immediately threatening, and as autumn advanced it focused on the trial of Charles X's ex-ministers, for whom the populace demanded the death penalty while suspecting that the government intended to spare them. The government feared that the trial might set off a renewed outbreak of revolution, this time aimed at the Orléanist regime, and the ministry was recast to give leadership to men thought best qualified to meet the grave threat. The completion of the trial in December without outbreak of violence and the subsequent retirement of Lafayette from his key post in command of the National Guard marked the firm establishment of the new regime. The victors of the revolution were Louis-Philippe, who had won a crown in August and fixed it firmly on his head in December, and the majority in the Chamber of Deputies, who had found a monarch apparently respectful of its wishes, placed its friends in public office, and forestalled a more far-reaching revolution.

Laffitte, who had been elevated to the presidency of the council in November because it was thought that he could appease the party of the Hôtel de Ville, remained in office until March 1831, when he was replaced by Casimir Périer. He retained most of Laffitte's ministers, who had no trouble in switching their allegiance to the more conservative Périer. They placed the narrowest interpretation on the Revolution of July. It had changed the person of the King and confirmed the responsibility of ministers to the majority in the Chamber of Deputies but had effected no fundamental shift in the seat of power and resulted in no mandate for such change. Even after the adoption of a new electoral law in April 1831, which lowered the tax qualifications and age requirements for electors and deputies, the slightly enlarged electorate returned a chamber little altered in composition from that of 1829. The new regime did differ from its predecessor in that there was larger place in it for businessmen like Laffitte and Périer and for liberal nobles like Broglie and Sébastiani, whose role had been limited to opposition. Nonetheless, political power was still firmly in the hands of the landed proprietors, the officeholders, and the professional men. In this respect the July Days had effected no revolution in France.

The revolution had wrought one revolutionary change, one that its principal beneficiaries had not intended and thoroughly deplored. It had brought the people, particularly the people of Paris, back into politics in a way they had not been involved since the 1790s. The government of the Restoration had scarcely considered them politically nor had the opposition. On July 22, 1830, even the *National* reproached Polignac for seeking popular support among the "lower levels," where people had neither the leisure nor the intellect to be concerned with government. But in the July Days the people emerged as a political force, and in the succeeding weeks and months, since they could not express themselves by the ballot of a narrowly limited suffrage, they resorted to direct action in the streets. The new monarchy was faced with demands that the government concern itself with popular wishes, and it had to cope with public disorders in support of these demands. It lived under constant apprehension that a demonstration might get out of hand, as in July 1830, and overthrow the regime. For the men of 1830 this was the frightening heritage of their revolution.

BIBLIOGRAPHY

I. ARCHIVES

1. *Archives nationales de France*

AP = Archives privées

115 AP: Archives des familles de Montholon et Semonville.

149 AP 1: Papiers de Jean-Henri-Claude Mangin, Préfet de Police, 1829-1830.

228 AP 1-2: Papiers d'André Dupin.

252 AP 2: Papiers de Lafayette.

271 AP 21-39: Papiers d'Odilon Barrot: 271 AP 21d²3 Voyage de Cherbourg, 2-15 Août 1830; 271 AP 21d²4 Préfecture de la Seine, 8 Août 1830-2 Mars 1831.

BB = Ministère de la Justice

BB^{17} A 75, 76, 77: Bureau du Cabinet du Ministre (Juillet 1830-Décembre 1831).

BB^{18} 1175-1181, 1182-1187 (Août 1829-Octobre 1830): Correspondance générale de la Division criminelle.

BB^{21} 370-380: Graces accordées, 1832-1833.

BB^{24} 85-115: Graces demandées et accordées et refusées, 1830-1831.

CC = Chambre et Cour des Pairs

CC 546-551: Procès politiques, Affaire du 25 Juillet 1830.

CC 552: Affaire du 9 Novembre 1830.

F = Ministère de l'Intérieur

F^{1b} I 166^{26}: Personnel administratif, Dossiers individuels (report on events in Rouen, July 27-August 6, 1830 by Président de la Commission provisoire du Département de la Seine-Inférieure).

F^{1c} III Seine 10, 11: Esprit public et Elections, 1827-1839.

F^{1d} III 33-41: Administration générale, Commission des récompenses nationales de 1830.

F^{1d} III 42-78: Commission des récompenses nationales, Dossiers individuels des combattants et blessés de Juillet.

F^{1d} III 79-81: Administration générale, Récompenses honorifiques, Evénements de Juillet 1830 dans les départements.

F^{1d} III 82: Administration générale, Evénements de Juillet 1830.

F^3 II Seine 27, 44: Administration communale, Série départementale (papers on ateliers de secours, 1830-1831).

F^7 3882-3884: Préfecture de Police de Paris, "Bulletin de Paris," 1828, 1829, 1830.

F^7 3894: Police générale, Etats journaliers des arrestations faites par la police municipale de Paris, 1830-1835.

F^7 4174: Police générale, Gendarmerie, Garde municipale, Garde nationale de Paris: rapports, janvier 1829-décembre 1830.

F^7 6668-6669: Police générale, Affaires politiques, Famille Bonaparte, 1818-1830.

F^7 6706: Police générale, Affaires politiques, Objets séditieux, Seine-Yonne, 1818-1830.

F^7 6740-6741: Police générale, Affaires politiques, Elections, 1820-1830.

F^7 6742: Police générale, Affaires politiques, Journaux, 1814-1830.

F^7 6767-6772: Police générale, Affaires politiques, Situation politique des départements, 1820-1830.

F^7 6777-6784: Police générale, Affaires politiques, Situation politique des départements, Rapports de Gendarmerie, 1829-1835.

F^7 6969: Police générale, Affaires particulières, 1830.

F^7 9728: Police générale, Suicides et accidents, Saône-et-Loire–Yonne, 1824-1830.

F^7 9786-9787: Police générale, Affaires administratives, Police des ouvriers, 1814-1830.

F^7 12329: Préfecture de Police de Paris, "Bulletin de Paris," 1830, 1831.

F^9 683: Affaires militaires, Gardes nationales, Département de la Seine, Paris, 1830-1848.

F^9 1154: Affaires militaires, Vainqueurs de la Bastille, Combattants de l'Ouest, Combattants de Juillet: récompense et secours, 1831-1835.

F⁹ 1155-1156: Affaires militaires, Combattants de Juillet, Affaires particulières.

F⁹ 1157-1159: Affaires militaires, Dommages de Juillet, 1830-1849.

F²⁰ 722: Statistique (data on bankruptcies, 1820-1840).

2. Archives du Département de la Seine et de la Ville de Paris

D³ 1-2: Morts, Ancien 8ᵉ Arrᵗ.

D 1AZ–D 4AZ: Dons et Achats: D 1AZ 165; D 2AZ 186; D 3AZ 162; D 3AZ 293; D 4AZ 259; D 4AZ 295ter; D 4AZ 298; D 4AZ 1181.

DM¹³ 1: Administration générale, Evénements politiques (1814-1894).

Vᵇⁱˢ = Maires d'Arrondissement
Vᵇⁱˢ 1; Vᵇⁱˢ 2; Vᵇⁱˢ 3; Vᵇⁱˢ 60; Vᵇⁱˢ 151; Vᵇⁱˢ 153; Vᵇⁱˢ 255; Vᵇⁱˢ 285; Vᵇⁱˢ 287; Vᵇⁱˢ 295; Vᵇⁱˢ 322.

VD³ 1, 2, 3 = Orphelins de Juillet

VD⁴ = Mairies
VD⁴ 4569; VD⁴ 4570; VD⁴ 4571; VD⁴ 4572; VD⁴ 4573; VD⁴ 4826; VD⁴ 4827; VD⁴ 4907; VD⁴ 4908; VD⁴ 5870; VD⁴ 5886; VD⁴ 5887; VD⁴ 5890.

VK³ 7-17 = Récompenses nationales

3. Archives de la Préfecture de Police de Paris

A/420: Evénements divers, 1830

4. Archives du Département de Seine-et-Oise

IV.M.1³⁰⁻³¹, Révolution de Juillet
IV.M.1³², Monarchie de Juillet

5. Archives historiques du Ministère de la Guerre

E⁵ 1: Correspondance militaire générale, 9-31 Août 1830
E⁵ 3: Correspondance militaire générale, Octobre 1830

E⁵ 5: Correspondance militaire générale, Décembre 1830
D³ 131: Correspondance générale, 1 Juillet-1 au 8 Août 1830

6. *Bibliotheque historique de la Ville de Paris*

NA 153, 154: Papiers Odilon Barrot; Série 23, Carton 1830: Miscellaneous letters and reports relating to Revolution of 1830; Série 23, FGms 320, 321, 322: Victor Crochon, *Souvenirs*, 3 vol. ms on Revolution of 1830; Série 23, FGms 443: Journées de Juillet, ms; Série 23, FGms 784: "Rapport de M. Censier sur les journées de Juillet 1830," ms.

7. *Bibliothèque nationale, Département des Manuscrits*

Mss Fr. 7986-7988, 11294-11295: Papiers relatifs à l'expédition des armées françaises en Afrique.

NA Fr. 11909: Lettres de Benjamin Constant à C.J.B. Hochet.

NA Fr. 20601: Correspondance et papiers d'Adolphe Thiers, avant 1830 et années 1830 à 1834.

NA Fr. 23640: Proclamations de Thiers et du Duc d'Orléans.

II. NEWSPAPERS AND PERIODICALS

Bibliographie de la France, 20ᵉ-24ᵉ Années (1831-1835).
Le Courrier français (Paris), March, July 15-August 15, October, December 1830.
Le Drapeau blanc (Paris), March 15-24, May 15-June 1, July 1-28, 1830.
La Gazette de France (Paris), August 10-20, 1829, March 15-24, May 18-25, July 10-August 10, October 15-November 15, December 15-31, 1830.
Le Globe, journal politique, philosophique et littéraire (Paris), July 1-August 10, 1830.
Journal des débats (Paris), August 10-30, 1829, March 14-24, April 12-13, May, June 1, 20-30, July, August, October 18-31, November 1-15, December 1830.
Le Moniteur universel (Paris), August 1829, January-December 1830.

Le National (Paris), January 3-11, 29, March 1-21, May, June 1, July, August 1-20, October 15-November 20, December 15-31.

La Quotidienne (Paris), March 15-21, 1830.

Le Temps (Paris), July 10-August 10, 1830.

The Times (London), March 15-August 15, 1830.

III. MEMOIRS, DIARIES, LETTERS

Abrantes, Laure Saint-Martin, Duchesse d'. *Mémoires sur la Restauration, ou souvenirs historiques sur cette époque, la Révolution de Juillet et les premières années du regne de Louis-Philippe Ier*. Paris, 1835-36. 6 vols.

Anchel, R. "Un Témoinage anglais sur les journées de Juillet: souvenirs de Lady Aylmer," *Revue d'histoire moderne*, 6 (1931), 349-69.

Appert, Benjamin. *Dix ans à la cour du roi Louis-Philippe et souvenirs du temps de l'Empire et de la Restauration.* Paris, 1846. 3 vols.

Apponyi, Rodolphe. *Vingt-cinq ans à Paris, 1826-1850: journal du comte Rodolphe Apponyi, attaché de l'ambassade d'Autriche-Hongrie à Paris.* 2d ed. Paris, 1913-26. 4 vols.

Audiffret-Pasquier, Etienne. *Histoire de mon temps: mémoires du Chancelier Pasquier.* 3d ed. Paris, 1895. 6 vols.

Bapst, Germain. *Le Maréchal Canrobert: souvenirs d'un siècle.* 2d ed. Paris, 1898. Vol. I, 560 pp.

Barante, Amable-Prosper, Baron de. *Souvenirs . . . 1782-1866.* Paris, 1890-91. 8 vols.

Barrot, Odilon. *Mémoires posthumes.* 3d ed. Paris, 1875-76. 4 vols.

Bérard, Auguste. *Souvenirs historiques sur la Révolution de 1830.* Paris, 1834. 507 pp.

Bertier de Sauvigny, Guillaume de, ed., "La Conspiration des légitimistes et de la duchesse de Berry contre Louis-Philippe 1830-1832 (Correspondances et documents inédits)," *Etudes d'histoire moderne et contemporaine*, III, XV, 1-125 (1950).

Bertier de Sauvigny, Guillaume de, ed., *La Révolution de 1830 en France*. Paris, 1970. 336 pp.

Boigne, Charlotte-Louise, Comtesse de. *Récits d'une tante: mémoires de la comtesse de Boigne, née d'Osmond*. Paris, 1921-25. 2 vols.

Bonnelier, Hippolyte. *Mémorial de l'Hôtel de Ville de Paris 1830*. Paris, 1835. 293 pp.

Broglie, Victor, Duc de. *Souvenirs, 1785-1870*. Paris, 1886. 4 vols.

Cuvillier-Fleury, Alfred Auguste. *Journal intime de Cuvillier-Fleury*. Paris, 1901, 1902. 2 vols.

Damas, Anne-Maxence, Baron de. *Mémoires, 1785-1862*. Paris, 1922, 1923. 2 vols.

Dix jours de 1830; souvenirs de la dernière révolution, par A.S. . . . , officier d'infanterie de l'ex-garde royale. Paris, 1830. 128 pp.

Dumas, Alexandre. *Mes mémoires*. New ed. Paris, 1884-92. 10 vols.

Dumont d'Urville, Jules. "Journal du Dumont d'Urville," In Achille de Vaulabelle, *Histoire des deux Restaurations jusqu'à l'avènement de Louis-Philippe (de janvier 1813 à octobre 1830)*. 5th ed. Paris, 1860. VIII, 465-83.

Dupin, André-Marie. *Mémoires de M. Dupin*. Paris, 1855-61. 4 vols.

Eschevannes, Comte de. "Les Journées de Juillet," *Revue de Paris*, 18e Année, IV (Aug. 1, 1911), 545-74.

Falloux, Alfred, Comte de. *Mémoires d'un royaliste*. Paris, 1888. 2 vols.

Foucauld, Jacques-Jean. *Mémoires sur les événements de juillet 1830*. Paris, 1851. 142 pp.

Gambrell, Herbert P. "Three Letters on the Revolution of 1830" [by Charles Ellet, Jr.], *Journal of Modern History*, I (1929), 594-606.

Guernon-Ranville, Martial, Comte de. *Journal d'un ministre*. Caen, 1873. 416 pp.

Guizot, François-Pierre. *Mémoires pour servir à l'histoire de mon temps, 1807-1848*. New ed. Paris, 1872. 8 vols.

Haussez, Charles, Baron de. *Mémoires du Baron d'Haussez, dernier Ministre de la Marine sous la Restauration.* Paris, 1896, 1897. 2 vols.

Haussonville, Gabriel-Paul, Comte de. *Ma jeunesse, 1814-1830.* Paris, 1885. 342 pp.

Herbelot, Alphonse de. *La Jeunesse libérale de 1830: lettres à Charles de Montalembert et à Léon Cornudet, 1828-1830.* Paris, 1908. 295 pp.

Lafayette, Marie, Marquis de. *Mémoires, correspondance et manuscrits.* Paris, 1837-38. 6 vols.

Laffitte, Jacques. *Mémoires de Laffitte (1767-1844).* Paris, 1932. 347 pp.

———. "Mes deux ministres (1830-1831)," *Revue des deux mondes,* 100ᵉ Année, 7ᵉ Période, 59 (Oct. 1, 1930), 650-76.

———. *Souvenirs de Jacques Laffitte raconté par lui-même.* Paris, 1844-45. 3 vols.

———. "Les Trois Glorieuses," *Revue des deux mondes,* 100ᵉ Année, 7ᵉ Période, 58 (July 15, 1930), 293-328.

Lecuyer, Raymond. *La Révolution de Juillet . . . impressions et récits contemporains (Mémoires de Alex. Mazas-Chronique de Rozet).* Paris, [n.d.]. 158 pp.

"Lettres à Casimir Périer [de Louis-Philippe]," *Revue des deux mondes,* 101ᵉ Année, 8ᵉ Période, 2 (March 15, 1931), 388-427.

Marmont, Auguste de, Duc de Raguse, *Mémoires du maréchal Marmont, duc de Raguse, de 1792 à 1841.* 3d ed. Paris, 1857. 9 vols.

Marnay, A.-J. de. *Mémoires secrets et témoinages authentiques: chute de Charles X, Royauté de Juillet, 24 février 1848.* Paris, 1875. 440 pp.

Marrast, Armand. *Programme de l'Hôtel de Ville ou récit de ce qui est passé depuis le 31 juillet jusqu'au 6 août 1830.* Paris, 1831. 8 pp.

Mazas, Alexandre. *Saint-Cloud, Paris et Cherbourg; mémoires pour servir l'histoire de la Révolution de 1830.* 2d ed. Paris, 1832. 406 pp.

Metternich-Winneburg, Clemens, Furst von. *Mémoires, documents et écrits divers.* Paris, 1880-84. 8 vols.

Montalivet, Marthe, Comte de. *Fragments et souvenirs.* Paris, 1899, 1900. 2 vols.

Montbel, Guillaume, Comte de. *1787-1831: souvenirs du comte de Montbel, ministre de Charles X.* Paris, 1913. 436 pp.

Mortemart, Casimir, Duc de. "Un Manuscrit sur les journées de juillet," *Le Correspondant,* 331 (Dec. 1930), 641-58, 801-23.

Polignac, Jules, Prince de. *Considérations politiques sur l'époque actuelle.* Paris, 1832. 122 pp.

Raikes, Thomas. *Private Correspondence of Thomas Raikes with the Duke of Wellington and Other Distinguished Contemporaries.* London, 1861. 404 pp.

Rambuteau, Claude, Comte de. *Memoirs of the comte de Rambuteau.* London, 1905. 324 pp.

Réal, Pierre-F., Comte. *Indiscretions of a Prefect of Police: Anecdotes of Napoleon and the Bourbons from the Papers of Count Réal.* London, 1929. 240 pp.

Rémusat, Charles de. *Mémoires de ma vie.* Paris, 1958-67. 5 vols.

Saint-Chamans, Alfred-Armand, Comte de. "Le Combat pour le roi, juillet 1830," *Revue de Paris,* 3e Année, 1 (Feb. 1, 1896), 481-514.

―――. *Mémoires du Général Comte de Saint-Chamans.* Paris, 1896. 542 pp.

Semonville, Charles, Marquis de. "Mémoire sur la Révolution de 1830," *Revue de Paris,* 1e Année, 5 (Sept. 1, 1894), 63-101.

Talleyrand-Périgord, Charles, Prince de. *Mémoires du Prince de Talleyrand.* Paris, 1953-55. 7 vols.

Tocqueville, Alexis. *Oeuvres et correspondance inédites de Alexis de Tocqueville.* Paris, 1861, 2 vols.

Veron, Louis. *Mémoires d'un bourgeois de Paris.* Paris, 1853-55. 6 vols.

Vienne, Henri. "Dix jours à Paris du dimanche 25 juillet au mardi 3 août 1830," *Mémoires* de la Société bourguignonne de géographie et d'histoire, 8 (1892), 63-125.

Villèle, Joseph, Comte de. *Mémoires et correspondance.* Paris, 1888-90. 5 vols.

Villeneuve-Bargemont, Guillaume, Comte de. "Les Journées de Juillet 1830; la veille et le lendemain d'une révolution: souvenirs d'un témoin," *Le Correspondant*, 208 (1902), 217-36.

Viollet le Duc, Emmanuel. "Lettres d'Emmanuel Viollet le Duc à sa femme," *Revue de Paris*, LXIXe Année, No. 6 (June 1962), pp. 96-109.

Vitrolles, Eugène, Baron de. *Mémoires.* Paris, 1950, 1951. 2 vols.

IV. ALMANACS, ANNUALS, DICTIONARIES, COLLECTIONS

Almanach royal pour l'an MDCCCXXIX. Paris, 1829. 949 pp.

Almanach royal pour l'an MDCCCXXX. Paris, 1830. 965 pp.

Almanach royal et national pour l'an MDCCCXXXI. Paris, 1831. 958 pp.

Biographie des membres du Sénat. Paris, 1852. 320 pp.

Biographie universelle et portative des contemporaines. Paris, 1836. 4 vols. and Supplement.

Bulletin des lois du Royaume de France. 1830, 1831, 1833, 1839, 1840.

Chambre de Commerce de Paris. *Statistique de l'industrie à Paris resultant de l'enquête faite par la Chambre de Commerce pour les années 1847-1848.* Paris, 1950. 1200 pp.

Hillairet, Jacques. *Dictionnaire historique des rues de Paris.* Paris, 1963. 2 vols.

Lamothe-Langnon, Etienne Leon, Baron de. *Biographie des préfets depuis l'organisation des préfectures (3 mars 1800) jusqu'à ce jour.* Paris, 1826. 432 pp.

Lesur, Charles. *Annuaire historique universel pour 1830.* Paris, 1832. 780 pp. text, 300 pp. appendix.

Mullié, C. *Biographie des célébrites militaires des armées de terre et de mer de 1789 à 1850.* Paris, 1851. 2 vols.

Nouvelle biographie générale depuis le temps le plus reculés jusqu'à nos jours. Paris, 1855-70. 46 vols.

Procès-verbal de la réunion des électeurs du deuxième arrondissement . . . offert à messieurs les électeurs par M. Jacques Lefebvre. Paris, n.d.

Robert, Adolphe, Edgar Bourloton, and Gaston Cougny, *Dictionnaire des parlementaires français.* Paris, 1891. 5 vols.

Seine, Département de la. *Recherches statistiques sur la ville de Paris et le Département de la Seine.* Paris, 1826-60. 6 vols.

Vapereau, Gustave. *Dictionnaire universel des contemporains.* Paris, 1858. 1802 pp.

V. Books and Articles

Aguet, Jean-Pierre. *Les Grèves sous la Monarchie de Juillet.* Geneva, 1954. 408 pp.

Alméras, Charles. *Odilon Barrot, avocat et homme politique (19 juillet 1791-6 août 1873).* Paris, 1951. 371 pp.

Aulard, Alphonse. "Thiers, historien de la Révolution française," *La Révolution française,* 66 (1914), 492-520; 67 (1914), 5-19.

Bastid, Paul. *Les Institutions politiques de la monarchie parlementaire française, 1814-1848.* Paris, 1954. 425 pp.

———. "Le Procès des ministres de Charles X," *Revue d'histoire moderne et contemporaine,* 4 (1957), 171-211.

Beach, Vincent W. *Charles X of France: His Life and Times.* Boulder, Colo., 1971. 488 pp.

———. "The Fall of Charles X of France: A Case Study of Revolution," *University of Colorado Studies,* Series in History, No. 2 (Nov. 1961), pp. 21-60.

———. "The Polignac Ministry: a Re-evaluation," *University of Colorado Studies,* Series in History, No. 3 (Jan. 1964), 87-146.

Beau de Lomenie, E. de. *Les Résponsabilités des dynasties bourgeoises.* Vol. 1, *De Bonaparte à MacMahon.* Paris, 1943. 345 pp.

Bertier de Sauvigny, Guillaume de. *The Bourbon Restoration.* Philadelphia, 1966. 499 pp.

———. *Le Comte Ferdinand de Bertier (1782-1864) et l'énigme de la Congrégation.* Paris, 1948. 572 pp.

Betley, J. A. *Belgium and Poland in international relations, 1830-1831.* The Hague, 1960. 298 pp.

Bibliothèque impériale. *Catalogue de l'histoire de France.* Paris, 1861. Vol. VII. 818 pp.

Blanc, Louis. *Histoire de dix ans, 1830-1840,* 12th ed. Paris, 1877. 5 vols.

Blanchard, René. "Le 10ᵉ Leger et la Révolution de Juillet 1830 à Nantes," *Revue de Bretagne,* 29 (1903), 10-19, 144-54, 220-29, 294-303, 395-418.

Bourgin, Georges. "La Crise ouvrière à Paris dans la seconde moitié de 1830," *Revue historique,* 198 (1947), 203-14.

Campbell, Peter. *French Electoral Systems and Elections Since 1789.* 2d ed. London, 1965. 155 pp.

Chapman, Brian. *The Prefects of Provincial France.* London, 1955. 245 pp.

Charléty, Sébastien. *La Monarchie de Juillet, 1830-1848.* Vol. v in *Histoire de France contemporaine,* ed. E. Lavisse. Paris, 1921. 410 pp.

Chauvet, Paul. *Les Ouvriers du livre en France de 1789 à la constitution de la Fédération du Livre.* Paris, 1956. 717 pp.

Chevalier, Louis. *Classes laborieuses et classes dangereuses à Paris pendant la première moitié du XIXᵉ siècle.* Paris, 1958. 566 pp.

———. *La Formation de la population parisienne au XIXᵉ siècle.* Paris, 1950. 312 pp.

Cobban, Alfred. *The Myth of the French Revolution.* London, 1955. 25 pp.

———. "The Vocabulary of Social History," *Political Science Quarterly,* 71 (1956), 1-17.

Contamine, Henry. "La Révolution de 1830 à Metz," *Revue d'histoire moderne,* 6 (1931), 115-23.

Daumard, Adeline, *La Bourgeoisie parisienne de 1815 à 1848.* Paris, 1963. 661 pp.

Demoulin, R. "L'Influence française sur la naissance de l'état belge," *Revue historique*, 223 (1960), 13-28.

Dolléans, Edouard. *Histoire du mouvement ouvrier.* 3d ed. Paris, 1947, 1948. 2 vols.

Droulers, Paul. *Action pastorale et problèmes sociaux sous la Monarchie de Juillet chez Mgr. d'Astros, Archévêque de Toulouse, censeur de La Mennais.* Paris, 1954. 445 pp.

Duchon, Paul. "Les Mémoires de Jacques Laffitte," *Revue des deux mondes*, 100e Année, 7e Période, 58 (July 15, 1930), 289-92.

Durand, Charles. *Les Auditeurs au Conseil d'Etat de 1803 à 1814.* Aix-en-Provence, 1958. 197 pp.

Durand, René. "La Révolution de 1830 en Côte d'Or," *Revue d'histoire moderne*, 6 (1931), 161-75.

Duvergier de Hauranne, Prosper. *Histoire du gouvernement parlementaire en France, 1814-1848.* Paris, 1857-1871. 10 vols.

Emerit, Marcel. "Une Cause de l'Expédition d'Alger: le trésor de la Casbah," *Actes* du 79e Congrès national des sociétés savantes, Alger (1954). Pp. 171-88.

Falloux, Alfred, Comte de. *L'Evêque d'Orléans.* Paris, 1879. 210 pp.

Festy, Octave. *Le Mouvement ouvrier au début de la Monarchie de Juillet.* Paris, 1908. 359 pp.

Ford, Franklin L. *Strasbourg in transition, 1648-1789.* Cambridge, 1958. 321 pp.

Fortier, A. "Dupont (de l'Eure); la Révolution de Juillet 1830," *Révolution de 1848*, 12 (1916), 129-55, 231-55.

Fourcassié, Jean. *Une Ville à l'époque romantique: Toulouse; trente ans de vie française.* Paris, 1953. 310 pp.

Gain, André. *La Restauration et des biens des émigrés.* Paris, 1929. 2 vols.

La Garde royale pendant les événemens du 26 juillet au 5 août 1830; par un officier employé à l'état-major. Paris, 1830. 128 pp.

Garnier, Jean-Paul. *Charles X: Le Roi—Le Proscrit.* Paris, 1967. 481 pp.

Gignoux, C.-J. *La Vie du Baron Louis*. 2d ed. Paris, 1928. 264 pp.

Gille, Bertrand. *Recherches sur la formation de la grande entreprise capitaliste, 1815-1848*. Paris, 1959. 164 pp.

Girard, Louis. *Etude comparée des mouvements révolutionnaires en France en 1830, 1848 et 1870-71* (Les Cours de Sorbonne). Paris, 1960. 2 fascicules.

————. *La Garde nationale, 1814-1871*. Paris, 1964. 388 pp.

Giraud-Mangin, M. "Nantes en 1830 et les journées de juillet," *Revue d'histoire moderne*, 6 (1931), 455-68.

Godechot, Jacques. *Les Révolutions, 1770-1799*. Paris, 1963. 410 pp.

Gonnet, Paul. "Esquisse de la crise économique en France de 1827 à 1832," *Revue d'histoire économique et sociale*, 33 (1955), 249-92.

Guizot, François. "De la session de 1828," in *Mélanges politiques et historiques* (Paris, 1859), pp. 467-96.

Guyot, Raymond. "La Dernière Négotiation de Talleyrand: l'indépendance de la Belgique," *Revue d'histoire moderne et contemporaine*, 2 (1900-1901), 573-94; 3 (1901-1902), 237-81.

Haussonville, Joseph, Comte de. *Histoire de la politique extérieure du gouvernement français, 1830-1848*. New ed. Paris, 1850. 2 vols.

Higonnet, Patrick-Bernard. "La Composition de la Chambre des Députés de 1827 à 1831," *Revue historique*, 239 (1968), 351-79.

Hillebrand, Karl. *Geschichte Frankreichs von der Thronbesteigung Louis Philippe bis zum Falle Napoleon III*. Gotha, 1877, 1879. 2 vols.

Howarth, T.E.B. *Citizen King: The Life of Louis-Philippe, King of the French*. London, 1961. 358 pp.

Huart, Suzanne d'. "Le Dernier Préfet de Police de Charles X: Claude Mangin," *Actes* du 80e Congrès national des sociétés savantes, Dijon (1959); section d'histoire moderne et contemporaine. Pp. 603-16.

Kent, Sherman. *Electoral Procedure under Louis-Philippe.* New Haven, 1937. 264 pp.

Kleinclausz, A. *Histoire de Lyon.* Lyon, 1952. 3 vols.

Koht, Halvedan. "The Class Struggle in Modern History," *Journal of Modern History*, 1 (1929), 353-60.

Labrousse, Ernest. *Le Mouvement ouvrier et les idées sociales en France de 1815 à la fin du XIXᵉ siècle* (Les Cours de Sorbonne). Paris, 1948. 3 fascicules.

Lafon, Annie-Marguerite. "La Legende napoléonienne à Paris de 1830 à 1840 à travers le théâtre." Typescript thesis, Diplome d'études supérieures d'Histoire, Faculté des lettres de Paris, 1959. 244 pp.

Ledré, Charles. *La Presse à l'assaut de la monarchie.* Paris, 1960. 270 pp.

Lefebvre, Georges. "Foules révolutionnaires," *Etudes sur la Révolution française* (Paris, 1954), pp. 271-87.

Lhomme, Jean. *La Grande Bourgeoisie au pouvoir (1830-1880).* Paris, 1960. 378 pp.

Limouzin-Lamothe, Roger. *Monseigneur de Quelen, Archévêque de Paris; son rôle dans l'Eglise de France de 1815 à 1839 d'après des archives privées.* Paris, 1955, 1957. 2 vols.

Lucas-Dubreton, Jean. *Le Culte de Napoleon, 1815-1848.* Paris, 1960. 468 pp.

——. *La Royauté bourgeoise, 1830.* Paris, 1930. 217 pp.

Maag, Albert. *Geschichte der Schweizertruppen in französischen Diensten während der Restauration und Julirevolution, 1816-1830.* Biel, 1899. 864 pp.

Mantoux, Paul. "Patrons et ouvriers en juillet 1830," *Revue d'histoire moderne et contemporaine*, 3 (1901-1902), 291-96.

——. "Talleyrand en 1830 après des mémoires contemporaines," *Revue historique*, 78 (1902), 266-87.

Mellon, Stanley. *The Political Uses of History: A Study of Historians in the French Restoration.* Stanford, 1958. 226 pp.

Morizet, André. *Du vieux Paris au Paris moderne; Haussmann et ses prédécesseurs.* Paris, 1932. 399 pp.

Nettement, Alfred. *Histoire de la Restauration*. Paris, 1860-1872. 8 vols.

Nouvion, Victor de. *Histoire du règne de Louis-Philippe Ier, roi des français, 1830-1848*. Paris, 1858-1861. 4 vols.

Perreux, Gabriel. "L'Esprit public dans les départements au lendemain de la Révolution de 1830," *Révolution de 1848*, 20 (1923), 252-61; 21 (1924), 10-30; 30 (1933-34), 229-48; 31 (1936), 98-106.

Pinkney, David H. "Laissez-faire or Intervention? Labor Policy in the First Months of the July Monarchy," *French Historical Studies*, 8 (1963), 123-28.

―――. "Les Ateliers de secours à Paris (1830-1831); précurseurs des Ateliers nationaux de 1848," *Revue d'histoire moderne et contemporaine*, 12 (1965), 65-70.

―――. "The Crowd in the French Revolution of 1830," *American Historical Review* (1964), 1-17.

―――. "The Myth of the French Revolution of 1830," *A Festschrift for Frederick B. Artz*, David H. Pinkney and Theodore Ropp, eds. Durham, N.C., 1964, pp. 52-71.

―――. "The Revolution of 1830 Seen by a Combatant," *French Historical Studies*, 2 (1961), 242-46.

Posener, S. "La Révolution de Juillet et le Département du Gard," *Mercure de France*, 221 (1930), 607-36.

Pouthas, Charles-H. *Guizot pendant la Restauration; préparation de l'homme d'état, 1814-1830*. Paris, 1923. 497 pp.

―――. "Les Ministères de Louis-Philippe," *Revue d'histoire moderne et contemporaine*, 1 (1954), 102-30.

―――. "La Réorganisation du Ministère de l'Intérieur et la reconstitution de l'administration préfectorale par Guizot en 1830," *Revue d'histoire moderne et contemporaine*, 9 (1962), 241-63.

Powers, Richard H. *Edgar Quinet: a Study in French Patriotism*. Dallas, 1957. 207 pp.

Prentout, Henri. "Caen en 1830," *Revue d'histoire moderne*, 6 (1931), 101-14.

Rader, Daniel L. "The Breton Association and the Press: Propaganda for 'Legal Resistance' before the July Revolution," *French Historical Studies*, 2 (1961), 64-82.

Raoul. "Une Lettre inédite sur les journées de juillet 1830," *Révolution de 1848*, 7 (1910-11), 272-73.

Recouly, Raymond. *Louis-Philippe, roi des français: le chemin vers le trône*. Paris, 1930. 434 pp.

Reinhard, Marcel. "Sur l'histoire de la Révolution française: travaux recents et perspectives," *Annales: économies-sociétés-civilisations*, 14ᵉ Année (1959), pp. 553-70.

Rémond, René. *La Droite en France de 1815 à nos jours*. Paris, 1954. 323 pp.

Renouvin, Pierre. *Histoire des relations internationales*. Paris, 1953-58. 7 vols.

Resnick, Daniel P. *The White Terror and the Political Reaction after Waterloo*. Cambridge, 1966. 152 pp.

Richardson, Nicholas. *The French Prefectoral Corps 1814-1830*. Cambridge, Eng., 1966. 263 pp.

Robin-Harmel, Pierre. *Le Prince Jules de Polignac, ministre de Charles X, 1780-1847*. Paris, 1941. 215 pp.

————. *Le Prince Jules de Polignac, ministre de Charles X, 1780-1847: sa vie de 1829 à 1847*. Avignon, 1950. 295 pp.

Rousselet, Marcel. *La Magistrature sous la Monarchie de Juillet*. Paris, 1937. 499 pp.

Rozet, Louis. *Chronique de juillet 1830*. Paris, 1832. 2 vols.

Rudé, George. *The Crowd in the French Revolution*. Oxford, 1959. 267 pp.

Simpson, F. A. *The Rise of Louis-Napoleon*. 3d ed. London, 1960. 400 pp.

Simon, Jules. *Victor Cousin*. Chicago, 1880. 220 pp.

Soboul, Albert. "The French Rural Community in the Eighteenth and Nineteenth Centuries," *Past and Present*, No. 10 (Nov. 1956), pp. 78-95.

Stoeckl, Agnes de. *King of the French: A Portrait of Louis-Philippe, 1773-1850*. London, 1961. 308 pp.

Talbott, John E. "The Good Workingman: Image and Reality in the Revolutions of 1830 and 1848," *Missouri Honors Review* (Univ. of Missouri), 1 (1964), 50-67.

Thureau-Dangin, Paul. *Histoire de la Monarchie de Juillet*, Paris, 1888-1900. 7 vols.

Tocqueville, Alexis de. *The Recollections.* New York, 1949. 332 pp.

Trognon, Auguste. *Vie de Marie Amélie, Reine des Français.* Paris, 1872. 487 pp.

Tulard, Jean. *La Préfecture de Police sous la Monarchie de Juillet.* Paris, 1964. 177 pp.

Vaulabelle, Achille de. *Histoire des deux Restaurations jusqu'à l'avènement de Louis-Philippe (de janvier 1813 à octobre 1830).* 5th ed. Paris, 1860. 8 vols.

Vedrenne-Villeneuve, Edmonde. "L'Inégalité sociale devant la mort dans la première moitié du XIXᵉ siècle," *Population*, 16 (1961), 665-98.

Viard, Pierre-Paul. "Les Aspects juridiques de la Révolution de 1830," *Revue d'histoire moderne*, 6 (1931), 89-100.

Vidalenc, Jean. *Le Département de l'Eure sous la monarchie constitutionnelle, 1814-1848.* Paris, 1952. 700 pp.

————. "La Journée du 28 juillet 1830," *Annuaire-Bulletin* de la Société de l'Histoire de France, Années 1948-1949. Pp. 34-47.

Viel-Castel, Louis de. *Histoire de la Restauration.* Paris, 1860-78. 20 vols.

Vovelle, M. and D. Roche. "Bourgeois, rentiers, propriétaires; éléments pour la définition d'une catégorie sociale à la fin du XVIIIᵉ siècle," *Actes* du 80ᵉ Congrès nationale des sociétés savants, Dijon (1959); Section d'histoire moderne et contemporaine. Pp. 419-52.

Weil, Georges-Denis. "La Magistrature inamovible et la Révolution de 1830," *La Droit: journaux des tribunaux*, 53ᵉ Année (June 6-9, 1889), pp. 533, 537, 541, 545.

Weill, Georges. *L'Eveil des nationalités et le mouvement liberal, 1815-1848.* Paris, 1930. 591 pp.

————. *Histoire du parti républicain en France (1814-1870).* Paris, 1928. 431 pp.

————. "La Révolution de Juillet dans les départements (août-septembre 1830)," *Revue d'histoire moderne*, 6 (1931), 289-93.

Whitridge, Arnold. "Joseph Napoleon in America," *History Today*, 9 (1959), 308-18.

Aberdeen, Lord, 41

Adélaïde, Madame, 147, 151, 277

age of combatants, 257, 272

"Aide-toi, le ciel t'aidera," 4, 14, 32, 46, 48, 52, 83, 89, 95, 191, 205, 297, 326

Alençon (Orne), 177

Algeria, 224, 288, 303, 309

Algiers, 14, 15, 16, 27, 40, 41; expedition against, 14-18, 24, 27, 34-35, 40, 59, 305; Dey of, 14-15, 17, 40

Ami de la Charte (Nantes), 209-10

Amiens, 201

Angers, 213-14

Angoulême, Duc d', 7, 15, 27, 28, 37, 51, 90, 92, 126, 133, 136, 154, 155, 165, 166, 167, 168, 169, 170, 179, 182, 185

Angoulême, Duchesse d', 73, 179

anti-clericalism, 58, 268-69

Apponyi, Rodolphe, 46, 197

Arago, François, 90, 125

Archbishop of Paris, *see* Quélen, Louis de

Archbishop's Palace, 135-36

Argentan (Orne), 177, 178, 179

Argout, Apollinaire de, 83, 132, 136, 138-39, 147-48, 326-27

Ariège, Department of the, 199

aristocrats, 279, 280

Arles, 223

army, defections, 134, 166, 167, 168; efforts to maintain order, 89, 92, 99-100, 102, 103-108, 110-22, 130-31, 134-35, 145; purge, 208, 288, 291; service of supply, 122

Army of Africa, 24, 34-35, 36, 38, 76, 145, 170, 221, 223, 224, 288

Artois, Comte de, 151. *See also* Charles X

ateliers de secours, 316-17, 336, 355

Athalin, Louis, 304

Aubert, François d', 85

Audry de Puyraveau, Pierre, 96, 123, 128, 138, 140, 142, 146, 153

Austria, 16, 36; Emperor of, 305

Auteuil, 184

Avignon, 220

Aylmer, Lady, 93, 196, 228, 246

Balzac, Honoré de, 68

Barante, Amable de, 197

Barbet, Henri, 201

Bar-le-Duc (Meuse), 71

Barrot, Odilon, before the Revolution, 48; in the Revolution, 85, 141, 152, 157, 162, 172-73, 174, 175, 180, 269; Prefect of the Seine, 248, 316, 322, 323, 324, 325, 327, 338; trial of ministers, 346, 347, 354, 355, 356, 361, 363, 364

Barrot papers, 235-36

Barthe, Félix, 83, 363

Bas-Meudon (Seine-et-Oise), 318

Bassano, Duc de, 143

Baude, Jean-Jacques, 94, 95, 99, 141, 200, 232, 363-64

Baudran, Marie, 305

Bavoux, Nicolas, 141, 171

Beau de Loménie, E., 275n-276n

Beauvais (Oise), 110

Belgium, 76; revolution, 291, 307-10, 334, 335-36

Belliard, Augustin, 304, 305

Béranger, Pierre-Jean de, 49-50

Bérard, Auguste, in the Revolution, 87, 88, 89, 96, 127, 128-29, 139; revision of Charter, 183-88, 189-92; support of Orléans, 148-49, 151, 152, 156, 157, 158n-159n, 159, 160, 161, 195n

Bercy, 122

Berenger, Alphonse, 340, 344-45, 349-50

Berlin, 305
Bernard, Louis, 174, 287, 292
Berry, Duc de, 51
Berry, Duchesse de, 90, 126, 311, 332
Bertier, Ferdinand de, after the Revolution, 311-12, 332-34; Polignac Ministry, 6-8, 10, 12, 24, 36, 38-39
Bertier de Sauvigny, Guillaume de, 8
Bertin de Vaux, Louis, 140
Besançon, 22
Bibliothèque du Roi, 229
Bibliothèque historique de la Ville de Paris, 236
Bignon, Edouard, 171n, 299, 300, 326
Blair, Captain de, 104
Blanc, Louis, 265, 266, 268
Blois, 155
Bois de Boulogne, 117, 136, 139
Bonaparte, Joseph, 51
Bonapartism, 291-93
Bonapartists, before the Revolution, 47, 49-52; in the Revolution, 143-45, 146, 147, 153-54, 195, 294, 296, 366
Bonnelier, Hippolyte, 141
Bordeaux, 69, 219
Bordeaux, Duc de, 51, 90, 143, 157, 164, 165, 169, 171, 172, 174, 176, 179, 183, 195n, 219, 311-12, 332, 333, 366
Bourbon, Duc de, 73
Bourbon-Vendée, 213
"Bourgeois King," 277, 278
"Bourgeois Revolution," 274-76
Bourmont, Louis de, commander Army of Africa, 145, 170, 197, 224; exile, 181, 311-12; Polignac Ministry, 7, 8, 9-10, 15, 26, 34, 43
bread, price of, 63, 64, 65-66, 69, 262-63, 265, 323
Brest, 214
Brittany, 69, 170, 171, 209, 212, 213, 311, 332
Broglie, Victor de, before the Revolution, 42; in the Revolution, 129; Minister of

Public Instruction, 218, 297, 299, 300, 301, 302, 310, 324, 325, 326, 327, 367; revision of Charter, 185, 186, 187, 188n, 195n; trial of ministers, 348
Brussels, 307
Bulletin des lois, 78, 79, 153
Burgundy, 71
businessmen, 83-84, 139, 279-80, 279n, 286

Cadet-Gassicourt, Charles, 95, 97, 121
Cadoudel Plot, 8
Caen, 110, 180, 206
Café de la Rotonde, 83
Calvados, Department of the, 33-34, 205-206
Capelle, Guillaume, 24, 28, 29, 43, 168, 181, 353n
Carbonari, 46, 47-48, 89, 97, 156, 268, 270-71, 271n, 289, 327
Carentan (Manche), 177
Carlists, 223-24, 311-13, 333, 348
Carrell, Armand, 13, 85, 259
casualties of street fighting, 121, 211
Cauchois-Lemaire, 85, 86-87
cemeteries, Eastern, 338, Montmartre, 234
Cevennes, 221
Chabrol, Gilbert de, 7, 12, 22, 25, 26, 27
Champs de Mars, 233
Channel Islands, 178, 180
Chantelauze, Jean de, arrest and trial, 180, 338, 343, 344, 352, 353n; before the Revolution, 28, 29, 33-34, 36, 39, 42-43, 76, 77-78, 80; in the Revolution, 89, 124
Charles X, abdication, 169, 171-72, 182, 185; Algerian Expedition, 15-16, 40-41; before accession, 3, 8, 151; coronation, 194; departure from France, 172-73, 174-79, 185, 191, 204-205, 212-13; economic depression, 65, 71-72; exile, 179, 181, 221, 311-12, 341; in the Revolution, 90, 92-93, 100-101, 103, 107-108,

109-10, 123, 125-27, 132-33,
136-37, 139, 143, 145, 147, 148,
149, 151-52, 155, 157, 164,
165-70, 195n, 197, 214-15, 327;
Martignac Ministry, 5-6;
Polignac Ministry, 5-7, 19,
21-24, 27-29, 30, 37, 39, 44-45,
46-47, 51, 52, 75-77, 186, 187,
193, 259; Villèle Ministry, 57
Charter of 1814, 11, 14, 20, 21,
87, 152, 164, 182, 183, 340, 342;
Article 8, 81; Article 9, 57;
Article 14, 11, 14, 26, 28, 29,
36, 37, 38, 39, 41, 45, 81, 182,
190, 342; revision of, 185-88,
189-92
Chartres, 177, 180
Chartres, Duc de, 294
Chateaubriand, François, 5, 11
Chatelain, René, 85, 86, 87
Cherbourg, 178, 179, 180, 213
Chevalier, ex-Carbonaro, 96, 97
Chevalier, Louis, 66, 68, 252
Chouans, 9, 213
Civil List, 242
Clauzel, Bertrand, 224
clergy, 30, 40-41, 57-58, 198-99,
302, 310-11, 366
Clermont (Meuse), 69
clubs, 324
Collin de Sussy, Jean-Baptiste,
149, 151
Column of July, 235, 250-51
"Comité directeur," 46
commercial moratorium, 239
Commission de la Souscription
nationale, 246, 247, 248
Commission des Dommages, see
Commission of Damages
Commission des Récompenses
nationales, 84, 121, 230, 246,
248, 249-50, 252, 255, 261, 264,
270, 271, 284
Commission municipal de Paris,
see Municipal Commission of
Paris
Commission of Damages, 238,
241-44
Compiègne, 110, 197, 349
Concordat of 1801, 57, 189, 310

Congress of Vienna, 307
Conseil de Salubrité, 230
Constant, Benjamin, 32, 45, 54,
152, 159, 189, 195n, 284, 337-38
Constitution of 1791, 342
Constitutionnel, 84, 85, 88, 94,
245, 287
construction workers, 82, 253, 260
Coste, Jacques, 127
Council of State, 283, 284-85, 292
coup d'état, 36, 37, 38, 39-40,
42-43, 48, 73-74, 77
Courbevoie (Seine), 102
Courrier de la Moselle (Metz),
207
Courrier des électeurs, 88
Courrier français, 85, 88, 94
cours prévôtales, 56, 83, 187
Court of Cassation, 239, 287, 292
Courvoisier, Jean, 7, 18-19, 20,
25, 26, 27
Cousin, Victor, 58
Coutard, Louis, 76
Cowes, 179, 181
Crémieux, Adolphe, 344
Cross of July, 248-49, 250
crowds, 91-92, 99-100, 104-108,
109, 111-13, 145, 253-73, 320,
353; motives, 258-69, 272-73

damage, compensation for,
227-28, 230, 241-45
Damas, Maxence de, 169, 179
Daumard, Adeline, 280n
Daumesnil, Pierre, 322, 338,
351, 354
Daumier, Honoré, 68
Dauphin, see Angoulême, Duc de
dead, burial, 227, 233-35;
numbers, 121, 211
death penalty, 318-19, 321, 324,
327, 343
Defection, The, 5, 11
Défenseur de la Monarchie
(Bordeaux), 219
Delacroix, Ferdinand, 256
Delessert, Benjamin, 123, 125,
151, 195n, 241
depression, economic, 59-66,
68-72, 210, 225, 262, 264-65, 313

deputies, reaction to Four
Ordinances, 87, 88-89, 93, 95-98,
123-26, 127-29, 139-40, 142,
144, 150-53
De Schonen, Auguste-Jean, 89,
138, 140, 142, 173, 174
Despinois, General, 209-12
Dieppe, 197
diplomatic corps, 150, 155, 165,
165n-166n
Doctrinaires, 158n-159n
Drapeau blanc, 58
Dreux, 177
Dubourg, "General," 140-41, 153
Dumas, Alexandre, 156
Dumont d'Urville, Jules, 178, 179
Dumoulin, Evariste, 85, 153-54,
294
Dumoustier, Pierre, 212
Duperré, Guy-Victor, 35
Dupin, André, before the
Revolution, 21; in the
Revolution, 84-85, 96, 158, 170,
170n, 171, 182, 195n; Minister
without Portfolio, 297, 299,
300, 301, 326; revision of
Charter, 189, 190, 192;
Vice-President, Chamber of
Deputies, 328, 348
Dupont de l'Eure, Jacques,
before the Revolution, 32;
Minister of Justice, 171, 171n,
194, 277, 283, 287, 292, 297, 300,
301, 302, 324, 326, 327, 359, 363
Duras, Duc de, 107-108
Duvergier de Hauranne, Prosper,
190-91

Ecole militaire, 117, 148, 236
Ecole polytechnique, 131, 135,
197, 207, 269, 335n, 337, 355-56.
See also Poltechnicans
Egypt, Pasha of, 15
election of 1827, 3, 4, 60, 84, 326
election of 1830, 23, 24-26, 25-27,
30, 31-32, 35-36, 37, 205-206
elections, ordinance on, 42, 76
Electoral Law of 1831, 367
electoral procedure, 22n
electors of Paris, in the
Revolution, 89, 93, 95, 96, 97, 98

émigrés, 289
Empire, 47, 257, 282, 283, 285,
289-90, 291, 292, 293, 298
England, 53, 246
Eu, chateau d', 54
Eure, Department of the, 203-205
European powers, recognition
of Louis-Philippe, 304-306
Evreux (Eure), 204
Exelmans, Remi, 143

Fabvier, Charles, 249, 350
Faubourg, du Roule, 270
Faubourg Montmartre, 314
Faubourg Saint-Antoine, 65, 68,
93, 107, 114, 231, 248, 255,
263, 323
Faubourg Saint-Honoré, 129-30
Faubourg Saint-Marceau, 346, 354
Ferdinand, King of Spain, 306,
333
Figaro, 85, 88
Fontainebleau, 110, 349
food riots, 69-71
food supply, Paris, 232-33
Foucauld, Jacques de, 79, 90, 99,
263
Fougères (Ille-et-Vilaine), 69
Four Ordinances, 3, 39, 42-43,
74-82, 137, 139, 148, 151, 268,
341, 365
France méridionale (Toulouse),
218
France nouvelle, 53, 88, 94

Gard, Department of the, 198,
214, 220-24, 250
Garde du Corps, 135, 154, 155,
167, 175, 176, 177, 178, 179,
180, 247
Garde municipale de Paris, 237,
339
Garde nationale mobile, 145, 238
Garnier-Pagés, Etienne, 139n
Gazette de France, 9, 21n
Gendarmerie d'élite, 176
Gérard, Etienne, before the
Revolution, 32, 291; in the
Revolution, 123, 125, 126, 127,
128, 134, 137, 140, 140n;

Minister of War, 170, 170n, 171, 177, 182, 291, 298, 325, 326

Ghent, 53

Girard, Louis, 140n

Girod de l'Ain, Amedée, 171, 314-16, 319, 323

Gironde, Department of the, 250

Glandevès, Georges de, 125, 132

Globe, 53, 79, 85, 88, 93, 260, 261, 284

Gourgaud, Gaspard, 143, 293

Granville (Manche), 180

Great Britain, 16, 41, 274, 304-305, 308-10

Greece, 303, 310

Guernon-Ranville, Martial de, arrest and trial, 180, 338, 344, 352, 353n; defeated in election, 205-206; Polignac Ministry, 12, 19, 21-22, 26, 27, 37, 38-39, 75, 125, 133, 258

Guizot, François, before the Revolution, 4, 32, 45, 48, 54, 58, 79-80, 205; in 1840's, 281; in the Revolution, 96, 123, 140, 151, 159n, 171, 171n, 173, 177, 182, 183, 185, 186, 187, 188n, 190-91, 195n; Minister of the Interior, 277, 282-83, 285-86, 297, 300, 302, 321, 324-25, 328

Hague, The, 307

Ham, fortress of, 355

Haussez, Charles de, after the Revolution, 156, 181, 258, 353n; Polignac Ministry, 7, 12, 15-16, 18, 24, 25, 26, 28-29, 34-35, 37, 41, 43, 47, 77, 82, 83, 84, 91-92, 124, 133; Prefect of the Gard, 220

Haute-Garonne, Department of the, 214, 217

Hennequin, Antoine, 343

Henry V, *see* Bordeaux, Duc de

"Hernani," 246

Higonnet, Patrick, 280n

history, official, of the Revolution, 239-40

Hôpital de la Charité, 242

Hôtel de Ville, 113, 117, 118, 119, 120, 128, 137, 141, 145, 151, 153, 154, 156, 160, 161, 161n, 162, 163, 164, 170, 235, 236, 270, 323, 328, 332

Hôtel de Ville, party of the, 157, 159, 337, 367

Hôtel de Ville, program of the, 187, 337, 357, 360, 364

Hugo, Victor, 68, 246

Hyde de Neuville, Jean, 161

immigrants in crowd, 257-56

Invalides, Hôtel des, 236, 247

Isle of Wight, 179

Issoudon (Indre), 317

Jesuits, 71, 268, 316

Journal de Paris, 85

Journal des débats, 9, 17, 21n, 28, 32, 48, 58, 85, 94, 365

Journal de Rouen, 200

Journal du commerce, 53, 88, 93, 261

Journal du Havre, 200

journalists, 84-88, 93-95, 96-98, 109, 139, 189, 225, 252, 255, 261, 262, 267, 281, 297

justice, administration of, 171, 228, 239

Kent, Sherman, 276

"King of the French," 188n, 194

Komierowski, Louis, 126, 127

Laborde, Alexandre de, 87, 141, 195n

La Bourdonnaye, François de, 6, 7, 8, 9, 11-12

Labrousse, Ernest, 252

Laclayette (Saône-et-Loire), 70

Lafayette, George de, 346

Lafayette, Marie-Joseph de, after the Revolution, 149, 152, 153-54, 156-57, 160-64, 163n, 168, 172, 173, 203, 235, 236, 248, 284, 297, 316, 323, 325, 326, 327, 335n; before the Revolution, 32, 45, 48, 79; command National Guard, 139, 140, 140n; in the Revolution, 123, 128, 139-41, 140n, 145, 193, 195n, 208, 269; resignation,

Lafayette, Marie-Joseph de, *(cont.)*
  358-64, 366; revision of
  Charter, 185, 186, 188, 189,
  191, 192; trial of ministers,
  331-32, 344, 345, 346, 347, 348,
  350, 352, 353, 357, 358
Laffitte, Jacques, before the
  Revolution, 13, 32, 45, 46,
  54, 61, 79; in the Revolution,
  123, 125, 127, 128, 134, 139,
  140, 146-48, 150, 151-53, 159,
  160, 161-62, 183-93, 195n;
  Minister without Portfolio,
  282, 289, 300, 301, 302, 324;
  president of ministry, 282,
  326-28, 334, 347, 348, 358,
  359-60, 365, 367
Lamarque, Maximilien, 170, 213
Lamartine, Alphonse de, 162
Langsdorff, 148
La Rochelle, 211, 214
law courts, purge, 286-88
Law of Sacrilege, 58
Lefebvre, Georges, 265, 266
Le Ferronays, Pierre de la, 6
"legitimacy, principle of," 309
legitimists, 144, 147, 296, 311-13,
  332-34, 366
Le Raincy (Seine-et-Oise), 147,
  151
Leroux, Pierre, 85, 260
Lhomme, Jean, 276n
Lieutenant-General of the
  Kingdom, 151, 152, 158-62,
  168, 169, 172, 195n. *See also*
  Orléans, Duc de
Limoges, 317
Lobau, Georges, 123, 125, 127,
  138, 140, 142, 143, 362-63
Loire valley, 69, 133, 155, 176
London, 305, 309, 334
losses, compensation for, 241-45
Louis XVI, 3, 179, 282
Louis XVIII, 3, 8, 45, 53, 151,
  268, 282, 316, 327
Louis, Joseph, 171, 171n, 282,
  298, 325-26
Louis-Napoleon, 290, 292, 293
Louis-Philippe, accession, 52,
  194-95, 367; after the
  Revolution, 282, 283, 291, 296,

299, 300, 301, 305, 306, 309,
  322, 325, 327, 332, 334; in
  1840's, 251, 381; resignation
  of Lafayette, 358-62; social
  position, 277; trial of ministers,
  330, 344, 356
Louvre, 111, 129, 130, 131, 133,
  134, 135, 140, 141, 228, 236,
  355, 356, 362
Low Countries, 178
Luddism, 70
Lulworth, 179, 311
Lunéville, 168
Luxembourg, 181
Luxembourg Garden, 331, 338,
  339, 350
Luxembourg Palace, 138, 149,
  150, 151, 152, 320, 331, 332,
  338, 339, 340, 345, 350, 351,
  353, 354, 363
Lyon, 69, 70, 214-17

MacDonald, Jacques, 54
Mâcon (Saône-et-Loire), 216
Madier de Montjau, Joseph,
  345, 349
Maine-et-Loire, Department of,
  213
Maintenon (Eure-et-Loir), 175,
  176, 177
Maison, Nicolas-Joseph, 173,
  174, 326, 334
Manche, Department of the, 33-34
Mangin, Jean-Claude, before
  the Revolution, 36, 43, 50,
  62, 66, 75, 229; flight, 141,
  235; in the Revolution, 89-90,
  93, 94, 95, 100, 107, 110,
  111, 196
Marais, 255
Market of the Innocents, 233
Marmont, Auguste de, Duc de
  Raguse, after the Revolution,
  155, 169, 174, 176, 178, 209;
  before the Revolution, 34-35,
  79-80, 90, 92; command in
  Paris, 76, 100-104, 109-22, 123,
  124, 125-26, 127, 129, 130-31,
  132, 133-35, 154, 197, 266, 267
Marrast, Armand, 82, 97
"Marseillaise, La," 221, 303

Marseille, 17, 27, 219
martial law, in Paris, 110-11
Martignac, Jean-Baptiste, in ministry, 5, 6, 7, 58; trial of ministers, 342-43, 345, 349
Mauguin, François, 138, 140, 142, 153, 156, 209
Mauriac (Cantal), 71
mayors, 286
Mazas, Alexandre de, 148
Meaux (Seine-et-Marne), 317
Méchin, Alexandre, 140
Medal of July, 248-49, 250, 257
Melun (Seine-et-Marne), 110
Mérilhou, Joseph, 85, 287, 326, 327, 363
Metternich-Winneburg, Clemens, 162, 305
Metz, 206-209
Michelet, Jules, 284
Midi, 168, 198, 214-15, 282, 332, 333
Mignet, François-Auguste, 13, 47, 85, 150
ministerial responsibility, 44-45
ministers of Charles X, trial of, 318, 323, 327, 328, 330-58, 366
Modena, Duchy of, 306
Molé, Louis-Mathieu, 283, 297, 298, 302, 308, 309, 325, 334, 335
Molitor, Gabriel-Jean, 194
Moniteur universel, 3, 7, 17, 25, 77-78, 79, 80, 81, 82, 87, 149, 153, 171n, 196, 258, 296, 325, 362
Montalivet, Marthe de, 326, 344, 346, 347, 350, 351, 353, 355, 359-63, 364
Montbel, Guillaume de, after the Revolution, 168, 181, 353n; Polignac Ministry, 7, 12, 21-22, 24, 25, 28, 30, 77-78, 258
Montmartre, 136
Montmorillon (Vienne), 71
Mortemart, Victor-Louis de, 137, 139, 147-52, 154, 155, 164, 168
Mortier, Edouard, 54
Municipal Commission of Paris, 89, 138, 140-42, 142n, 144, 149, 153, 156, 161, 163, 164,

170, 203, 209, 231, 232, 239-40, 245, 299, 362, 364
Municipal Council of Paris, 316
Municipal Guard of Paris, *see* Garde municipale de Paris
Musée Carnavalet, 161n

Nadaud, Martin, 265
names, ship and street, 232
Nantes, 209-12, 214, 244, 271-72
Naples, 178
Napoleon I, 49-50, 52, 65, 143, 285, 289, 290, 291, 292, 299
Napoleon II, *see* Reichstadt, Duc de
Napoleon III, 291
Napoleonic Code, 57
Napoleonic Legend, 49-50
National, 13, 32, 52, 53, 85, 86, 87, 88, 93-94, 95, 96, 259, 261, 367
National Guard, after the Revolution, 145, 148, 151, 160, 161, 166, 171, 172, 173, 175, 180, 194, 228, 235-37, 245-46, 314-16, 320-21, 322, 323, 333; change of command, 358-63, 366; in the provinces, 166, 177, 178, 180, 198, 203, 204, 206, 207-209, 211, 214, 215-16, 219, 221, 317; in the Revolution, 269, 270; reestablishment, 131, 136, 139-40, 139n, 140n, 141, 197, 303; trial of ministers, 330-32, 337, 339, 341, 344, 345-54, 356-58
National Guard, of Bordeaux, 219; of Brest, 214; of Caen, 206; of Carentan, 177; of Cherbourg, 178; of Evreux, 204; of Le Havre, 203, 238; of Lyon, 214-16; of Metz, 207, 209; of Nantes, 211; of Nîmes, 221; of Paris, 360-62, 365; of Rouen, 201-203, 238
"National lands," 55, 57
Nemours, Duc de, 182, 356
Nettement, Alfred, 268
Neuilly, 78, 146, 151, 153, 322
Nevers (Nièvre), 69
Ney, Michel, 9

Nicholas I, Tsar of Russia, 305, 307, 333

Nîmes, 80, 198, 214, 220-24, 344

nonintervention, principle of, 308-10, 335

Normandy, 71-72, 145; fires, 33-34, 76, 203-204, 205; revolution, 198, 199-206

Notre Dame of Paris, 267

Odéon Theater, 339

Odier, Antoine, 140

officeholders, 279-80, 286

office-seeking, 55, 284

One Hundred Days, 213, 287, 290, 291, 292, 293, 299

Orange, House of, 307

Orléanists, before the Revolution, 52-55; in the Revolution, 143-51, 154, 172, 183

Orléans, 110, 145

Orléans, Duchesse de, 78, 147, 151, 182, 193

Orléans, Louis-Philippe, Duc de, and the crown, 144-53, 157, 165, 188, 192-93, 296; before the Revolution, 14, 19, 52-54, 78; Lieutenant-General of the Kingdom, 158-64, 167, 168, 169, 170-72, 181-83, 184, 185, 188, 191, 192, 195n, 198, 203, 239, 246, 299, 357, 360. *See also* Louis-Philippe

Orne, Department of the, 33

"Orphans of July," care of, 228-29

Oudard, secretary of Duc d'Orléans, 146

Ouvrard, Gabriel-Julien, 73

Pajol, Claude, 174, 175

Palais-Bourbon, 151, 152, 160, 181, 184, 188, 189, 194, 236, 363

Palais-Royal, 52, 54, 103, 153, 157, 159n, 160, 163, 170, 181, 192, 258, 260, 263, 266, 277, 303, 316, 320, 321, 322, 323, 331-32, 346, 354, 355, 356, 357, 360, 361

Palais-Royal, Garden of, 82, 90-91, 98, 99, 228, 263, 321

Palmerston, Lord, 335

Panthéon, 235, 338

Parlement de Paris, 282, 283

"party of movement," 296

"party of resistance," 296

Passy, 318

Pasquier, Etienne, 41, 194; trial of ministers, 340, 342, 344, 346, 347, 349, 350, 351, 352

Paultre de Lamothe, 216

paving streets, 229-30

peasant protests, 199

peerage, hereditary, attack on, 187, 188-89, 190-91, 193

Penal Code, 342, 351

Périer, Augustin, 151

Périer, Casimir, before the Revolution, 20, 38, 45, 54; heads ministry, 367; in the Revolution, 87, 89, 96-97, 123, 125, 127, 137, 138, 140, 142, 153, 171n, 194, 195n, 218; Minister without Portfolio, 282, 295, 299, 300, 302, 324, 325-26; President, Chamber of Deputies, 328

Persil, Jean, 341-42

Petit Luxembourg, 338, 345, 350

Peyronnet, Charles de, arrest and trial, 180-81, 338, 343, 352, 353n; Minister of the Interior, 24, 27-28, 33, 35, 37-38, 39-42, 43, 89, 94, 124, 165, 326-27

Philadelphia, 335n

Pillet, Léon, 85, 86

Pilote (Caen), 206

Placide de Justin, 79

Plougoulm, official historian, 240

Poland, revolution in, 33, 335

policing after the Revolution, 235-36

Polignac, Jules de, arrest and trial, 180, 181, 318, 338, 341, 342, 350, 351, 352, 358; before the Revolution, 6-8, 10, 12, 14-18, 24-26, 27-28, 30, 33-34, 36, 37-38, 43, 48, 62, 71, 73, 75, 76, 259, 305, 307-308, 367; in the Revolution, 91-92, 93, 101,

102, 103, 110, 112, 124, 126,
128, 132-33, 137
Polignac Ministry, 3, 6-8, 9-11,
14-26, 27-28, 34-35, 37-40,
41-43, 52, 55-59, 61-62, 80, 132,
136, 145, 381
Polytechnicians, 154, 166, 208, 270
Pont l'Evêque-Lisieux
(Calvados), 205
Pope, 310
Pozzo di Borgo, Charles-André,
93, 298, 309
Précurseur (Lyon), 215
Prefect of Police of Paris, and
labor troubles, 314-16; trial of
ministers, 319, 323, 341, 343-44
prefects, purge of, 285, 290-91
press, ordinance on, 42, 76,
80-81, 89-90
printers, 82, 83, 98, 252,
260-62, 267, 273
procurers-general, purge of,
283-84, 288, 291
professional men, 279-81, 286
proprietors, 279, 281, 286
prostitutes, 228, 229
provinces, revolution in, 166,
196-226
Provins (Seine-et-Marne), 110,
349
Protestants, 198, 214, 220-23
Prussia, 16, 305, 307, 308, 334,
335; King of, 308
public works, 316-17
purge, of deputies, 278-79; of
officeholders, 276-77, 283-84,
285, 288, 290-91

Quélen, Louis de, 40-41, 310-11
Quinet, Edgar, 47, 284
Quinsonnas, Emmanuel, 113,
114-16, 118, 122
Quotidienne, 21, 322

Raguse, duc de. *See* Marmont,
Auguste de
Rambouillet, 90, 92, 242;
march on, 168, 172-75, 181, 203;
royal retreat to, 166-67, 169,
175, 176, 180, 181
Ravez, Auguste, 6

Reichstadt, Duc de, 50, 51, 95,
128, 143, 153-54, 294, 348
relief of combatants and
dependents, 246-47, 248, 250
religion, 189-90, 191-92
Rémond, René, 276n
Rémusat, Charles de, before the
Revolution, 79, 82, 259; in the
Revolution, 85, 86, 88, 96,
97-98, 128, 129, 156-57;
Laffitte Ministry, 326;
revision of Charter, 186,
190-91; trial of ministers, 348,
352
Rennes, 214
republicans, 46-47, 48-49, 95,
143, 145, 146, 147, 156, 163,
183, 189, 195, 296, 302, 366
Restoration, 282, 283, 284, 285,
292, 293, 295, 297, 310, 326, 367
Revolution of 1688, 53
Revolution of 1789, 47, 257, 271,
272, 273, 274, 282, 283, 288, 292
Rhine, 333
Richelieu, Cardinal de, 285
Rigny, Henri de, 2, 7, 171n
Rome, 310
Rouen, 166, 173, 199-203, 204, 317
Royal Bodyguard, *see*
Garde du Corps
Royal Court of Paris, 89
Royer-Collard, Pierre, 20, 23, 24
Rueil (Seine-et-Oise), 102
Russia, 16, 304, 305, 307, 333,
334, 335

Saint-Chamans, Alfred de, 114,
118, 119-21, 259, 263
Saint-Cloud, 39, 73, 74, 79, 90,
92, 101, 126, 128, 129, 132,
136, 139, 154-55, 165, 165n,
201, 242; convalescent home,
247; tax resistance in, 318
Saint-Cyr, 154
Saint-Denis, 102, 318
Saint-Helena, 293
Saint-Leu, 73
Saint-Lo, 180
Saint-Omer, 168
Saint-Pélagie Prison, 242
Saint-Petersburg, 304, 305, 335

Saint-Quentin, 317
sanitation problems, 230-31
Sarreguemines (Moselle), 207
Sauvo, editor of *Moniteur universel*, 77-78, 149
Sauzet, Paul, 343, 344
Scheldt River, 308
Sébastiani, Horace, before the Revolution, 38-39; in the Revolution, 127, 151, 152, 158, 192, 195n; Minister of Foreign Affairs, 326-27, 334, 335, 346, 367; Minister of the Navy, 298, 299, 300, 325
Second Empire, 290, 291
Seine-et-Oise, Department of, 250
Seine-Inférieure, Department of the, 250, 292
Semonville, Charles de, 54; in the Revolution, 132, 133, 136, 137-38, 149, 157; trial of ministers, 331, 338, 344, 346
Sèvres, 148, 154-55, 165, 174, 318
Sicily, King and Queen of, 277-78
Sidi-Ferruch, 16, 35
Société de la Morale chrétienne, 327
Société des Amis de la Liberté de la Presse, 327
Société des Amis de l'Ordre, 312
Soissons, 317
Sorbonne, 58
Soult, Nicolas, 281-82, 291, 326, 327, 347, 355, 365
Spain, 306
Spitzer, Alan, 271n
Stock Exchange, 61, 73, 82-83, 106, 229, 301
street lighting, 231
strikes and demonstrations, 273, 313-18
students, 48, 189, 269-70, 337, 355-56, 357, 363
Swiss Guard, 102, 118, 130, 133, 134, 135, 167, 169, 192, 222, 288, 303
Switzerland, 181, 303
Sylphe, 88

Talleyrand-Périgord, Charles-Maurice de, 13,
45, 51, 54, 158, 165n-166n, 309-10, 335
Talon, Mathieu, 114, 117-19, 120
tax resistance, 13, 14, 42, 70, 317-18
Temps, 73, 88, 93-94, 95, 99, 127, 141, 200, 261
theaters, 50, 229, 244, 339
"The 221," 21-22, 32, 35, 83, 91, 213, 297, 328
Thiers, Adolphe, before the Revolution, 13, 45, 47, 52; in the Revolution, 85, 86, 87, 88, 95, 96, 97, 128, 146-47, 149, 150, 195n; Minister of Foreign Affairs, 326-27, 334, 335, 346, 367
Thionville (Moselle), 207
Times (London), 57, 58
Tocqueville, Alexis de, 55
Toulon, 27, 34, 40
Toulouse, 214, 217-18
Tours, 155, 165, 180, 317
Treilhard, Achille, 85, 331, 336, 337, 341, 343-44, 347, 356, 363
Trévise, Duc de, 194
Trianon Palace, 90, 165, 166, 167, 180, 181, 242
Tribunal de Commerce, 83, 239
Tribune des départements, 48, 82, 88, 94
Tricolor, 113, 170, 177, 178, 181, 182, 192, 193, 197, 198, 201, 204, 206, 207, 212, 216, 217, 219, 223, 224, 267, 268, 303
Tuileries Garden, 228, 242
Tuileries Palace, 23, 111, 119, 124, 128, 129, 130, 131, 132, 134, 135, 137, 236, 242, 270, 277, 363
Turkey, Sultan of, 15

United States Military Academy, 335n
United States of America, 163, 246, 334n-335n
Ussel (Corrèze), 71

Val-de-Grace, hospital, 266
Valognes (Manche), 178
Vaucluse, Department of the, 219-20

INDEX

Vaulabelle, Achille de, 97, 265, 268
Vendée, 108, 133, 168, 170, 176, 198, 209, 211, 212, 213, 332
Verdier, Jean, 216
Verneuil (Eure), 204
Versailles, 102, 154-55, 164, 166, 167, 320-22, 349
Vienna, 304, 305
Viennet, Jean, 161-62
Villèle, Joseph de, 4-5, 25-26, 28, 57, 58, 59-60
Villemain, François, 58, 96, 159
Vincennes, 110, 120, 316, 320, 347, 350, 351, 353, 354, 355; chateau of, 88, 103, 181, 338, 346, 350
Vitrolles, Eugène de, 51, 54, 74-75, 126, 136, 137-38, 139, 148-49

Vougy, Vicomte de, 107

Wall, Comte de, 92, 98-99, 103, 113, 114
war, threat of, 302-303, 365, 366
Waterloo, 10, 293, 362
Weill, Georges, 47
Weld, Sir Thomas, 179
Wellington, Duke of, 305, 309
White Terror, 9, 10
widows, care of, 228-29
William and Mary of England, 53
William, King of the Netherlands, 307
William III of England, 53, 128, 146, 310
women in the Revolution, 256
wounded, care of, 121, 227, 245, 247; numbers, 121